ANNUAL EDITIONS

Computers in Society

04/05

Eleventh Edition

EDITOR

Paul De Palma

Gonzaga University

Paul De Palma has degrees from St. Louis University, Temple University, and the University of California at Berkeley where he was a Woodrow Wilson Fellow. When he discovered computers, he was working on a doctorate in English. He retrained and spent a decade developing software for two large companies on the East Coast. He joined the Gonzaga faculty as a professor of computer science in 1990. His professional interests include artificial intelligence and the social implications of computing. Professor De Palma is currently conducting research into the use of genetic algorithms, loosely based on the ideas of natural selection, for structural engineering. He is also working on a collection of essays about the experience of computing entitled *Dim Sum for the Mind.*

McGraw-Hill/Dushkin

530 Old Whitfield Street, Guilford, Connecticut 06437

Visit us on the Internet

http://www.dushkin.com

Credits

1. **Introduction**
   Unit photo—© 2004 by PhotoDisc, Inc.
2. **The Economy**
   Unit photo—Courtesy of Robin Gallagher
3. **Work and the Workplace**
   Unit photo—TRW, Inc. photo
4. **Computers, People, and Social Participation**
   Unit photo—© 2004 by Sweet By & By/Cindy Brown.
5. **Societal Institutions: Law and Politics**
   Unit photo—TRW Inc. photo
6. **Risk and Security**
   Unit photo—Apple Computer, Inc. photo
7. **International Perspectives and Issues**
   Unit photo—© 2004 by PhotoDisc, Inc.
8. **Philosophical Frontiers**
   Unit photo—Matsushita Electric Company Photo

Copyright

Cataloging in Publication Data
Main entry under title: Annual Editions: Computers in Society. 2004/2005.
1. Computers in Society—Periodicals. I. De Palma, Paul, *comp.* II. Title: Computers in Society.
ISBN 0–07–284717–4 658'.05 ISSN 1094–2629

Eleventh Edition

Cover image © 2004 PhotoDisc, Inc.
Printed in the United States of America 1234567890BAHBAH54 Printed on Recycled Paper

Editors/Advisory Board

Members of the Advisory Board are instrumental in the final selection of articles for each edition of ANNUAL EDITIONS. Their review of articles for content, level, currentness, and appropriateness provides critical direction to the editor and staff. We think that you will find their careful consideration well reflected in this volume.

Staff

To the Reader

In publishing ANNUAL EDITIONS we recognize the enormous role played by the magazines, newspapers, and journals of the public press in providing current, first-rate educational information in a broad spectrum of interest areas. Many of these articles are appropriate for students, researchers, and professionals seeking accurate, current material to help bridge the gap between principles and theories and the real world. These articles, however, become more useful for study when those of lasting value are carefully collected, organized, indexed, and reproduced in a low-cost format, which provides easy and permanent access when the material is needed. That is the role played by ANNUAL EDITIONS.

In a now famous scene from the 1968 movie, *The Graduate,* the hapless main character, Ben, is pulled aside at his graduation party by one of his father's business associates who asks him about his plans. As Ben fumbles, the older man whispers a single word in his ear: "plastics." The question is just what would Ben, now a middle-aged man himself, say to a new graduate today? Surely not "plastics," even though petrochemicals, for good and ill, have transformed the way we live over the past three decades. Odds are that computers have replaced plastics in the imaginations of today's graduates, this despite the current slump in the industry's fortunes. To test this hypothesis, I did a Google search on "plastics." It produced 2, 470, 000 hits, an indication that Ben was offered good advice. I followed this with a search on "computers," to which Google replied with an astonishing 30,700, 000 articles. You can learn more about Googling in "The World According to Google." For now, the point is that computers are a phenomenon to be reckoned with.

In culling forty-six articles for the eleventh edition of *Annual Editions: Computers in Society* from the sea of contenders, I have tried to continue in the tradition of former editor Kathryn Schellenberg. The writers are journalists, computer scientists, lawyers, and academics, the kinds of professions you would expect to find in a collection on the social implications of computing. Their writing is free from both the unintelligible jargon and the breathless enthusiasm that is so often found in writing about computers.

Annual Editions: Computers in Society 04/05 is organized around important dimensions of society rather than of computing. The book's major themes are the economy, community, politics considered broadly, and the balance of risk and reward. In a field as fluid as computing, the intersection of computers with each of these dimensions changes from year to year. In this edition, several articles consider the growing problem and growing costs of unwanted e-mail, rather than the importance of e-commerce which, in just a few years, has moved into the mainstream.

But computing is about more than the economy. More than any other technology, computers force us to think about limits. What does it mean to be human? Are there kinds of knowledge that should not be pursued? When combined with the truly revolutionary discoveries in biology, computers require that we ask the really big questions: what is possible and what is to be feared?

A word of caution. As Kathryn Schellenberg pointed out in the tenth edition, "Each article has been selected for its informational value, but to say that an article is 'informative' does not necessarily imply that the information is correct or valid." This is as true of the facts presented as it is of the points of view. Several articles in unit 2, for instance, assert that nearly half of all e-mail is spam. Yet, when reading startling assertions, it is well to remember that writers gather facts from other sources who gathered them from still other sources that may ultimately rely upon a selective method of fact-gathering. "The Computers and the Dynamo," originally written for the *American Scientist,* examines this very issue. I hope you approach these articles as you might approach a good discussion among friends. You might not agree with all their opinions, but you come away perhaps nudged in one direction or another by reasoned arguments.

This book includes several features that I hope will be helpful to students and professionals. Each article listed in the *table of contents* is followed by a short abstract with key concepts in bold type. The social implications of computing, of course, are not limited to the seven broad areas represented by the unit titles. A *topic guide* lists each article by name and number, along with still other dimensions of computers in society.

We want *Annual Editions: Computers in Society* to help you participate more fully in some of the most important discussions of the time. Your suggestions and comments are very important to us. If you complete and return the postage-paid article rating form in the back of the book, we can try to incorporate your thoughts into the next edition.

Paul De Palma
Editor

Contents

The concepts in bold italics are developed in the article. For further expansion, please refer to the Topic Guide and the Index.

UNIT 3
Work and the Workplace

Eight articles in this unit look at what happens when most of us work in an office: we are angry, watched, and dangerously prone to write intemperate e-mails. Computing has even altered the old debate about whether immigration displaces native born workers.

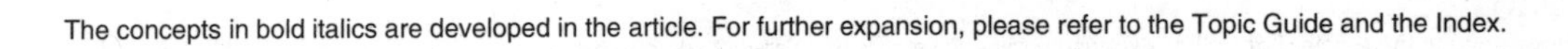
The concepts in bold italics are developed in the article. For further expansion, please refer to the Topic Guide and the Index.

UNIT 4
Computers, People, and Social Participation

Five selections discuss the complexity of computing devices, virtual community and its temptations, the inclusion of women and African Americans in computer science, and the meaning of "to google."

UNIT 5
Societal Institutions: Law and Politics

New technologies often have unintended consequences that require a rethinking of legal and political structures. Seven articles demonstrate that this is true in the debates surrounding intellectual property, "e-democracy," and governing the Internet itself.

The concepts in bold italics are developed in the article. For further expansion, please refer to the Topic Guide and the Index.

UNIT 6
Risk and Security

With the spread of computers and computer networks, comes an entirely new set of risks. Seven selections examine computer security, terrorism, and the vulnerabilities of digital documents.

The concepts in bold italics are developed in the article. For further expansion, please refer to the Topic Guide and the Index.

UNIT 7
International Perspectives and Issues

From Indian software engineers to satellite-delivered American television, computer technology is an international phenomenon. Five articles look at aspects of this phenomenon.

The concepts in bold italics are developed in the article. For further expansion, please refer to the Topic Guide and the Index.

UNIT 8
Philosophical Frontiers

Five articles explore these questions: What does it mean to be human? Are there kinds of knowledge that should not be pursued? What is possible and what is to be feared?

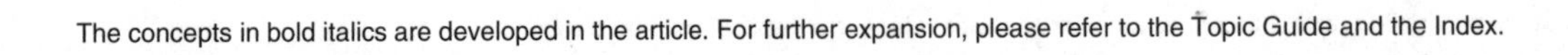
The concepts in bold italics are developed in the article. For further expansion, please refer to the Topic Guide and the Index.

Topic Guide

This topic guide suggests how the selections in this book relate to the subjects covered in your course. You may want to use the topics listed on these pages to search the Web more easily.

On the following pages a number of Web sites have been gathered specifically for this book. They are arranged to reflect the units of this *Annual Edition.* You can link to these sites by going to the DUSHKIN ONLINE support site at *http://www.dushkin.com/online/.*

ALL THE ARTICLES THAT RELATE TO EACH TOPIC ARE LISTED BELOW THE BOLD-FACED TERM.

Legal issues

Networks

Philosophical issues

Politics

Privacy

Regulation

Robotics

Stress

Technological failure and risk

Technological revolution

Terrorism

Workplace

World Wide Web Sites

The following World Wide Web sites have been carefully researched and selected to support the articles found in this reader. The easiest way to access these selected sites is to go to our DUSHKIN ONLINE support site at *http://www.dushkin.com/online/*.

AE: Computers in Society 04/05

The following sites were available at the time of publication. Visit our Web site—we update DUSHKIN ONLINE regularly to reflect any changes.

General Sources

Livelink Intranet Guided Tour

http://www.opentext.com/

Livelink Intranet helps companies to manage and control documents, business processes, and projects more effectively. Take this tour to see how.

UNIT 1: Introduction

Beyond the Information Revolution

http://www.theatlantic.com/issues/99oct/9910drucker.htm

Peter Drucker has written a three-part article, available at this site, that uses history to gauge the significance of e-commerce—"a totally unexpected development"—to throw light on the future of, in his words, "the knowledge worker."

Short History of the Internet

http://w3.ag.uiuc.edu/AIM/scale/nethistory.html

Bruce Sterling begins with the development of the idea for the Internet by the cold war think tank, the Rand Corporation, and goes on to explain how computer networking works. There are links to other sites and to further reading.

UNIT 2: The Economy

CAUCE: Coalition Against Unsolicited Commercial Email

http://www.cauce.org

This all-volunteer organization was created to advocate for a legislative solution to the problem of UCE, better known as spam. Read about the fight and how you can help at this Web page.

E-Commerce Times

http://www.ecommercetimes.com/

E-Commerce Times is a gateway to a wealth of current information and resources concerning e-commerce.

The End of Cash (James Gleick)

http://www.around.com/money.html

This article, previously published in the *New York Times,* on June 16, 1996, discusses the obsolescence of cash.

Fight Spam on the Internet

http://spam.abuse.net

This is an anti-spam sight that has been in operation since 1996. Its purpose is to promote responsible net commerce, in part, by fighting spam. Up-to-date news about spam can be found on the home page.

The Linux Home Page

http://www.linux.org

This Web site explains that Linux is a free Unix-type operating system, originally created by Linus Torvalds, that is causing a revolution in the world of computers. The site features the latest news about Linux, and everything else you would need to know to switch to the service.

Mersch Online: E-Cash Links

http://www.mersch.com/links/moneyzz.htm

This page has a good series of links to other sources of information about E-cash.

The Rise of the Informediary

http://www.ait.unl.edu/crane/misgrad/sglee/informediary.htm

The author of this site explains what an informediary is and what an informediary does. He also shows why the informediary is so important in today's business environment.

Smart Cards: A Primer

http://www.javaworld.com/javaworld/jw-12-1997/jw-12-javadev.html

This article by Rinaldo Di Giorgio brings the smart card to life with a real-world smart-card example. Five pages explain what a smart card is, how it is used, its limitations, and its strengths.

Smart Card Group

http://www.smartcard.co.uk

This Web site bills itself as "the definitive Web site for Smart Card Technology. At this site you can download Dr. David B. Everett's definitive "Introduction to Smart Cards."

UNIT 3: Work and the Workplace

American Telecommuting Association

http://www.knowledgetree.com/ata-adv.html

What is good about telecommuting is examined at this site that also offers information regarding concepts, experiences, and the future of telecommuting.

Cisco E-Learning

http://www.cisco.com/warp/public/10/wwtraining/elearning/

E-learning is Internet-enabled learning. This site explains why e-learning is important and contains an e-learning glossary.

Computers in the Workplace

http://www.msci.memphis.edu/~ryburnp/cl/cis/workpl.html

In this lecture, some of the advantages of computers in the workplace are examined as well as some of the negative aspects, including issues of training, ethics, and privacy.

InfoWeb: Techno-rage

http://www.cciw.com/content/technorage.html

Techno-rage is becoming more and more common. This site provides information and resources regarding techno-rage and techno-stress.

STEP ON IT! Pedals: Repetitive Strain Injury

http://www.bilbo.com/rsi2.html

Data on carpal tunnel syndrome are presented here with links to alternative approaches to the computer keyboard, and links to related information.

What About Computers in the Workplace

http://law.freeadvice.com/intellectual_property/computer_law/computers_workplace.htm

This site, which is the leading legal site for consumers and small businesses, provides general legal information to help people understand their legal rights in 100 legal topics—including the answer to the question, "Can my boss watch what I'm doing?"

www.dushkin.com/online/

UNIT 4: Computers, People, and Social Participation

Adoption Agencies
http://www.amrex.org/
Here is an example of the much-talked-about new trend of online adoption agencies.

Alliance for Childhood: Computers and Children
http://www.allianceforchildhood.net/projects/computers/index.htm
How are computers affecting the intellectual growth of children? Here is one opinion provided by the Alliance for Childhood.

The Core Rules of Netiquette
http://www.albion.com/netiquette/corerules.html
Excerpted from Virginia Shea's book *Netiquette*, this is a classic work in the field of online communication.

How the Information Revolution Is Shaping Our Communities
http://www.plannersweb.com/articles/bla118.html
This article by Pamela Blais is from the Planning Commissioners Journal, Fall 1996 issue, and deals with our changing society. It points out and explains some of the far-reaching impacts of the information revolution, including the relocation of work from office to home.

SocioSite: Networks, Groups, and Social Interaction
http://www2.fmg.uva.nl/sociosite/topics/interaction.html
This site provides sociological and psychological resources and research regarding the effect of computers on social interaction.

UNIT 5: Societal Institutions: Law and Politics

ACLU: American Civil Liberties Union
http://www.aclu.org
Click on the Supreme Court's Internet decision, plus details of the case *Reno v. ACLU,* and the ACLU's campaign to restore information privacy; "Take Back Your Data"; and cyber-liberties and free speech for opinions on First Amendment rights as they apply to cyberspace.

Information Warfare and U.S. Critical Infrastructure
http://www.twurled-world.com/Infowar/Update3/cover.htm
The "twURLed World" contains a pie chart of URLs involved in IW (information warfare) as well as report main pages that list Internet domains, keywords in contexts and by individual terms, and listing of all URLs and links to details.

Issues in Telecommunications and Democracy
http://www.benton.org/publibary/workingpapers/working8.html
This article by Daniel A. Mazmanian, part of the Benton Foundation's Communication Policy Working Papers series, discusses the issues surrounding telecommunications in the twenty-first century. Other papers in the series can be found at http://www.benton.org/publibrary/index.html.

Living in the Electronic Village
http://www.rileyis.com/publications/phase1/usa.htm
This site addresses the impact of information in technology on government. Shown is the executive summary, but seven other sections are equally pertinent.

Patrolling the Empire
http://www.csrp.org/patrol.htm
Reprinted from *CovertAction Quarterly,* this article by Randy K. Schwartz details the plans of NIMA (National Imagery and Mapping Agency) for future wars by helping to fuse high-tech surveillance and weaponry.

United States Patent and Trademark Office
http://www.uspto.gov/
This is the official homepage of the U. S. Patent and Trademark Office. Use this site to search patents and trademarks, apply for patents, and more.

World Intellectual Property Organization
http://www.wipo.org/
Visit the World Intellectual Property Organization Web site to find information and issues pertaining to virtual and intellectual property.

UNIT 6: Risk and Security

AntiOnline: Hacking and Hackers
http://www.antionline.com/index.php
This site is designed to help the average person learn how to protect against hackers.

Copyright & Trademark Information for the IEEE Computer Society
http://computer.org/copyright.htm
Here is an example of how a publication on the Web is legally protected. The section on Intellectual Property Rights Information contains further information about reuse permission and copyright policies.

Electonic Privacy Information Center (EPIC)
http://epic.org
EPIC is a private research organization that was established to focus public attention on emerging civil liberties issues and to protect privacy, the First Amendment, and constitutional values. This site contains news, resources, policy archives, and a search mechanism.

Internet Privacy Coalition
http://www.epic.org/crypto/
The mission of the Internet Privacy Coalition is to promote privacy and security on the Internet through widespread public availability of strong encryption and the relaxation of export controls on cryptography.

Center for Democracy and Technology
http://www.cdt.org/crypto/
These pages are maintained for discussion and information about data privacy and security, encryption, and the need for policy reform. The site discusses pending legislation, Department of Commerce Export Regulations, and other initiatives.

Survive Spyware
http://www.cnet.com/internet/0-3761-8-3217791-1.html
Internet spying is a huge problem. Advertisers, Web designers, and even the government are using the Net to spy on you. CNET.com provides information about spyware and detecting spying eyes that will help you eliminate the threat.

An Electronic Pearl Harbor? Not Likely
http://www.nap.edu/issues/15.1/smith.htm
Is the threat of information warfare real? Yes. Do we need to be completely concerned? Probably not. This site tries to dispel some of the myths and hoaxes concerning information warfare.

UNIT 7: International Perspectives and Issues

Encryption in the Service of Human Rights
http://www.aaas.org/spp/dspp/cstc/briefing/crypto/dinah.htm
Here is a briefing paper from the Human Rights Watch concerning encryption in the service of human rights. What role does encryption play in the Human Rights Movement?

Information Revolution and World Politics Project

http://www.ceip.org/files/projects/irwp/irwp_descrip.ASP

This project, launched by the Carnegie Foundation in 1999, has as its purpose top analyze the political, economic, and social dimensions of the world-wide information revolution and their implications for U.S. policy and global governance.

National Security in the Information Age

http://www.terrorism.com/documents/devostthesis.html

This thesis project by Matthew G. Devost from the University of Vermont explores the new role that national security will play in the information age.

Satellite Imagery in Court

http://www.crowsey.com/spacearticle.htm

This article explains how satellite imagery works and predicts that it will be an important tool in the future. The article also asks whether or not satellite imagery technology will invade our homes and impinge upon our human rights.

UNIT 8: Philosophical Frontiers

Introduction to Artificial Intelligence (AI)

http://www-formal.stanford.edu/jmc/aiintro/aiintro.html

This statement describes A.I. Click on John McCarthy's home page for a list of additional papers.

Kasparov vs. Deep Blue: The Rematch

http://www.chess.ibm.com/home/html/b.html

Video clips and a discussion of the historic chess rematch between Garry Kasparov and Deep Blue are available on this site.

PHP-Nuke Powered Site: International Society for Artificial Life

http://alife.org/

Start here to find links to many alife (artificial life) Web sites, including demonstrations, research centers and groups, and other resources.

We highly recommend that you review our Web site for expanded information and our other product lines. We are continually updating and adding links to our Web site in order to offer you the most usable and useful information that will support and expand the value of your Annual Editions. You can reach us at: *http://www.dushkin.com/annualeditions/*.

UNIT 1

Introduction

Unit Selections

1. **From Movable Type to Data Deluge**, John Gehl and Suzanne Douglas
2. **Whom to Protect and How?** Robert J. Blendon et al.
3. **Five Things We Need to Know About Technological Change**, Neil Postman

Key Points to Consider

- All American school children learn that the first message Samuel F.B. Morse transmitted over his newly invented telegraph were the words, "What hath God wrought?" What they, perhaps, do not learn is that Morse was quoting from the poem of Balaam in the Book of Numbers, chapter 23. (http://www.cforc.com/kjv/numbers/23.html) Read the text of this poem. The overview to this unit presents two ways to understand technical and scientific discoveries. In which camp is Morse? Explain your answer.
- Early on in *Walden,* Thoreau remarked that "Our inventions are wont to be pretty toys, which distract our attention from serious things. They are but an improved means to an unimproved end, an end that it was already but too easy to arrive at.... We are in great haste to construct a magnetic telegraph from Maine to Texas; but Maine and Texas, it may be, have nothing important to communicate." Substitute "Internet" for "magnetic telegraph." Do you agree or disagree with Thoreau? Defend your answer.
- The invention of the computer is often compared in social impact to the invention of moveable type in the fifteenth century. Do you agree? Why or why not.

Links: www.dushkin.com/online/
These sites are annotated in the World Wide Web pages.

Beyond the Information Revolution
http://www.theatlantic.com/issues/99oct/9910drucker.htm

Short History of the Internet
http://w3.ag.uiuc.edu/AIM/scale/nethistory.html

This book, *Annual Editions: Computers in Society,* is part of a larger series of books published by McGraw-Hill/Dushkin. The series contains over 70 titles, among them American History, Sociology, and World Politics. It is instructive that not one of them carries the final prepositional phrase "in Society." Why is that? Here is a first approximation. History, sociology, world politics, indeed, most of the other titles in the Annual Editions series are not *in society,* they *are society.* Suppose we produced an edited volume entitled "History in Society." If such a volume contained reflections on the social implications of the academic study of history, it would have a tiny readership, indeed. But you know that when we speak of computers in society, we are not talking about the social implications of the academic study of computing. So this raises a question. Is it possible to study computers thoroughly without studying their social dimension?

Until recently most people interested in the philosophy and sociology of science considered it value-neutral.[1] That is, a given technology, it was thought, carried no ethical values of its own. The ethics of this or that technology depended on what was done with it. A vestige of this thinking is still with us. When people say, "Guns don't kill people. People kill people," they are asserting that technology somehow stands outside of society, waiting to be put to use for good or ill. The concern about intoxicated drivers is similar. All of us would live happier, safer lives if campaigns to remove drunken drivers from their cars were successful. But this would not get to the heart of highway carnage, which has to do with federal encouragement for suburbs, local patterns of land use, and a neglect of public transportation. Driving while drunk would not be the issue it is if driving were not so vital to American life and driving would not be so vital to American life if a cascade of social and political decisions had not come together in the middle of the twentieth century to favor the automobile. The article "Five Things We Need to Know About Technological Change" makes this point eloquently: "Embedded in every technology there is a powerful idea."

The idea that technology can be studied apart from its social consequences owes part of its strength to the way many people imagine that scientific discoveries unfold. It is commonly imagined that scientists are disinterested observers of the natural world. In this view, science unfolds, and technology unfolds shortly after, according to the laws of nature and the passion of scientists. But, of course, scientists study those things that are socially valued. The clearest expression of scientific social value in the United States is National Science Foundation and National Institute of Health funding. We should not be surprised to learn that the medical and computing sciences are funded generously or, indeed, that our research physicians and computer scientists are paid more than English professors. The article, "Whom to Protect and How?" says that when Americans were asked to rate 11 items that interested them on a scale, they ranked new medical discoveries highest, followed in fourth and fifth place by new scientific discoveries and new technologies.

Perhaps a more accurate view of the relationship between technology and computing to society is that social values affect technical discovery which, in turn, affects social values. It is this intricate dance between computers and society, now one leading, now the other, that the writers in this volume try to understand. Before we begin that discussion, it seems reasonable to understand what is meant by the word "computer." You will find in this volume a decided bias toward networked computers. A networked computer is one that can communicate with many millions of others through the global Internet. As recently as 1996, less than 1 in 5 Americans had used the Internet. Just as we mean "networked computers" when we use the word "computer" today, in the late eighties someone using the word would have meant a stand-alone PC, running, maybe, a word processor, a spread sheet, and some primitive games. A decade prior to that, the word would have referred to a large, probably IBM, machine kept in an air-conditioned room and tended by an army of technicians. Before 1950, "computer" would have meant someone particularly adept in arithmetic calculations. The point here is that as the meaning of a single word has shifted, our understanding of the dance has to shift with it.

That this shift in meaning has occurred in just a few decades helps us understand why so many commentators—two in this unit—use the word "revolution" to describe what computing has wrought. Just as technologies come with hidden meanings, so do words themselves. Thus the word "revolution" when it is applied to political upheaval usually describes something thought bad, or at least chaotic. The American Revolution is the single exception. Not so when the word is applied to computing. Computing is thought to change quickly, but, more, it is thought to bring many benefits. One of the surveys cited in the second article indicated that 90 percent of Americans believe that science and technology will make their lives easier and more comfortable. The real question to ask is, whether or not Americans believe it, is it true? First, does the spread of computing constitute a revolution, or just, in Thoreau's words, "an improved means to an unimproved end." Second, revolutionary or not, have we grown smarter, healthier, happier with the coming of the computer? This is still an open question to a shrinking number of commentators. Before their number shrinks still further, we owe ourselves the pleasure of reading the article, "Five Things We Need to Know About Technological Change," by Neil Postman, an eloquent commentator on technology.

1. For a fuller discussion of these issues see: Johnson, Deborah G. (2001). Is the Global Information Infrastructure a Democratic Technology? In R. Spinello & H. Tavani (Eds.), Readings in Cyber Ethics (pp. 77–90). Sudbury, MA: Jones and Bartlett Publishers.

FROM MOVABLE TYPE TO DATA DELUGE

Instant, global news and the hypertext web are carrying us into realms of "information" access that alter knowledge foundations laid by Gutenberg's printing technology.

BY JOHN GEHL AND SUZANNE DOUGLAS

Marshall McLuhan—the pundit best known for his slogan "the medium is the message"—described the information age as an age of "all-at-onceness," in which space and time are overcome by television, jets, and computers. In such an all-at-once world, linear, "cause-effective" thinking processes give way to a "discontinuous integral consciousness," so that points of view and specialist goals are replaced by an overall awareness of the mosaic world of a "retribalized" society. McLuhan's seminal work, *Understanding Media,* was written in the early sixties. It's time to ask whether he was right: Is the modern world more "all-at-once" than ever?

It would certainly seem so. The media world that existed in McLuhan's time can now be remembered as almost genteel. Back then, in the United States there were just three TV networks and an orderly schedule of mass-consumption shows like *Ed Sullivan* and *I Love Lucy;* now, thanks (if thanks is the right word) to cable, satellite, and computer networks, we are given all news all the time, all comedy all the time, all MTV all the time, all shopping all the time, all anything you want all the time. Could anything be more "all-at-once" than that?

Correct answer: yes. The digital revolution, with its glut of evermore compelling and evermore intrusive (and less apparent) technologies, continues to develop at the frenetic pace of Moore's law (the accurate prediction by Intel cofounder Gordon Moore that microprocessor power will double every 18 months). And things will get even worse (or even better, if you prefer).

George Gilder, author of the privately circulated *Gilder Technology Report,* foresees a fundamental technological shift with "catastrophic consequences for some and incredible profits for others." He says the future will bring us universal technology "as mobile as your watch, as personal as your wallet," a technology that will be able to recognize speech, navigate streets, collect your mail, and even cash your paycheck.

And he is not alone in predicting radical lifestyle changes driven by technology. Others say that soon you will be sporting wearable computers that can, among other things, continuously monitor your vital signs and general health. The world was fast enough in the twentieth century, but now it's getting faster and faster and faster—so fast that it's experienced as "all-at-once."

In the face of such rapid technological advance, it's no wonder that "blur" has become the latest buzzword for how information is experienced (and thus how the world itself is experienced). The relentless immediacy of today's media leaves no time for reflection before the next onslaught of "news"—making one wonder whether there's truly any real news, real information, left to report.

Gutenberg's Legacy

Before the invention of the movable-type printing press, the fact that books had to be hand-copied assured that they were expensive and rare.

Printing empowered Luther, Calvin, and others who sought to reform the Roman Catholic Church, even as it also catalyzed the standardization of vernacular language and heightened nationalistic identity.

Through stimulating literacy and educational reform, printing was a primary instrument in the formation of an educated public that could participate in democratic political processes.

As the first mechanization of a complex craft, printing can be considered the original ancestor of the Industrial Revolution.

Electronic publishing continues the print tradition started by Gutenberg, while the multimedia, hypertext Internet goes beyond it.

TECHNOLOGICAL FOUNDATIONS

Johannes Gutenberg struggled for more than 10 years to build his printing press by inventing movable metal type and integrating it with adaptations of the technologies of paper, oil-based ink, and the winepress. He then required about 5 years to typeset and print his Bible, completing it in about 1455.

We can gain perspective on his invention's historical debt by examining the components that went into Gutenberg's printing press:

- A punch and mold system. Gutenberg's singular contribution to printing was developing a system that allowed mass production of the movable type used to reproduce a page of text. These letters would be put together in a type tray, which was then used to print a page of text. If a letter broke, it could be replaced. When sufficient copies of one page had been printed, the type could be reused for the next page or book.
- The screw-type press for wine or olive oil. This had been used for centuries throughout Europe and Asia. Gutenberg adapted it to printing.
- Block-print technology. Marco Polo brought knowledge of block printing from Asia at the end of the thirteenth century. Gutenberg modified the block format to hold his movable type as it was used in a press.
- Mass production papermaking techniques. Paper was brought from China to Italy in the twelfth century but was thought too flimsy for books. Gutenberg's press made it more feasible to use paper and spurred the development of better papers.
- Oil-based inks. These had been around since the tenth century but were smeared on the vellum used to make books. Gutenberg improved the formulation, allowing the ink to stick to and spread smoothly across his metal type.

—Daniel Munyon

GUTENBERG'S INVENTION

This kind of quickening has occurred once before—though at a slower pace and on a smaller scale—when Gutenberg's invention of the movable-type printing process eliminated the need for books to be laboriously and expensively hand-copied for limited distribution to the elite, those very few people rich enough and educated enough to use them. In doing so, Gutenberg gave the world far more than that famous Bible; he gave it the conditions for revolution. The process he invented opened the way for smaller and more portable texts, lowered the cost of books, and encouraged a great surge in literacy, individualism,… and rebellion. Added to a growing discontent with the Catholic Church, printing played a key role in ushering in the Reformation (as well as the later Renaissance), and created the conditions for nationalism itself.

In 1439 in Mainz, Germany, goldsmith Johannes Gutenberg found he'd been given bad information about the date of a religious fair where he and his investors had planned to sell small mirrors to the pilgrims. What does an entrepreneur do about a missed opportunity? Create another opportunity. The goldsmith convinced his investors to back an alternative project—one involving the making of individual letters of metal so as to combine and recombine them to print words on paper. Seventeen years later he produced his first and best-known printed document: the Gutenberg Bible.

Among the results of this strategic redirection were a new Europe and an entirely new world. In their 1995 book, *The Axemaker's Gift: A Double-Edged History of Human Culture,* James Burke and Robert Ornstein write:

> The effect of Gutenberg's letters would be to change the map of Europe, considerably reduce the power of the Catholic Church, and alter the very nature of the knowledge on which political and religious control was based. The printing press would also help to stimulate nascent forms of capitalism and provide the economic underpinning for a new kind of community.

Although ecclesiastic and civil authorities at first looked benignly on the apparently pious nature of the act of publishing the Bible in German (and, soon thereafter, in all the other European languages), the publisher's intentions were far less important than the publishing consequences. Using the vernacular languages legitimized those languages, detracted from Rome's authority, and made it easier for monarchs to enforce their laws and extend bureaucratic control far beyond what had been previously possible.

Bibles were just the beginning; they were followed by an immense number of almanacs, technical books, and scholarly treatises, as Gutenberg was imitated by scores of competitors. The most interesting of these competitors may have been Christophe Plantin, a printer who ran the biggest publishing house in Europe. As Burke and Ornstein explain, Plantin and his fellow printers were "the first real capitalists."

> In Plantin's shop, university professors and ex-abbots acted as proofreaders and text editors, scholars of all subjects checked text for factual accuracy, artists prepared woodcuts and engravings, craftsmen printed or advised

McLUHAN "ALL-AT-ONCE"

University of Toronto communications theorist Marshall McLuhan (1911–1980) became a dominant force in the 1960s and was hailed by Tom Wolfe as an intellectual peer of Newton, Darwin, Freud, Einstein, and Pavlov. It is because of McLuhan that we use the word *media* in its current sense and talk about the "global village."

Though his slogan "the medium is the message" mystified some and infuriated many, McLuhan never said that the message (i.e., the content) of a particular TV show or book has no importance. He merely wanted to point us in another direction. Look at this, he was saying, forget the message for a second and see what the medium itself is doing to us, to our very "nervous systems"; you can't watch thousands upon thousands of hours of television without becoming a changed person. McLuhan said that we are as unaware of the psychic and social effects of the new technology as a fish of the water it swims in. We remain blissfully ignorant of what the media do to us.

And just how do the media affect us (or "massage" us, as he liked to say, punning on the word *message*)? They do it by altering the balance of our senses. Prehistoric, or tribal, man existed in a harmonious balance of all five senses, but two great inventions—first the phonetic alphabet and later the movable-type printing press—upset that balance by rewarding a single sense, sight, as the eye chased across a page in a linear hunt for the end of a sentence. The inventions had an unfortunate side effect. Because they rewarded "linear thinking," man effectively lost his senses—and became fragmented, individualistic, specialized, and detached.

But then came the electric media (telegraph, radio, films, telephone, computer, and television). What then? Well, the "Gutenberg galaxy" (as McLuhan dubbed it) yielded to the information age (another McLuhanism), with its various competing media.

Possessing a Cambridge Ph.D. in English and a scholar's love of literature, this icon of the twentieth century described himself as a person who had "nothing but distaste for the process of change" and who personally preferred a stable environment "of modest services and human scale." How did a dedicated humanist come to lead an intellectual revolution? With both humility and irony, McLuhan explained simply: "I ceased being a moralist and became a student."

As a student of media, he "probed" (another of his favorite words) into every field, with what he proudly proclaimed as "no fixed point of view." He defined media broadly to include "any technology whatever that creates extensions of the human body and senses, from clothing to the computer." What he foresaw was a "retribalizing" of mankind as it allows modern multimedia to restore the balance of the senses that was destroyed by the rise of literacy.

One manifestation of this retribalization will take place in politics, and McLuhan predicted that "the day of political democracy as we know it today is finished." Here is just one example why:

> The people wouldn't have cared if John Kennedy lied to them on TV, but they couldn't stomach LBJ even when he told the truth. The credibility gap was really a communications gap. The political candidate who understands TV—whatever his party, goals or beliefs—can gain power unknown in history. How he uses that power is, of course, quite another question. But the basic thing to remember about the electric media is that they inexorably transform every sense ratio and thus recondition and restructure all our values and institutions. The overhauling of our traditional political system is only one manifestation of the retribalizing process wrought by the electric media, which is turning the planet into a global village.

As the man said, the medium is the message.

—J.G. and S.D.

on books relating to their own area of expertise, and merchants became involved as financial backers.

Printing led to the prominence of specialists and experts, who wrote books on every subject and fed Europe's growing demand for information of all kinds—the old, reliable kind and the novel, heretical kind that fomented dissent and upset all the traditional relationships that had sustained medieval Europe. Because of portable, printed books (and later newspapers), people could study the Bible without relying on a priest, learn a subject without going to a master, and think thoughts without asking for permission. Things would never be the same again, because ideas were now as free as air. The genie was out of the bottle.

And that genie—we now know—was at the head of a long family tree.

NATIONALISM AND THE INDUSTRIAL REVOLUTION

In a 1964 interview, McLuhan explained that nationalism didn't exist in Europe "until typography enabled every literate man to see his mother tongue analytically as a uniform entity. The printing press, by spreading mass-produced books and printed matter across Europe, turned the vernacular regional languages of the day into uniform closed systems of national languages—just another variant of what we call mass media—and gave birth to the entire concept of nationalism."

After books came newspapers. During the seventeenth and eighteenth centuries they spread across Europe and the

ENGRAVED BY WILLIAM SHARP IN 1793/ LIBRARY OF CONGRESS

Ideas widely circulated in printed pamphlets played a critical role in the American Revolution. "Common Sense" (1776), by Anglo-American political theorist Thomas Paine, set forth arguments for independence that were to influence the revolutionary movement in France in 1789 as well.

New World, fomenting change and allowing vying factions to express individual opinions. Social transformation was wrought not only by the free flow of ideas empowered by the printed word but by the fundamentally new approach to machine use that was embodied in the printing process. McLuhan explained:

> Printing, remember, was the first mechanization of a complex handicraft; by creating an analytic sequence of step-by-step processes, it became the blueprint of all mechanization to follow. The most important quality of print is its repeatability; it is a visual statement that can be reproduced indefinitely, and repeatability is the root of the mechanical principle that has transformed the world since Gutenberg. Typography, by producing the first uniformly repeatable commodity also created Henry Ford, the first assembly line and the first mass production. Movable type was archetype and prototype for all subsequent industrial development. Without phonetic literacy and the printing press, modern industrialism would be impossible. It is necessary to recognize literacy as typographic technology, shaping not only production and marketing procedures but all other areas of life, from education to city planning.

ENTER THE DIGITAL REVOLUTION

If only McLuhan were still alive! In these last years of the twentieth century, the Internet and the World Wide Web have changed the very nature of communication by radically realigning the relationships between the people involved in a communications process. Whereas books, newspapers, radio, and television are all essentially "one to many" broadcast media (i.e., one source transmitting to many readers, listeners, or viewers), the Internet allows a surfer to exercise complete control over what is now an "interaction with" rather than a "reception of" news or information. Hypertext links and "search engines" allow Internet users to become entirely and quickly free of the confines of the information sender's intended message. Whereas the communication process has in the past typically implied an assumption that the message sender had more information than the message receiver, now the relationship is effectively reversed. The one with control is not the one with the message but the one with the mouse.

Control of the mouse also provides control of the clock, and these developments combine to dramatically revise the relationship between the consumer of news and information and the medium through which news and information are delivered. Rather than passively waiting for the six o'clock, 30-minute scripted presentation of whatever it is the "major" networks want you to know, you can now check your favorite Web sites (AP? MSNBC? Excite? the Drudge Report?) for regularly updated reports on news you can tailor to your specific profile. You can even have the news shipped to your desktop, pushed on you rather than

KEN WEBER/THE WORLD & I

Electronic technologies such as the CD have already opened new options, both for storing the printed word and for interacting with it via the personal computer.

laboriously pulled off the Web. You are the boss.

THE DEATH OF NEWS

On the other hand, being the boss isn't what it used to be. Having control doesn't mean getting what you want. If what you want is real information, you may have a problem, because the ubiquity, immediacy, and relentless repetition of media communication have resulted in the decline of the very commodity all these media purport to be selling: news.

News is surprise. In the classic formulation, news is when man bites dog. It's a "classic" formulation because the event described is not just news, it's big news, for when it happens it is extremely surprising.

But there is less and less surprise in the "global village" (one of many expressions coined by McLuhan). When the news is constant and continuous and always with us, when we are saturated with news, there is no real news. Real news is from elsewhere. When everyone is in the same room (or the same global village), there is no real news, because everyone can see what everyone else is doing. Surprise is impossible. News is impossible. The people in the room don't need information about what's going on there.

And so as we become increasingly submerged in a steady, enveloping stream of "news" and "information" presented live by Web or television from places all over the globe, we are now at last in McLuhan's world of "all-at-onceness." Whereas the notion of news requires discrete "news events," the current reality is a miasma of worldwide data "smog," continuous news "updates," and disguised argumentation, happening all at once on our computers and TV sets.

NEWS IN THE NEXT CENTURY

It's too late to turn back the tide of the information deluge. The best we can hope to do is make some sense of what the state of constant information means, and what this "all-at-onceness" means for the idea of "news" as it evolves into the next century. The launching of the first communications satellites meant that suddenly people all over the world could see and hear about events as they were happening and form opinions based on that experience, rather than waiting for interpretation by newswriters and editors. Now, by accessing the World Wide Web with its hypertext linkages—specified words or phrases that can be used to call up related text or images—anyone can essentially create a unique and completely personal version of the news. (This assumes, of course, that he has the stamina to wade through the never-ending onslaught of information overload, compressed news cycles, Web reports that challenge traditional news sources, and news overlaid with split screens and simultaneous events. It assumes, too, a talent for extracting from the stream of 1s and 0s some kernel of information that qualifies as "surprise.")

JOHN HARRINGTON/THE WORLD & I

With the Internet, we can immerse ourselves in a globe-girdling news stream that transcends the limitations of time, distance, content, and linearity imposed by type and photos printed on paper.

Left on the cutting-room floor will be many of the traditional news organizations that found themselves too analogue, too linear, too exhausted and distracted to keep up. But don't worry about the big news organizations; they will somehow find a way of surviving. Save your worry for the people. Will the people survive the end of the information age? Will the Republic?

An optimist may hope that the information age will yield to an age of knowledge, when surfers of fact will become seekers of truth.

It could happen.

Of course, a pessimist may fear that the Internet will devolve into the mindlessness of television, creating a citizenry that can't think or read, is unfit for jury duty, and can be entertained (just barely and only momentarily) but not enlightened.

The pessimist may continue to fear that all the world's intelligence will be embedded in machines and none in ordinary people; that those ordinary people will live out their lives in a new Dark Age, filled with dread and awe, worshiping the mysterious and incomprehensible machines that surround them, like magical trees in a primeval forest.

Which will it be? We'll have to wait to find out and hope for the best. Perhaps the pessimist is taking just one part of human nature—the "thinking" part—too seriously. The mathematician and philosopher Alfred North Whitehead once said: "It is a profoundly erroneous truism, repeated by copybooks and by eminent people when they are making speeches, that we should cultivate the habit of thinking of what we are doing. The precise opposite is the case. Civilization advances by extending the number of important operations which we can perform without thinking about them."

And so maybe it will be okay if we surrender our thinking (or most of it) to machines.

Maybe.

ADDITIONAL READING

James Burke and Robert Ornstein, *The Axemaker's Gift: A Double-Edged History of Human Culture,* Grosset/Putnam, New York, 1995.

Marshall McLuhan, *Understanding Media: The Extensions of Man,* McGraw-Hill, New York, 1964.

John Gehl and Suzanne Douglas are editors and publishers of the print magazines Exec *and* Educom Review *and the Internet newsletters* Innovation, Edupage, *and* Energy News Digest, *which can be found at http://www.newsscan.com.*

This article originally appeared in *The World & I,* January 1999, pp. 24-33. Reprinted by permission of *The World & I,* a publication of The Washington Times Corporation. © 1999.

Access Denied

Whom to Protect and How?

The Public, the Government, and the Internet **Revolution**

by Robert J. Blendon, John M. Benson, Mollyann Brodie, Drew E. Altman, Marcus D. Rosenbaum, Rebecca Flournoy, and Minah Kim

The United States is now in the second stage of a major technological transformation. What began in the 1980s as the Computer Revolution has extended its reach and become the Computer and Internet Revolution. The second stage of the revolution is not only transforming American life, but also leading to calls for federal government protection from perceived threats presented by specific Internet content. Because of First Amendment concerns and the difficulty of regulating this international technology, the government will find it hard to provide the kind of oversight the public wants.

During the first stage of the Computer and Internet Revolution, computer use grew rapidly. Between 1985 and 1999, the share of Americans who used a computer at work or at home more than doubled, from 30 percent to 70 percent. The increase in home computer ownership was even more striking, quadrupling from 15 percent in 1985 to 60 percent by century's end (table 1).

The Internet stage of the revolution started in the mid-1990s. Only five years ago, fewer than one in five Americans (18 percent) had ever used the Internet. As the new century begins, nearly two-thirds (64 percent) have used the Internet some time in their lives. In 1995 only 14 percent of Americans said they went online to access the Internet or to send or receive e-mail. By 1997 that share had more than doubled, to 36 percent, and today more than half (54 percent) go online. Virtually all Americans younger than 60 say they have used a computer (92 percent), and most have used the Internet (75 percent) or sent an e-mail message (67 percent).

The rapid spread of the new technology is not without precedent. Television ownership in the United States exploded from 6 percent in 1949 to 52 percent in 1953 to 83 percent by 1956. Still, the increase in computer use and, in the second wave, Internet use is remarkable.

Most Americans see the computer's impact on society as mainly positive. Just over half believe that the computer has given people more control over their lives

Although much is made of the Internet's almost limitless capabilities, at this point people are most likely to use it to get information. Americans use the Internet at home to learn about entertainment, sports, and hobbies (38 percent), current events (37 percent), travel (33 percent), and health (28 percent). Fewer use the Internet to shop (24 percent), pay bills (9 percent), and make investments (9 percent).

A Beneficent Revolution

America's Internet Revolution is taking place among people already disposed to believe strongly in the benefits of new technology. When asked to rate on a scale of 0 to 100 their interest in 11 issues, Americans ranked new medical discoveries highest (an average of 82), followed in fourth and fifth places by new scientific discoveries (67) and new inventions and technologies (65).

Table 1. Share of the Public with Access to Computers at Home and at Work, 1985–99

PERCENT	1985	1990	1995	1997	1999 (a)	1999 (b)
Computer at work	25	32	39	38	42	44
Computer at home	15	22	36	42	54	60
Computer at neither	70	58	46	43	35	30

Source: NSF, 1985–1999 (a); NPR–Kaiser–Kennedy School, 1999 (b)

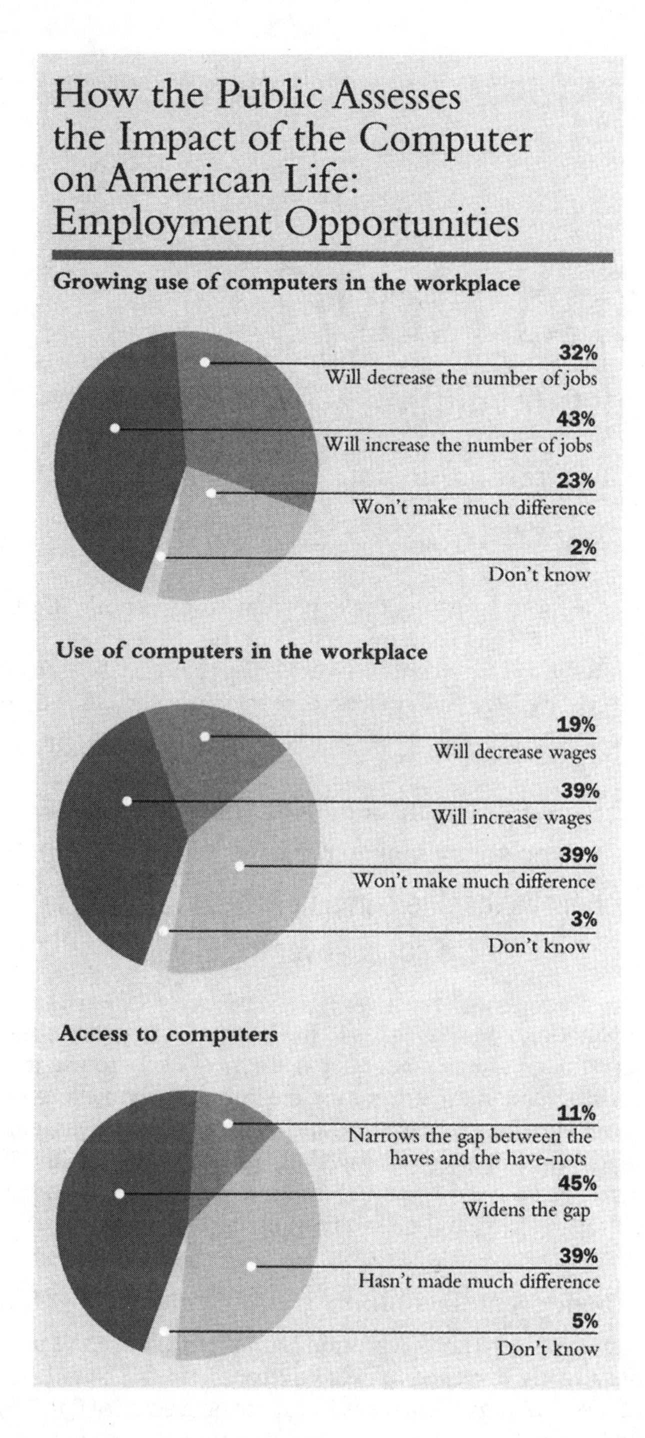

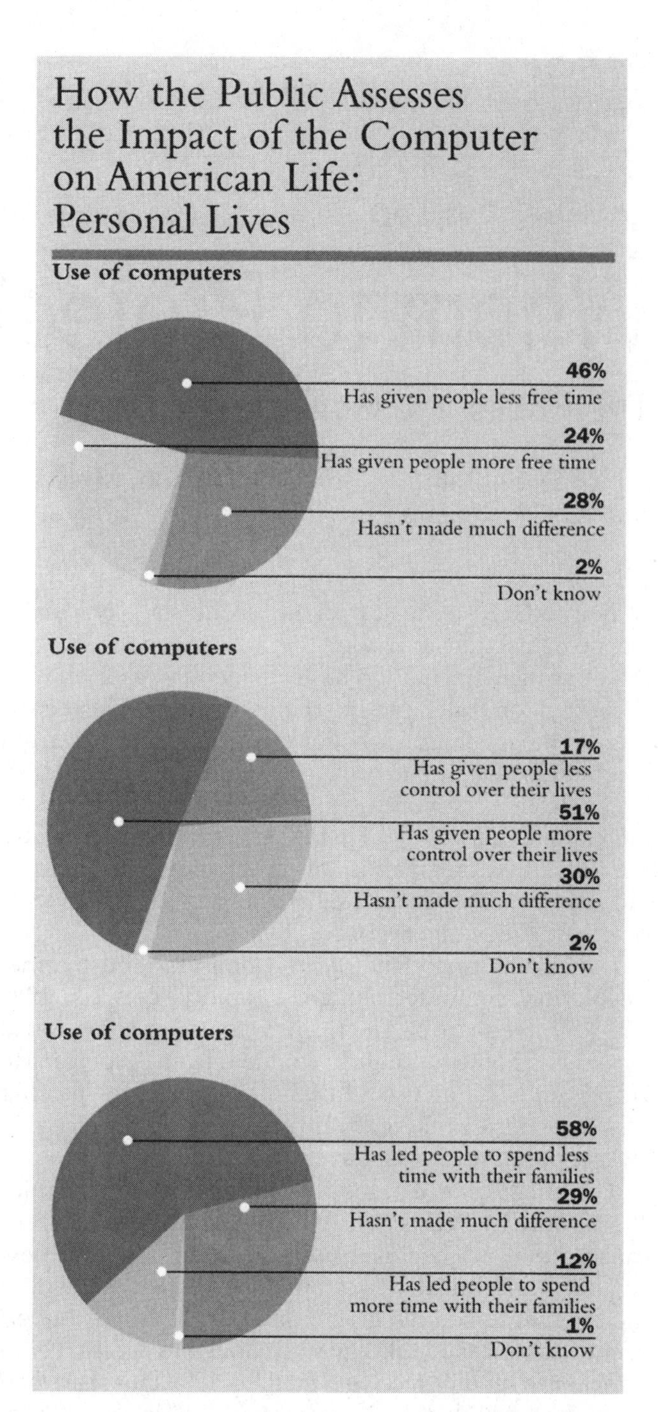

Large majorities of Americans believe that science and technology make lives healthier, easier, and more comfortable (90 percent) and that science and technology will provide more opportunities for the next generation (84 percent). Three-fourths of Americans (74 percent) believe that the benefits of scientific research have outweighed the disadvantages.

The experiences of the past two decades have left most Americans feeling quite positive about the general impact of computers on national life and receptive to the possibilities of the Internet. Asked to choose, from a list of eight options, the two most significant technological developments of the 20th century, Americans put the computer (named by 62 percent) at the top of the list by a large margin over the automobile (34 percent), television (21 percent), and the airplane (16 percent). The landslide vote for the computer may be due in part to its novelty, but Americans clearly regard the computer as a major technological discovery.

Most Americans see the computer's impact on society as mainly positive. Just over half believe that the computer has given people more control over their lives (17 percent believe it has diminished their control). More than eight out of ten see computers as making life better

Table 2. What the Public Believes the Government Should Do about Key Issues Involving the Internet

PERCENT	ISSUE IS A PROBLEM			
	GOVERNMENT SHOULD DO SOMETHING	GOVERNMENT SHOULD NOT BE INVOLVED	ISSUE IS NOT A PROBLEM	DON'T KNOW
Dangerous strangers making contact with kids	79	15	3	1
The availability of pornography to kids	75	20	4	1
The availability of information about how to build bombs and other weapons	75	15	8	1
False advertising	62	20	12	4
Pornography and adult entertainment	61	26	10	3
The ability to purchase guns	61	14	18	5
Loss of privacy	54	29	14	2
Hate speech, information that attacks people based on their race, religion, or ethnicity	53	27	15	5
Violent games	51	31	15	3

Source: NPR–Kaiser–Kennedy School, 1999

for Americans (9 percent think computers are making life worse). Sixty-eight percent believe the Internet is making life better (14 percent believe it is making life worse). Americans are more evenly divided in their views on the impact of television: 46 percent believe that TV is making life better, 34 percent think it is making life worse.

Most Americans also view the computer industry positively. More than three out of four (78 percent) think computer software companies serve consumers well, while only 7 percent think their service is poor. Only banks (73 percent) and hospitals (72 percent) have comparably positive ratings, but both have higher negatives (24 percent each). Nearly two-thirds (65 percent) of Americans believe that the Internet industry is doing a good job serving its consumers; again, only 7 percent think it is doing a bad job.

Despite some early fears, most Americans do not think the use of computers in the workplace displaces workers or depresses wages. A plurality (43 percent) think the growing use of computers will create more jobs; 32 percent think it will mean fewer jobs; about a quarter think it will not make much difference. Americans are evenly divided, at 39 percent each, on whether the use of computers will raise wages or not have much effect; but only 19 percent believe it will lower wages.

In two areas—the amount of free time and time spent with family and friends—Americans do not believe computers have improved life. Only one-fourth (24 percent) of the public believes that computers have given people more free time. Nearly half think computers have actually reduced free time. And more than half (58 percent) say computers have led people to spend less time with families and friends.

What Role for Government?

The first wave of the Computer and Internet Revolution led many Americans to see a role for government in narrowing a "digital divide" in American society, a problem that continues to concern the public today. Nearly half (45 percent) believe that access to computers widens the gap between the haves and the have-nots, while only 11 percent believe that it narrows the gap; 39 percent think it has not made much different. A majority of Americans (57 percent) believe the government should help low-income people get access to computers and the Internet, and 78 percent say the government should help low-income children.

The Internet Revolution is leading to a broader range of public concerns, accompanied by calls for more government involvement in specific areas. Eighty-five percent of Americans cite as a major problem the possibility of dangerous strangers making contact with children; 84 percent, the availability of pornography to children; and 73 percent, the availability of information about how to build bombs and other weapons.

In addition, more than half (56 percent) of Americans regard the loss of privacy as a major problem with computers or the Internet. Although few (4 percent) have ever had an unauthorized person gain access to their financial records or personal information over the Internet, privacy concerns are increasing demands for regulation. More than half (59 percent) of Americans worry that an unauthorized person might gain such access, including 21 percent who say they are very worried. More than three-fourths (81 percent) of people who ever go online say they are concerned about threats to their personal privacy when using the Internet, including 42 percent who say they are very concerned.

What do these trends indicate about a possible new role for government in regulating the Internet? On the one hand, the coming years will witness an upsurge in use of the Internet for a wide variety of purposes, and the public is unlikely to want across-the-board government regulation of the Internet. On the other, most Americans are likely to support legislation to address their specific concerns about the content of the Internet.

POLLS USED

The results reported here are drawn primarily from a survey conducted by the National Public Radio–Henry J. Kaiser Family Foundation–Kennedy School of Government survey project, November 15–December 19, 1999. Other data come from polls by the National Science Foundation (1985, 1990, 1995, 1997, 1999); the Pew Research Center for the People and the Press-Princeton Survey Research Associates (1995, 1997, 2000); CBS News-*New York Times* (1995); CBS News (1999); the Gallup Poll (1949, 1953, 1956); Harris Interactive (2000); the Henry J. Kaiser Family Foundation–Kennedy School of Government (2000), Louis Harris & Associates-Dr. Alan F. Weston–Privacy and American Business–Price Waterhouse, Inc.(1998); and *Newsweek*–Princeton Survey Research Associates (1999). Results of the NSF polls may be found at http://www.nsf.gov/sbe/srs/seind00/pdf. Results of all other polls cited may be obtained from the Roper Center for Public Opinion Research, Storrs, Connecticut.

Many people are wary of having the government regulate what can be put on the Internet, but they are more willing to accept regulation when it comes to specific threatening content. At least at this point, only about a third of Americans see the need for more government regulation of the Internet industry or the general content of the Internet. But when specific content seen as threatening, such as pornography and bomb-making information, is mentioned, 60 percent favor government restrictions, even if they would impinge on freedom of speech. More than half (57 percent) say that "the federal government needs to regulate what is on the Internet more than television and newspapers because the Internet can be used to gain easier access to dangerous information."

Three-quarters of Americans say the government should "do something" about the possibility of dangerous strangers making contact with children and about the availability both of pornography to children and of information on how to build explosives (see table 2). A majority also says the government should do something about false advertising (62 percent), the availability of guns (61 percent), pornography (61 percent), the loss of privacy (54 percent), and hate speech (53 percent).

More Americans are worried about specific threats like pornography and bomb-making information on the Internet than about First Amendment issues involved in regulating these threats. When asked which worried them more, 53 percent said they were more concerned that government would not get involved enough in regulating pornography and bomb-making information on the Internet. Only 26 percent were more concerned that government would get too involved in censorship of the Internet.

Public concerns about specific threats on the Internet are not likely to dissipate as more people go online. While Internet users are less likely than nonusers to believe that the content of the Internet needs more regulation than TV or newspaper content, about half of Internet users (as against 65 percent of nonusers) favor this additional regulation in general. In addition, a majority of Internet users believe the government should do something about most of the same specific threats mentioned by nonusers.

The next decade will see an explosion of growth and change in the world of the Internet. Like the advent of television half a century ago, the Internet Revolution will lead to fundamental and in most cases positive changes in the way Americans live. The number of Americans who use the Internet for nearly every activity is likely to double or triple.

Between a Rock and a Hard Place

In the midst of this extraordinary ferment, public pressure will build in favor of more government involvement in regulating specific parts of the Internet's content. Regulatory efforts will raise a number of First Amendment issues, if not with the public, at least within the judicial system. Given that information on the Internet flows almost seamlessly across national borders, the U.S. government—or any other—will find it extremely difficult to limit access to information the public thinks is dangerous. Policymakers are likely to be caught between growing public pressure to protect against perceived threats to national and personal well-being and the limits of their ability to regulate specific Internet content.

Robert J. Blendon, of the John F. Kennedy School of Government and the Harvard School of Public Health; John M. Benson and Minah Kim, of the Harvard School of Public Health; Mollyann Brodie, Drew E. Altman, and Rebecca Flournoy, of the Henry J. Kaiser Family Foundation; and Marcus D. Rosenbaum of National Public Radio are part of a team conducting ongoing polling on Americans' attitudes about domestic policy issues.

Five Things We Need to Know About Technological Change

Neil Postman

Editor's note: Address by Neil Postman to New Tech '98 conference, Denver, Colorado, March 27, 1998

Good morning your Eminences and Excellencies, ladies, and gentlemen.

The theme of this conference, "The New Technologies and the Human Person: Communicating the Faith in the New Millennium," suggests, of course, that you are concerned about what might happen to faith in the new millennium, as well you should be. In addition to our computers, which are close to having a nervous breakdown in anticipation of the year 2000, there is a great deal of frantic talk about the 21st century and how it will pose for us unique problems of which we know very little but for which, nonetheless, we are supposed to carefully prepare. Everyone seems to worry about this—business people, politicians, educators, as well as theologians.

> The human dilemma is as it has always been, and it is a delusion to believe that the tehnological changes of our era have rendered irrelevant the wisdom of the ages and the sages.

At the risk of sounding patronizing, may I try to put everyone's mind at ease? I doubt that the 21st century will pose for us problems that are more stunning, disorienting or complex than those we faced in this century, or the 19th, 18th, 17th, or for that matter, many of the centuries before that. But for those who are excessively nervous about the new millennium, I can provide, right at the start, some good advice about how to confront it. The advice comes from people whom we can trust, and whose thoughtfulness, it's safe to say, exceeds that of President Clinton, Newt Gingrich, or even Bill Gates. Here is what Henry David Thoreau told us: "All our inventions are but improved means to an unimproved end." Here is what Goethe told us: "One should, each day, try to hear a little song, read a good poem, see a fine picture, and, if possible, speak a few reasonable words." Socrates told us: "The unexamined life is not worth living." Rabbi Hillel told us: "What is hateful to thee, do not do to another." And here is the prophet Micah: "What does the Lord require of thee but to do justly, to love mercy and to walk humbly with thy God." And I could say, if we had the time, (although you know it well enough) what Jesus, Isaiah, Mohammad, Spinoza, and Shakespeare told us. It is all the same: There is no escaping from ourselves. The human dilemma is as it has always been, and it is a delusion to believe that the technological changes of our era have rendered irrelevant the wisdom of the ages and the sages.

> ...all technological change is a trade-off... a Faustian bargain.

Nonetheless, having said this, I know perfectly well that because we do live in a technological age, we have some special problems that Jesus, Hillel, Socrates, and Micah did not and could not speak of. I do not have the wisdom to say what we ought to do about such problems, and so my contribution must confine itself to some things we need to know in order to address the problems. I call my talk *Five Things We Need to Know About Technological Change.* I base these ideas on my thirty years of studying the history of technological change but I do not think these are academic or esoteric ideas. They are the sort of things everyone who is concerned with cultural stability and balance should know and I offer them to you in the hope that you will find them useful in thinking about the effects of technology on religious faith.

First Idea

The first idea is that all technological change is a trade-off. I like to call it a Faustian bargain. Technology giveth and technology taketh away. This means that for every advantage a new technology offers, there is always a corres-ponding disadvantage. The disadvantage may exceed in importance the advantage, or the advantage may well be worth the cost. Now, this may seem to be a rather obvious idea, but you would be surprised at how many people believe that new technologies are unmixed blessings. You need only think of the enthusiasms with which most people approach their understanding of computers. Ask anyone who knows something about computers to talk about them, and you will find that they will, unabashedly and relentlessly, extol the wonders of computers. You will also find that in most cases they will completely neglect to mention any of the liabilities of computers. This is a dangerous imbalance, since the greater the wonders of a technology, the greater will be its negative consequences.

Think of the automobile, which for all of its obvious advantages, has poisoned our air, choked our cities, and degraded the beauty of our natural landscape. Or you might reflect on the paradox of medical technology which brings wondrous cures but is, at the same time, a demonstrable cause of certain diseases and disabilities, and has played a significant role in reducing the diagnostic skills of physicians. It is also well to recall that for all of the intellectual and social benefits provided by the printing press, its costs were equally monumental. The printing press gave the Western world prose, but it made poetry into an exotic and elitist form of communication. It gave us inductive science, but it reduced religious sensibility to a form of fanciful superstition. Printing gave us the modern conception of nationwide, but in so doing turned patriotism into a sordid if not lethal emotion. We might even say that the printing of the Bible in vernacular languages introduced the impression that God was an Englishman or a German or a Frenchman—that is to say, printing reduced God to the dimensions of a local potentate.

Perhaps the best way I can express this idea is to say that the question, "What will a new technology do?" is no more important than the question, "What will a new technology undo?" Indeed, the latter question is more important, precisely because it is asked so infrequently. One might say, then, that a sophisticated perspective on technological change includes one's being skeptical of Utopian and Messianic visions drawn by those who have no sense of history or of the precarious balances on which culture depends. In fact, if it were up to me, I would forbid anyone from talking about the new information technologies unless the person can demonstrate that he or she knows something about the social and psychic effects of the alphabet, the mechanical clock, the printing press, and telegraphy. In other words, knows something about the costs of great technologies.

Idea Number One, then, is that culture always pays a price for technology.

Second Idea

This leads to the second idea, which is that the advantages and disadvantages of new technologies are never distributed evenly among the population. This means that every new technology benefits some and harms others. There are even some who are not affected at all. Consider again the case of the printing press in the 16th century, of which Martin Luther said it was "God's highest and extremest act of grace, whereby the business of the gospel is driven forward." By placing the word of God on every Christian's kitchen table, the mass-produced book undermined the authority of the church hierarchy, and hastened the breakup of the Holy Roman See. The Protestants of that time cheered this development. The Catholics were enraged and distraught. Since I am a Jew, had I lived at that time, I probably wouldn't have given a damn one way or another, since it would make no difference whether a pogrom was inspired by Martin Luther or Pope Leo X. Some gain, some lose, a few remain as they were.

Let us take as another example, television, although here I should add at once that in the case of television there are very few indeed who are not affected in one way or another. In America, where television has taken hold more deeply than anywhere else, there are many people who find it a blessing, not least those who have achieved high-paying, gratifying careers in television as executives, technicians, directors, newscasters and entertainers. On the other hand, and in the long run, television may bring an end to the careers of school teachers since school was an invention of the printing press and must stand or fall on the issue of how much importance the printed word will have in the future. There is no chance, of course, that television will go away but school teachers who are enthusiastic about its presence always call to my mind an image of some turn-of-the-century blacksmith who not only is singing the praises of the automobile but who also believes that his business will be enhanced by it. We know now that his business was not enhanced by it; it was rendered obsolete by it, as perhaps an intelligent blacksmith would have known.

The questions, then, that are never far from the mind of a person who is knowledgeable about technological change are these: Who specifically benefits from the development of a new technology? Which groups, what type of person, what kind of industry will be favored? And, of course, which groups of people will thereby be harmed?

...there are always winners and losers in technological change.

These questions should certainly be on our minds when we think about computer technology. There is no doubt that the computer has been and will continue to be advantageous to large-scale organizations like the military or airline companies or banks or tax collecting institutions. And it is equally clear that the computer is now indispensable to high-level researchers in physics and other natural sciences. But to what extent has computer technology been an advantage to the masses of people? To steel workers, vegetable store owners, automobile mechanics, musicians, bakers, bricklayers, dentists, yes, theologians, and most of the rest into whose lives the computer now intrudes? These people have had their private matters made more accessible to powerful institutions. They are more easily tracked and controlled; they are subjected to more examinations, and are increasingly mystified by the decisions made about them. They are more than ever reduced to mere numerical objects. They are being buried by junk mail. They are easy targets for advertising agencies and political institutions.

In a word, these people are losers in the great computer revolution. The winners, which include among others computer companies, multi-national corporations and the nation state, will, of course, encourage the losers to be enthusiastic about computer technology. That is the way of winners, and so in the beginning they told the losers that with personal computers the average person can balance a checkbook more neatly, keep better track of recipes, and make more logical shopping lists. Then they told them that computers will make it possible to vote at home, shop at home, get all the entertainment they wish at home, and thus make community life unnecessary. And now, of course, the winners speak constantly of the Age of Information, always implying that the more information we have, the better we will be in solving significant problems—not only personal ones but large-scale social problems, as well. But how true is this? If there are children starving in the world—and there are—it is not because of insufficient information. We have known for a long time how to produce enough food to feed every child on the planet. How is it that we let so many of them starve? If there is violence on our streets, it is not because we have insufficient information. If women are abused, if divorce and pornography and mental illness are increasing, none of it has anything to do with insufficient information. I dare say it is because something else is missing, and I don't think I have to tell this audience what it is. Who knows? This age of information may turn out to be a curse if we are blinded by it so that we cannot see truly where our problems lie. That is why it is always necessary for us to ask of those who speak enthusiastically of computer technology, why do you do this? What interests do you represent? To whom are you hoping to give power? From whom will you be withholding power?

I do not mean to attribute unsavory, let alone sinister motives to anyone. I say only that since technology favors some people and harms others, these are questions that must always be asked. And so, that there are always winners and losers in technological change is the second idea.

Third Idea

Here is the third. Embedded in every technology there is a powerful idea, sometimes two or three powerful ideas. These ideas are often hidden from our view because they are of a somewhat abstract nature. But this should not be taken to mean that they do not have practical consequences.

> The third idea is the sum and substance of what Marshall McLuhan meant when he coined the famous sentence, "The medium is the message."

Perhaps you are familiar with the old adage that says: To a man with a hammer, everything looks like a nail. We may extend that truism: To a person with a pencil, everything looks like a sentence. To a person with a TV camera, everything looks like an image. To a person with a computer, everything looks like data. I do not think we need to take these aphorisms literally. But what they call to our attention is that every technology has a prejudice. Like language itself, it predisposes us to favor and value certain perspectives and accomplishments. In a culture without writing, human memory is of the greatest importance, as are the proverbs, sayings and songs which contain the accumulated oral wisdom of centuries. That is why Solomon was thought to be the wisest of men. In Kings I we are told he knew 3,000 proverbs. But in a culture with writing, such feats of memory are considered a waste of time, and proverbs are merely irrelevant fancies. The writing person favors logical organization and systematic analysis, not proverbs. The telegraphic person values speed, not introspection. The television person values immediacy, not history. And computer people, what shall we say of them? Perhaps we can say that the computer person values information, not knowledge, certainly not wisdom. Indeed, in the computer age, the concept of wisdom may vanish altogether.

> The consequences of technological change are always vast, often unpredictable and largely irreversible.

The third idea, then, is that every technology has a philosophy which is given expression in how the technology makes people use their minds, in what it makes us do with our bodies, in how it codifies the world, in which of our senses it amplifies, in which of our emotional and intellectual tendencies it disregards. This idea is the sum and substance of what the great Catholic prophet, Marshall McLuhan meant when he coined the famous sentence, "The medium is the message."

Fourth Idea

Here is the fourth idea: Technological change is not additive; it is ecological. I can explain this best by an analogy. What happens if we place a drop of red dye into a beaker of clear water? Do we have clear water plus a spot of red dye? Obviously not. We have a new coloration to every molecule of water. That is what I mean by ecological change. A new medium does not add something; it changes everything. In the year 1500, after the printing press was invented, you did not have old Europe plus the printing press. You had a different Europe. After television, America was not America plus television. Television gave a new coloration to every political campaign, to every home, to every school, to every church, to every industry, and so on.

That is why we must be cautious about technological innovation. The consequences of technological change are always vast, often unpredictable and largely irreversible. That is also why we must be suspicious of capitalists. Capitalists are by definition not only personal risk takers but, more to the point, cultural risk takers. The most creative and daring of them hope to exploit new technologies to the fullest, and do not much care what traditions are overthrown in the process or whether or not a culture is prepared to function without such traditions. Capitalists are, in a word, radicals. In America, our most significant radicals have always been capitalists—men like Bell, Edison, Ford, Carnegie, Sarnoff, Goldwyn. These men obliterated the 19th century, and created the 20th, which is why it is a mystery to me that capitalists are thought to be conservative. Perhaps it is because they are inclined to wear dark suits and grey ties.

I trust you understand that in saying all this, I am making no argument for socialism. I say only that capitalists need to be carefully watched and disciplined. To be sure, they talk of family, marriage, piety, and honor but if allowed to exploit new technology to its fullest economic potential, they may undo the institutions that make such ideas possible. And here I might just give two examples of this point, taken from the American encounter with technology. The first concerns education. Who, we may ask, has had the greatest impact on American education in this century? If you are thinking of John Dewey or any other education philosopher, I must say you are quite wrong. The greatest impact has been made by quiet men in grey suits in a suburb of New York City called Princeton, New Jersey. There, they developed and promoted the technology known as the standardized test, such as IQ tests, the SATs and the GREs. Their tests redefined what we mean by learning, and have resulted in our reorganizing the curriculum to accommodate the tests.

A second example concerns our politics. It is clear by now that the people who have had the most radical effect on American politics in our time are not political ideologues or student protesters with long hair and copies of Karl Marx under their arms. The radicals who have changed the nature of politics in America are entrepreneurs in dark suits and grey ties who manage the large television industry in America. They did not mean to turn political discourse into a form of entertainment. They did not mean to make it impossible for an overweight person to run for high political office. They did not mean to reduce political campaigning to a 30-second TV commercial. All they were trying to do is to make television into a vast and unsleeping money machine. That they destroyed substantive political discourse in the process does not concern them.

Fifth Idea

I come now to the fifth and final idea, which is that media tend to become mythic. I use this word in the sense in which it was used by the French literary critic, Roland Barthes. He used the word "myth" to refer to a common tendency to think of our technological creations as if they were God-given, as if they were a part of the natural order of things. I have on occasion asked my students if they know when the alphabet was invented. The question astonishes them. It is as if I asked them when clouds and trees were invented. The alphabet, they believe, was not something that was invented. It just is. It is this way with many products of human culture but with none more consistently than technology. Cars, planes, TV, movies, newspapers—they have achieved mythic status because they are perceived as gifts of nature, not as artifacts produced in a specific political and historical context.

> The best way to view technology is as a strange intruder.

When a technology become mythic, it is always dangerous because it is then accepted as it is, and is therefore not easily susceptible to modification or control. If you should propose to the average American that television broadcasting should not begin until 5 PM and should cease at 11 PM, or propose that there should be no television commercials, he will think the idea ridiculous. But not because he disagrees with your cultural agenda. He will think it ridiculous because he assumes you are proposing that something in nature be changed; as if you are suggesting that the sun should rise at 10 AM instead of at 6.

Whenever I think about the capacity of technology to become mythic, I call to mind the remark made by Pope John Paul II. He said, "Science can purify religion from error and superstition. Religion can purify science from idolatry and false absolutes."

What I am saying is that our enthusiasm for technology can turn into a form of idolatry and our belief in its beneficence can be a false absolute. The best way to view technology is as a strange intruder, to remember that technology is not part of God's plan but a product of human creativity and hubris, and that its capacity for good or evil rests entirely on human awareness of what it does for us and to us.

Conclusion

And so, these are my five ideas about technological change. First, that we always pay a price for technology; the greater the technology, the greater the price. Second, that there are always winners and losers, and that the winners always try to persuade the losers that they are really winners. Third, that there is embedded in every great technology an epistemological, political or social prejudice. Sometimes that bias is greatly to our advantage. Sometimes it is not. The printing press annihilated the oral tradition; telegraphy annihilated space; television has humiliated the word; the computer, perhaps, will degrade community life. And so on. Fourth, technological change is not additive; it is ecological, which means, it changes everything and is, therefore too important to be left entirely in the hands of Bill Gates. And fifth, technology tends to become mythic; that is, perceived as part of the natural order of things, and therefore tends to control more of our lives than is good for us.

If we had more time, I could supply some additional important things about technological change but I will stand by these for the moment, and will close with this thought. In the past, we experienced technological change in the manner of sleep-walkers. Our unspoken slogan has been "technology über alles," and we have been willing to shape our lives to fit the requirements of technology, not the requirements of culture. This is a form of stupidity, especially in an age of vast technological change. We need to proceed with our eyes wide open so that we many use technology rather than be used by it.

Five Things We Need to Know About Technological Change, address to New Tech 98 (a conference), Denver, Colorado, March 27, 1998.

UNIT 2

The Economy

Unit Selections

4. **Beyond the Bar Code**, Charlie Schmidt
5. **How You'll Pay**, Evan I. Schwartz
6. **You've Got Spam**, Jonathan Krim
7. **Start-Up Finds Technology Slump Works in Its Favor**, John Markoff
8. **The Computer and the Dynamo**, Brian Hayes
9. **Bringing Linux to the Masses**, Fred Vogelstein

Key Points to Consider

- The overview to this unit says, "you may be surprised to learn... that some economists doubt the relationship between increased output per worker, that is, productivity, and information technology." Are you surprised? Things change quickly. What do economists say now?
- Does the assertion that up to 40 percent of all e-mail traffic is now spam seem too large? Use the Internet to find the source for this figure.
- The definition of what constitutes an operating system was an important part of the Department of Justice's recent antitrust suit against Microsoft. What is an operating system? Have you ever used Linux? Since it's free, why do you think your computer does not come with Linux already installed? The etymology of the word "Linux" is interesting. Trace it to its roots in a research project at Bell Labs in the 1970s.

Links: www.dushkin.com/online/
These sites are annotated in the World Wide Web pages.

CAUCE: Coalition Against Unsolicited Commercial Email
http://www.cauce.org

E-Commerce Times
http://www.ecommercetimes.com/

The End of Cash (James Gleick)
http://www.around.com/money.html

Fight Spam on the Internet
http://spam.abuse.net

The Linux Home Page
http://www.linux.org

Mersch Online: E-Cash Links
http://www.mersch.com/links/moneyzz.htm

The Rise of the Informediary
http://www.ait.unl.edu/crane/misgrad/sglee/informediary.htm

Smart Cards: A Primer
http://www.javaworld.com/javaworld/jw-12-1997/jw-12-javadev.html

Smart Card Group
http://www.smartcard.co.uk

Living in the United States at the beginning of the twenty-first century, it is hard to imagine that the accumulation of wealth once bordered on the disreputable. Listen to William Wordsworth, writing 200 years ago:

> The world is too much with us; late and soon,
> Getting and spending, we lay waste our powers:
> Little we see in Nature that is ours;
> We have given our hearts away, a sordid boon!

These are words that would quicken the pulse of any opponent of globalization. And no wonder. Writing a generation after James Watt perfected the steam engine, England was in the grips of the Industrial Revolution. Just as the developed world appears to be heading away from an industrial towards a service economy, so Wordsworth's world was moving from an agrarian to an industrial economy. And just as the steam engine has become the emblem of that transformation, the computer has become the symbol of this one.

Now, people did not stop farming after the Industrial Revolution, nor have they stopped producing steel and automobiles after the Information Revolution, although many commentators write as if this is exactly what has happened. It is true that we in the United States have largely stopped working in factories. In the last three decades, the number of employed Americans increased by over 50 million. During this same period, the decline in manufacturing jobs was in the hundreds of thousands. A large handful of these new workers are software developers, computer engineers, Web-site developers, manipulators of digital images—the glamour jobs of the information age. A much larger portion provide janitorial, health, food, and other services, leading to the charge that the American economy works because we take in one another's laundry. It is also often said that the fabulous productivity of American factory workers, augmented by computers, frees the rest of us to provide services. You may be surprised to learn, however, that some economists doubt the relationship between increased output per worker, that is, productivity, and information technology.

One area in which computers play an indisputable role is in the global economy. Over the past two decades, more and more of American manufacturing has migrated to countries with lower labor costs. It is impossible to imagine how a global manufacturing network could be coordinated without computers. Products manufactured abroad—with or without the productivity benefits of computers—pass through a bewildering array of shippers and distributors until they arrive on the shelves of a big box retailer in a Phoenix suburb or just-in-time to be bolted to the frame of an automobile outside of St. Louis. Or imagine how Federal Express could track its parcels as they make their way from an office in a San Jose suburb to one in New York. The ability to track manufactured items is about to improve significantly, according to Charlie Schmidt in "Beyond the Bar Code." With the help of tiny and inexpensive radio tags, a company like Gillette, can know the location of each razor blade that it manufactures, from the shipper to the distributor to the retailer to the consumer. (Cooperate by installing a tag reader in your medicine cabinet, and each time you toss a razor in the trash, another is on the way, or so the visionaries hope.) Personal microprocessors might even play a part in how you will pay for the razor blades—and use the subway and buy gas and make phone calls—if developers of "smart cards" have their way ("How You'll Pay," by Even I. Schwartz).

Recall what Neil Postman said in the first unit, "Technology giveth and technology taketh away." No sooner did computers, through the global economy and through more productive factories, enable so many of us to work in offices outfitted with computers, that economists began to notice something odd happening. The annual cost of what they call "end-user" operations exceeded, significantly, the cost of the computer itself. These "end-user" operations include trying to figure out why your software won't work with your printer, rearranging icons on your desktop, and in fact, anything that you do with your computer that you are not being paid to do.

As this volume of *Annual Editions: Computers in Society* goes to press, we are the in the midst of technology taking back something even more significant than the apparent low cost of computing. When computer scientists designed the protocols of ARPANET, the precursor of the Internet, for the Department of Defense in the seventies, e-mail happened almost serendipitously. It was not long before e-mail constituted the bulk of the traffic over the network. Among all the features of the Internet, e-mail remains among the most important. But there is a dark cloud on the horizon. Spam, or unsolicited e-mail, now accounts for 40 percent of the e-mail sent in the United States, according to Jonathan Krim, writing for the *Washington Post.* Microsoft and AOL have recently joined forces to push for legislation to regulate spam. Finally, this would not be America—and it certainly would not be computing—if someone did not find a way to make money when technology bites back, as it does in the case of spam. John Markoff, of *The New York Times,* profiles one of the Silicon Valley entrepreneurs who is making money after the tech bust by developing (what else?) software to block spam.

If the estimate that 40 percent of e-mail traffic is spam strikes you as an exaggeration, you will appreciate Brian Hayes excellent essay, "The Computer and the Dynamo." In the winter of 2000, stories began to circulate in reputable periodicals like the *Wall Street Journal* and *Computer* (published by a professional society of electrical engineers), that by 2010 "fully half of all electricity generated in the United States would go to keep computer hardware humming." When Hayes discovers that the story, like all stories, is more complex, we learn a lesson not just about the economy but about how to read critically as well.

There is another way in which the computer figures largely in the economy. For many years it has been thought of as an object that ambitious young men and women might use to achieve great wealth quickly. Even if the dot-com crash has battered this myth, it still resonates with Americans. After all, many of the world's richest men made their fortunes in computing. And they are still rich. Most spectacularly, Bill Gates's billions have come overwhelmingly from the hold that his company's operating systems have had on the small computer market since the very beginning. Fred Vogelstein's piece, "Bringing Linux to the Masses," shows how one man thinks there is money to be made by nipping at the heels of the Microsoft empire.

Try to imagine spaces in the United States, public or private, free from commercial endorsements of any sort. Once you perform this little experiment, you realize that the economy touches all aspects of our lives—our homes, our work, our play, our study, even our prayer. "Money makes the world go round," Joel Gray sang in *Cabaret* 30 years ago. Computers are there to help us earn it, collect it, and keep track of it.

Beyond the Bar Code

WITHIN A FEW YEARS, UNOBTRUSIVE TAGS ON RETAIL PRODUCTS WILL SEND RADIO SIGNALS TO THEIR MANUFACTURERS, COLLECTING A WEALTH OF INFORMATION ABOUT CONSUMER HABITS—AND ALSO RAISING PRIVACY CONCERNS.

BY CHARLIE SCHMIDT

IT'S 2010, AND AN ORDINARY DAY ON AN ASSEMBLY LINE. A bottle of root beer gets stamped with an innocuous little tag that immediately begins sending messages into cyberspace. The tag radios the soda company's Web site to report the bottle's whereabouts, allowing computers to track the bottle as it moves from the factory, through warehouses and distribution centers, and into a refrigerator at a corner drugstore. When the bottle is sold, the manufacturer is alerted and makes a new one to take its place. Finally, facing reincarnation at a recycling plant, the bottle radios its "last words" to a robotic separator that lifts it from a pile of plastic and newspaper and tosses it into a container of broken glass.

Manufacturers hoping to recoup some of the billions lost every year to theft, counterfeit, and depleted stocks have been closely watching a technology that promises to track the locations of individual products, from perfume bottles to car parts, in real time. At the heart of this scenario is a little device called a "radio frequency identification tag"—a silicon chip that boots up and transmits a signal when exposed to the energy field of a nearby reader. The ultimate goal is to put a radio tag on virtually every manufactured item, each tracked by a network of millions of readers in factories, trucks, warehouses and homes, transforming huge supply chains into intelligent, self-managing entities. Dick Cantwell, vice president of global business management at Gillette, says that the devices for reading the tags are "going to be a ubiquitous part of construction, whether you're building stores or homes.... We see this as a tremendous opportunity and we intend to make full use of the technology as it becomes available."

The radio tag has been around for more than half a century, largely relegated to specialized industries. Some of its first uses were for tracking livestock and government freight-train cargo; today highway tolls throughout the United States and abroad are outfitted with readers that pick up signals from a tag in your car as you drive by. Insiders in this field believe the technology won't blanket the consumer market, though, until someone produces a radio tag costing in the neighborhood of a penny—an assumption that has sent engineers back to the drawing board.

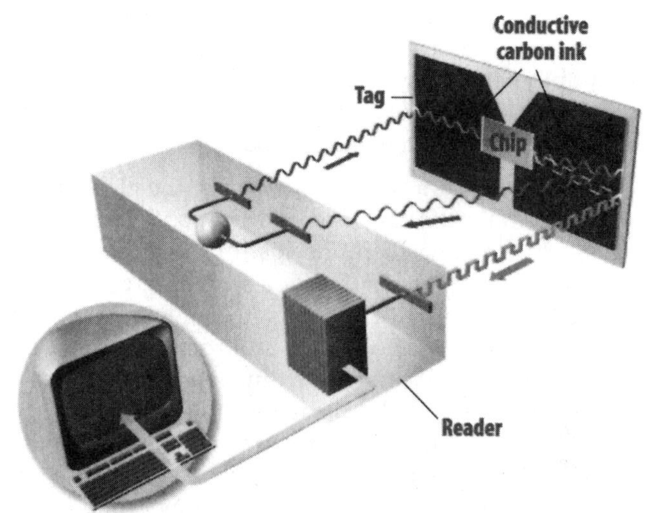

SLIM FILMS

Motorola's Radio Tag

In order to communicate with nearby readers, conductive carbon ink on the tag's surface intercepts a reader's electric field, generating a current between the tag and the reader to power the chip. The tag then transmits data stored on the chip to the reader, which decodes it and passes it on to a computer.

When the penny barrier is finally broken, manufacturers hope to use these tags as a next-generation bar code linking manufactured items to online databases containing product-specific information. Steve Halliday, vice president of technology at AIM, a trade association for manufacturers of tagging technology, says, "If I talk to companies and ask them if they want to replace the bar code with these tags, the answer can't be anything but yes. It's like giving them the opportunity to rule the world."

PENNIES OR LESS

Designed to speed up checkout counters and eliminate the drudgery of physical price marking, the bar code has come a long way since 1974—when it was introduced into retail sales on a pack of chewing gum in an Ohio supermarket. Far exceeding initial expectations, five billion codes are scanned every day in 140 countries. But even as retailers tip their hat to the bar code's success, few deny that a more sophisticated kind of tagging would be a great improvement. Bar codes identify only classes of products, not individual items, whereas a digital numbering scheme built into a tag has the capacity to identify *every single manufactured* item that is currently made and sold. Bar codes also have to be deliberately scanned at specific orientations; tags need only be within a reader's range. "Once the infrastructure is in place, managing inventory in warehouses and retail stores could become highly automated," says Alan Haberman, co-founder and governor-at-large of the Uniform Code Council, the organization that administers the bar code.

While attractive in concept, saturating the global supply chain with radio tags and readers poses huge challenges—chief among them the cost of the tag, typically more than a dollar. That's fine for a choice Hereford steer but much too expensive for consumer items. The high cost results from the silicon chip and from the antenna, a pricey metal coil that serves two functions. First, it uses a magnetic field emitted by the reader to power the chip. Then, when the chip is powered, the antenna transmits data from the chip back to the reader. Most manufacturers of radio tags, including Texas Instruments and Everett, WA-based Intermec, have developed tags based on this model, which is known as "inductive coupling."

It is the cost of the inductively coupled tags, hovering around a dollar, that lit a fire under Noel Eberhardt, vice president for advanced technology at Motorola. "The words that burned in my ears were 'this is interesting technology, but it's too expensive,'" Eberhardt says. "So I set out to build the lowest-cost silicon chip possible. And my first objective was to get rid of that coil."

In late 1995, Eberhardt started collaborating with Neil Gershenfeld, director of the MIT Media Lab's Physics and Media Group, on a cost-effective design. Eberhardt experimented with "capacitive coupling," an alternative method in which the tag is powered not by magnetic forces but by electrostatic charges emitted by the reader, charges similar to those that cause your clothes to stick together when you pull them out of the dryer. Using this mechanism, he found that coil antennas could be replaced with conductive carbon ink printed on paper which would pick up the electrostatic charges from the reader and create a current across the chip. The silicon chip—itself less than three millimeters square—could be mounted atop a sheet of paper lined with the special ink.

Without the metal coil, the cost of the tag dropped to less than 50 cents. The added flexibility of the paper material also meant Eberhardt's prototype tag could function when bent, cut or crumpled, as long as a remnant of the carbon ink-based antenna remained connected to the chip. Eberhardt and Gershenfeld announced their innovation in February 1999. Within weeks of the announcement, Motorola released the first and so far the only capacitively coupled tag.

TWO STEPS FORWARD

While Eberhardt's work moved the field closer to the penny tag, one lingering issue is whether low-cost tags will have a long enough range to make them practical. The range of Motorola's tag, for example, is limited to slightly more than a centimeter. Painting the antenna over an entire box extends the range to about 60 centimeters, but this won't help much on something as small as a can of tuna fish. Higher-cost tags, like Intermec's inductive tag, can transmit signals up to five meters but at a price beyond the reach of the typical consumer market. Echoing industry sentiments, Winston Guillory, vice president of the tag's business unit at Intermec, predicts that short-term applications will probably be limited to warehouse, rather than retail, management. And as for the penny tag, Guillory admits to a certain skepticism. "You hear all this talk about it," he says. "But it's never been delivered."

Despite the skepticism, many companies are in hot pursuit of the penny tag and its glittering potential payoff. Steve Van Fleet, International Paper's program manager for e-packaging, says the technology will benefit his company's clients by eliminating the "shrinkage" due to lost, stolen or spoiled goods that consumes three to five percent of everything they make. Last year, International Paper partnered with Motorola to use their radio tag on some of the 8.6 million metric tons of corrugated crates, boxes and other packages the paper company makes annually. Explains Van Fleet, "Say I have 5,000 cases on a truck that's supposed to be going to Cincinnati, but the driver goes to St. Louis and diverts 1,000 cases to the black market. Without the tags, we have limited visibility to detect this. But if we put readers in the truck, I can inventory these cases remotely using geographic information systems software on a laptop."

In addition to reducing shrinkage, such identification technology could help companies create a more realistic picture of how their products move through the supply chain and into the world. At Gillette, for example, sales information is transferred across warehouses, distribution centers and retail stores in batches by telephone, fax or e-mail. Since the information isn't matched with demand in real time, manufacturers often get stuck making too little, then too much, product in an attempt to

What's My Number?

Researchers at MIT's Auto-ID Center have developed a numbering scheme called the "Electronic Product Code" that will identify consumer products individually—not just by type, as today's Universal Product Code does. Stored in the memory of the tag's chip, the code uses 96 bits of information: an 8-bit header, two sets of 24 bits each identifying the manufacturer and product type, and a 40-bit serial number. Ninety-six bits can encode enough information to uniquely identify trillions upon trillions of objects. When readers lining warehouse or retail store shelves intercept a tag's radio signal, which contains the product code, they use the numbering scheme to direct networked computers to an Internet database called the "Object Naming Service." Designed and supported by the Auto-ID Center, the database system reads the portion of the code identifying the manufacturer and directs computers to the manufacturer's server address.

In order for tags to communicate with different servers regardless of the type of computer or software encountered, engineers at MIT are also developing a format called "Product Markup Language." In the future, files written in this format will contain information on things like shipping, expiration dates, recycling and advertising. Instructions for machines that change a product in some way could also be included in these files. For example, a specific frozen-food file would have cooking instructions for microwave ovens. A dynamic data file could describe physical changes that occur as a product ages or is consumed. So while the Electronic Product Code initially identifies a physical item, the Product Markup Language describes the item, and the Object Naming Service links the two, communicating product information between a manufacturer and an aisle in your local supermarket.

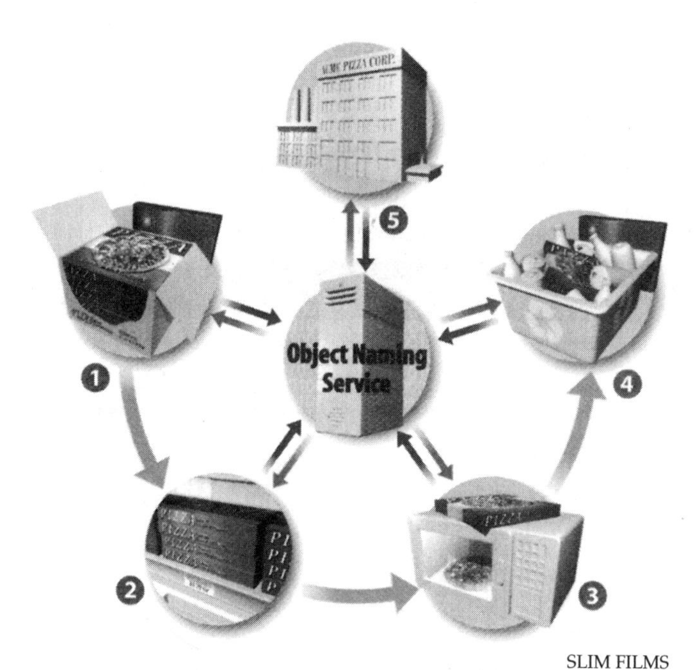

SLIM FILMS

Naming Network

The Object Naming Service, developed at MIT's Auto-ID Center, routes radio tag information from (1) warehouses, (2) store shelves, (3) microwave ovens and (4) recycling facilities back to the (5) manufacturer. That way, Acme Pizza knows when stock is low, when to send cooking instructions over the Internet to a customer's microwave oven and when to make another pizza to replace the one that's just been consumed.

keep up with the market. Economists call this the "bullwhip effect."

Getting the cost of the radio tag down to a penny isn't the only major technology challenge in this field. Another is linking the tags to the Web. That effort is being led by an MIT-based consortium of academic and industry partners called the Auto-ID Center. Kevin Ashton, the center's director, anticipates the arrival of the penny tag in five years and says he is now focusing, not on the tag, but on how to create a network architecture that squeezes as much profit out of it as possible. "And profit," says Sanjay Sarma, research director at the center, "will ultimately depend on a system that allows for the seamless flow of data throughout the entire supply chain."

The system will have to scale to unprecedented proportions, potentially handling *trillions of items* annually, making it one of the largest systems ever built. "It's an enormous undertaking," Ashton concedes. The Auto-ID Center, formed in 1999, with 11 corporate members including Gillette, Procter & Gamble, International Paper, Sun Microsystems and the Uniform Code Council, is simplifying the task by hooking on to an existing system: the Internet. "Initially, it was expected that tags would need quite a lot of memory," recalls Ashton. But Sarma, along with Sunny Siu and Auto-ID Center co-director David Brock, designed a cost-saving system that makes tags extremely simple and transfers all the information about a product to the Web—a description of its constituent parts, for example, or a record of its trajectory through the supply chain. The only information actually on the tag is an

Auto-ID Center invention called the "Electronic Product Code," a counterpart of the bar code that assigns a searchable number to each object (see box, "What's My Number?").

GETTING PERSONAL

According to Cantwell, Gillette and many other companies envision using tags to download promotional material to displays mounted on store shelves, or even to shoppers' handheld computers. By simply scanning a product in front of a networked reader linked to a computer monitor, customers could one day retrieve user instructions, specifications and other product information to help them decide, for instance, which toothbrush is more flexible or which soup has less sodium.

Talk to Cantwell awhile longer, and he's likely to bring up Gillette's next goal: using readers to track consumer use of its products at home. Gillette sees the technology engaged in direct consumer marketing, which would rely on personalized information obtained from readers installed where products are actually used—in your refrigerator, say. While this scenario may be decades away, the coming era of ubiquitous computing could bring Internet access to every household appliance. "Smart" fridges could monitor tagged products, learn your food preferences and shopping schedule, and then buy all your groceries for you. And, if you let them, companies like Gillette will monitor personal use of their products. Throw one of their razors into the trash, and another one would be on its way.

That's a vision that, predictably, has marketers salivating. But are you ready for a system that surrounds you and monitors your family's day-to-day activities? Watchdog organizations like the Center for Democracy and Technology, a Washington, DC-based public interest group focused on civil liberties, worry about new challenges to privacy. "Imagine putting a frozen pizza into a microwave that downloads cooking instructions from Pizza Hut," suggests the group's staff counsel, Alan Davidson. "Is Pizza Hut going to track the server of that microwave? Will they find out where and when you bought the pizza, and are they logging this transaction? Suddenly they have a detailed record that describes your personal activities."

One of the greatest challenges facing the creators of such an infrastructure, predicts Davidson, will be finding ways to allow consumers to opt in or out of the system as it becomes more pervasive. "It's not clear how that's going to happen," he says. "But it's important if companies want to prevent a public backlash against these systems."

In some ways, the technology itself has certain limitations that minimize privacy concerns. The range of a tag seldom exceeds five meters, nor can the tags be read through walls or other thick barriers. What's more, Electronic Product Codes identify objects, not people. The only way for a manufacturing company to link the two is through an automatic debiting system or credit card, for which the consumer would most likely have to give consent. Sarma acknowledges that privacy and security are concerns at the Auto-ID Center, adding that industrial uses, for which these issues are minimal, are certain to emerge before consumer applications. "Security concerns will be resolved long before we get to the consumer," he says. "We are bringing a lot of technical and organizational resources to bear on this issue."

Before implementing the tagging system, the Auto-ID Center will have to seek consensus from the Uniform Code Council and its European counterpart, a process that could take two to five years. While the online infrastructure now being created could set the stage for an explosion of radio-based identification technology across the consumer marketplace, in all likelihood the change will start slowly. First in warehousing, out of the average consumer's sight. Then among some isolated and expensive retail items worthy of the investment. Until, finally, a Wal-Mart salesman shows you the latest refrigerator on the market, complete with Internet connectivity, the ability to analyze its own contents—and optional online access to your wallet.

Tag Teams

Some companies manufacturing radio tags

COMPANY	LOCATION	APPLICATIONS
BiStar Technology	Oxfordshire, UK	Warehouse management, article tracking, building-access control
Intermec	Everett, WA	Supply-chain management, vehicle tracking, access control, mobile commerce
Motorola	Rolling Meadows, IL	Warehouse management, ski-lift tickets, building access, high-value consumer goods tracking
Philips Semiconductors	Eindhoven, Neth.	Airline baggage tracking, supply-chain management, tracking of retail articles
SCS	San Diego, CA	Airline baggage tracking, warehouse management, garment tracking
Texas Instruments	Dallas, TX	Tracking books in libraries, airline baggage handling, express parcel identification

Fair game: Subway riders in Washington use smart cards equipped with a memory chip and radio transponder.

how you'll pay

Smart cards, radio tags, and microchip buttons are going to revolutionize the way you buy things.

By Evan I. Schwartz

To catch the future of payment schemes, go underground. Beneath the streets of the nation's capital, more than 60 percent of peak-time riders on the Metro (Washington, DC's subway network) have switched from magnetic-stripe tickets to "smart cards" embedded with memory chips and radio transponders. Riders can load as much as $200 into their SmarTrip cards at a kiosk or over the Internet. Antennae built into subway turnstiles pick up radio signals from the cards and convert them into streams of bits that denote the embarkation point and subtract money from the card's memory. Similar systems are being planned for other U.S. cities, and next year London will adopt these newfangled fare cards for its famous double-decker buses and massive Underground subway network.

But the ultimate destiny of such electronic-payment devices goes way beyond multibillion-dollar public-transit projects. Smart cards and rival gadgets are rapidly evolving into technology platforms that could trigger changes in everything from urban commerce and suburban shopping sprees to national security. Commuters could eventually use such devices not only to buy coffee and newspapers, but also to store bus transfers, hold medical records and drug prescriptions, download coupons, and redeem tickets to museums and sporting events. "The current thrust is to reduce or eliminate the cash handled by these fare collection systems," says David de Kozan, vice president of market planning and support at San Diego-based Cubic Transportation Systems, which supplies cards and readers to the Washington and London transit networks. "But the technology can also provide other tools. You could rent out spaces on the card for different applications."

And so the competition to produce and popularize the most secure, the most convenient, and the most versatile high-tech payment system is heating up. One contestant in this race is indeed the smart card, which incorporates not only a memory chip but also a microprocessor. Touted for more than a decade and already popular in Europe, the cards have yet to make it big in the United States, Washington's Metro notwithstanding. Meanwhile, radio wave transponder tags that supply identification data, as well as coin-size microprocessors that store security codes and encrypted money are gaining ground.

The merchants, banks, and device manufacturers that figure out and deliver what people want from these technologies stand to reap a rich bounty of profits and transaction fees on the $5.7 trillion in annual credit- and debit-card purchasing worldwide—not to mention tens of billions of dollars more in the market for secure identification, subway payment, and other applications.

It won't be easy. Credit card companies and banks have long pined for a large-scale rollout of microchip-based payment devices mainly because storing customers' identity data chips has proved a more secure and reliable way to prevent fraud than encoding data on a traditional magnetic stripe. And because consumers are not liable for transactions conducted using their stolen identities, merchants and banks eat the estimated $4 billion in annual losses. In high-profile tests—most notably Visa's trial at the 1996 Olympic Games in Atlanta and a 1998 Citibank and Chase Manhattan experiment on Manhattan's Upper West Side—stored-value smart cards have been resounding flops. Not only that, the costs of implementing a new system are formidable. Diana Knox, senior vice president of emerging channels at Visa

U.S.A., estimates that it would cost $11 billion to replace magnetic-stripe cards and upgrade U.S. authorization terminals and networks. "The infrastructure hurdles are enormous, and there isn't much money in processing small transactions," Knox says.

MERCHANTS, BANKS, AND DEVICE MAKERS THAT FIGURE OUT THE BEST PAYMENT TECHNOLOGIES WILL REAP A RICH BOUNTY FROM THE $5.7 TRILLION IN ANNUAL CREDIT- AND DEBIT-CARD TRANSACTIONS

That is why smart cards have for years been a technology in search of compelling applications. Yet it is a quest that is quickly gaining new urgency—and not just beneath the streets of Washington and London. Retailers such as Target Stores are introducing smart cards that can receive and redeem digital coupons and other incentives. And over the next few years, the credit card industry will mandate that many European, Asian, and Latin American countries replace magnetic-stripe credit cards with smart cards. Toni Merschen, senior vice president for chip and mobile commerce at MasterCard International's laboratory in Waterloo, Belgium, says, "We have a big global migration ahead of us."

Smarter Cards

The potential of the smart card to handle many different applications has revived hopes for making the technology as commonplace in the United States as it is becoming overseas. Advances in the technology itself are driving the possibilities in the marketplace. Three years ago smart cards boasted the processing power of a 1980 Apple II computer; today's versions are approaching the level of a 386-class PC, circa 1990. Most smart cards can hold 32 kilobytes of data, and their embedded microprocessors can execute simple application programs stored in 64 kilobytes of flash memory.

That's enough computing power to run multiple payment, customer loyalty, health-care, and security applications on a single card. "It is essentially a PC without the keyboard or display," says Neville Pattinson, director of business development for New York City–based SchlumbergerSema, a top maker of microprocessor cards. The cost has dropped below $5 apiece for quantities of thousands, and smart cards with the power of a Pentium-class PC are within reach this decade, he says.

Perhaps the biggest push for smart cards is coming from large organizations that want them for their employees. In one of the largest smart-card rollouts under way, the U.S. Department of Defense is issuing a Common Access Card to every member of the armed services. Each card includes a photograph and a microchip that authenticates identity whenever the card holder enters an agency facility or logs onto its computer network. The card will also encrypt and decode employees' e-mail. More than a million of these cards have been deployed, and the department plans to issue the cards to all its 3.5 million officers, service members, and civilian employees within the next year.

Prompted in part by the security concerns that crystallized after September 11, other government agencies are following suit. The Aviation and Transportation Security Act and other recent legislation mandate that the Department of Transportation, the Border Patrol, and other agencies investigate a universal worker-identification device that would hold biometric data such as fingerprints and digital "faceprints." The devices would be automatically monitored at checkpoints or spot-checked by roving security officials. Workers may need the cards to log onto agency and airport computer networks, as well as to gain physical entry into facilities. "Post-September 11, there are secure-identification projects going on all around the world," says Ed MacBeth, senior vice president of marketing at ActivCard, a Fremont, CA, company that is supplying software for the Defense Department's card. "The card has to be smart enough to identify the user," MacBeth says. "It's no longer good enough just to flash a photo ID."

Although government agencies are rolling out the largest number of cards, the technology is turning up at major corporations, as well as college campuses and other large institutions. Hewlett-Packard, Microsoft, and Sun Microsystems are all issuing cards to tens of thousands of employees for building access and for logging into their corporate computer networks. Some employers are enhancing cards with such applications as electronic-cash accounts that can be used at their company cafeterias. Managing the cards is getting so complicated that companies are contracting the work out to banks.

Paying by Waving

But are smart cards too smart for their own good? Developers of technologies that compete with smart cards argue that it's precisely the complexity of those cards that will spell their doom in the marketplace. For such everyday applications as buying gasoline, smart cards may be impractical: they require new equipment and authorization procedures. "We've been hearing the pitch about smart cards for 10 years," says Joe Giordano, a business development vice president at ExxonMobil. "But there isn't a need for the technology unless it has a real benefit for the consumer."

FASTER FILL-UPS: EXXONMOBIL'S SPEEDPASS TRANSMITS A CUSTOMER'S INFORMATION TO A GAS PUMP OR CHECKOUT REGISTER, WHICH BILLS THE CREDIT CARD.

That's what prompted Giordano to develop an alternative technology for streamlining the purchase of gasoline. Brainstorming on an airplane trip nearly 10 years ago, he sketched a simple payment idea on some cocktail napkins on his tray table. He envisioned a toe-size device that would hang on a key chain. "It needed to be durable, reliable, simple, and lightweight," Giordano recalls thinking at the time. Wave it in front of a gas pump, and a customer's identification code would be picked up from the device's built-in radio transponder. A customer would no longer have to find her wallet, pull out her credit card, and swipe it through a reader. Before Giordano got off the plane, he had even come

Digital Payment's Big Three

MAKERS	APPLICATIONS	STORED INFORMATION	DEVICE TALKS TO READER	READER TALKS TO NETWORK
Smart card				
SchlumbergerSema (New York, NY) **Gemplus** (Gemenos, France)	Customer loyalty program at Target Stores	Personal-identification data; programs that formulate special offers, discounts, and loyalty certificates	Swiped through a checkout counter reader, a card's embedded microprocessor communicates via its gold-plated contact pad.	Transactions are authorized via data lines, and purchasing information used to formulate loyalty offers is uploaded to the store's database.
Speedpass				
ExxonMobil Speedpass Network (Fairfax, VA)	McDonald's drive-through service	Customer's identification code	A radio transmitter inside the McDonald's order box signals to nearby Speedpass transponder to emit its unique identification code.	The unique code and purchase amount are sent over the standard credit-card authorization network.
iButton				
Dallas Semiconductor (Dallas, TX)	Canadian vending machines	Digital-cash accounts	When an iButton is touched to a vending machine's receptor, the sale is debited from the chip's memory.	The self-contained system does not communicate with any network.
	Segway starter key	Vehicle identification data and codes for controlling top speed and steering sensitivity	Touching the Segway key to the receptor on the handlebar identifies the driver and adjusts the vehicle's settings.	The self-contained system does not communicate with any network.

up with a name for this device: Speedpass.

Giordano successfully sold the idea in a series of corporate strategy meetings. Nearly six million people now use the Speedpass, and the payment system has been installed at more than 7,500 Exxon and Mobil service stations. Unlike the smart card, Speedpass has no onboard computer chip or memory. It consists of a radio transponder programmed to transmit a digital code that identifies its user. A radio receiver inside the gas pump constantly scouts the immediate airwaves for the presence of a Speedpass, and when it finds one, it simply picks up the code numbers that authorize payment from the customer's credit card. (Similar radio tags are embedded in the FastLane, FasTrak, and E-Zpass units millions of U.S. motorists use to pay highway tolls.)

ExxonMobil is now taking this simple message to other retailers. Giordano, currently vice president of the company's Speedpass Network unit, is signing deals with fast-food restaurants and grocery stores. The Speedpass is being tested in Chicago-area McDonald's restaurants and at Stop and Shop supermarkets around Boston. At a McDonald's restaurant, the reader is incorporated into the drive-through order box. At Stop and Shop, Speedpass readers are built into automatic teller machines in special checkout lanes. In addition, Giordano has signed a deal with Timex to build the devices into watches that will be available in 2003. The goal, he says, is to make Speedpass a "ubiquitous form of customer ID and payment."

Button-Down Solution

The wild card in the electronic-payment competition against smart cards comes in a smaller package. The iButton—a 16-millimeter diameter steel canister containing a microchip—has advantages over both technologies. The iButtons, made by Dallas Semiconductor, are activated when they are placed in contact with a receptor pad on, say, a vending machine. As soon as it touches the pad, the iButton transmits data directly to the chip inside the receptor. The device can be made into a ring, worn on a necklace, or built into a wide array of garments, says Dallas Semiconductor vice president Michael Bolan, iButton's coinventor.

Unlike a Speedpass, which stores nothing but the user's identification code, an iButton can hold electronic cash, coupons, and other data. In that sense, it does resemble a smart card, but Dallas Semiconductor claims that the steel button is more rugged than the plastic card. And cheaper, too: Bolan says that his company supplies the devices for less than $1 each in large quantities. By contrast, SchlumbergerSema's Pattinson confirms that smart cards typically cost at least $4 each.

In addition, because the iButton isn't a major-brand credit card, there are no transaction fees, which range from two to six percent of every MasterCard, Visa, or American Express payment. The iButton's chief drawback is that, unlike other payment technologies, it adheres to no recognized standard: it stores and communicates data in a proprietary format.

THE 65 MILLION iBUTTONS IN USE PAY FOR SUBWAYS IN ISTANBUL, PARKING METERS IN SOUTH AMERICA, AND VENDING MACHINES IN CANADA. UP NEXT: TURNING ON THE SEGWAY.

In iButton's most extensive installation so far, it serves as a subway pass in Istanbul, Turkey. Riders entering the station simply touch their buttons to a reader, which deducts the payment from electronic cash stored on the button. Five million people now use the so-called Istanbul Purse, which is also gaining acceptance as a form of payment among the city's merchants.

All told, according to Dallas Semiconductor, there are more than 65 million iButtons in use worldwide. That includes large installations in parking meters in Brazil and Argentina, gas stations in Moscow and Mexico City, bus terminals in China, hospitals in Switzerland, apartment buildings in Korea, and vending machines in Canada.

One application should drive that number even higher. Dean Kamen, inventor of the self-balancing Segway electric scooter, which is expected to hit the market in 2003, has selected the iButton as the Segway's all-purpose starter key and security device. To activate the vehicle, the user touches the steel canister, mounted on a key-size piece of plastic, against small metal contacts on the handlebar. The Segway owner can program the chip with a variety of access features, including top speed and steering sensitivity. Companies with Segway fleets can use that ability to control their users' driving behavior.

Fraud Busters

Although most Americans have yet to encounter any of these portable payment and identification devices, the technologies are proliferating throughout the rest of the world. Smart cards were introduced more than a decade ago, and in the past few years they have gained real momentum; more than 685 million smart cards were shipped last year alone, 60 percent of them going to Europe and 30 percent to Asia, according to Gartner Group, a market research firm in Stamford, CT. "My colleagues from the States think it's hilarious," says Clare Hirst, a London-based analyst with Gartner. "They come over here and say, 'you've got chip cards for everything.'"

Most of the smart cards in Europe are postage stamp-size SIMs, or subscriber identity modules, that give a mobile-phone owner the option of requiring a password for placing calls. These cards, which large numbers of Europeans have been using for a decade, not only store identity data but also hold phone numbers, address lists, and other personal information. Users can pop their cards into new phones, retain all their collected data, and begin charging calls to their own accounts. Due to the far lower incidence of telephone fraud in the United States, U.S. phone companies have been policing scams only after they have happened. Thus, Americans are just starting to gain experience with chip card technology already familiar to Europeans.

Europeans have deep-seated reasons for their devotion to stopping fraud and their rapid adoption of smart cards. Because government-owned telecommunications companies have precluded a competitive business environment in Europe, even local calls are expensive. "There is no such thing as a free local call in Europe," says Pattinson, of SchlumbergerSema. To reduce telecommunications costs, European merchants process credit card transactions in batches rather than individually in real time, the standard practice in the United States. By the time European merchants check authorization, the thieves have made their getaway. It's simple for store clerks and waiters to "clone" credit cards: they quickly skim the data from magnetic-stripe credit cards and transfer the information to new cards for use somewhere else. This procedure makes it easier for thieves using stolen or cloned cards.

Smart cards go a long way toward thwarting such popular crimes, and they save European retailers a bundle: because the money is in memory, there is no need for costly phone-based verification. Before the introduction of smart cards in Europe, card cloning and theft resulted in fraud rates as much as 10 times higher than those in the United States, says MasterCard's Merschen. Key features of today's smart cards were invented in France in the mid-1970s to combat this very problem. "It's easy to hack into a card with a mag stripe," says Peter Buhler, manager of IBM's Secure Systems Research Group in Zurich, Switzerland. "Smart card chips are resistant to tampering."

Europe is now going one step further. The Europay-MasterCard-Visa global consortium, or EMV, has set a series of deadlines by which all banks in Europe and many parts of Asia and Latin America must issue smart cards to their customers. By 2005 the switch to smart cards should be complete in many countries. Though its edict lacks the force of law, the consortium can use strong financial incentives and punishments to impose nearly universal acceptance. "EMV has said it will no longer absorb the cost of fraud in those regions," says Gartner's Hirst. "So if they don't comply, the banks and merchants will have to take on the cost of the fraud themselves."

This liability transfer is "the ultimate enforcement measure," says Visa's Knox, who notes that there will be "real financial consequences for those who fail to adopt smart cards." The cost of moving so many banks and merchants to smart cards is expected to total billions of dollars, but in much of the world, the antifraud benefit is expected to justify the expense, she says. In the United States, however, where fraud rates are so much lower, the savings reaped from reducing fraud would not justify a comparable action, Knox adds.

Yet the United States could very well be forced to join the global conversion, Gartner's Hirst predicts. "If fraud isn't as easy in other regions, the crime will shift to the U.S.," she says, "or it will look high in comparison." ActivCard's MacBeth agrees. "If the rest of the world deploys smart cards, and that eliminates much of the fraud elsewhere," he says, "the criminals will focus on the United States, and we could become the last bastion of magnetic-stripe fraud." This, he says, would force the United States to replace its infrastructure. "We wouldn't have much of a choice."

Shopping's Next Wave

Or the current infrastructure could be bypassed altogether. In the future, portable computing devices and smart cards will become one and the same, perhaps lessening the importance of stationary card readers. Diana Knox of Visa says the credit card networks are already experimenting with smart card capabilities in cell phones and handheld computers. Long-advertised scenarios in which a cell phone user zaps money through the air to a vending machine or to a friend's cell phone will become commonplace, she predicts. "At the end of the day," she says, "it's not about the devices as much as it is the payment network. Visa can be inside the phone or inside a personal digital assistant."

SHOPS COULD TARGET SMART-CARD HOLDERS IN THE VICINITY WITH WIRELESS TRANSMISSIONS THAT PROMOTE DISCOUNTS ON EVERYTHING FROM T-SHIRTS TO BOOKS AND BACKPACKS.

That might be wishful thinking. As PayPal, the online payments pioneer, has shown in the fast-growing market for person-to-person payments over the Internet, cost and complexity must be much lower before consumers will accept the technology (*see "Digital Cash Payoff,"* TR *December 2001*). In eBay auctions, PayPal introduced the ability to transfer cash to anyone with an e-mail address. Thus online sellers could accept money from far-flung strangers without opening expensive Visa and MasterCard merchant accounts. Once PayPal struck the right formula, millions of users flocked to the system, providing the critical mass of success that led to eBay's $1.5 billion acquisition of PayPal in October.

Such rapid market acceptance helps explain why so much energy is now being channeled into finding plausible applications for new payment technologies and why the SmarTrip system in Washington's Metro is considered such an important market test. Another key trial is under way at Target Stores, the third largest U.S. retailer. Target is issuing microprocessor-equipped Visa smart cards to its customers. Checkout lanes with smart-card readers will be programmed to monitor purchasing patterns and load coupons, promotional offers, and loyalty incentives into each card's 16 kilobytes of memory. To better integrate Internet commerce with what happens in its stores, Target is giving free smart-card readers to shoppers, who plug the devices into their home PCs to access a special Web site. Eventually, customers will be able to download electronic coupons and review new offers. "This is the first test of its kind in the world," says Visa's Knox. "Many merchants are cautiously watching what is happening at Target."

The next wave of applications is bound to bring more creative ideas, says Ted Selker, who heads the MIT Media Lab's context-aware computing group. His experiments have included putting chips in clothing, furniture, and other everyday items. Selker foresees a day when airport shops will target smart-card holders in the vicinity with wireless transmissions that promote discounts on everything from T-shirts to books and backpacks. Another possibility: as a customer approaches a rack of clothing in a store, wireless readers in the clothes hangers glean his size information from the smart card in his wallet, causing lights on the hangers of outfits that are his size to flash. Selker says the goal isn't so much to wow as to figure out "how do you add functions that can simplify people's lives?"

In the meantime, payment devices will assuredly proliferate—to the point that the average person might carry four or five variations of smart cards. No single technology will likely dominate; rather, radio tags, chip buttons, and smart cards will catch on wherever their qualities are best suited. A person might have an iButton for secure access to her apartment building, a Speedpass to buy gasoline and convenience store items, a smart card for riding the subway and storing tickets to events around town, a multiapplication card for corporate access and health-care data, and even a cell phone with a smart chip that can transfer money to the phone of a friend.

Just don't be too surprised to find that your digital fingerprints are floating through the air along with your money. As the payment technologies take off, you'll be able to do just about anything with your smart card or Speedpass or iButton. And then you'll be asking whether you can do anything without them.

You've Got Spam

And so does everyone else—accounting for 40 percent of e-mails sent in America

By Jonathan Krim
Washington Post Staff Writer

The flood of unsolicited messages sent over the Internet is growing so fast that spam may soon account for half of all U.S. e-mail traffic, making it not only a hair-pulling annoyance but also an increasing drain on corporate budgets and possibly a threat to the continued usefulness of the most successful tool of the computer age.

Spam continues to defy most legal and technical efforts to stamp it out. The surge has spurred calls for national legislation, but deep divisions remain regarding what constitutes spam and how best to regulate it. In the meantime, spammers, Internet providers, company network administrators and anti-spam vigilantes are locked in a ferocious electronic arms race. Many spammers have become so adept at masking their tracks that they are rarely found. They are so technologically sophisticated that they adjust their systems on the fly to counter special filters and other barriers thrown up against them. They can even electronically commandeer unprotected computers, turning them into spam-launching weapons of mass production.

"The spammers are evil folks," said Matt Korn, America Online Inc.'s vice president for network operations. "As hard as we're working, they are working 24 hours a day. That's the level to which this battle has escalated."

Roughly 40 percent of all e-mail traffic in the United States is spam, up from 8 percent in late 2001 and nearly doubling in the past six months, according to Brightmail Inc., a major vendor of anti-spam software. By the end of this year, industry experts predict, fully half of all e-mail will be unsolicited. (About 40 percent of U.S. Postal Service mail is business marketing.)

MANY COMPANIES WITH LEGITIMATE products rely on the ability to reach millions of existing and potential customers through e-mail, and they argue that their solicitations are not spam. But of the total volume of unsolicited mail pouring into e-mail boxes, much is pornographic, comes from scam artists or contains viruses.

"We're seeing a slow degradation of the medium," said Jason Catlett, a computer scientist and founder of Junkbusters Corp., an anti-spam and privacy advocacy group. "Many people don't get on the Internet or abandon it because they don't like the trash that they see."

According to Ferris Research Inc., a San Francisco consulting group, spam will cost U.S. organizations more than $10 billion this year. The figure includes lost productivity and the additional equipment, software and manpower needed to combat the problem.

Robert Mahowald, research manager for IDC, said his firm estimates that for a company with 14,000 employees, the annual cost to fight spam is $245,000. And, he said, "there's no end in sight."

THE FRONT LINE IN THE WAR against spam is inside an unmarked building in Northern Virginia, where a bank of computer screens tracks the volume of e-mail pouring into the system used by America Online's 35 million subscribers.

On a recent afternoon, an unexpected spike suggested the work of spammers using one of their favorite new weapons, the "dictionary" attack.

With special software, spammers can generate millions of e-mails using combinations of letters and numbers, such as JaneH79, placed in front of the @aol.com portion of the address. Enough are generated that many match real e-mail accounts.

That's when Charles Stiles and an anti-spam team take over. They work in a separate backroom because some of the Web sites they need to examine to track down owners are so sexually explicit that colleagues might find the workplace offensive.

The group first determines whether AOL's spam filters, which block 1 billion messages a day, need to be adjusted. Meanwhile, a large monitor displays the code for the network address of the computer that sent the suspected spam. The address is automatically cross-checked against a list of registered owners.

But there is an immediate problem: Some of the addresses show up on the display as "unknown." Many others are obvious fakes, making it difficult to track down the senders to get them to stop, or to sue them if they don't.

Similar scenarios play out every day at every Internet provider, from giants such as AOL, Microsoft Corp. and EarthLink Inc. to tiny firms that serve a few thousand customers. And in general, the efforts are about as effective as plugging a water-main break with chewing gum.

Although there are anti-spam laws in 26 states, including Virginia and Maryland, the direct-marketing industry and some Internet retailers have successfully lobbied Congress against a federal law.

That posture has softened as the volume of spam—and complaints from irate businesses and home-computer users—has skyrocketed. Marketers now say that while they prefer technological solutions, a national law would be helpful and more effective than a patchwork of state regulations that vary in strength and approach.

Microsoft, AOL, Verizon Communications Inc., EarthLink and other Internet providers also are aggressively pushing for national legislation.

But prospects for getting a law passed are unclear. Industry and many anti-spam activists are divided over how to combat the problem, and even on how spam should be defined.

Marketers of legitimate products worry that their messages are getting lost in the din, threatening what has become a thriving business. Although Web site advertising fell victim to the dot-com implosion, marketing via e-mail has been an Internet bright spot, growing to a $1.4 billion industry last year, according to Jupiter Research.

These companies want any law to distinguish their ability to distribute such e-mail from messages that have deceptive subject lines, commit fraud or are designed to thwart detection of the sender so they cannot be stopped on demand.

"We want to make sure we can get to who the bad guys are," said Louis Mastria, spokesman for the powerful Direct Marketing Association. "Accountability is paramount."

But anti-spam activists argue that any piece of unsolicited commercial e-mail sent in bulk is spam, even if it comes from "legitimate" businesses.

"Spam is postage-due marketing," Catlett said. "It's obvious to every Internet user that if every company out there can send them junk whenever they feel like it until they're told to stop, junk e-mail will overrun them."

What worries the anti-spam community most is what happens if legitimate marketers step up their e-mailings to try to rise above the clutter.

"There are 24 million small businesses in the country. If just 1 percent of those got hold of your e-mail address, and each of them sent you one e-mail a year, that's 657 messages in your inbox every day. And that's just small businesses," said John C. Mozena, a founder of the Coalition Against Unsolicited Commercial Email.

Mozena, Catlett and others argue that only an outright ban on unsolicited commercial e-mail will make a dent in the volume of spam, as happened when junk faxes were banned in 1991.

"Almost none of them [state laws] do more than regulate the manner of spamming," said David E. Sorkin, who teaches technology and privacy law at the John Marshall Law School in Chicago. "I view them as counterproductive.... You may ameliorate some of the symptoms, but you are not dealing with the problem itself. Then legitimate marketers will start to think it's okay, so volume goes way up."

The practical effect of such a ban would be an "opt-in" system, in which companies would have to wait for consumers to request commercial e-mail before it could be sent. This was the system adopted by the European Union last year.

Marketers and most Internet providers oppose requiring opt-in, preferring the "opt-out" system that most firms use. In opt-out, a consumer's approval to receive solicitations via e-mail is assumed unless he or she requests otherwise.

Amazon.com Inc., the largest Internet retailer and an active lobbyist on the issue, also does not support an outright spam ban.

"We don't do unsolicited commercial e-mail," said Paul Misener, the firm's vice president for global public policy. "But we get really concerned when there are hard-line rules aimed at one medium. We send out thousands of e-mails every day. What if we make a mistake? Accidents happen, and the real harm is minuscule."

Only one state, Delaware, bans unsolicited commercial bulk e-mail. But Steven Wood, a lawyer with the state attorney general's office, said the state has yet to have a successful prosecution because it is so difficult to track spammers down. Most states do little enforcement on their own. Instead, their laws are used by companies as grounds to sue spammers.

Some in the industry also worry that an outright ban on spam would violate free-speech provisions of the Constitution. But many legal experts argue that a properly written ban would stand a good chance of passing constitutional muster, as the junk-fax law did.

Like junk faxes, spam imposes a cost on users, occupying space in e-mail boxes and on networks and the computer servers that power them. That cost can outweigh protections on commercial speech, as long as restrictions are not based on the content of the e-mail, lawyers said.

Analysts say the best chance for legislative action is the return of a bill sponsored in the last session of Congress by Sens. Conrad Burns (R-Mont.) and Ron Wyden (D-Ore.), which would outlaw e-mail with deceptive subject lines and forged code that masks a sender's identity.

Burns said he hopes to join forces with House members, such as Rep. Heather A. Wilson (D-N.M.), who also have proposed spam legislation. Burns said he is optimistic his bill will pass this year and that President Bush will sign it.

So far, the White House has been silent on legislation, although the Federal Trade Commission plans a three-day symposium on the problem late next month.

Bruce P. Mehlman, assistant secretary for technology policy at the Commerce Department, said the administration would wait to see what is proposed.

"Consumers are choking on spam, and it is clogging the arteries of the Internet," he said. "Personally, I believe we need to find ways to help consumers protect themselves... provided they would be effective, have minimal impact on innovation and preserve consumer choice. The best anti-spam solutions may well be technologically based and market-driven."

EVEN ON THEIR BEST DAYS, Charles Stiles and the AOL anti-spam team are reduced to playing defense.

They filter out as much as they can, act on customer complaints and try to contact as many spam originators as possible. AOL, like all major Internet providers, also offers users additional spam-fighting tools.

But some in the anti-spam community are more aggressive, waging a daily electronic war that is largely invisible to the average computer user.

At the quieter end of the battlefield, activists such as Chip Rosenthal, a computer consultant in Texas, create e-mail accounts for the express purpose of attracting spam.

"If they hit one of my spam traps, I launch probes" to figure out the location of the senders' computers, Rosenthal said.

Sometimes, Rosenthal identifies unprotected computers that were unwittingly taken over by a spammer, launching spam without the owners' knowledge.

But Rosenthal is part of a loose network of anti-spam advocates whose primary goal is to collect and publicize "blacklists" of spammers' Internet addresses. These are then incorporated into spam filters used by small Internet service providers, company system administrators and individual users, blocking any e-mail that comes from those addresses.

The most complete of these blacklists is kept by the Spamhaus Project, a British-based organization that serves as a clearinghouse for not only spammers' addresses and contact information but also biographical sketches of what is known about the most notorious, who have nicknames such as Dr. Fatburn, the Ballman and CPUguys.

Spam Sense

Experts say that despite the rise in the volume of spam, there are things you can do to better keep it under control.

- Don't click the "unsubscribe" link. Spammers have co-opted the system and use the unsubscribe link to confirm you have an active e-mail account. They then sell your name to other spammers. Better to just delete the e-mail.
- Use a long e-mail name. The longer your e-mail handle, with letters and numbers included, the lower the chance that a computer-generated e-mail name will match yours. Spammers use software to generate thousands of e-mail names in the hopes that they will match existing accounts.
- Have multiple accounts. By using separate accounts for e-commerce and personal use, you decrease the chances that your personal address will get spammed.
- Avoid chat rooms and Web-based discussion groups. Spammers are constantly harvesting the Internet for new addresses. They do so by using software to search Web pages for names. Online chat rooms and news groups are easy targets.
- Limit how often your e-mail address appears on any Web page. This may be difficult, or undesirable, for many businesspeople.
- Avoid online contests and surveys. These are another prime vehicle for spammers to gather e-mail names.
- Check out new filtering software. Technology is evolving, and many creative solutions are being introduced.

—Jonathan Krim

Spammers sometimes attack the blacklist builders, such as Julian Haight, who runs SpamCop.net.

Haight said an unknown spammer recently sent thousands of e-mails, disguised to look as if they came from SpamCop, to network owners, claiming they were originating spam, were about to be blacklisted and should call Haight's telephone number if they had questions. Haight said his inundated phone was nearly rendered useless by the ruse.

But the anti-spam community has its own rogue elements who use the detailed blacklist information to launch attacks against spammers by flooding their computers with... spam.

In a celebrated incident last year, one of the country's largest bulk e-mailers, Alan Ralsky of Michigan, found his home address, telephone number and pictures of his house posted online in a coordinated effort to make his life miserable after the Detroit Free Press wrote a story about his business.

The anti-spammers also signed him up for hundreds of catalogues, advertising fliers and contest mailing lists that jammed his mailbox.

Ralsky could not be reached for comment. His attorney, Robert Harrison, said he doubted Ralsky would talk to the media again.

"They hit me with spam, too," Harrison said.

On top of everything else, the anti-spam team at AOL has to keep an eye on its own members.

Although spammers disguise their movements by ricocheting e-mail blasts off of several computers, or use networks based overseas, the originators could be AOL account holders.

Like all Internet providers, AOL monitors its networks for unusually high volumes of outgoing mail and will shut down those with abnormally high numbers.

In the past, spammers could automate the process of creating new accounts, which is especially attractive with free, Web-based e-mail systems such as those run by Yahoo Inc. and Microsoft. Both companies recently changed their registration steps to make that more difficult.

BUT THE REALITY IS THAT MASS e-mailing is too lucrative for spammers to be discouraged by most obstacles thrown in front of them.

Each e-mail sent costs a fraction of a cent. A gray market for spamming products, including software that disguises the sender's address, or "scrapes" Internet sites for e-mail addresses that are then sold as lists, is flourishing.

Random dictionary attacks are especially effective because they enable the spammers to confirm which addresses are legitimate by monitoring which ones don't bounce back. The working addresses are then added to lists that are sold and resold within the spammer community.

Internet providers, as well as third-party software companies, also are giving their customers ever-improving software to help filter spam from their individual e-mail boxes. But many users still encounter annoying "false positives," in which important e-mail, or e-mail with seemingly innocuous keywords, gets blocked.

And even for legitimate network owners, the allure of having thousands of e-mail addresses at their fingertips is difficult to resist.

AOL has, on rare occasion, entered into marketing deals in which retailers have paid the company to distribute solicitations to members.

"Like other companies, AOL has reserved the right to occasionally present e-mail offers on behalf of trusted partners," said spokesman Nicholas J. Graham. "This has taken place, however, only a handful of times in the past several years. Additionally, AOL has also always allowed members to completely opt out from any such mailings at any time."

Recently, a vendor of an anti-spam product was accused of spamming.

Seattle-based Spam Arrest LLC is one of a handful of firms offering what some see as a promising new technology. When someone sends an e-mail to a user of Spam Arrest, he or she gets an automatically generated e-mail back asking to verify that the sender is a live person.

After the sender confirms by identifying a word or picture on the screen, the original e-mail is allowed to get to its destination. This thwarts auto-generated e-mail.

But the software also allows Spam Arrest to capture senders' e-mail addresses, and it recently sent them a solicitation for the Spam Arrest software.

"It was a one-time mailing," said Spam Arrest chief executive Cameron Elliott. "We'll probably choose not to do this again."

Start-Up Finds Technology Slump Works in Its Favor

By John Markoff

SAN FRANCISCO, March 23—Silicon Valley is continuing to hemorrhage thousands of jobs, but there are some here who say that the time has never been better for creating a start-up company.

On Monday, Phil Goldman, whose career as a software designer has included stints at Apple, General Magic, WebTV and Microsoft, will introduce a service that he says will permanently end e-mail spam for consumers who are being driven to distraction by unsolicited pitches for diet schemes and offers of great wealth from Nigeria.

Mr. Goldman, 38, who is self-financing his company, **Mailblocks,** said that the falling cost of new technologies and the slumping technology economy are making it relatively easy to enter new markets.

"It's incredibly inexpensive to buy computers, and network bandwidth is essentially free and there is surplus equipment," he said. At the same time, innovation has been frozen because Silicon Valley's venture capitalists are largely sitting on the sidelines.

"It's like a guy crawling in the desert who sees the oasis, but who can't quite get there," he said.

Mailblocks, based in Los Altos, Calif., is entering the crowded e-mail market with the premise that consumers will pay a small annual fee for a solution to spam.

The consumer e-mail market is currently dominated by Yahoo, Hotmail and America Online, which provide free basic services that are supported through advertising.

There are also already dozens of commercial add-in products that try to recognize and block spam. Moreover, Internet service providers in recent months have begun to make new efforts to respond to growing consumer frustration with spam.

In addition to legislative proposals before Congress and state legislatures, there are efforts under way within the direct marketing industry to try to deal with spam. And last week, the Internet Engineering Taskforce, a committee of technology experts that sets Internet standards, met in San Francisco to listen to proposals for technical solutions to spam.

The Mailblocks antispam service is based on a so-called challenge-response mechanism to block bulk mail sent automatically to e-mail accounts. When a customer receives a new message from an unknown correspondent, the system will intercept the message and automatically return to the sender a digital image of a seven-digit number and a form to fill out. Once a human being views that number and types it into the form—demonstrating that he or she is a person and not an automated mass-mailing machine—the system will forward the e-mail to the intended recipient.

Phil Goldman is chief executive of the start-up Mailblocks, based in Los Altos, Calif. Its e-mail service promises to block spam.

Analysts who have seen the Mailblocks system are impressed by it, but some said it would be hard for a new entrant to become anything more than a niche player in the e-mail market. The International Data Corporation, a research house, estimates that there are about 700 million electronic mailboxes in the world and that the number will grow to 1.2 billion in 2005.

"It's a really nice product, and it's pretty easy to use," said Jim Nail, a senior analyst at Forrester Research, a computer and communications industry research firm. "The question is how big a market. Do people want to pay anybody anything for these features?"

Mr. Goldman said he was trying to imitate the strategy of Google, the dominant Web search engine company, which entered its market late but quickly became the leading service in its field because of its ability to provide more useful Web searches.

Mailblocks will charge an annual fee of $9.95 for its personal e-mail service, which will give users 12 megabytes of mail storage and 6 megabytes of allowances for attachments. Charter members will receive two additional years of free service.

Mr. Goldman plans for Mailblocks to offer related services in the future, like personalized domain names, calendaring, contact list management and other personal information functions.

The idea of a challenge-response system to protect against bulk electronic mail has been familiar to the technology community for several years. A number of programmers, in fact, have developed their own home-brew challenge-response systems, and so have several small companies including Mailcircuit and Frontier.

Mr. Goldman said he had come upon the idea independently in 2001, only to discover there were already many patents in the area. He contacted the inventor who held the first patent covering the idea and acquired that patent, as well as another in the same field.

With the depressed job market, Mr. Goldman said it had been easy to find a small team of people who were passionate about building an easy-to-use consumer mail system. The technology trends that are currently driving costs down will make it possible for the new start-up to "be patient" during the period that the business is being built.

Mailblocks has 15 employees, and Mr. Goldman said he estimated that he would need to add one employee for each million new e-mail customers the company attracts.

THE COMPUTER AND THE DYNAMO

Brian Hayes

Blackouts were rolling across California last winter when I first began to hear stories about the gluttonous energy appetite of computers, and how Silicon Valley might be partly to blame for the power crisis. Computers and the infrastructure of the Internet, the reports said, were consuming 8 percent of the nation's electricity supply. Or maybe the figure was 13 percent. In any case, by 2010, fully half of all electricity generated in the U.S. would go to keep computer hardware humming.

I first heard these numbers mentioned—without explanation or attribution—in a television newscast. They have turned up in many other places as well, from *USA Today* and the *Wall Street Journal to Computer* (the magazine of the IEEE Computer Society). They have been cited in testimony before various Congressional committees. And during the 2000 presidential campaign, George W. Bush quoted the 8 percent figure in a speech on energy policy. His remarks were promptly echoed in a Doonesbury cartoon.

The estimates of computer and network power consumption struck me as quite remarkable. If they were correct, we were approaching a notable inflection point in human affairs, where we expend as much effort in moving information as we do in moving matter. But I had my doubts about those numbers. Bits are so much lighter than atoms. Perhaps a decimal point had slipped out of place. Could it really be true that roughly a tenth of the output of all those gargantuan power plants was being squeezed through the finespun filigree of conductors on silicon chips? It seemed preposterous—but, then again, something like a tenth of all electricity squeezes through the finespun filaments of lightbulbs. The question was not to be answered by mere hand-waving.

The Coal-Burning Internet

It wasn't hard to trace the story back to its source. Typing the words "8 percent computer electricity consumption" into a search engine produced lots of leads. (The search engine told me how many seconds it spent on the query, but not how many kilowatt-hours.) All trails led to Peter Huber and Mark P. Mills, writers and consultants who publish a newsletter called *Digital Power Report*. In particular, I was directed to an article of theirs titled "Dig More Coal—The PCs Are Coming," which appeared in *Forbes* in 1999.

The *Forbes* article includes all the essential elements of the story: "At least 100 million nodes on the Internet, drawing from hundreds to thousands of kilowatt-hours per year, add up to 290 billion kWh of demand. That's about 8% of total U.S. demand. Add in the electric power used to build and operate stand-alone (unnetworked) chips and computers, and the total jumps to about 13%. It's now reasonable to project that half of the electric grid will be powering the digital-Internet economy within the next decade."

Other statements of Huber and Mills are no less electrifying. Utilities have to burn a pound of coal, they calculate, for every two megabytes of data moving across the Internet. A "server farm" housing computers that serve Web pages has the power needs of a small steel mill. And then there is their most provocative claim: A Palm Pilot connected to the Internet consumes as much energy as a household refrigerator. (Of course that power doesn't come out of AAA batteries; it's the handheld unit's share of the power used by Internet routers and servers.)

Unfortunately, Huber and Mills don't always make it easy to trace the line of reasoning that led them to their

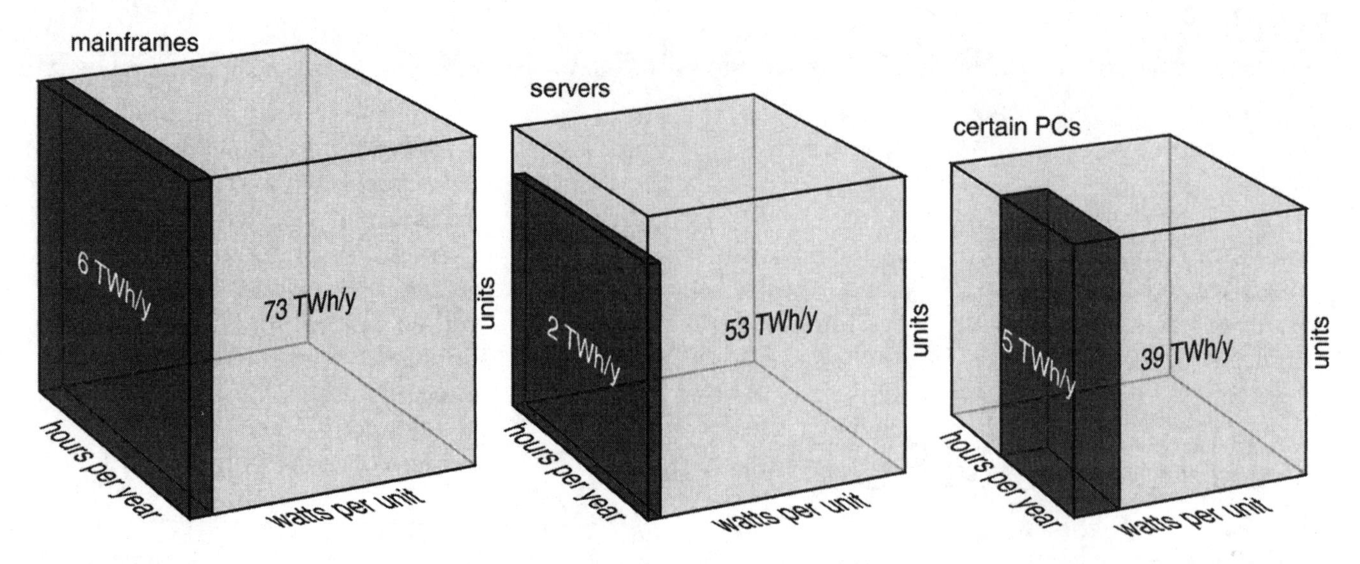

Figure 1. Estimates of power consumption by computers differ by an order of magnitude. The cubes represent estimates published by Mark P. Mills; in each category, multiplying the number of units by the power demand per unit and the hours of use per year yields a total consumption in terawatt-hours per year (Twh/y). The smaller dark-shaded blocks reflect the analysis of Jonathan Koomey and his colleagues at Lawrence Berkeley National Laboratory.

conclusions. As far as I can tell, the Palm Pilot–refrigerator equation is not explained anywhere. The extrapolation from 8 or 13 percent today to 50 percent a decade hence is also presented without any supporting documentation. (Moreover, another version of this prediction says 30 to 50 percent in two decades.)

The longest and most explicit presentation of these ideas appears in a report titled *The Internet Begins with Coal*, authored by Mills alone. Even there, however, certain blanks remain unfilled. A crucial starting point for the numerical estimates is an assumption that "your typical PC and its peripherals require about 1,000 watts of power," but the documentation for this number is vague and confusing. A footnote mentions as one source of information an "online configuration tool" provided by a manufacturer of uninterruptible power supplies, but that tool's rating for the configuration that Mills discusses is not 1,000 watts but only 205 watts. Mills then remarks: "The 1,000 W figure for the PC nominally accounts for the power needs of otherwise unaccounted microprocessor devices on the network." Those devices remain unaccounted, so that four-fifths of the power drain attributed to PCs comes from unidentified "behind-the-wall components."

This shadow world of unseen power loads is also mentioned in the *Forbes* article. "For every piece of wired hardware on your desk," Huber and Mills write, "two or three pieces of equipment lurk in the network beyond—office hubs and servers, routers, repeaters, amplifiers, remote servers and so forth." Taken literally, this statement implies that there are 200 or 300 million hubs, routers, etc.—two or three for each of the 100 million desktop computers that Huber and Mills count as being connected to the Internet. The preponderance of hidden devices is hard to fathom, since the Internet has a treelike structure, in which the leaf nodes—desktop PCs—ought to be more numerous than machines along the trunk and branches. Elsewhere, Huber and Mills themselves assume there are only 7 million routers and Web servers.

Such gaps in documentation are no definitive refutation of the Huber and Mills thesis, but they don't inspire great confidence. Neither does the provenance of the report. *The Internet Begins with Coal* was published by an organization called the Greening Earth Society, where Mills serves as science advisor. The name of this group might evoke images of the Green Party and Greenpeace, but the agenda is rather different. The name reflects a conviction that higher concentrations of atmospheric CO_2 are "beneficial to humankind and all of nature," because they promote plant growth. The society was created by the Western Fuels Association, a consortium of electric utilities and coal-mining companies, whose main business, of course, is digging up C and combining it with O_2. Both the society and the association argue that coal-fired power plants will remain essential to continued prosperity; in particular, they disparage the notion that the Internet will usher in a new economy without smokestacks, where demand for electricity would remain static or decline.

The fact that an argument serves the publisher's economic interest certainly does not invalidate the argument. But when interests and arguments are so closely aligned, readers can be expected to give the supporting evidence rather careful scrutiny.

Net Savings

The mirror image of the Greening Earth Society is the Center for Energy and Climate Solutions, a division of the

Global Environment and Technology Foundation, which describes itself as "a nonprofit dedicated to building the infrastructure for sustainable development." The center's director, Joseph Romm, presents a view diametrically opposite to that of Huber and Mills. The Internet has not inflated energy use, he says, but instead produces a net savings of energy, mainly through "dematerialization." For example, software delivered online saves energy that would have been expended on manufacturing and shipping. Other efficiencies of electronic commerce allow companies to reduce inventory levels, saving the energy needed to build and operate warehouses. Telecommuting saves gasoline.

The trouble is, measuring these diffuse effects of computer and communications technology is probably even harder than documenting the direct electricity demand of the Internet. Furthermore, the two trends are not mutually exclusive; in principle, Romm and Mills could both be right. The Internet economy could be saving energy overall but still consuming more electric power—in effect siphoning energy out of automobile gas tanks and dumping it onto the coal heaps of electric generating stations.

On the specific issue of electricity consumption, Romm points out that growth in demand actually slackened at just about the time the Internet boom began. Before 1996, according to Romm's figures, electricity output was growing at 2.9 percent per year, but since then the growth rate has been only 2.2 percent. Therefore, if computers and the Net have suddenly introduced enormous new loads, other uses of electricity must have held steady or declined.

The governmental body charged with gathering statistics about the production and consumption of electricity is the Energy Information Administration, or EIA, within the Department of Energy. Their figures on consumption come from surveys of three sectors—residential, commercial and industrial—which each consume about a third of the nation's kilowatt-hours.

The EIA data on computer power demand were summarized in February 2000 by Jay E. Hakes, who was then the Administrator, in Congressional testimony. In the residential sector, Hakes said, PCs account for about 2 percent of electric power consumption, and in the commercial sector about 3 percent. Because computers are not a significant factor in the industrial energy budget, the computer's share of total electricity use works out to 1.6 percent.

One might suppose that the government statistics would carry enough weight to put an end to the argument, but there are enough complications and inconsistencies to leave room for doubt. In the residential survey, a PC was defined as a CPU and a monitor, but printers and other accessories were relegated to a different category, "electronics," which also included some audio and video equipment. The electronics category accounted for 10 percent of residential electricity use—five times the PC segment. How much of that 10 percent should be allocated to computer peripherals? In the commercial survey, laser printers were included in the computer category, but "Internet-related infrastructure equipment" was counted under another heading. Although it seems implausible that any rearrangement of the data could make up the difference between 1.6 percent and 8 or 13 percent, the differences in classification make comparisons awkward.

How Much and How Many

Another group of energy analysts has undertaken a direct rebuttal of the Huber-Mills thesis. At the Lawrence Berkeley National Laboratory, Jonathan G. Koomey heads the Energy Analysis Department of the Environmental Energy Technologies Division, which has carried out numerous studies of energy consumption, mostly funded by the Department of Energy and the Environmental Protection Agency. When the *Forbes* article appeared, Koomey immediately disputed its conclusions, citing data from his own group's survey of energy use by computers and other office equipment.

Koomey and his colleagues question nearly all the assumptions that underlie the Huber-Mills energy estimates, starting with the power demands of individual machines. A desktop PC is not a 1,000-watt device, Koomey says, even if the nameplate attached to the chassis gives a rated power in this range. For a 500-megahertz Pentium III computer and a 17-inch monitor, Koomey's measurements indicate that power demand is no greater than 150 or 200 watts, even including a share of the electricity consumed by a workgroup laser printer. For the somewhat larger computers used as servers, Huber and Mills specify 1,500 watts, and Koomey reduces it to 300. In the case of mainframe computers the disparity is even greater. For these machines Huber and Mills adopt a figure of 250 kilowatts (half for the computer itself and half for air conditioning). Koomey finds that only exotic supercomputers with hundreds of processors approach this level of power use, and that a more realistic estimate for a typical mainframe is 10 or 20 kilowatts.

There are also disagreements about counting. Relying on a compilation of computer sales statistics, Mills asserts that the inventory of computers in use is growing by 40 million a year. Koomey points out that some fraction of the new computers are not additions to the stock but replacements for retired equipment. (The EIA says that computers in offices are nearing "saturation," with four computers for every five employees.)

In August 2000 the LBNL group released a new report on power consumption by computers and network equipment, with further supporting data published in February 2001. The survey includes energy used by all kinds of office machinery, including not only computers and their peripherals but also unrelated devices such as copiers and fax machines. The conclusion: The entire spectrum of equipment dissipates 74 terawatt-hours per year, which is about 2 percent of U.S. electricity consumption. Adding in an allowance for a few other items that Huber and Mills count (such as the energy needed to manufacture computers, and a share of the energy consumed by telephone switchgear) brings the total to 3.2 percent—still only a fourth of the 13 percent level claimed by Huber and Mills.

The debate between Huber and Mills and their critics has been conducted via letters to the editor, press releases and public e-mails. The tone has not always been collegial. In February 2000, when Mills testified before the House Subcommittee on National Economic Growth, Natural Resources, and Regulatory Affairs, he seized the opportunity to defend his ideas against the attacks by Koomey and others. Koomey responded with a memo offering further rebuttal. He wrote: "In the past year and a half, I have been witness to an extraordinary event: an analysis based on demonstrably incorrect data and flawed logic has achieved the status of conventional wisdom, in spite of my and my colleagues' best efforts to refute its assertions. The results continue to be cited by an unsuspecting press, and even by people who ought to know better."

A further year and a half later, the "conventional wisdom" is still very much in circulation. A few weeks ago, Roger N. Anderson of the Lamont-Doherty Earth Observatory published an op-ed essay in the *New York Times* alluding to the Huber-Mills conclusions, with no hint that they might be controversial.

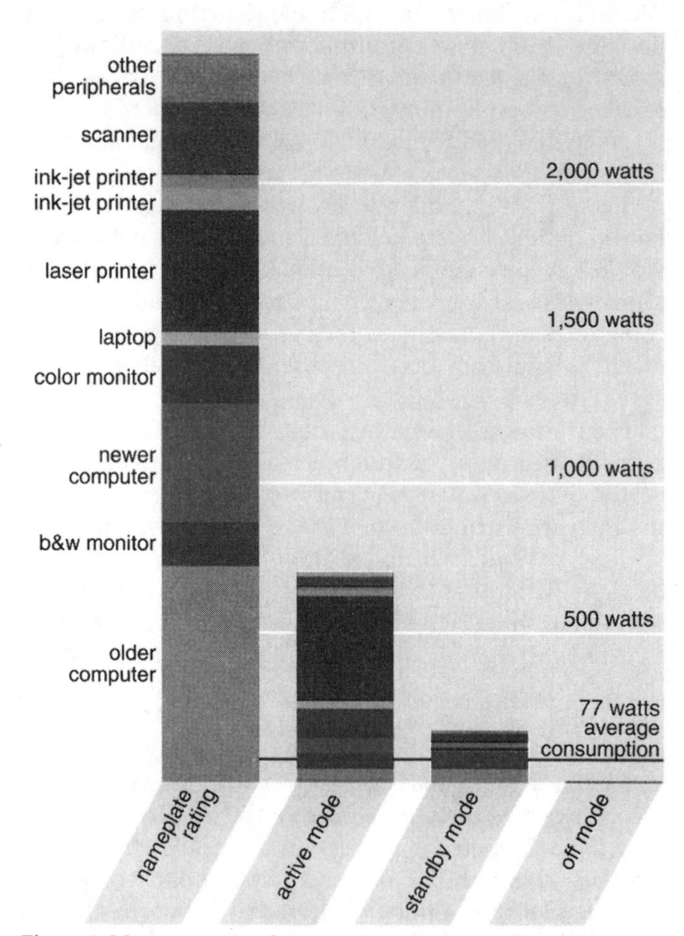

Figure 2. Measurements of computer energy use in the author's own household give a mixed message. On the one hand, actual energy consumption is far lower than what equipment nameplates and owner's manuals would suggest. But the 77 watts of average consumption/demand (horizontal line/at bottom of graph) is a non-negligible fraction of total energy use.

Meanwhile, the Home Fires Burn

After reading so many disparate claims about the wattage of PCs, I became curious about my own computers' contribution to the energy budget. If national statistics are hard to pin down, maybe I could at least figure out what proportion of my own household electric bill feeds my digital habits. To make a first crude estimate, I went around the house with a flashlight, crawling under desks to read the power ratings on nameplates. I knew that the result of this exercise would be an overestimate; in fact it proved useless even as an upper bound.

Adding up all the nameplate data suggested that the computer equipment in my home could draw as much as 2,400 watts. This is a fair amount of power; it would fully load a 20-ampere circuit. That the actual consumption can't be anywhere close to this level became apparent when I dug out the old utility bills. For the past two years the average electricity demand for the whole house was 868 watts—roughly a third of the nameplate rating for the computer equipment alone.

Obviously, I needed a better measurement technology. To this end I was aided by Ethan Brand, of Brand Electronics in Whitefield, Maine, who lent me a digital power meter that measures both demand in watts and cumulative energy consumption in watt-hours. After crawling back under the desk to plug in this instrument, I soon had a clearer picture. A computer rated at 400 watts actually draws about 50 watts in active use; in its standby or "sleep" mode the power consumption falls to 3 watts. The color monitor attached to this computer uses more power than the CPU—97 watts in active mode, 6 watts when sleeping.

Adding up figures for all of the monitored equipment, I found that the most I could manage to consume was about 700 watts—and I could get near that level only by having three computers simultaneously spit out pages from three printers, while at the same time I scanned a photograph and burned a CD-ROM. The typical wattage reading, at times when I was working, ranged from 150 to 170 watts. Note that this is right on target according to Koomey.

But that's not the end of the story. I left the monitor attached to the big bundle of power cords under the desk, measuring total energy consumption over 10 days. In 240 hours, some 18,540 watt-hours of electricity flowed through the meter. That works out to an average demand of 77 watts, which implies that computer equipment is responsible for some 9 percent of my electricity consumption.

Of course it would be foolish to extrapolate from my home office to the entire national economy. I have no reason to believe my experience is representative; on the contrary, as someone who writes about computers, I surely spend more time at the keyboard than most people do. But, the fact remains, the proportion of my electric bill that goes to bit-shuffling is far greater than I ever would have guessed. I had assumed that my power consumption would be so dominated by air conditioning, refrigeration, water heating and lighting that the computing load would barely be detectable. Now I know otherwise.

Personal Virtues

For Huber and Mills, the power demands of computers and the Internet signal inevitable future growth in overall electricity consumption. But you can equally well look at the situation as an opportunity for conservation. If computers really were responsible for some large fraction of the nation's energy consumption, then measures to make the machines more efficient would have a major impact. And even if computers do not make up such a fat slice of the energy pie, they may nonetheless be an attractive target for conservation measures, because there's so much room for improvement. Cutting another 10 percent off the energy consumption of a refrigerator or a water heater is an engineering challenge, but the energy per operation and per device in computers has been falling for decades, and that trend will surely continue. Indeed, there is no intrinsic limit to it; in principle, computing can be done without energy loss.

In the 1940s, the ENIAC had 18,000 vacuum tubes and consumed 174 kilowatts—roughly 10 watts per tube. If modern silicon chips required 10 watts per transistor, a Pentium would suck 100 megawatts out of the power grid, and the computer on your desk would easily swallow the entire output of a nuclear plant. Instead, a few tens of watts are enough to power a chip with transistors numbering in the tens of millions.

For the most part, these gains in transistor efficiency have been exploited not to minimize the power consumption of each chip but to maximize the number of transistors per chip, while keeping the power density just below the melting point. There is little incentive to do otherwise. This is the muscle-car era of computer design; what sells hardware is performance, not fuel economy. Until the electric bill for running a machine begins to approach the purchase price, no one is going to care much about energy consumption.

But energy use in computers may well decline anyway, even without economic impetus. Laptop computers offer a proof by example that electric power can be reduced by an order of magnitude without greatly impairing computer power. Some of the technologies and components of laptops will find their way into desktop machines, again not because lower power consumption is a selling point but because smaller fans, heat sinks and power supplies can save the manufacturer a few dollars. Flat-panel displays are already migrating from laptops to desktops.

Power-management systems that put idle machines and monitors to sleep have also had an effect. In the 2000 office-equipment survey, Koomey and his colleagues find that such reduced-power modes save 23 terawatt-hours per year; if everyone used the sleep modes, they would save another 17 terawatt-hours.

At the end of the day, I am left with the sense that the issue of computer power consumption is not going to be the determining factor in national energy policy. Even if the Huber-Mills analysis were correct, most of our kilowatts would still be flowing into the real world, not into cyberspace. Fluctuations in prices and the weather have a bigger impact on power demand than any conceivable events on the World Wide Web. Computers will not save the coal mines, nor will they save the planet.

But efficiency is more than a matter of economics and industrial policy; it has an aesthetic aspect, and even an ethical one. As Vice President Cheney recently observed, energy conservation is a sign of personal virtue. There is satisfaction in accomplishing more with less, in wringing the most results out of the least resources. For a long time this was a prominent strand in the mental habits of computer enthusiasts. To waste a CPU cycle or a byte of memory was an embarrassing lapse. To clobber a small problem with a big computer was considered tasteless and unsporting, like trout fishing with dynamite. Not even rolling blackouts will roll us back to that quaint age of frugal computing, but there is much to admire in its ethos.

Bibliography

Anderson, Roger. 2001. Wattage where it's needed. *The New York Times*, June 6, 2001. http://www.nytimes.com/2001/06/06/opinion/06ANDE.html

Angel, Jonathan. 2001. Emerging technology: Energy consumption and the new economy. *Network Magazine*, January 5, 2001. http://www.networkmagazine.com/article/NMG20010103S005

Bryce, Robert. 2000. Power struggle. *Interactive Week*, December 19, 2000. http://www.zdnet.com/intweek/stories/news/0,4164,2666038,00.html

Energy Information Administration. 2000. *Annual Energy Outlook 2001, with Projections to 2020.* http://tonto.eia.doe.gov/FTPROOT/forecasting/0383(2001).pdf

Hakes, Jay. 2001. Residential and commercial buildings electricity use. Update to testimony by former EIA Administrator Jay Hakes to the House Committee on Government Reform. http://www.eia.doe.gov/oiaf/speeches/pdf/0329eia.pdf

Huber, Peter, and Mark P. Mills. 1999. Dig more coal—the PCs are coming. *Forbes*, May 31, 1999, pp. 70–72. http://www.forbes.com/forbes/1999/0531/6311070a_print.html

Kawamoto, Kaoru, Jonathan G. Koomey, Bruce Nordman, Richard E. Brown, Mary Ann Piette and Alan K. Meier. 2000. Electricity used by office equipment and network equipment in the U.S. http://enduse.lbl.gov/Info/KawamotoACEEE.pdf

Karamoto, Kaoru, Jonathan G. Koomey, Bruce Nordman, Richard E. Brown, Mary Ann Piette, Michael Ting and

Alan K. Meier. 2001. Electricity used by office equipment in the U.S. http://enduse.lbl.gov/Info/Kawamoto ACEEE.pdf

Koomey, Jonathan, Kaoru Kawamoto, Bruce Nordman, Mary Ann Piette and Richard E. Brown. 1999. Initial comments on "The Internet Begins with Coal." Memorandum to Skip Laitner, EPA Office of Atmospheric Programs, December 9, 1999. http://enduse.lbl.gov/Info/LBNL-45917b.pdf

Koomey, Jonathan G. 2000. Rebuttal to testimony on 'Kyoto and the Internet: The energy implications of the digital economy.' http://enduse.lbl.gov/Info/annotatedmillstestimony.pdf

Mills, Mark P. 1999. The Internet begins with coal: A preliminary exploration of the impact of the Internet on electricity consumption. Arlington, Va.: the Greening Earth Society. http://www.greeningearthsociety.org

Mills, Mark P., Amory Lovins and others. 1999. Exchanges between Mark Mills and Amory Lovins about the electricity used by the Internet. Archive of electronic mail messages. http://www.rmi.org/images/other/E-MMABLInternet.pdf

Romm, Joseph, with Arthur Rosenfeld and Susan Herrmann. 2001. The Internet economy and global warming: A scenario of the impact of e-commerce on energy and the environment. The Center for Energy and Climate Solutions. http://www.cool-companies.org/energy/ecomm.doc

Brian Hayes is Senior Writer for American Scientist. *Address: 211 Dacian Avenue, Durham, NC 27701; bhayes@amsci.org*

Bringing Linux to the Masses

He took on the music labels with MP3.com. Now, with Lindows, Michael Robertson is challenging Bill Gates. Does he have what it takes to crack Windows?

BY FRED VOGELSTEIN

FOR AS LONG AS ANYONE CAN REMEMBER, MICHAEL ROBERTSON has been fighting with someone or something. He sparred with his political science professors in college because they were too liberal; he started MP3.com in 1997 and tussled with his co-founders and investors when they wouldn't do things his way. And he fought with the music industry, which accused his company, a distribution site for digital music, of piracy. When the major labels sued MP3.com, Robertson spent millions battling them, lost—and yet still walked away with $115 million when Vivendi Universal bought what remained of his company.

Now Robertson has a new fight on his hands, this time with an opponent that makes the recording industry look like a 98-pound weakling: Bill Gates. Over the past year Robertson's latest company, Lindows, has crafted software that mimics the look, features, and feel of Windows. The major difference is this: Instead of developing proprietary code, Robertson has taken advantage of the free Linux operating system and its legion of freelance programmers to cobble together his product. Oh, and Lindows and its Office-like offerings are at least half the price of Windows and Office. Microsoft's not taking the challenge lightly. Within weeks of Lindows's formation, Microsoft sued the company for trademark infringement, saying the copycat name is getting a free ride on the $1.2 billion Microsoft has invested in marketing Windows.

Silicon Valley has proved to be Death Valley for those who've challenged Microsoft's core operating systems business. But don't count Robertson out just yet. Even his detractors—and there are plenty—say he's on to something powerful here: the increasing popularity of Linux and the increasing frustration with Microsoft.

Over the past two years Linux has spread like a virus through corporate data centers. Companies once dependent on expensive proprietary systems from Sun, IBM, or Hewlett-Packard have replaced them with dirt-cheap Dell or no-name boxes that are Intel-powered and loaded with Linux. Linux now runs nearly 10% of all servers and is growing at about 23% a year. PC users have yet to latch on—less than 1% of all computers run Linux—but a survey last year by *CIO* magazine found that almost 30% of chief technologists were considering moving their companies' PCs to Linux. Already almost every major electronics maker, from HP in printers to Epson in scanners, is making sure it has Linux-compatible offerings. And Sun has poured millions of dollars into its Star Office software suite, which gives Linux users programs that work like—and more important, are compatible with—PowerPoint, Word, and Excel.

LOW PRICES PERSUADED SCOTT TESTA TO CONVERT HIS FIRM TO LINDOWS

Microsoft's legendary hardheadedness has helped fuel this small fire. Starting with Office 2000, the company put padlocks on its software, preventing it from being installed on more than one machine. The idea was to stamp out piracy; instead it stamped out what had become commonplace among home and small-business users: using one copy on multiple PCs. That has driven up the cost of Windows and Office sharply. "It's not fair to a small guy like me," says Charles Russell, a 72-year-old insurance investigator in Santa Rosa, Calif., who has recently been experimenting with Lindows. "It cost me $600 to upgrade my three computers to Windows XP."

Robertson isn't the only one hoping to cash in. Software companies like Red Hat, Mandrake, and Suse all offer Linux products that compete with Windows. But Lindows has a few things those companies don't: It has Robertson's bombastic personality to sell it, and it has a better pitch—that it is easier to install and use. Wal-

Throwing stones at Windows

	Lindows	Windows XP
Founder Approximate net worth	Michael Robertson $100 million	Bill Gates $45 billion
Year introduced	2001	2001
Underlying technology	Linux	Windows NT
License terms	Multiple computers	One computer
Typical install time	Under 30 minutes	An hour-plus
Cost with PC and typical software at Walmart.com	$298	$750
Cost for Testa to install Mindbrige	$10,000	$20,000

Mart, which began selling Lindows-ready PCs on its website in September, has had such success with the offering that by Christmas it was having trouble meeting demand.

"In every business sector there is always room for a low-cost provider," says Robertson between bites of a turkey sandwich and gulps of cherry Gatorade. "Computer users only have one choice right now, and that's Microsoft."

SPEND A COUPLE OF HOURS WITH ROBERTSON, AND YOU FEEL AS if you've been granted an audience with a cult leader. At 35, his fine blond hair and craggy face make him look as benign as an over-the-hill surfer. Everything else about him is icy. Employees at MP3.com recall a ruthless perfectionist who would burst in on meetings to dress down associates or explode at teammates for bad plays during lunchtime basketball games. "You miss a shot on his team, and he's all over you like you're the worst athlete in the world," says one of his former colleagues. "He's not even that good."

That drive has been to his advantage. Close to a dozen people who have worked for, with, or against Robertson say that he is one of the most uncompromising and competitive businessmen they have ever met. In 1999, at age 31, he turned down $10 million from VC heavyweight Sequoia. The company had wanted 60% of MP3.com in exchange for its money. Robertson's terms were $10 million for 20%—take it or leave it. Sequoia took it. "He's a zealot, and he's fearless," says Lise Buyer, who covered MP3.com as an analyst for CS First Boston. "I'm just not sure I'd want to sit on his board."

The idea for Lindows came in the dying days of MP3.com. Robertson built his company on Linux, an operating system he learned about during his eight-year stint running PC tech support at the San Diego Super Computer Center. He knew the system worked well in the back office. But in talks with his engineers in early 2001 he found himself surprised by how much they liked running it as a desktop operating system.

That wasn't the experience of most users. Those who toyed with Linux for the desktop—and there were plenty of sites offering such homegrown software—quickly gave up. Exchanging documents with Windows users was next to impossible, configuring PCs to run the programs took forever, and attempting to find printers, scanners, or even mice compatible with Linux was often fruitless. Microsoft, for all its faults, was dedicated to writing desktop software. Linux was just a disparate and unorganized society of software geeks coding for other software geeks.

After trying out a handful of Linux titles himself, Robertson concluded that what the group lacked was a strong leader with a profit motive. In the summer of 2001, he earmarked $5 million of his money for the new venture, and at the end of August he quit MP3.com along with three associates. Three days later Lindows was open for business. The company had little but a deliberately antagonistic name. "Software business plans are a waste of time," he says. "The time it takes to write one is always better spent writing and testing the software. Then you have real results rather than marketing projections."

Robertson counted on his own peculiar form of marketing to build his brand. As he and his programmers mapped out the system's look and feel, Robertson started drumming up press by making outrageous claims. He declared that Lindows would run every Windows program. In fact, it ran Office but not much else. In the summer of 2002 he declared a strategic alliance with AOL, but in reality no such alliance existed.

It wasn't until September 2002 that Lindows became a real threat. The company's sales chief, Larry Kettler, had spent the first part of the year looking for a way to get his product onto store shelves but found that few retailers were willing to clog precious shelf space with an untested newcomer, especially one that catered to the tiny Linux retail market. On a whim he called Microtel Computer, a Los Angeles and Taiwanese maker of generic computers that was selling PCs without operating systems on Walmart.com. Kettler wondered if Microtel might be interested in selling those with Lindows too. It was lucky timing. Microtel's U.S. sales chief, Rich Hindman, had been hunting for a vendor after receiving thousands of e-mails for nearly a year from customers requesting Linux machines. For just $500 a month, Lindows would allow Microtel to sell an unlimited number of copies of its software. Microsoft, by contrast, charged $100 per machine, says Hindman. "Lindows did everything they could to make it happen," he says.

Soon the companies were selling a $199 Lindows Microtel PC. It was a bare-bones configuration: no monitor, a no-name chip, no speakers. By autumn the machines were selling well enough—2,000 to 3,000 a month—that a clearly agitated Steve Ballmer, Microsoft's CEO, declared to a Gartner conference that "somebody is losing [money] there." After all, a similar Microtel machine with Windows XP costs $299. Customers didn't care about the economics. They wanted cheap PCs. Demand was so strong that in December, Wal-Mart suspended sales for four weeks to allow Microtel to meet its backlog.

Even with limited distribution, users are seeking out the product. Not that it is bug-free: Lindows doesn't run on many computers, particularly older models. But the price is proving tempting. Scott Testa, CEO of Mindbridge, a 60-person software company in Norristown, Pa., switched all his PCs to Lindows weeks after they were available on Wal-Mart's website. He had been using Dell PCs, but when it came time to buy more, he chose 30 Microtel boxes running Lindows. "They're as good as Dells for half the price," he says.

This all sounds potentially dangerous for Microsoft, but can Lindows become a viable business? After all, Microtel is now paying about 25 cents a copy on average, and in January it will start distributing the machines on Amazon.com and on CompUSA's site, dropping the price per copy even further. That's fine for Robertson. He's hoping Lindows consumers will then pony up $99 a year for unlimited downloading at a Lindows site full of Linux software. Among the offerings are Sun's Star Office, which typically sells for $80, and thousands of other Linux titles. Historically it has been hard for all but the geekiest to find, download, and install Linux programs. Robertson's so-called Click & Run Warehouse divides the Linux world into neat shopping aisles with automatic downloads and installs. Robertson won't say how many have anted up for the service but admits that 30,000 customers "isn't that far off the mark."

It will take more than that to topple Microsoft, of course. But Robertson has at least gotten the Linux community fired up about one of their original visions: making Linux the world's dominant operating system. "I haven't always agreed with him, but he's helped me and my company tremendously," says Jeremy White, founder and CEO of Codeweavers, which makes emulator software that allows users to run Microsoft Office 2000 and a few other programs on Linux platforms. "I had felt Linux on the desktop was not a real possibility. Michael was the person who kicked me in the rear and said, 'It is.'" It's a good thing. In this fight Robertson will need all the help he can get.

FEEDBACK *fvogelstein@fortunemail.com*

UNIT 3

Work and the Workplace

Unit Selections

Key Points to Consider

- The issue of immigration to the United States is controversial. Do you agree with AnnaLee Saxenian's arguments? Why or why not?
- In "You're Hired, Now Go Home," Jeanne Allert cites four traits to look for when hiring an individual to do virtual work. What traits would you add?
- Do you agree that e-mail is more likely to foster careless and intemperate remarks than conversation or conventional letters? Explain.
- Were you surprised to learn that an employer may be tracking employee Web sites, reading their e-mail? How do you feel about this?
- Suppose you learned that your university is reading student e-mail to protect itself from sexual harassment suits and its students from sexual harassment itself. How would you feel? Have the courts said anything about a university's rights and obligations in these matters? What is the policy at your university?

Links: www.dushkin.com/online/
These sites are annotated in the World Wide Web pages.

American Telecommuting Association
http://www.knowledgetree.com/ata-adv.html

Cisco E-Learning
http://www.cisco.com/warp/public/10/wwtraining/elearning/

Computers in the Workplace
http://www.msci.memphis.edu/~ryburnp/cl/cis/workpl.html

InfoWeb: Techno-rage
http://www.cciw.com/content/technorage.html

STEP ON IT! Pedals: Repetitive Strain Injury
http://www.bilbo.com/rsi2.html

What About Computers in the Workplace
http://law.freeadvice.com/intellectual_property/computer_law/computers_workplace.htm

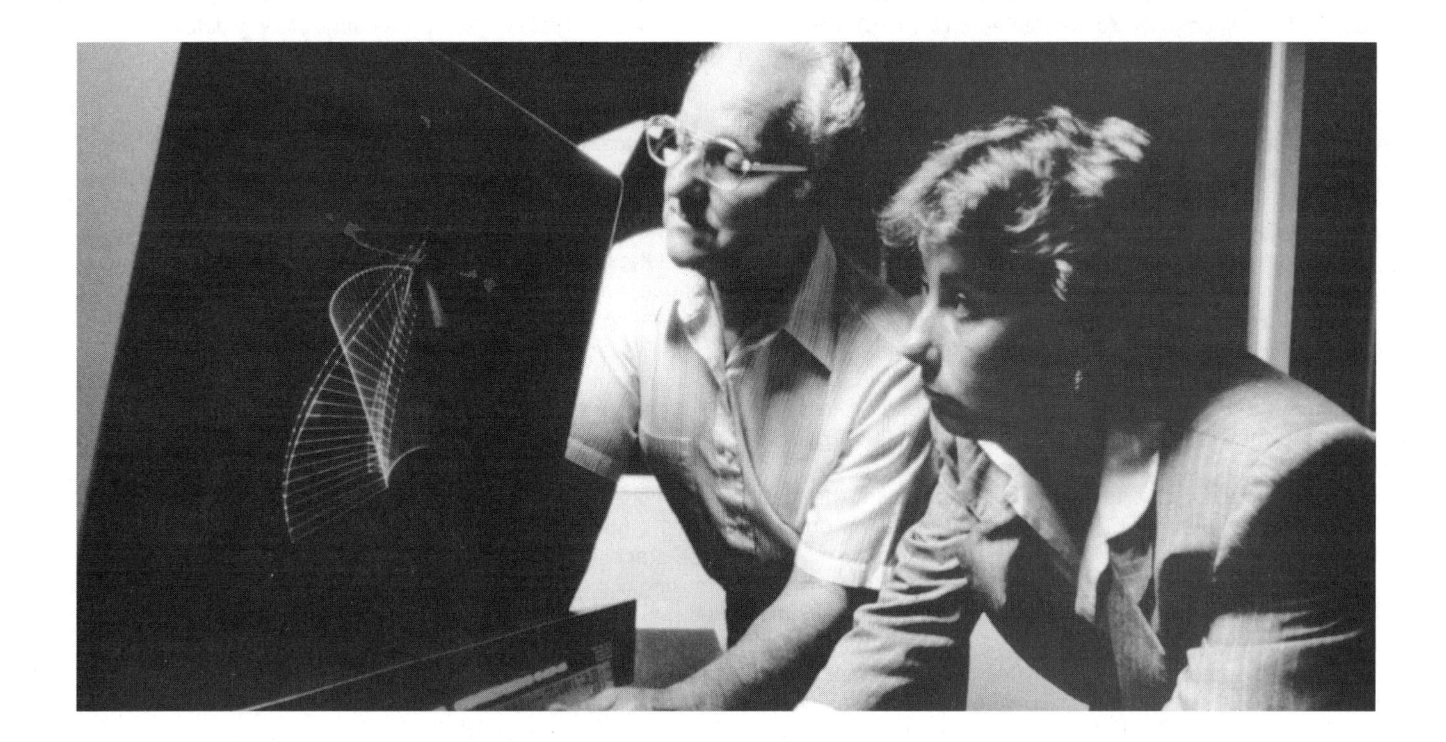

Work is at the center of our lives. The kind of work we do plays a part in our standard of living, our social status, and our sense of worth. This was not always the case. Read some of the great Victorian novels and you will find a society where paid employment, at least among the upper classes, by and large does not exist. Even those men from the nineteenth century and before whose discoveries and writings we study and admire, approached their work as an avocation. It is hard to imagine Lord Byron kissing his wife goodbye each morning and heading off to the English Department, where he will direct a seminar in creative writing before he gets to work on a sticky line in "Childe Harold's Pilgrimage." Or think of Charles Darwin donning a lab coat and supervising an army of graduate students while he touches up his latest National Science Foundation proposal. A hundred or more years ago, there were a handful of professions—doctor, lawyer, clergyman, military officer a larger handful of crafts—joiner, miller, cooper, an army of agricultural workers; and an increasing number of displaced peasants toiling in factories—places that William Blake referred to as England's "Dark Satanic Mills."

To be more precise, the U.S. Census records tell us that there were only 323 different occupations in 1850, among them, the butcher, the baker, and the candlestick maker, which all children read about. The butcher is still with us, as well as the baker, but both of them work for national supermarket chains, using digitally-controlled tools and manage their 401k's online. The candlestick maker has morphed into a refinery worker, watching digital displays in petrochemical plants that light up the Louisiana sky. Today, the Canadian National Occupational Classification lists more than 25,000 occupational titles. Throughout the twentieth century, it was feared that first machines and then computers, would render work obsolete, transforming us into country gentlemen like Charles Darwin in the utopian view or nomadic mobs of starving proletarians in the distopian.

It appears instead that fabulously productive farms and factories—as well as a developing world willing to make our shoes, clothing, and electronics for pennies an hour—have opened up opportunities that did not exist in Darwin's time. We are now sales clerks, health care workers, state license examiners, light truck drivers, and equal opportunity compliance officers, and, yes, also software engineers, database analysts, Web-site designers, and entrepreneurs. Some of the more interesting and better paid of these new occupations are increasingly held by foreign-born individuals. AnnaLee Saxenian observes in "Brain Circulation: How High-Skill Immigration Makes Everyone Better Off," that "more than a quarter of Silicon Valley's highly skilled workers are immigrants" This raises questions about whether the growth in numbers of foreign-born professionals displaces native workers, while at the same time draining talent from countries too poor to lose it.

These workers, both foreign and native born, along with other professional and semi-professional people in occupations created in the last half century, work in offices equipped with computers that are attached to the Internet. E-mail is just another way to do business. But it has its dangers. As Nicholas Varchaver writes, when the Justice Department discovered that Bill Gates wrote, "How much do we need to pay you to screw Netscape," its antitrust case was made that much stronger. Years of research have documented that people tend to be more frank when using e-mail. If you have been on the receiving end of a blistering attack from a friend or colleague, this will not be news. As it happens, many corporations are beginning to learn that they sometimes pay a price for their employee's overheated writings. In response, they are beginning to train them in e-mail temperance, since electronic communication can be subpoenaed.

It should come as no surprise to anyone who has suffered through the seemingly arbitrary, and almost always, cryptic and unhelpful, error messages that stand between you and what you would like to do with your computer, that tech rage is a phenomenon in offices across the country. Chris Wood, in "Dealing With Tech Rage" discusses some reasons for this growing problem and how it might be alleviated.

Sara Boehle in "They're Watching You," tells us what can happen when corporations fear incriminating e-mail. Her employer has software that not only tracks which Web sites she visits, but records how long she spends at each site. In fact, as corporations shed more of their middle managers, fewer people are left to oversee the rest who remain in their cubicles. This leaves monitoring software to do the job, an approach that has been adopted by General Electric and the Norwegian energy company, Asea Brown Boveri.

Justice Louis Brandeis wrote in 1890 that the most cherished of American rights is the "right to be left alone." Increasingly, this is a right to be cherished at home. Almost three-fourths of large U.S. companies record and review either their employees' phone calls, e-mail, computer files, or Web use. Boehle quotes Lewis Maltby of the National Workrights Institute who says, "You don't have any Constitutional rights at work because the Constitution only applies to the government, not to the private sector."

"Security vs. Privacy" and "Searching for Answers," written by Jonathan Segal, a lawyer specializing in litigation and unionization avoidance, give an insider's account into what employers may do to maintain workplace security, broadly defined. "Simply put," he says, "if you tell employees that they have no right to privacy, they probably don't." He recommends that employers reserve the right to randomly search employees, along with their belongings, desks, computers, e-mail, voice mail, and Internet activities. Yet reserving the right, he tells us, in only half the story. Random searches may contribute to a hostile atmosphere and the right of an employer to monitor U.S. Postal Service mail and telephone calls is circumscribed by federal law. Circumscribed, but not prohibited, as you will learn when you read this fascinating article.

In *Bleak House,* Charles Dickens satirizes the snail's pace of legal machinery. An important social dimension of computing that appears in this unit and elsewhere in the book, is that the technology changes far more quickly than the laws to regulate it. Thus the federal Wiretap Act prohibits the interception of most telephone calls. In order not to run afoul of the law, Segal advises employers to wait until an electronic transmission has been received to review it. The computer, of course, obliges by making copies of all sent and received e-mail, a luxury not available to an employer who wants to listen in on his employee's phone calls. Perhaps, one day, case law will clarify and broaden an employee's expectation of privacy with respect to e-mail. Until that day, because courts have already ruled that corporations are liable for damage caused by their employee's e-mail, companies have the incentive, the right, and, with sophisticated software, the ability to monitor it.

Brain Circulation

How High-Skill Immigration Makes Everyone Better Off

By AnnaLee Saxenian

Silicon Valley's workforce is among the world's most ethnically diverse. Not only do Asian and Hispanic workers dominate the low-paying, blue-collar workforce, but foreign-born scientists and engineers are increasingly visible as entrepreneurs and senior management. More than a quarter of Silicon Valley's highly skilled workers are immigrants, including tens of thousands from lands as diverse as China, Taiwan, India, the United Kingdom, Iran, Vietnam, the Philippines, Canada, and Israel.

Most people instinctively assume that the movement of skill and talent must benefit one country at the expense of another. But thanks to brain circulation, high-skilled immigration increasingly benefits both sides

---

Understandably, the rapid growth of the foreign-born workforce has evoked intense debates over U.S. immigration policy, both here and in the developing world. In the United States, discussions of the immigration of scientists and engineers have focused primarily on the extent to which foreign-born professionals displace native workers. The view from sending countries, by contrast, has been that the emigration of highly skilled personnel to the United States represents a big economic loss, a "brain drain."

Neither view is adequate in today's global economy. Far from simply replacing native workers, foreign-born engineers are starting new businesses and generating jobs and wealth at least as fast as their U.S. counterparts. And the dynamism of emerging regions in Asia and elsewhere now draws skilled immigrants homeward. Even when they choose not to return home, they are serving as middlemen linking businesses in the United States with those in distant regions.

In some parts of the world, the old dynamic of "brain drain" is giving way to one I call "brain circulation." Most people instinctively assume that the movement of skill and talent must benefit one country at the expense of another. But thanks to brain circulation, high-skilled immigration increasingly benefits both sides. Economically speaking, it is blessed to give *and* to receive.

"New" Immigrant Entrepreneurs

Unlike traditional ethnic entrepreneurs who remain isolated in marginal, low-wage industries, Silicon Valley's new foreign-born entrepreneurs are highly educated professionals in dynamic and technologically sophisticated industries. And they have been extremely successful. By the end of the 1990s, Chinese and Indian engineers were running 29 percent of Silicon Valley's technology businesses. By 2000, these companies collectively accounted for more than $19.5 billion in sales and 72,839 jobs. And the pace of immigrant entrepreneurship has accelerated dramatically in the past decade.

Not that Silicon Valley's immigrants have abandoned their ethnic ties. Like their less-educated counterparts, Silicon Valley's high-tech immigrants rely on ethnic strategies to enhance entrepreneurial opportunities. Seeing themselves as outsiders to the mainstream technology community, foreign-born engineers and scientists in Silicon Valley have created social and professional networks to mobilize the information, know-how, skill, and capital to start technology firms. Local ethnic professional associations like the Silicon Valley Chinese Engineers Association, The Indus Entrepreneur, and the Korean IT Forum provide contacts and resources for recently arrived immigrants.

Combining elements of traditional immigrant culture with distinctly high-tech practices, these organizations simultaneously create ethnic identities within the region and aid professional networking and information exchange. These are not traditional political or lobbying groups—rather their focus is the professional and technical advancement of their members. Membership in Indian and Chinese professional associations has virtually no overlap, although the overlap within the separate communities—particularly the Chinese, with its many specialized associations—appears considerable. Yet ethnic distinctions also exist within the Chinese community. To an outsider, the Chinese American Semiconductor Professionals Association and the North American Chinese Semiconductor Association are redundant organizations. One, however, represents Taiwanese, the other Mainland Chinese.

> The most successful immigrant entrepreneurs in Silicon Valley today appear to be those who have drawn on ethnic resources while simultaneously integrating into mainstream technology and business networks.

Whatever their ethnicity, all these associations tend to mix socializing—over Chinese banquets, Indian dinners, or family-centered social events—with support for professional and technical advancement. Each, either explicitly or informally, offers first-generation immigrants professional contacts and networks within the local technology community. They serve as recruitment channels and provide role models of successful immigrant entrepreneurs and managers. They sponsor regular speakers and conferences whose subjects range from specialized technical and market information to how to write a business plan or manage a business. Some Chinese associations give seminars on English communication, negotiation skills, and stress management.

Many of these groups have become important cross-generational forums. Older engineers and entrepreneurs in both the Chinese and the Indian communities now help finance and mentor younger co-ethnic entrepreneurs. Within these networks, "angel" investors often invest individually or jointly in promising new ventures. The Indus Entrepreneur, for example, aims to "foster entrepreneurship by providing mentorship and resources" within the South Asian technology community. Both the Asian American Manufacturers Association and the Monte Jade Science and Technology Association sponsor annual investment conferences to match investors (often from Asia as well as Silicon Valley) with Chinese entrepreneurs.

> The long-distance networks are accelerating the globalization of labor markets and enhancing opportunities for entrepreneurship, investment, and trade both in the United States and in newly emerging regions in Asia.

Although many Chinese and Indian immigrants socialize primarily within their ethnic networks, they routinely work with U.S. engineers and U.S.-run businesses. In fact, recognition is growing within these communities that although a start-up might be spawned with the support of the ethnic networks, it must become part of the mainstream to grow. The most successful immigrant entrepreneurs in Silicon Valley today appear to be those who have drawn on ethnic resources while simultaneously integrating into mainstream technology and business networks.

Transnational Entrepreneurship

Far beyond their role in Silicon Valley, the professional and social networks that link new immigrant entrepreneurs with each other have become global institutions that connect new immigrants with their counterparts at home. These new transnational communities provide the shared information, contacts, and trust that allow local producers to participate in an increasingly global economy.

Silicon Valley's Taiwanese engineers, for example, have built a vibrant two-way bridge connecting them with Taiwan's technology community. Their Indian counterparts have become key middlemen linking U.S. businesses to low-cost software expertise in India. These cross-Pacific networks give skilled immigrants a big edge over mainstream competitors who often lack the language skills, cultural know-how, and contacts to build business relationships in Asia. The long-distance networks are accelerating the globalization of labor markets and enhancing opportunities for entrepreneurship, investment, and trade both in the United States and in newly emerging regions in Asia.

Taiwanese immigrant Miin Wu, for example, arrived in the United States in the early 1970s to pursue graduate training in electrical engineering. After earning a doctorate from Stanford University in 1976, Wu saw little use for his new skills in economically backward Taiwan and chose to remain in the United States. He worked for more than a decade in senior positions at Silicon Valley–based semiconductor companies including Siliconix and Intel. He also gained entrepreneurial experience as one of the founding members of VLSI Technology.

By the late 1980s, Taiwan's economy had improved dramatically, and Wu decided to return. In 1989 he started one of Taiwan's first semiconductor companies, Macronix Co., in the Hsinchu Science-based Industrial Park. Wu also became an active participant in Silicon Valley's Monte Jade Science and Technology Association, which was building business links between the technical communities in Silicon Valley and Taiwan.

> In this complex mix, the rich social and professional ties among Taiwanese engineers and their U.S. counterparts are as important as the more formal corporate alliances and partnerships.

Macronix went public on the Taiwan stock exchange in 1995 and in 1996 became the first Taiwanese company to list on Nasdaq. It is now the sixth biggest semiconductor maker in Taiwan, with more than $300 million in sales and some 2,800 employees. Although most of its employees and its manufacturing facilities are in Taiwan, Macronix has an advanced design and engineering center in Silicon Valley, where Wu regularly recruits senior managers. A Macronix venture capital fund invests in promising start-ups in both Silicon Valley and Taiwan—not to raise money but to develop technologies related to their core business. In short, Miin Wu's activities bridge and benefit both the Taiwan and Silicon Valley economies.

A New Model of Globalization

As recently as the 1970s, only giant corporations had the resources and capabilities to grow internationally, and they did so primarily by establishing marketing offices or manufacturing plants overseas. Today, new transportation and communications technologies allow even the smallest firms to build partnerships with foreign producers to tap overseas expertise, cost-savings, and markets. Start-ups in Silicon Valley are often global actors from the day they begin operations. Many raise capital from Asian sources, others subcontract manufacturing to Taiwan or rely on software development in India, and virtually all sell their products in Asian markets.

The scarce resource in this new environment is the ability to locate foreign partners quickly and to manage complex business relationships across cultural and linguistic boundaries. The challenge is keenest in high-tech industries whose products, markets, and technologies are continually being redefined—and whose product cycles are exceptionally short. For them, first-generation immigrants like the Chinese and Indian engineers of Silicon Valley, who have the language, cultural, and technical skills to thrive in both the United States and foreign markets, are invaluable. Their social structures enable even the smallest producers to locate and maintain collaborations across long distances and gain access to Asian capital, manufacturing capabilities, skills, and markets.

These ties have measurable economic benefits. For every 1 percent increase in the number of first-generation immigrants from a given country, for example, California's exports to that country go up nearly 0.5 percent. The effect is especially pronounced in the Asia-Pacific where, all other things being equal, California exports nearly four times more than it exports to comparable countries elsewhere in the world.

Growing links between the high-tech communities of Silicon Valley and Taiwan, for example, offer big benefits to both economies. Silicon Valley remains the center of new product definition and of design and development of leading-edge technologies, whereas Taiwan offers world-class manufacturing, flexible development and integration, and access to key customers and markets in China and Southeast Asia. But what appears a classic case of the economic benefits of comparative advantage would not be possible without the underlying social structures, provided by Taiwanese engineers, which ensure continuous flows of information between the two regions.

The reciprocal and decentralized nature of these relationships is distinctive. The ties between Japan and the United States during the 1980s were typically arm's-length, and technology transfers between large firms were managed from the top down. The Silicon Valley-Hsinchu relationship, by contrast, consists of formal and informal collaborations among individual investors and entrepreneurs, small and medium-sized firms, and divisions of larger companies on both sides of the Pacific. In this complex mix, the rich social and professional ties among Taiwanese engineers and their U.S. counterparts are as important as the more formal corporate alliances and partnerships.

Silicon Valley-based firms are poised to exploit both India's software talent and Taiwan's manufacturing capabilities. Mahesh Veerina started Ramp Networks (initially Trancell Systems) in 1993 with several Indian friends, relatives, and colleagues. Their aim was to develop low-cost devices to speed Internet access for small businesses. By 1994, short on money, they decided to hire programmers in India for one-quarter of the Silicon Valley rate. One founder spent two years setting up and managing their software development center in the southern city of Hyderabad. By 1999 Ramp had 65 employees in Santa Clara and 25 in India.

Having used his Indian background to link California with India, Veerina then met two principals of a Taiwanese investment fund, InveStar, that folded in Taiwan. In less than three months, Veerina set up partnerships for high-volume manufacture of Ramp's routers with three Taiwanese manufacturers (it took nine months to establish a similar partnership with a U.S. manufacturer). The Taiwanese price per unit was about half what Ramp was paying for manufacturing in the United States, and Ramp increased its output one-hundred-fold because of relationships subsequently built by Veerina with key customers in the Taiwanese personal computer industry. Ramp also opted to use the worldwide distribution channels of its Taiwanese partners. And when Ramp designed a new model, the Taiwanese manufacturer was prepared to ship product in two weeks—not the six months it would have taken in the United States.

Veerina attributes much of his success to InveStar's partners and their network of contacts in Taiwan. In a business where product cycles are often shorter than nine months, the speed and cost savings provided by these relationships provide critical competitive advantages to a firm like Ramp. InveStar sees as one of its key assets its intimate knowledge of the ins and outs of the business infrastructure in Taiwan's decentralized industrial system. By helping outsiders (both Chinese and non-Chinese) negotiate these complicated networks to tap into Taiwan's cost-effective and high-quality infrastructure and capability for speedy and flexible integration, such firms provide their clients far more than access to capital.

> Americans should resist viewing immigration and trade as zero-sum processes.

As Silicon Valley's skilled Chinese and Indian immigrants create social and economic links to their home countries, they simultaneously open foreign markets and identify manufacturing options and technical skills in Asia for the broader U.S. business community. Traditional Fortune 500 corporations as well as newer technology companies, for example, now increasingly turn to India for software programming and development talent. Meanwhile, information technology-related sectors in the United States rely heavily on Taiwan (and more recently China) for their fast and flexible infrastructure for manufacturing semiconductors and PCs, as well as their growing markets for advanced technology components. And these distant resources are now just as accessible to new start-ups like Ramp as to more established corporations.

These new international linkages are strengthening the economic infrastructure of the United States while providing new opportunities for once peripheral regions of the world economy. Foreign-born engineers have started thousands of technology businesses in the United States, generating jobs, exports, and wealth at home and also accelerating the integration of these businesses into the global economy.

A New Policy Environment

The Silicon Valley experience underscores far-reaching transformations of the relationship between immigration, trade, and economic development in the 21st century. Where once the main economic ties between immigrants and their home countries were remittances sent to families left behind, today more and more skilled U.S. immigrants eventually return home. Those who remain in America often become part of transnational communities that link the United States to the economies of distant regions. These new immigrant entrepreneurs thus foster economic development directly, by creating new jobs and wealth, as well as indirectly, by coordinating the information flows and providing the linguistic and cultural know-how that promote trade and investment with their home countries.

Analysts and policymakers must recognize this new reality. In the recent U.S. debate over making more H1-B visas available for highly skilled immigrants, discussion began—and ended—with the extent to which immigrants displace native workers. But these high-tech immigrants affect more than labor supply and wages. They also create new jobs here and new ties abroad. Some of their economic contributions, such as enhanced trade and investment flows, are difficult to quantify, but they must figure into our debates.

Economic openness has its costs, to be sure, but the strength of the U.S. economy has historically derived from its openness and diversity—and this will be increasingly true as the economy becomes more global. As Silicon Valley's new immigrant entrepreneurs suggest, Americans should resist viewing immigration and trade as zero-sum processes. We need to encourage the immigration of skilled workers—while simultaneously improving the education of workers here at home.

AnnaLee Saxenian is a professor of city and regional planning at the University of California at Berkeley.

From the *Brookings Review,* Winter 2002, pp. 28-31.

The perils of e-mail

It was supposed to make life easier. Now e-mail has become a prosecutor's No. 1 weapon and the surest way for companies to get sued. How e-mail became e-vidence mail--and why the solution is often worse than the problem.

by Nicholas Varchaver

IT WAS THE SORT OF E-MAIL MOST PEOPLE DELETE WITH NARY a glance. The bland subject heading read: "E-mail content training to begin in October." But the message inside was anything but routine. Merrill Lynch was ordering its 50,000-plus employees to attend a reeducation camp of sorts. "It is imperative that every employee knows how to use e-mail effectively and appropriately," wrote Merrill president Stanley O'Neal and chairman David Komansky. "E-mail and other forms of electronic communication are like any other written communication, and are subject to subpoena." Before sending an e-mail, they advised, "Ask yourself: How would I feel if this message appeared on the front page of a newspaper?"

Good question. And one O'Neal and Komansky would get a chance to answer. Some thoughtful Merrill staffer, apparently, zapped the e-mail to the Reuters news service (or to someone else who did), from which it traveled to the pages of the *New York Post*, the *Boston Herald*, and the *Houston Chronicle*, and to *Lou Dobbs Moneyline* on CNN. Take two seconds to think about it, and two lessons emerge: (1) E-mail is inspiring a very real and growing fear in corporate boardrooms, and (2) that fear can't do anything to stop electronic messages from careening out of control.

Sure, 2002 was the Year of Corporate Scandal. But really it wouldn't be fair to give all the credit to grasping, conniving executives and malevolent, sneaky bookkeepers. No, as those corporate honchos offer their plea bargains, they'll all be able to name an accomplice: e-mail.

For prosecutors, it has become the star witness—or perhaps an even better weapon than that. Think of e-mail as the corporate equivalent of DNA evidence, that single hair left at the crime scene that turns the entire case. In theory you can explain it away, but good luck trying.

So ubiquitous has the smoking e-mail become that some lawyers have taken to calling it "evidence mail." Says Garry Mathiason, whose law firm, Littler Mendelson, defends giant corporations in employment cases: "I don't think there's a case we handle today that doesn't have some e-mail component to it."

Who knew that a nation could become so transfixed by *writing*? There was the Stephen King of e-mail prose—former Merrill Lynch analyst Henry Blodget—whose output was as prolific as it was haunting. Former Salomon Smith Barney analyst Jack Grubman favored a terser style—he's reportedly a BlackBerry man—for what he would later claim were his fictional musings. But literary style notwithstanding, their e-mails shared a common plot: jacking up stock ratings to please investment-bank clients. Does anybody think the nation's biggest brokerages would have agreed to hand over $1.5 billion in settlements if not for this electronic paper trail?

Nor was the pox limited to the Wall Street houses. Like forgotten land mines, unfortunate e-mails involving Enron, WorldCom, Qwest, Global Crossing, and Tyco exploded sporadically throughout the year. There was even damaging e-mail *about* e-mail, as happened with the J.P. Morgan Chase banker who warned a colleague to "shut up and delete this e-mail."

But even that seemingly obvious fix can bring its own perils. Five big Wall Street brokerages coughed up $8.25 million in fines in December for failing to preserve electronic messages, as securities rules require. And one cannot forget Arthur Andersen, whose destruction of Enron-related transmissions led to a criminal conviction and eventually to the accounting firm's implosion. While the degree of punishment was exceptional, the fact of it wasn't: Judges are increasingly imposing penalties on companies that can't turn over old e-mails when the court demands them.

And so it boils down to this, to borrow an old phrase: Companies can't live with e-mail, and they definitely can't live without it. As we've seen it's increasingly a legal albatross—and, at the very least, a fast track to public humiliation. But then it's also the most important business technology since the advent of the telephone. It's invaluable in allowing far-flung offices to communicate and it lets employees work from anywhere. It has freed us from the tyranny of phone tag and given us an effortless way to transmit lengthy documents without so much as a busy fax signal. If you have any doubt how much the technology has worked its way into your daily life, just ask yourself this: How many times a day do you check your e-mail?

How to reconcile these two contradictory notions—that e-mail is both salvation and threat? As we're about to show you, there is no easy answer. In fact, this may be one of the most daunting, high-stakes conundrums facing corporate America today.

But one thing is certain: Imposing a technological solution to a behavioral problem, as many companies are trying, seems doomed to failure. After all, e-mail didn't cause Blodget to write what he did—it simply did a good job of recording him.

IT'S NOT AS IF WE'VE NEVER BEEN WARNED. ONLY FOUR years ago Microsoft was flayed at its antitrust trial for endless indelicate e-mails, such as the one in which Bill Gates asked, "How much do we need to pay you to screw Netscape?" A decade before that an early form of e-mail provided key evidence in the 1987 Iran-Contra investigation. As it happens, many of the smoking guns consisted of e-mails that Oliver North had erased. Or thought he did.

Now, 15 years later, it sounds obvious to say that "delete" doesn't mean delete. It sounds schoolmarmish to say, "Careful what you write." We know that already. But still, neither lesson has sunk in.

So what is it about e-mail that makes it seem like electronic truth serum? Some years back, researchers at the University of Texas conducted an experiment. They asked volunteers to sit in a cubicle by themselves and respond to a series of personal questions. The subjects had to speak into a microphone, which, they were told, would record what they said. Half the group sat in cubicles with a large mirror facing them; the others had no mirror. The researchers found that the mirrorless subjects were noticeably more willing to speak and more likely to say revealing things. E-mail, which at heart is a solitary way of communicating, may convey that same mirrorless feeling.

Perhaps that explains our apparent tendency to confess electronically. In *Alphabet to E-Mail: How Written English Evolved and Where It's Heading*, linguist Naomi Baron notes that 25 years of research reveal that "people offer more accurate and complete information about themselves when filling out questionnaires using a computer than when completing the same form on paper or through a face-to-face interview. The differences were especially marked when the information at issue was personally sensitive."

That's great news for D.A.s and advice columnists, but a nightmare from the corporation's vantage point. "Companies are really struggling with this," says Jay Ehrenreich, senior manager of PricewaterhouseCoopers' cybercrime prevention and response group. For starters, we're drowning in electronic paperwork. The ease of e-mail means we send and receive more documents than ever before. And as document-management consultant Bob Williams of Cohasset Associates points out, the rise of word processing and e-mail has led to the gradual extinction of the secretary—the person who paid attention to filing and purging. If the typical middle manager were to file papers the way he stores e-mails, his office would be filled with five-foot pillars of vellum and bleached bond. Is it any wonder that embarrassing e-mails keep popping up?

Many corporate managers have concluded that the best solution to this mess is the mass purge. If your business isn't, say, a brokerage or health-care company, both of which have specific rules on how long they must keep records, you can trash e-mails whenever you want, as long as you do so pursuant to the terms of a formal policy. And so companies are cleaning out their electronic closets, now typically wiping all e-mail messages from their servers after 30 to 90 days.

Others limit individuals' storage capacity. For example, Boeing restricts staffers to 15 megabytes of e-mail in their in-box. If they exceed the limit, the system won't allow them to send any e-mail. In theory, employees will judiciously eliminate messages that have outlived their usefulness.

Purging has other benefits—it allows companies to free server space for more productive uses. But as a litigation-avoidance tool it's "pissing into the wind," in the earthy words of Tom Campbell, founder of Kobo.biz, a company that offers high-end web-based e-mail. Purges don't delete the messages that are stored on employees' hard drives; they don't eliminate the ones that people print out and file away; and they don't eradicate the e-mails that have been sent or forwarded to people outside the company. In other words, a huge percentage of e-mails will escape most purges.

More fundamentally, do businesses want the legal tail to wag the commercial dog? How many documents do you want to throw out in hopes of avoiding future litigation? "To purge the contents of the entire e-mail system," says consultant and lawyer Randolph Kahn, co-author of the forthcoming book *E-Mail Rules*, "is to potentially dispose of records with business significance that are needed to protect the company's business and legal interests."

And, believe it or not, e-mail can actually come to the rescue of corporations in litigation. In employment cases, says lawyer Mathiason of Littler Mendelson, e-mail evidence is as likely to help a company as it is to hurt it. He cites a recent mediation in which a company was sued be-

Are you sure you want to send this message?

Great (and not-so-great) moments in e-mail history

E-mail for Sale

1982: The first easy-to-use e-mail system debuts.

Ollie's Phantom Deletions

1987: Iran-Contra protagonist Oliver North testifies that he assumed e-mails would be vaporized when he deleted them. Faced with a mountain of incriminating reconstructed messages, he says, "Wow, were we wrong."

Spam I Am

1994: First report of mass, unsolicited e-mail. Mail-order brides rejoice. Everyone else cringes.

A New Big Brother

1997: Software that lets companies monitor worker e-mail is released.

Me and My Big Mouth

Microsoft's antitrust trial spotlights Bill Gates' indiscreet e-mails. In one, he recounts asking AOL execs, "How much do we need to pay you to screw Netscape?"

Love Stinks

2000: The "I Love You" virus causes $8.7 billion of damage to computer systems worldwide.

XXX

2000: Dow Chemical fires 74 and suspends 435 for trading X-rated e-mail.

The Swire Effect

2000: Londoner Claire Swire rhapsodizes about oral sex with her boyfriend—only to see the e-mail forwarded to mailboxes across the globe.

Boss From Hell

2001: Cerner CEO Neal Patterson berates 400 managers electronically. The e-mail lands on Yahoo, and Cerner stock drops 28% within a week.

Attention, Prozac Users!

June 2001: Eli Lilly "outs" 700 Prozac users when it inadvertently reveals their addresses in a mass e-mail.

Buy This P.O.S.

2002: Merrill Lynch pays $100 million after e-mails from ex-Internet analyst Henry Blodget emerge. He calls one stock "a piece of crap" while rating it "accumulate."

Obstruction of Judgement

2002: Arthur Andersen's David Duncan pleads guilty, and the firm is convicted of destroying Enron-related e-mails and papers.

Nurserygate

2002: Salomon Smith Barney's Jack Grubman claims in e-mails to have raised AT&T's rating to help Citigroup CEO Sandy Weill. Why? So Weill could help Grubman's twins get into a fancy preschool.

cause a male executive had allegedly sexually harassed a female employee. Mathiason's team retrieved lurid e-mail attachments that the woman had sent to her ostensible harasser, undercutting her claim that she'd been a victim. Says Mathiason: "The attachments were so gross and so disgusting that, first of all, one of our paralegals wouldn't even look at them, and I could hardly blame that person. We threw those out in the mediation, and the claim went down from $1 million to $10,000."

But for good or ill, e-mails are fundamentally survivors. They are the cockroaches of mass communication. Even if e-mails have been purged from a server, for instance, they may survive on the company's backup tape. And while it can be difficult and expensive to retrieve files from backup tapes, that doesn't get companies off the hook: Courts expect you to produce the e-mails anyway.

Consider one recent case involving a GMAC subsidiary, Residential Funding Corp. In a breach-of-contract lawsuit, RFC had won a $96 million jury award against DeGeorge Financial Corp. That is, until a New York federal appeals court weighed in. At issue was RFC's inability to deliver old e-mails at trial. The fact that RFC had hired a leading electronic discovery firm to recover the messages from backup tapes—and that the effort had failed—was no excuse, the judges said. A company can be punished, the appellate court found, even if its failure to provide e-mails was caused by negligence rather than bad faith. The case was sent back to the trial court and settled in December with an unspecified payment to DeGeorge.

IF PURGING ISN'T THE ANSWER, CAN E-MAIL MONITORING come to the rescue? These days, 47% of companies engage in the practice, according to the ePolicy Institute, a research and consulting firm in Columbus. There's no getting around the Orwellian flavor of all this scrutiny, though perhaps it's leavened by a certain absurdism in the corporate incarnation: Even the watchers are watched. Witness the very large company that brought in PWC's Ehrenreich as a precautionary measure during the layoff of some of its IT staff. The consultants scanned the hard drives of the soon-to-depart IT employees, hoping to stave off any potential sabotage. That's when they discovered that one IT staffer had quietly snooped into a senior executive's electronic in-box and retrieved some hardcore pornographic e-mails. Rather than report it to his higher-ups, he was gleefully sharing the material with his fellow techies.

Even when monitors do what they're supposed to do, they gear their efforts largely to warding off sexually explicit and junk e-mails—not ferreting out the Blodgets and Grubmans among us. Adam Ludlow, senior network engineer at electronics manufacturer Brother Industries, estimates that spam- and obscenity-hunting software blocks 7,000 of the 20,000 e-mails that arrive at Brother's U.S. servers every day. "MAILsweeper [a software program] probably blocks 2,000 e-mails a day just with the word 'Viagra' in it," he says.

The software also filters what is going in the other direction, waylaying messages with objectionable language. "I don't let any profanity leave this establishment," Ludlow says. He has programmed the software, which Brother bought from a company called Clearswift, not only to search for obscene phraseology, but also to seek out certain technical language. The latter prevents employees from sending, say, new-product designs to any e-mail address that isn't on an approved list.

It's both impressive and chilling—and still only nascent. According to International Data Corp., companies spent $139 million on content-oriented e-mail monitoring in 2001, compared with the $1.67 billion they shelled out for software that blocks viruses. IDC predicts that e-mail monitoring software sales will grow to a $662 million market by 2006.

Companies that sell monitoring software say they've been getting a lot of interest lately. Says Ivan O'Sullivan, vice-president for worldwide corporate development at Clearswift (whose 2,000 U.S. customers include AT&T, Bank of America, Continental Airlines, and General Electric): "In terms of requests for proposals, I haven't ever seen it as hot and busy as it was in the last three months of 2002."

Wall Street houses, in particular, are looking to tighten their monitoring, O'Sullivan says. In the past, they employed software to identify suspicious messages after they were sent and delivered. Now, he says, "more people want to do *pre*-review of messages in the financial space, rather than look at things after the fact." In pre-review, messages are electronically shanghaied and then "quarantined" until, say, a compliance supervisor reads them. Only with the supervisor's approval is a message routed to its intended recipient. Second, whereas investment banks mostly monitored e-mails that went to people outside the firm, according to O'Sullivan, they're now looking to monitor communications within the firm too. (Need we point out that the infamous Wall Street e-mails were all intracompany messages?)

Better living through software, right? Perhaps. But there are plenty of dangerous things a person can say without using a single hot-button word or combination. Consider two phrases: "This is an accommodation for an important client" and "This company is very important to us from a banking perspective." Both excerpts are from the Merrill Lynch e-mail collection. In the context of allegations that Merrill inflated stock ratings to please investment-banking clients, the phrases are extremely damning.

But if every e-mail that mentions an accommodation for a client sets off an alarm bell, companies will need battalions of censors to comb through the resulting deluge of "suspicious" messages. Even clearly inflammatory wording, such as the Blodget assessment that a stock was "a powder keg," is caught only if the phrase in question is common enough to be included on a programming list. As O'Sullivan acknowledges, "Ultimately, we're not a substitute for good management. We're a tool that organizations who wish to comply can use to assist them in their compliance."

Aggressive monitoring can actually create surprising risks for multinational corporations, which the great majority of the FORTUNE 500 are. Privacy-protection laws for employees are much stricter in Europe than in the U.S. Three Deutsche Bank executives now face prison time in Spain for doing something American companies routinely do: examining an employee's e-mail. Microsoft was fined after a few of its Spanish employees *voluntarily* submitted personal data to a company website, which sent the information to the human resources department in Redmond, Wash.

The buzz phrase for e-mail consultants in recent years is "having a policy." In theory, companies are shielded from liability by putting their e-mail rules in writing—something four-fifths of American companies already do. "But where employers drop the ball," says Nancy Flynn of the ePolicy Institute, "is that only 24% do any kind of training. So you can't expect your employees to know what to do and what not to do if you don't train them."

Companies such as Boeing and Intel have long had classes on e-mail and Internet use, which focus on commonsense rules and advice (with an occasional quirky mandate: Intel's policy forbids chain letters). Boeing even requires an annual refresher course.

Training, perhaps, is the best tonic—at least when it comes to simple concepts, such as not using offensive language. But can we ever train people when the core of the message is "Don't say anything stupid"? And ultimately, of course, e-mail is simply a recording medium. Though no company would ever admit to such a view, you get the feeling that more than one CEO is thinking, I don't care how you act—just don't write it down. And that, of course, is not an e-mail problem.

NOW THAT SOME BUSINESSPEOPLE APPEAR TO CRAVE A RE-turn to a world where every exchange isn't recorded, it's worth recalling that there was a time when just the opposite was true. In the earliest days of the telephone, according to *America Calling: A Social History of the Telephone to*

1940, some businessmen actually resisted the new technology because they couldn't conceive of buying, selling, and negotiating without a permanent paper record.

Indeed, the history of the telephone offers lessons for corporate managers wrestling with e-mail. For all its universal acceptance, e-mail has been in widespread use for less than ten years. We simply haven't figured it out yet. By comparison, it took decades to evolve uses for the phone that seem completely natural now. For nearly half a century, the Bell companies scorned the idea of using a phone to socialize; they marketed it for its business and utilitarian purposes only.

Like the telephone, e-mail is occasionally blamed for long-developing changes that it didn't necessarily create (but did accelerate): the increasing overlap of home and work life and the tendency of written language to resemble speech. Both have fed people's tendency to write irreverent, loose e-mail.

Add to that more recent technological developments, such as the popularity of the BlackBerry, which both heighten the intermingling of work and home and accentuate people's tendency to fire off a quick electronic note. Where once an employee would compose himself and dictate a memo to a secretary, who might bring it back for inspection an hour later, a manager is more likely now to thumb-type a two-line e-mail while standing on the sidelines at her daughter's soccer game.

As young as it is, e-mail is already being followed by an even faster technology that could be more dangerous still. Instant messaging is rising fast in corporate America; some 45% of Internet users at work currently have access to consumer IM services such as those from AOL, MSN, and Yahoo, according to ComScore Media Metrix. Such systems generally leave little electronic trace unless a user intentionally takes steps to preserve messages. But for the same reason that companies monitor, block, and save e-mail messages, they're likely to eventually do the same with IM.

Among teenagers and college students, IM plays the role that e-mail does for older people, argues Baron: It's casual and written in "spoken" style. Students, she says, save e-mail for more formal correspondence with parents and professors.

So our e-mail problem may disappear—only to be replaced by an IM problem. Says Paul Saffo of the Institute for the Future: "By the time we get all four corners of e-mail nailed down, the important communications are going to be instant-messaging. And no one will know what to do with that."

REPORTER ASSOCIATE *Katherine Bonamici*
FEEDBACK *nvarchaver@fortunemail.com*

Article 12

The Great Prosperity Divide

Unemployment is at a 30-year low and corporate profits are surging. But much of today's work force can't afford the education and training needed to succeed in the New Economy. Can public-funded training replace the career ladders now denied many American workers?

Kevin Dobbs

Sarah Schaefer leans forward and rests her head in her hands. It's 5:30 p.m. and she's been on the go for 13 hours. She cleaned her apartment. She took her daughters—ages 3 and 5—to day care. She made a cross-town commute—all before an eight-hour shift in the customer service department at American Express Financial Services in Minneapolis. Now she will muster the energy to pick up the kids and get groceries and make dinner.

So it goes—just to get by.

Schaefer, a 25-year-old single parent, is bone tired. More than her job, more than any single chore, she is exhausted by the knowledge that tomorrow means more of the same. "It's a struggle, but if I worried about it as much as I could, I don't think I'd even wake up in the morning," she says.

She has maintained this rigorous routine for five years, but finds herself in a financial hole. In the midst of unprecedented economic prosperity, with corporate profits soaring and employers seemingly desperate for workers, Schaefer wonders why she can't get ahead. She is a high school graduate, she has two years of college to her credit, and she works for a successful company, yet her income barely covers her monthly bills. Any unexpected expenses go on a credit card or go unpaid.

She takes home about $1,400 a month. Thanks to state aid, day care claims only $120 of that. Still, there are utility, food, rent and insurance payments. All told, she pays out a minimum of $1,140, leaving $260 a month for clothing, household items and miscellaneous needs. Inevitably, bills stockpile. She has had her electricity cut off and her telephone service disconnected for months at a time. "I cut it very, very close every month," she says.

Schaefer shares these experiences with thousands of American workers. She sees them every day—at work, at day care, around her neighborhood. Most of the talk about the New Economy centers on a roaring stock market or Internet start-ups, so it is easy to forget that nearly two-thirds of household incomes are stagnant or declining, that half of Americans have no assets, that credit card debt is growing at an annual rate of more than 7 percent.

We forget because the country boasts exceptionally low unemployment, modest inflation increases, and accelerated productivity growth. By these statistical measures, we are on a roll.

Life is good in the New Economy. Problem is, more than two-thirds of today's labor force does not work in the New Economy—in high-tech occupations like software development, computer services or telecommunications. Instead, these workers are employed in such areas as construction and education and customer service, where real wages have not risen noticeably or have actually declined in recent years.

Retail, service, education and manufacturing workers—and the companies that employ them—all are falling behind. Computers can be used to cut some processing costs, but because such industries are so labor-intensive, employers still must ante up the dollars to physically produce products and deliver customer service. Even health care, the nation's largest industry, accounting for one-sixth of the gross national product, is lagging. Real wages stagnated in the '90s, thanks to health care reform and managed care programs that reduced profits and forced job cuts even among highly skilled professionals like physical therapists and nurse practitioners.

According to the Bureau of Labor Statistics and reports from economists, average real wages for New Economy jobs climbed more than 10 percent over the past five years, while all other incomes merely held steady or declined until 1998, when modest increases at last reflected the demands of a shrinking labor pool.

It comes down to this: If you don't have a New Economy job, you will continue to lose ground relative to those who do, even as overall national wealth continues to mount. The scenario creates a majority class of workers that is steadily falling behind. Knowledge Universe founder Michael Milken, speaking at Online Learning '99, a September conference in Los Angeles sponsored by TRAINING's parent company, estimated that 70 percent of the work force is ill-prepared for advancement. "Two Americas have been built," he said.

Technology and Inequality

The rush to invest in computers dramatically alters the typical workplace and ups the relative demand for high-tech workers. Consequently, writes economist James Galbraith in his 1998 book *Created Unequal* (The Free Press), those who are most skilled see their pay climb much more rapidly than everyone else.

Investments in technology, of course, are premised on the productivity gains and profit increases it allows. Most New Economy businesses' products or services are centered on information. Computers have dramatically increased the speed and efficiency of information processing, which has lowered production costs and bolstered opportunities for expansion. This is not the case for the rest of the economy, where traditional industries cannot rely as heavily on the spread of information. They are not posting big gains and cannot afford to accommodate significant wage increases.

As a result, industries in the information-technology sector are steadily distancing themselves. Federal statistics show that New Economy companies are expanding their work forces at a 4 percent annual clip and are increasing productivity by as much as 30 percent per year. Their counterparts are expanding employment half as quickly and productivity is rising only a tenth as fast. Profits and labor demand, then, are much greater in the information sector.

Disillusioned Work Force

Despite the booming economy, more than half of recent hires are troubled by sharp income disparities they observe at work. That's the finding of a recent report about the attitudes of young American workers released by Peter Hart Research Associates for the AFL-CIO. The firm interviewed 750 workers ages 18–34 and found that only 40 percent believe their employers treat them fairly. By the time people reach their late 20s, they generally feel that employers fail to help their workers advance economically by sharing profits or providing anything more than cost-of-living raises. And 60 percent don't feel employers can be trusted. Moreover, while they're aware that a large number of new jobs are being created, two-thirds of young workers view them as predominantly low-paying positions.

—K.D.

Staunch free-market proponents say not to worry. The demand for New Economy workers simply alerts the labor force to get more information-technology training. Over time it all takes care of itself, they contend, because college students migrate toward majors that are in demand, and those already in the work force go back to school to acquire new skills. Eventually, supply meets demand, and when that happens the premium for technology workers tapers off, thus satisfying labor needs and narrowing the income gap.

With more students in college than ever before and specialized online universities popping up like dandelions, it seems the message is getting through. "People *are* taking notice," says William Dickens, an economist at the Brookings Institution in Washington, DC.

But Dickens is quick to note a flaw in the free-market scenario: Many people can't afford to respond, in large part because college education costs continue to climb faster than inflation. The average annual cost of attending a four-year private college for the 1999–2000 school year is $23,650, reports New York-based College Board. That's more than 60 percent of the $38,900 annual pretax income of the average American family of four.

'An awful lot of people in the bottom half are falling farther behind those at the top.'

—WILLIAM DICKENS
ECONOMIST, BROOKINGS INSTITUTION

Moreover, the College Board says, nearly 60 percent of all student aid now comes in the form of student loans. And lower-income families are backing away from such heavy debts, meaning parents' income tends to determine children's ability to get advanced education. That's bad news for children growing up in low-income households; the average college grad makes $14,000 more per year than the typical high school educated employee, according to the Bureau of Labor Statistics. The gap widens with each additional year of education.

Experts doubt college costs will stop rising faster than other prices, which means paying for higher education—and acquiring the necessary skills to fit into the New Economy—is likely to present an ever more daunting burden to lower- and middle-income families. "An awful lot of people in the bottom half are falling farther behind those at the top," says Dickens.

'For people in the lower-income brackets, sometimes I don't think the economy will ever change enough.'

—SARAH SCHAEFER
MINNEAPOLIS

Sarah Schaefer, in Minneapolis, typifies the dilemma. She spent two years in college, but the expenses were staggering. She quit in favor of full-time work and was left with hefty student-loan debt and no new marketable skills. Her hope now is that she'll defy the odds and earn enough to help her kids get to college. But she has her doubts: "For people in the lower-income brackets, sometimes I don't think the economy will ever change enough."

Of course, the intent here is not to suggest that *everyone* should train for IT careers. Like any industry, there are only so many positions to fill. Economists like Dickens and Galbraith simply point out that New Economy growth at once creates new wealth and a heightened need for skilled labor. The problem is that not enough people are meeting that demand and too few are sharing in the prosperity the technology age has fostered. Thus the income divide yawns wider than necessary.

The Training Gap

Still, economic prosperity *has* trickled down, and many in the blue-collar ranks have made some strides. Surely, at least, we can say more have jobs, as unemployment levels hover around 30-year lows. But is low unemployment necessarily an indicator that people are employed well?

MIT economist Lester Thurow says no. In his 1999 book *Building Wealth: The New Rules for Individuals, Companies and Nations in a Knowledge-Based Economy* (Harper Collins), he notes that jobs have never been more plentiful, yet "wages have been falling for more than half the work force" and "careers are in very short supply." In fact, between 1993 and 1998, the number of temporary jobs—which often have few benefits and lower wages—expanded from 238,600 to 412,500. That was a higher rate than the job growth in the software and electronic industries combined, representing a sizable portion of the work force that is trying to break into the New Economy but can't, according to the Washington Policy Institute.

Thurow explains it this way: Knowledge is the new basis for wealth. When new knowledge makes old skills obsolete, firms want workers who have that knowledge. Yet in an era of downsizing and efficiency, most companies do not want to pay for extensive training or retraining. The 1990s, despite the economic boom, saw more than 5 million job cuts. The old career ladders are gone, and individual workers are responsible for finding their own routes to better jobs with better pay.

Employees, fully aware of this, jump ship when even a slightly better opportunity surfaces. Companies therefore don't want to invest in people who are likely to change jobs. Conversely, workers are unlikely to invest in training for positions with quickly changing job descriptions because it is too costly and time consuming.

"Without career ladders, how does anyone rationally plan an educational investment? No one wants to waste investment funds on skills that will go unused," Thurow argued last year in an *Atlantic Monthly* article. "... the basic problem in the United States is that every employer wants a free ride in the training system."

Consequently, even though job opportunities abound, the ability to acquire New Economy skills and the wages that accompany them is rare. Many people are left underemployed or working temp jobs for meager pay and scant benefits. Fewer than 5 percent of American adults are unemployed, for instance, but one in six has no health insurance. At the same time, companies complain about a shortage of skilled workers, and they look to government for help. IT trade groups are currently pushing for corporate tax breaks to offset the costs of technology training.

Thurow and others prefer levying a training tax. Employers could deduct their training expenses, so if they spent a certain percentage of their income on training, they would not pay the tax. "It makes employers invest as if there were career ladders," says Thurow. Still others would address the problem through regional training programs that create partnerships among employers, unions and educators—much like the plan championed by President Clinton during his tour of the country's most impoverished areas last summer. They would develop specific programs to meet labor demands in growth industries, with the intent of transferring people from low-paying jobs to higher-income professions.

Many economists, however, insist that corporate America would shun a training tax and argue that publicly funded training programs serve merely as stop-gap measures that temporarily lessen the effect of the problem. Says Dickens, "There really are no obvious solutions. The only true hope is that economic trends will reverse themselves over time."

But what if the next reversal simply halts economic expansion? When growth slows, the income gap is likely to render social and political unease. The New Economy, after all, thrives on a free market policy that is oblivious to career ladders. But we also know from Galbraith and others that workers outside New Economy industries want job security, and *they* make up the majority of the voting public. If the economy turns sour, tension will mount.

Social Mobility

The critical question is this: Can the average person, over the course of a career, steadily work his way into increasingly better-paying jobs? Traditionally, Americans have accepted some disparity in pay as long as there is opportunity for personal improvement, says Iowa State University sociologist Cornelia Flora.

'People are under increasing financial pressure. They are working longer hours, and they still can't attain the basics of a middle-class existence.'

—ROBERT FRANK
ECONOMIST, CORNELL UNIVERSITY

Evidence does suggest that such opportunities exist. Between 1988 and 1998, adjusting for inflation, the average 30-year-old man earned $30,000 and the typical 40-year-old earned $40,000. Even if wages are stagnant, people still see rising income as they age. But this ignores the key issue of relativity deprivation. As Flora points out, "When you see other people getting very rich and they're not working any harder than you, you tend to ask, 'Why are they doing so well and I am not?'"

As the economy continues to flourish, the people earning the most are seeing far greater gains than the average worker. Two Washington, DC, think tanks found in a recent study that the ratio of top executive to production worker pay has ballooned in recent years, from 42-to-1 in 1980 to 419-to-1 in 1998. Had the two groups' pay increased at an identical rate, the typical factory worker would now earn $110,400 a year, rather than the actual average of $29,270, report the Institute for Policy Studies and United for a Fair Economy (see "Wage Disparity").

With such great disparity comes the potential for social upheaval. As the wealthy get wealthier, they buy more expensive cars, more extravagant homes. As this happens, prices ratchet up for everyone, making it increasingly difficult for the average person to acquire major assets. The median price for a home tops $200,000 in Los Angeles, New York and Boston, and continues to rise in most major metropolitan areas. In absolute numbers, more Americans than ever own houses, but only half of all people living in the country's central cities can afford to buy their own home. As such prices climb, as a result of increased spending from the wealthy, the effects of income disparity become blindingly obvious.

Wage Disparity

In the past year several studies were released concerning the income gap separating corporate executives and the average worker. Some of the most staggering findings come from a pair of think tanks in Washington, DC. The Institute for Policy Studies and United for a Fair Economy find that the average annual compensation for chief executives of large companies increased fivefold in recent years, from $1.8 million in 1990 to $10.6 million in 1998. It has risen 500 percent over the past 15 years, a pace three times faster than corporate profits and seven times greater than blue-collar wages. In 1998 alone, executive pay climbed 26 percent, compared with a 2.7 percent gain for the average worker. If worker pay had increased at an identical pace, the minimum wage would top $22 an hour, rather than the current $5.15. Microsoft Corp. chairman Bill Gates alone has amassed as much wealth as the bottom 40 percent of the American population.

—K.D.

There are other barriers, as well: rising child-care, health care and transportation costs. People are working harder and longer just to cover these expenses. This explains why, even though the economy is strong, the average household is taking on more debt. "People are under increasing financial pressure," says Cornell University economist Robert Frank, author of *Luxury Fever: Why Money Fails to Satisfy in an Era of Excess* (The Free Press, 1999). "They are working longer hours, and they still can't attain the basics of a middle-class existence."

All of this, Galbraith argues, leads to "a high degree of inequality" that further distances "the haves from the have-nots, transforming the U.S. from a middle-class democracy into something that more closely resembles an authoritarian quasi democracy with an overclass and an underclass."

For people like Sarah Schaefer, the working world becomes a place of subdued desperation. "To me, it's just how it's always been," she says.

She can't afford college and therefore can't break into the higher-paying jobs of the New Economy. Without that earning power, she can't buy a home and acquire the assets needed for security, not to mention social mobility. Schaefer wants nothing more than to buy a home and raise her children in a quiet neighborhood. For now, though, she finds herself living in a dilapidated apartment complex on the north side of Minneapolis, an area known for rampant crime.

"I get myself up at 4 a.m. just to get my kids ready and get to work on time, and still I come home to this," she says. "There are shootings in the streets and drug dealers in the hallways. It's a place I'd never choose to live, especially with kids. But it's all I can afford."

And so it goes, unnoticed in most prominent circles but profoundly affecting much of America's work force. The economy has turned viciously against unskilled workers, and escape routes are narrow and expensive. For now, at least, most have jobs.

"There are a lot of people—I see them every day—who are doing the best they can and just getting by," Schaefer says. "We're just hoping nothing bad happens. I know if I lost my job right now, I'd be screwed. *Screwed.*"

Shortly after being interviewed for this article, Schaefer was laid off by American Express.

Kevin Dobbs *is an associate editor of TRAINING. kdobbs@trainingmag.com*

"You're Hired, Now Go Home"

Here's how to hire virtual workers and keep them connected.

By Jeanne L. Allert

Do you remember going to career workshops in college that taught you to research a prospective employer, plan carefully what you would wear, and rehearse responses to expected questions? I recall one advice book recommending that you spend a morning and an afternoon hanging out in the lobby of a prospective employer, observing when people come and go, what they wore, and how they interacted to see whether it was a place you'd fit in.

What if the prospective employer is a startup, there is no dress code or commuting patterns to observe, and most of your interview conversations have been via email? What if there is no "place" to fit into?

A virtual company is where work is performed outside of the definition of *place*. There's no factory floor, no retail store, no conference room, no cubicle farm. Virtual work is primarily the manufacture, retail, and distribution of intellectual property. Some of that intellectual property can lead to a product, as in the case of software or Website development, but not only is there no physical place, there are often no established policies or practices. Virtual companies have to rewrite a lot of the traditional rules and make many of them up as they go along.

Main Points

- A virtual company is where work is performed outside of the definition of *place*.
- Virtual work opens up a wider net of potential employees, but it also narrows your options because of the needle-in-a-haystack characteristics that virtual employees need to have.
- It's to your advantage to employ people who have some level of comfort solving their own technology problems, among other necessary skills.

In the sparse collection of advice for managers about hiring virtual employees, you'll find that most of the recommendations are for telecommuters. A telecommuter is someone who spends some part of his or her work time outside of the office. In the case of telecommuting employees, managers can still rely on the structure and amenities of the physical office to provide support. But what about managers who work exclusively in a virtual context? I have been a manager of telecommuting employees for six years, and now I am a company officer in a completely virtual enterprise.

Interviewing

The literature on virtual work suggests that you have to hire the "right kind of person" for this type of work. I agree, but what is the right kind? It's true that virtual work opens up a wider net of potential employees, in that you can consider a stay-at-home parent, a disabled person or retiree, or even someone in another state or country. But virtual work also narrows your candidates because of the needle-in-a-haystack characteristics you have to identify.

Here are some traits to look for.

Values- or mission-based. Candidates who see the larger picture of what you're trying to create and share your passion for the work will adjust better to virtual work. There will be days when any employee would question, "Why am I doing this?" Without readily available colleagues to boost morale, a virtual worker can create a pool of doubt. Ask candidates what motivates them to work. What internal rewards do they need? What activities do they do in which time and effort don't seem to matter? Look for signs that they are motivated from within.

Multiple communication skills. One advantage in remote interviewing is that you get a fair indication of how well a candidate communicates on the phone, by email, and in writing. Those skills are essential to success in virtual work. Virtual employees must be able to communicate instructions, understanding, disagreement, and their own unique personalities—using the tools of virtual work. During the interview process, you should seek to have a candidate communicate with you using all modes of communication. Pay careful attention to tone and how well candidates get their ideas across.

Decision-making confidence. Equally important to good communication skills is an employee's level of initiative, especially around problem solving. Virtual workers are on their own. Should a complication or problem arise, you don't want them sitting around waiting for help. Look for people who try—right or wrong—to fix their own problems. Ask questions during interviews about problems candidates have encountered in the past and how they solved them. Probe into how candidates reacted when problems arose and how they felt resolving them.

Tech savvy. Maybe this seems obvious, but I'm not referring to a candidate's ability to use email or word processing. It's to your advantage to identify people who have some level of comfort solving their own technology problems. Have they ever ordered ISP service at home? Have they ever installed a new PC or software? Have they ever called a help desk and been coached through a problem? You can't afford to have a technician make house calls with each little computer mishap. You need people who understand their systems enough to troubleshoot or find the help they need.

Hiring

Truth be told: I've never hired a virtual worker I haven't met. Even though I've had some long-term work relationships with people exclusively online, I don't recommend it for employees. Ultimately, face-to-face interaction is important to building and solidifying the kind of relationship people have working together.

Here are some bases to cover in the hiring process.

Set expectations. In extending a job offer, make sure you have communicated everything that you expect the employee to provide for him- or herself and, specifically, what the company will provide. In a physical office, there's always a copy room full of paper and supplies. In the virtual workplace, will employees be expected to purchase their own supplies? Is the company providing hardware, software, connectivity, cell phone, second phone line, fax machine, answering machine, home office insurance, and so forth? Have all of the details spelled out in the offer package.

Introductions. So, the candidate accepted and is ready to start. How do you introduce him or her to the rest of the company if you're not in the same place? My suggestion: Make the hiring of a new person an occasion. Get a digital camera and take the person's picture. Have her write up a short bio and route it on email to the other employees. Create an employee Website (secure access recommended), and let employees update their personal information on their own with news and announcements. Have a luncheon, dinner, or teleconference to celebrate a new employee's arrival and introduce him. That's certainly no worse than the obligatory parading of the new employee around the office, and it may actually put the new person at ease to see faces and learn names.

Orientation

I've known of several large organizations where the employee orientation process was a precrafted routine, such as a scavenger hunt, in which new employees get a checklist of who to meet and what they'll need. I've also been a manager in companies where new employees were ushered into an elaborate Hell Week of presentations, workshops, and speeches—complemented by the onerous three-ring binder of "essential information" that might or might not get opened.

Generally, employers create orientation programs to acclimate new people and get them into a productive mode in the least amount of time possible. In a virtual environment, that's one of the hardest tasks.

Here are some suggestions.

Start busy. Create a bridge between the new employee's former work life and the new one by scheduling appointments and meetings tightly, at least in the beginning. Map out his or her commitments over the first few weeks, set goals and due dates, and find occasions to meet in person. You might arrange to meet a new employee at a local coffee shop for an hour once a week during his or her first month on the job. That can be valuable time for you to gain feedback and assess his or her progress. Taper off the meetings as you both become comfortable.

Find a buddy. Mentoring is a popular form of orientation that can also work in a virtual context. However, the reasons you select a particular buddy for a new employee should probably have less to do with job skills and more to do with similar personal circumstances.

In our company, only two of us are parents. There's an unspoken fraternity among people who have to deal with carpools and sick kids and snow days; it's a different level of peer support. Similarly, I can't relate to the 22-year-old whose distractions might be dating or planning the weekend. If you create a peer pairing, you should consider what kind of support is needed. It's good to let employees create their own support network and find each other. You need only to encourage them and make accommodations.

Support structures

You've already made great strides in setting your virtual employee on a right course. But unlike some traditional offices where new employees are wooed for a few weeks and then forgotten, the manager of a virtual enterprise must remain attentive. You need to put into place a variety of structures that will support employees and encourage their self-sufficiency.

Home-office setup. Give your virtual workers guidelines for setting up their home offices, including recommended equipment and space allocation. If possible, make a site visit to offer suggestions and identify other ways the company can be supportive. That includes obvious support such as equipment installation and guidelines for not so obvious items such as how to answer their home-office phone during business hours and why having a six-year-old record the answering machine message might not be a good idea.

Service providers. When you're running a virtual enterprise, you often must outsource services that would usually be part of internal operations—such as mail service couriers, office-supply providers, copier services, and travel agents. Be sure to educate your employees on how to take advantage of those services to save them time and save you money.

Job definition. A clearly defined job description is imperative (but challenging) in a small, virtual enterprise. It's critical from the standpoint of giving employees direction and structure. At the same time, considering the fast pace of growth and change, nothing is carved in stone. It takes more management, but you would do well to revisit people's job descriptions at least every six months. Again, make sure that employees see a clear connection between their job tasks and the company's mission.

Training. Make no assumptions about an employee's aptitude for your internal communications systems (email, voicemail, intranet, extranet) and provide training on all of them. Such systems are often employees' only link to the world outside of their home offices. They must know when and how to use those tools. They are part of your company's culture, which needs everyone to be a full participant.

Time management. If your workers are home-based, you can recoup (theoretically) hours not spent on commuting, going out for lunch, and socializing with other employees. You might think that would make managing time easier, but two negative forces are at work. One, a home office opens up a host of distractions: the laundry, a sick child, the TV. Such temptations are out of sight, out of mind to office workers, but they loom in the minds of home-based employees. What's more, the middle of a workday is a great time to get your oil changed, grocery shop, or catch a short line at the bank. It can be hard to go back to the computer.

Another—and actually bigger—threat to virtual workers is not working too little but working too much. Because work is only a couple steps away, it's easy to start at 6:30 a.m. and find yourself still at the keyboard at 11 p.m. I'm notorious for forgetting to eat; I just get caught up in what I'm doing. So, I force myself to break up the day. I've also logged on to the network late at night and sent "Stop working and get some sleep!" messages to employees who were still logged on.

Give your virtual employees a clear definition of what constitutes a workday or workweek. If there's room for flexibility, they might see it as a perk to be able to take care of personal errands during the day and, thus, would be willing to work into the night. You, however, must set the lower and upper limits of how much work should get done in the designated time. Monitor it periodically. We can all slip back into bad habits.

Virtual workers need to have a daily sense of connectedness to colleagues, the company, and the larger purpose.

Social connection. Work is inherently a social enterprise, and the work you're doing is—in some way—connected to providing a product or a service to society. Virtual workers need to have a daily sense of connectedness to colleagues, the company, and the larger purpose. Because the work at our company is Internet-based, the entire staff is online almost all day long. We use AOL Instant Messenger as a lifeline to each other. There's something affirming about logging on at 8:20 in the morning and seeing the names of your colleagues appear on your buddy list. It's akin to taking roll call and a lifesaver at 10 at night when you're tying up the last of a report and you see a co-worker from the opposite coast still available for a question.

I make an effort to connect in some way to every employee at least twice a week. A quick email or instant message can be enough to say, "How are you doing?" or "I'm glad you're with us."

It's also mandatory to appear at the weekly staff meeting and devote part of every meeting to social activity. There's always food, and conversation about people's lives flows freely. That's our time to reconnect and feel part of the same enterprise. It's rejuvenating and sustains us for the week ahead. If your group can't meet in person with such frequency, encourage members to get together on their own, or plan more grandiose gatherings less often.

As the manager of a virtual enterprise, you set the tone and the culture of the organization. New employees will take their cue from you, so you must set them on a productive course by your systems and your actions. It can be challenging and time-consuming to manage that way, but a virtual enterprise should never be viewed as an easier way to work. It can, however, provide for a whole new set of rewards to benefit not only your employees, but also your business.

Jeanne L. Allert *is principal and owner of Ellipsis Partners, a completely virtual company and an Internet consulting firm that specializes in providing strategy, design, education, and marketing services to the nonprofit sector. Allert is also an international speaker on technology topics and serves as adjunct professor at Loyola College in Baltimore. You can reach her at jallert@ellipsispartners.com.*

From *Training & Development,* March 2001, pp. 55-58.

Article 14

DEALING WITH TECH RAGE

Ever feel like hurling your computer out the window? You're not alone

By Chris Wood

You know the feeling. Some people get it when their VCRs flash "12:00... 12:00... 12:00..." But even folks who long ago sussed out their stereos can be driven to fury by a fickle cellphone, some cruelly misnamed piece of "productivity" software or a message in Deep Geek accusing them of committing Fatal Error 12.v. Be honest: haven't *you*, at least once, *really* wanted to heave your PC out the nearest window? Thought so.

High-tech gadgets and their associated software promise to make life better, more productive, *simpler*. But new and powerful software is by nature complex. Each new program, gadget or communication device—even the latest set of endless voicemail prompts at the gas company—creates new demands on time and attention. When smart technology makes people feel dumb, some snap. While it is difficult to isolate the effect of information technology on people's stress levels—as compared, say, with working long, hard days in an environment of corporate cutbacks—what's been dubbed "IT rage" is setting off alarm bells for business, researchers and the world's biggest software maker, Microsoft Corp.

Instances are anecdotal, but studies indicate that IT rage, or "techno-stress," is mounting. Eighty per cent of Canadian managers and executives surveyed late last year by Alberta's Athabaska University admitted to stress at work over pressure to adopt new technology. Focus groups conducted for the study revealed tales of laptops hurled at walls and screaming matches over software glitches. An earlier survey by Marlboro, Mass.-based Concord Communications Inc. found that 83 per cent of corporate IT managers had seen enraged workers violently abuse computer equipment. The most common targets: keyboards, followed by mouses and monitors. But what sets off an explosion need not be any quirk of a particular piece of soft- or hardware. Often it is a secondary effect of technology, such as an endless avalanche of e-mail. "We think a lot of IT rage comes from badly designed systems," says Peter Carr, the Athabaska business dean who oversaw the survey. "People haven't really understood how big the change is they're trying to make."

E-mail leads the list of mixed blessings. While it undoubtedly improves speed and cuts the cost of sending messages, it has quickly become an insatiable consumer of time. The average middle manager, according to one count, gets upwards of 100 e-mails a day. Productivity expert Dan Stamp, whose Vancouver company Priority Management Systems Inc. has clients in 15 countries, deplores the way e-mail dominates many managers' work lives. "People start the day by making the fundamental mistake of opening their e-mail, instead of working to a plan," Stamp says. "The best hour and a half of the day is spent on complete rubbish."

Larry Rosen and Michelle Weil, U.S. psychologists who authored the 1997 book *TechnoStress: Coping with Technology @Work @Home @Play*, have identified no fewer than seven different forms of the affliction. These range from the never-ending process of learning how to use new technologies to the blurring of work and home life as a result of innovations like e-mail, call-forwarding and wireless phones. "Nearly everyone tells us they are trying to do too many things at the same time," says Rosen, who teaches at California State University, Dominguez Hills. Comparing data over four years, Rosen and Weil found that skepticism towards technology has risen steadily—even in the New Economy study area of Southern California.

Other experts blame any backlash against technology in part on exaggerated expectations that powerful new software will also be simple and easy to use. In fact, learning to use new systems may crush some people's self-confidence. Many technol-

HOW TO KEEP YOUR COOL

Experts recommend these ways to help limit IT rage:

Set boundaries. Put aside time each day to turn the technology off and devote attention to family or private pursuits.

Choose with care. Ask whether a new device really will simplify your life, or just add new complexity.

Lower expectations. Prepare to invest time before you become adept enough at new technologies to reap their full benefits.

Balance priorities. Work according to your own plan rather than the demands of your technology. Check your e-mail when it is convenient, not whenever it comes.

ogies, notes Stamp, "are becoming so sophisticated, so complex, that the average joe can't ever get on top of them." Adds John Pickett, publisher of *CIO Canada* magazine, a Toronto publication aimed at IT executives, and co-sponsor of the Athabaska study: "Users find the first time they use a new IT system, they're not as competent as they used to be on the old one. They feel, 'I don't know how to do this job anymore.'"

At Microsoft Canada, marketing manager Susan Sharp refuses to accept that her company has raised false expectations about how easy its products are to use. She simply promises that "you'll see moving forward that software is only going to become more friendly." Even so, Sharp has gone on the offensive against the perception that technology is a hazard to quality of life. In December and January, Microsoft Canada equipped five Canadian executives with personal technology products, including Office 2000 software and gadgets like a Pocket PC and a portable printer, and trained them in their use. The goal, says Sharp, "was to demonstrate that technology really isn't as overwhelming as people think, that business professionals can achieve success and a better balance between their private and professional lives."

One participant was London, Ont., mother, grandmother and entrepreneur Brenda Macdonald. The president of Coyle and Greer Awards Canada Ltd., a company that makes plaques and other commemorative items, Macdonald has one daughter still living at home. A husband who spends most week nights in Toronto, where he is president of Jacuzzi Leisure Products Inc., means much of the parenting burden falls on Macdonald. "I don't have enough hours in the day," she complains. "I thought, if I could get up to speed on the technology it might assist me." She found it had on the day she needed to take her daughter to the orthodontist—and used her time in the waiting room to go through e-mail she had transferred to her Pocket PC. Like other participants, though, Macdonald credits her success as much to the training as to the new technology she now uses.

Training, however, does not come in the box with most technology products. Perhaps it should. According to Stamp, a growing number of businesses buying productivity software for their employees also invest in training them how to use the new tools—at a cost of $300 to $500 a day per worker. Drill into Microsoft Canada's Web site, meanwhile, and you can find a time-limited free offer of several CD-ROM discs containing tips on using its most popular office programs.

Computers may one day help reduce the stress themselves. Researchers at IBM are working on something called the "Emotion Mouse." Measuring skin temperature, sweat and heart rate, it is designed to know when a user is about to blow—and perhaps suggest, on-screen, that he or she take a break. But until then, Canadians left to master technology on their own may need to fall back on a humbler prescription. Breath deeply. Count to 10. And dare we suggest: read the manual.

They're Watching YOU

WORKPLACE PRIVACY IS GOING... GOING...

BY SARAH BOEHLE

I visited a pornographic Web site at work, and Gordon Alexander knows it.

Thing is, I never told Alexander about my visit to the Internet's underbelly, nor did he pass by my cubicle when risqué photographs were splashed across my monitor. So is he some sort of clairvoyant? Nope. He's the MIS manager at the Minnesota office of Bill Communications (which owns TRAINING Magazine), and he's using the latest in employee surveillance aids: Internet monitoring software. From his desktop, Alexander has a bird's-eye view into the Internet surfing habits of the 100 or so employees here in Minneapolis. And the software he uses is so advanced that not only can he track and record which Web sites workers visit, he can also determine how much time they spend at each site.

Welcome to the 21st century workplace, where such tactics are no longer the exception but the norm. According to a survey this year by the American Management Association (AMA), nearly three-quarters of major U.S. firms now record and review some form of their employees' communications—either telephone calls, e-mail, Internet connections or computer files. That's more than double the number of just two years ago.

Of all surveillance methods, Internet and e-mail monitoring have seen the most explosive growth recently, with 54.1 percent of companies now monitoring their employees' Internet connections and 38.1 percent reviewing e-mail messages.

What's behind this rush to Orwellian oversight? Employers cite lost productivity, decreased bandwidth, corporate espionage and legal liability as some of the reasons, fearing that employee abuse of e-mail and the Internet will damage their bottom lines. All this, coupled with the fact that monitoring software is now faster, cheaper and more flexible than ever before, has made it tough for employers to resist.

With the proliferation of Internet and e-mail monitoring, the boss's eyes are everywhere. Is this any way to run a business?

Ray Boelig, CEO of Elron Software in Burlington, MA, a leading purveyor of Internet and e-mail surveillance tools, believes that the rise in monitoring isn't a sign that companies are overly paranoid. "Monitoring is essential," Boelig says. "Organizations need to look at the proper use of their assets. They have a responsibility to make sure that their workplace is a nonhostile environment."

In fact, employers don't just have a moral obligation to maintain a nonhostile working environment, they're legally required to do so. The Communications Decency Act of 1996 says that an employer can be held liable for the activities of its employees. Logging on to playboy.com over the lunch hour, for example, might seem fairly harmless to one employee, but if a co-worker who doesn't share that viewpoint sees those lewd images, she might construe them as sexual harassment and sue the employer for allowing a hostile work environment to exist.

How to Create an Effective Monitoring Policy

The American Management Association recently called on employers to raise the level of dialogue with workers over the use of electronic monitoring in the workplace. "... [M]onitoring is such a new area filled with so many misconceptions of what is proper, appropriate and legal, that employees and employers need to have a clear, mutual understanding of what each may and may not do," says Ellen Bayer, the AMA's global practice leader on human resources issues.

In an effort to ensure fair and effective surveillance practices, Bayer recommends that company policies be:

- Clearly defined and disseminated to all employees through all communication channels from paper to electronic media.
- Addressed in recruitment, orientation and training.
- Discussed in face-to-face meetings between managers and employees, allowing for questions to be answered and concerns aired.
- Illustrated through specific examples of misuse, accompanied by a consistent explanation regarding the application of standards.

—S.B.

E-mail is even more nettlesome. Under federal law, sending and receiving e-mail via an employer's computer is no different than writing a memo on company letterhead—meaning that any off-color e-mails circulating around the office can set employers back millions of dollars. Chevron Corp. learned this lesson the hard way when it settled a sexual-harassment lawsuit for $2.2 million over offensive e-mail postings such as "25 reasons why beer is better than women." Corporate behemoths like Citigroup and Morgan Stanley Dean Witter have also been taken to court by employees who allegedly received e-mail at work containing racist jokes.

But do a few isolated lawsuits really warrant a bandwagon approach to prying into the doings of millions of U.S. employees? Privacy watchdogs would answer with an emphatic no. But employers point to statistics that show some cause for concern.

Last year, Elron Software commissioned a study by market research firm NFO Interactive in Northwood, OH, that revealed some chilling trends. According to the survey, the number of employees who admitted to sharing confidential business information via e-mail with other companies weighed in at 20.6 percent. The poll also found that nearly three-quarters of respondents sent or received adult-oriented e-mail at work, and 64.4 percent admitted to sending or receiving sexist or racist e-mail. And according to a 1998 Internet-abuse study conducted by NFO and Elron, 62 percent of organizations reported catching employees accessing sexually explicit Web sites on company computers.

While the Elron/NFO surveys undoubtedly raised red flags among corporate management types, Lewis Maltby, who is president of The National Workrights Institute in Princeton, NJ, takes a more skeptical view. "I would be suspicious," he says of such studies. "There's a lot of junk data that has come out from advocates who are more interested in pushing their agenda than in being straight with the [research]." Nevertheless, Maltby admits that employers have legitimate concerns. "The Web is seductive," he says. "The risk that employees will spend all day surfing the Web instead of working is vastly greater than the risk that they'll goof off in some other, less entertaining way."

The Gray Zone

In 1890, in one of the most seminal essays on privacy ever written, Louis Brandeis and Samuel Warren proclaimed that the right most valued by the American people was "the right to be left alone." Brandeis and Warren were worried that then-modern-day technology such as photography and the tabloid press were invading "the sacred precincts of private and domestic lives," and they warned that "[n]umerous mechanical devices threaten to make good the prediction that what is whispered in the closet shall be proclaimed from the housetops." If Brandeis and Warren could see the wired world of today, they'd likely turn over in their graves.

'Say some woman is sitting at her desk writing her husband a very intimate e-mail about their anniversary plans that evening, and the next thing you know the boss is reading it. That's practically like having a microphone in the bedroom.'

—Lewis Maltby, The National Workrights Institute

Thanks to the expeditious advance of technology and the advent of the World Wide Web, the most minute details of our everyday lives are now on display for the world to see—often without our knowledge. Each time we swipe our frequent-buyer savings card at the local supermarket, our grocer surreptitiously tracks what food we eat, even how much dog food or kitty litter we buy. "Cookies," which are pieces of computer code dropped from Web sites onto users' hard drives, record where we travel on the Net, what purchases we make, which passwords we create, and any personal information we disclose. This data is then used for marketing purposes or sold to third parties.

Privacy 101

Eric Schmidt knows the value of education. Before he landed a job as chief information officer at Bricker & Eckler LLP in Columbus, OH, six-and-a-half years ago, he spent a large portion of his career as director of information services at Ohio State University. So when Bricker & Eckler decided to install Elron Software's Internet Manager and E-Mail Inspector, he rallied hard for a first-rate policy and training program to be put in place before the software hit the firm's computer network.

"Education can solve 90 percent of your problems," says Schmidt, who claims that a number of companies he's talked to have installed monitoring technology without telling anyone. "If you don't let [employees] know up front, it's not playing fair. You've first got to tell folks what your expectations are."

So Schmidt put together a monitoring policy that was quite explicit. It stated that office computers were the law firm's property and that there was no expectation of privacy. It detailed how, when, and to what extent monitoring would take place. And it provided employees with several examples of inappropriate usage.

From the outset, Schmidt wanted to avoid creating what he calls a "Stalinesque" working atmosphere. Rather than relying on human nature or attempting to create "block lists" of inappropriate sites—a Sisyphean task, considering the amount of pornographic material currently on the Net—the firm uses Elron's SmartList technology, which screens the language of Web sites before they're visited and blocks users from those deemed unacceptable.

Bricker & Eckler refrains from monitoring the content of text-based e-mail messages—a tactic it believes infringes on employee privacy. Instead, Schmidt gathers a random sampling of e-mail attachments every few months and reviews them to make certain that employees are not downloading software illegally or sending classified information or inappropriate pictures and jokes over the company network.

The next step was education. Coordinating with Bricker & Eckler educational specialist Rick Anderson, Schmidt put together a training program for new and existing employees that explained the reasons behind the firm's decision to install monitoring software, set the ground rules, and gave staffers an opportunity to ask questions. And education doesn't stop there; every six to eight weeks, Schmidt sends out "gentle reminders" of the monitoring policy. He also includes links to the policy on every page of the firm's intranet, which is the mandatory home page for all attorneys and support staff.

Thus far, the approach seems to be working. According to Schmidt, only one employee has been reprimanded for excessive personal Internet surfing, and that person is still employed by the company. Morale hasn't plummeted either—though Schmidt admits to receiving his fair share of ribbing from staffers. "Yeah," he chuckles. "I sometimes get stuff like, 'How's Big Brother doing today?'"

—S.B.

Public outcry against such intrusions has reached a boiling point in recent months, leading consumer rights advocates to lobby Congress to enact legislation that would limit the types of information companies are allowed to collect on the Web. Should such legislation pass, however, it is doubtful that any protections will extend to the millions of Americans subjected to monitoring on the job.

Not that monitoring is anything new to the business world. In the manufacturing industry, it has been used for decades to track employee productivity and to record inventory. Cyclometers (which measure typing output) were in place by 1913, and employers began monitoring employee telephone calls for "quality assurance purposes" in the 1920s.

What *has* changed is the sophistication of surveillance software and the types of information it allows employers to gather—which is precisely what disturbs privacy advocates. Although most concur that employers have valid reasons for watching their employees, the fear that these methods are becoming too meddlesome is nonetheless blossoming. Maltby and many other privacy advocates argue that those employers who routinely read their employees' e-mail and compile individualized lists of all Web sites workers visit are creating a nightmare for themselves as well as their employees. "If someone has a problem today, they don't write to 'Dear Abby.' They go to the Web with their darkest, most personal secrets," says Maltby. "Do employers really want to know one of their employees is HIV-positive or just got divorced? These are not things employers have any right to know or even want to know, but they're going to routinely find out if they keep going down the road they're on."

Not surprisingly, fallout from such spying can be ugly. In fact, this year more than half of employers reported reprimanding employees—ranging from a formal warning to termination—for abusing company telecommunications equipment. Yet at its most insidious, the result of snooping is not termination or some draconian penalty; it is loss of privacy.

Although multimillion-dollar e-mail- and Internet-oriented lawsuits make for juicy headlines, it is spying of a more mundane ilk that threatens to hit workers the hardest. The latest software, for example, can monitor employees' every keystroke, even allowing managers to view workers' desktops in real time—i.e., what they're working on minute by minute—on the sly.

Extrapolate a bit, and it is not hard to imagine the machinations running through some pointy-haired boss's brain. "Hmm… Smith didn't log on to the company network until 8:30 a.m. even though work was scheduled to begin at 8." (Never mind that Smith has been in the office since 6:30 this morning working from hard copy; the boss has no record of that.) Or, "Interesting. Julie spent two hours reading *The Wall Street Journal* online this afternoon. I'll make a note of that on her next performance review." (So what if Julie was doing research pertinent to her job.)

Holy Grail?

Then there's online learning. The latest generation of training management software can monitor and record every moment of a student's progress through an online course. To be sure, there are tangible benefits. Dave Mandelkern, executive vice president and chief technology officer for e-learning provider Docent Inc. in Mountain View, CA, calls reporting software the "Holy Grail" of the training industry. "Traditionally, getting data back on what students thought and what they learned was extraordinarily difficult," says Mandelkern. "Now, for the first time, we've got this built-in two-way communications mechanism that allows us to capture that data." Reporting software is also invaluable in helping employers to improve their e-learning programs, allowing them to determine the effectiveness of specific test questions or course modules by gauging student performance.

'I don't think most employers want to lurk around and catch people. It's just that they don't really think through the implications of spying on their employees.'

—Richard Sobel, Harvard University

For all its attractiveness, though, tracking software sometimes borders on the intrusive, going so far as to monitor students' activity down to the mouse click and to record what they say in course chat rooms and asynchronous forums. Ostensibly, these features are for students' own good; yet they raise some concerns, especially when studies show that many people are more open with their thoughts on the Web, revealing personal information online that they otherwise wouldn't share in face-to-face environments.

So why aren't employees asking questions about it? Although there are no hard numbers as to how many companies inform their workers that online classrooms are monitored, it appears that most employees are currently unaware they're being watched. Dave Evangelisti, vice president of marketing for e-learning management software provider Pathlore in Columbus, OH, estimates that less than half of Pathlore's customers tell their students that monitoring is in place. "A lot of companies are not prone to abusing this cache of information," notes Evangelisti. "But anytime you have employees interact with software and ask them to put in comments and give their feedback and then capture that information, the potential for abuse is definitely there."

The Electronic Boss

Evangelisti also points out that it is important for employers to use such information in the right way, and to refrain from determining employee performance based on limited data gleaned from monitoring, such as test scores and time spent completing specific assignments.

This opens up a larger debate, which is that electronic surveillance, in its sundry forms, not only has the potential to encroach upon worker privacy, it also could change the way in which employee job performance is assessed.

Indeed, with continuing corporate downsizing leaving fewer and fewer middle managers to supervise employees in person, the likelihood that monitoring software will soon play a larger role in the performance-assessment process is increasing—and many pundits doubt its effectiveness.

MIT professor and *Fortune* columnist Michael Schrage attacked this phenomenon recently in a column decrying the best-practices databases that have spread like wildfire in world-class organizations such as General Electric and Asea Brown Boveri. Likening them to "database-driven blackmail," Schrage argued that such knowledge management systems are poised to squash innovation because they define, in set terms, the best way to go about doing things without giving employees rein to think up new, and possibly better, practices of their own.

'There's no doubt that an employer who wants to can monitor just about everything—except what a person thinks.'

—Jim Bruce, EMA, the E-Business Forum

Schrage also lambasted the tracking features of such systems, citing their sometimes arbitrary determination of "good" performance as a detriment to all. "You ignore checking in with these databases at your peril," he wrote. "Dis [them], and you may lose your promotion, your job, or your employment lawsuit—whether you're suing because you've been fired, or being sued for firing.... And if your performance evaluation isn't based in part on how well you draw upon these best-practice resources, then what's the point of having them?"

Which begs the question: Do employers actually realize any of the gains in productivity they trumpet as a reason for turning to monitoring software in the first place?

"This kind of piecework keeping track of everything people do is really not the way to get people to do their best jobs and feel best about companies. It makes employees feel like children or potential miscreants," says Richard Sobel, a political scientist at Harvard University who works on privacy policy and who opposes workplace monitoring. "The environments that respect people and their privacy tend to see results in productivity, good ideas, and in people giving their best efforts."

Unfortunately, there is virtually no research on the effects of monitoring on employees whose work is more complicated than data entry or customer service. But several studies of telecommunications and clerical workers suggest that electronically monitored workers experience higher levels of depression, tension and anxiety, lower levels of productivity, and more health problems than unmonitored employees.

Studies also indicate that the most creative thought takes place during periods of seclusion or daydreaming, meaning that if workers know or suspect they are being watched, there's a good chance their ability to think freely and creatively will suffer.

Your Privacy Ends at the Office Door

While federal, state and local government employees benefit from some degree of legal protection of their privacy, private businesses (particularly those whose employees are not unionized) are free to monitor their workers' every move with near total impunity. "You don't have a right to privacy at work," says Maltby. "You don't have a right to free speech. You don't have a right to due process. You don't have any Constitutional rights at work because the Constitution only applies to the government, not to the private sector."

There are, however, a few exceptions. The Federal Electronic Communications Privacy Act prohibits employers from deliberately eavesdropping on purely personal conversations that an employee may have at work. Yet while this legislation includes telephone calls and audio-equipped video devices, it does not protect purely personal communications that occur through means other than the spoken word, such as e-mail or other Web-based forms of communication.

And here's something most workers don't know. Even when employers promise *not* to monitor their employees, courts are supporting companies' right to break such promises without notice. In 1994, a Pennsylvania case between Michael A. Smyth and the Pillsbury Co. helped to establish this precedent. According to court documents, Smyth, an at-will employee, was fired based on an indiscreet private e-mail message that he sent from his home computer to a supervisor at work. The message, which referred to the company's sales management and made threats to "kill the back-stabbing bastards," was later read by company executives who terminated Smyth for "inappropriate and unprofessional comments" made over the company's e-mail system.

Smyth filed a wrongful-discharge action against Pillsbury, alleging that the company had repeatedly promised its employees that all e-mail would remain confidential and that no employee would be fired based on intercepted e-mail. Yet the court dismissed Smyth's claim, saying that because Pillsbury owned the computer system to which the message was sent, it could intercept the e-mail without invading its workers' legitimate expectations of privacy.

In some instances, employers have even nosed into their employees' company-owned home computers. Consider the case of Ronald F. Thiemann, the respected dean of the Harvard Divinity School who was forced to resign in 1998 after pornographic images were discovered on a university-owned computer located in his home. Reportedly, none of the pornography found was illegal. Yet in Harvard's and many other employers' view, the very fact that Thiemann accessed the images via his employer's computer was grounds for dismissal.

What's the Solution?

In 1993, in one of the most sweeping federal actions governing workers' privacy to date, Sen. Paul Simon of Illinois and Rep. Pat Williams of Montana made a failed attempt to enact legislation that would have required employers to more clearly define their privacy policies and to refrain from monitoring employees' personal communication.

'Even though their intentions may be honorable, many of the mechanisms in place invariably infringe on people's privacy rights.'

—Kevin Conlon, CWA

Jim Bruce, outside counsel to EMA, the E-Business Forum in Arlington, VA—which represents the e-business and messaging industries and is a staunch supporter of employers' right to monitor workers—opposed the legislation because of the way in which it was drafted. "The problem was that nobody in Congress or anyone else could forecast all the types of electronic monitoring that could be done in the workplace," says Bruce.

The good news is that even in the absence of government intervention, a majority of employers are beginning to institute monitoring policies of their own accord. This year's AMA survey, for instance, revealed that 88 percent of companies now have established Internet and e-mail usage policies and also inform their employees of them. That's real progress, considering that a 1993 *Macworld* poll determined that less than one-third of companies that monitored their workers gave advance warning, and only 18 percent had established a written policy.

Yet the privacy problem is far from solved. The reason, experts say, is that most companies' electronic monitoring policies and training programs are woefully inadequate. "The standard notice form employers use today communicates virtually nothing," says Maltby. "It basically says, 'We reserve the right to monitor any form of electronic communications for any reason at any time in the future.' What does that tell employees? How? When? Is it going to be e-mail monitoring? Voice mail? Web site monitoring? Is it going to happen all the time or on certain, specified occasions? And is it going to include everything or just things that are work-related?"

Indeed, the 1999 Elron study offers some evidence that few employees understand the scope of their company's monitoring practices. It found that nearly two-thirds of workers are unaware that a policy exists—despite the fact that, as the AMA points out, 88 percent of employers claim that they have such a policy and inform their employees of it.

The key to bridging this divide, experts say, is better communication. Even some of those who support an employer's right to monitor are urging companies to improve their policies and to take more proactive measures with their educational initiatives (see box, How to Create an Effective Monitoring Policy). The EMA recently released an updated version of its Privacy Toolkit booklet, which provides guidelines for writing effective electronic monitoring policies. Next fall, the EMA also intends to debut a set of interactive training tools that will help employers to better communicate both their policies and the ramifications of Internet and e-mail abuse to workers. "I believe that the next stage is going to be education and employee understanding of what company policies are," says Lauren Haywood, the EMA's acting president and CEO.

These are hopeful trends. However, barring the unlikely event that federal legislation sets clear guidelines as to what's fair game for employee monitoring and what's not, Kevin Conlon, district counsel for the Communication Workers of America, urges workers to take responsibility for protecting themselves. "Like it or not, the presumption should be that there is no such thing as privacy in the workplace," he says. "Everything is subject to scrutiny, and employees need to start living their work lives accordingly."

Sarah Boehle *is an associate editor of* TRAINING. sboehle@ trainingmag.com

Security vs. Privacy

To ensure a secure environment for all workers, avoid violating the privacy of any one individual.

By Jonathan A. Segal

First of a two-part series.

Since Sept. 11, employers have focused—quite appropriately—on upgrading workplace security. But security measures will be compromised if employers do not clearly retain the right to search communications moving across their systems, or persons and items on their premises. Employers that fail to secure these rights may find themselves facing the wrong end of an invasion of privacy suit from the very employees they have attempted to protect.

This article discusses preventive steps employers should take to avoid such a clash of rights.

Basis for Right of Privacy

There are several potential legal restrictions on employer searches, including the following:

Constitutional restrictions. The Fourth Amendment to the U.S. Constitution prohibits unreasonable searches and seizures. Generally, the constitution restricts only government action, not private action.

As a result, private sector employers can search employees without violating the federal Constitution. However, some state constitutions have been interpreted to restrict private sector searches. (See, for example, *Pettus v. Cole*, 49 Cal. App. 4th 402 (Ct. of App. 1996).)

Common law restrictions. Most states recognize a common law right to privacy; these rights apply equally to public- and private-sector employees.

Statutory restrictions. Several federal and state statutes create enforceable privacy rights. For example, the federal Electronic Communications Privacy Act (ECPA), which comprises the federal Wiretap Act and the Stored Communications Act, generally prohibits interceptions of wire, electronic and oral communications. This includes e-mail, voice mail and Internet activities.

Many states also have wiretap laws. Some of these state laws are more restrictive than federal law.

The underlying question is: Did the employee have a reasonable expectation of privacy?

Employee Relations

Even where there are no legal barriers, employee relations considerations remain. While employees appear willing to give up some of their privacy for security, this willingness is not open-ended.

As always, employers must consider how employees will perceive their actions. Employers who go too far, even under current circumstances, risk an employee relations backlash.

Reasonable Expectation of Privacy

Regardless of the legal theory behind a claim, the underlying question is essentially the same: Did the employee have a reasonable expectation of privacy?

To have a viable claim, employees must do more than show they subjectively believed they had a right to privacy. Generally, employees must show that their expectation was objectively reasonable under the circumstances.

We can't completely control our employees' subjective expectations, but we can create the circumstances that determine whether such expectations are objectively reasonable.

Generally, there are three approaches employers can take:

Tell employees they have no expectation of privacy. Simply put, if you tell employees they have no right to privacy, they probably don't. When employers clearly state that there is no expectation of privacy, it's hard to argue that a reasonable person could have such an expectation.

Employer silence. Some employers are reluctant to issue a sweeping statement destroying privacy rights, so they say nothing.

Employers that remain silent do not necessarily lose the right to search. However, in the absence of a clear policy, a jury will decide if employees had a reasonable expectation of privacy. In contrast, if there is a clear policy destroying privacy rights, an employer has a good shot at preventing a case from ever getting to a jury.

Establish privacy rights. Some employers unwittingly take a third approach: Rather than destroy privacy rights, they create them by including statements in their handbooks or other policies saying they respect employee privacy.

While employers should try, where possible, to respect employee privacy, they should not make affirmative statements regarding that privacy.

Recommendation: Employers should destroy employee expectations of privacy by issuing broadly worded search policies.

Some employers avoid issuing separate search policies but rather bury the search statement in another policy—for example, in the policy on workplace violence or substance abuse. This approach may avoid an immediate negative reaction from workers; however, it also may limit the employer's right to search.

For example, if your statement reserving the right to search appears only in your weapons policy, employees reasonably could argue that they believed your right to search was limited to prohibited weapons. In that case, where will you be if you have reason to believe employees are stealing confidential information or selling illegal drugs?

From a legal perspective, employers are better served issuing stand-alone search policies.

When to Search

Employer policies must address when they can search. Generally, there are three options:

Reserve the right to search randomly. Some policies state that the employer has the right to search randomly—at any time and for any reason.

In terms of legal notice, reserving the right to search randomly is the best option. Employees who are told that their belongings, communications and persons may be searched randomly will have difficulty convincing a jury that an expectation of privacy was reasonable.

However, such language may offend employees. While most employees understand the need for employers to reserve their right to search, they might balk at the possibility of being searched without cause.

Limit the right to search to reasonable cause. To deal with employee relations concerns, some employers limit the right to search to situations in which there is reasonable cause that specific items will be found.

Limiting the right to search in this way will allay some employee discomfort; however, it may be too restrictive legally. In an emergency involving workplace safety and security, employers may not have the luxury of searching only those individuals or work areas where they have reason to believe that weapons, explosives, etc., will be found.

No qualifying language (random or reasonable cause). The third option is to reserve the right to search, without adding either random or reasonable cause language. By not including any limitations, employers can argue that there are none. At the same time, employers are not flaunting the absence of limitations by stating expressly that there are none.

This approach is in the middle of the continuum in terms of legal notice and employee relations.

Recommendation: While the first two options may work best in some workplaces, I believe the last option is best in general.

What to Search

Even if employers reserve the right to search in general terms, there may be disputes regarding whether that right extends to certain items or places. To avoid such disputes, the policy should clearly state—by way of examples only—its broad application. Here are some key examples:

Persons and belongings. The policy should clearly state that it covers employees and their belongings when on the employer's premises. Define premises broadly to include owned and leased facilities, surrounding grounds, parking areas, etc.

But even if employers reserve the right to search, don't employees retain some privacy regarding the contents of their wallets, pocketbooks or briefcases? Stay tuned. Next month's Legal Trends column will focus on this and other implementation issues.

Work areas and lockers. A search policy should cover employees' work areas, including their desks. Make clear in your policy that you retain the right to search desks, even if they are locked.

By the same token, your policy should clearly state that you have the right to search employee lockers—even if they are locked. To reinforce this message, provide the locks to be used on employee lockers.

Automobiles. Do you also have the right to search employees' automobiles? Yes, if they are on your premises and if you specifically reserve this right.

Is this going too far? No. If you don't reserve this right, where do you think employees will keep forbidden items?

Computer equipment. Sometimes, the key to determining what employees have done—or intend to do—is found in the documents they create on the company's computer system. Do employers have the right to review these documents? The visceral answer is yes. After all, it's the company's computer.

However, it may not be that simple. Before using an employer's computer system, employees are given a "confidential password." Could this create a reasonable expectation of privacy?

There is the risk that these passwords—which employers provide to protect confidentiality for their benefit—could be interpreted by employees as establishing a right of privacy for their benefit. To minimize this risk, reserve the right to review all documents employees create or store on the computer system—even on company laptops—regardless of where they are used.

E-mail, voice mail and Internet. For similar reasons, employers should make clear that the right to search applies to employee e-mail, voice mail and Internet activities. Otherwise, employees may believe their passwords grant them privacy rights.

Search policies should clearly state that when employees use company e-mail, voice mail and Internet services, they agree to allow the employer to review and monitor all messages they send, store or receive on the system, or any searches they make or web sites they visit using the employer's Internet server.

Does the right to search include e-mail messages sent by employees from home using the company's server? How about Internet searches conducted and web sites visited via the company server? Yes, if the policy is clear on this point.

However, even if employers reserve their right to search employee communications, they must be mindful of potential restrictions from the federal ECPA and comparable state laws. This too will be discussed next month.

Regular mail. Federal law provides criminal penalties for obstructing the delivery of mail. But the Postal Service takes the position that mail is "delivered" when it reaches the employer. Accordingly, employers can read personal mail sent to employees at work without violating federal law.

However, such a practice might constitute an invasion of privacy under state common law. (For example, see *Doe v. Kohn, Nast & Graf, P.C.*, 866 F. Supp. 190 (E.D. Pa. 1994).) Accordingly, inform employees that you reserve the right to review all mail they receive, even items marked "personal" or "confidential."

Telephone communications. Telephones, which leave no paper trail, may be the instrument of choice for planning (or carrying out) wrongdoing. Accordingly, policies should clearly state that you reserve the right to monitor telephone calls on your telephone lines.

However, we all have had personal telephone conversations that our employers have no legitimate need to hear. Next month, one of the issues this column will focus on is how to implement the right to monitor telephone calls without intruding upon an employee's legitimately private conversations.

Conclusion

Employers should reserve their right to search as broadly as possible. Of course, reserving the right is one thing. Implementing it correctly is quite another.

Next month's Legal Trends column [Ed. note: See *HR Magazine*, March 2002] will focus on implementation traps and how to avoid them.

Author's note: This article should not be construed as legal advice or as pertaining to specific factual situations.

Jonathan A. Segal, Esq., is a partner in the Employment Services Group of Wolf, Block, Schorr and Solis-Cohen LLP, a Philadelphia-based law firm. His practice concentrates on counseling clients, developing policies and strategic plans, and training managers to avoid litigation and unionization.

Article 17

Searching for answers

Don't search employees in a way that leaves them questioning your legal authority.

By Jonathan A. Segal

Second in a two-part series.

Last month*, this column discussed the steps employers should take to preserve their right to search employees' persons and work areas and to monitor employees' communications. However, there is a difference between reserving a right and exercising that right. For example, while employers should use broad terms when stating their right to search, they should be more circumspect when implementing that right. This article discusses how to avoid common traps in the implementation process.

When to Search

Absent emergencies or other special circumstances, employers should conduct searches only when and where they have reason to believe they will find the specific object of the search. Random searches likely will result in employee anger and resentment—with concomitant costs in productivity.

When deciding whether reasonable cause exists, focus on specific observed or alleged behaviors, not the EEO profile of the person being searched. In other words, do not consider an employee's race, ethnicity, religion or membership in any group when deciding whether reasonable cause exists.

Employers are well-positioned to rebut discrimination and other claims when they have legitimate, non-discriminatory reasons for searching a particular person, area, communication, etc. Accordingly, when you have reasonable cause for a search, document that cause.

When emergencies dictate that you conduct more sweeping searches (for example, searching all employees instead of one or two for whom you may have reasonable cause), document the specifics of the emergency and the legitimate, non-discriminatory reason for the scope of the search.

Employee Objections

Consider this hypothetical situation: You believe an employee has in her purse a computer disk containing confidential customer information. When you ask to search the purse, she says she first wishes to remove personal medical information.

If you allow her to remove the confidential item, she may remove the disk—if she has it. But, if you don't let her remove the item—which you have no legitimate need to see—a jury may rule that you unreasonably invaded her privacy.

A similar issue may arise with drug testing: An employer wants to search an employee's urine for illegal drugs. The problem: Lawful medical prescriptions may be present as well. The solution to this second scenario can be helpful in the first as well.

When conducting drug testing, employers often use an independent Medical Review Officer (MRO). (MROs are required in certain states and for tests mandated by the federal government.)

Here's how the MRO process works: The employee provides a specimen to the collection site, which sends it to the laboratory. Results are reported to the MRO. If the results are positive, the MRO contacts the employee to determine if there is a legitimate explanation for the positive result. If there is, the MRO tells the employer the result was negative, and the employer never learns of any medication that appeared in the test results.

Employers should borrow the MRO concept for workplace searches. If employees indicate they have confidential items in their briefcases, desks, etc., offer them the option of having the object or area searched by a third party.

The employer then would ask the third party one question: Is the suspected item or any other prohibited item present? The third party would answer "yes" or "no" without disclosing the existence of any medical or other confidential information. If employees reject the offer of a third party search, document this fact.

Failure to Cooperate

When employees refuse to cooperate with a search, don't physically touch them. Doing so could spark a civil harassment claim or even a criminal charge of assault and battery.

For this and other reasons, have a witness to all searches who can testify regarding what was done—and what wasn't done. It's a good idea for the witness to be the same gender as the person being searched. And if the individual being searched is a bargaining unit employee, a union shop steward should be present.

In general, when employees refuse to cooperate, do not detain them against their will. Doing so could give rise to a claim for false imprisonment. Instead, inform employees that continued failure to cooperate is cause for immediate discharge. (Of course, this admonition is stronger if there is comparable language in your policy.)

Ordinarily, individuals who still refuse to cooperate can be discharged. In such cases, document what employees were told and how they responded.

Sometimes, deciding not to detain employees can risk irreparable harm to the company. (For example, an employee could have unique information on a pilfered disk and may destroy that data if given the chance.) In these circumstances, you should balance the legal risk of detaining the employee for a short time (to allow law enforcement to arrive) against the business risk of not detaining the individual. When a critical business reason exists for detaining an employee, document the business exigency.

Snail Mail

Federal law prohibits the obstruction of mail delivery. But, according to the U.S. Postal Service, mail is delivered when it reaches the workplace. Accordingly, employers do not violate federal law if they open personal mail addressed to employees.

However, intercepting employee mail may violate common law. Under common law, employees can bring two potential privacy claims: "intrusion upon seclusion" and "public disclosure of a private fact."

"Intrusion upon seclusion," as applied to employers, goes something like this: If employers intrude upon the seclusion, or solitude, of employees in a way that a reasonable person would find highly offensive, the employees can bring an invasion of privacy claim. (For example, see *Borse v. Piece Goods Shop, Inc.*, 963 F.2d 611 (3d Cir. 1992).) Not exactly crystal clear, is it?

The "public disclosure of a private fact" standard is equally vague: Employers may be sued when they publicly disclose a private fact about an employee in a way that a reasonable person would find highly offensive.

To minimize the potential for these common law privacy claims, reserve—in writing—your right to search all mail you receive, then take the following steps:

- Tell employees not to receive personal mail at work. This limits your exposure to personal information.
- If you open a letter and determine it is personal, stop reading. In other words, if you realize you are reading a love letter, don't keep reading to determine how much the correspondents love each other.
- Keep confidential any personal information you discover when reading employees' mail. Disclose such information only as necessary to take disciplinary or other corrective action (or to defend an adverse employment action upon which it is based).

Telephone Calls

Employer monitoring of telephone calls is subject to the federal Wiretap Act. State wiretap laws, which may be more restrictive, apply as well.

Generally speaking, the federal Wiretap Act prohibits the interception, recording or disclosure of wire, electronic and aural communications through any electronic, mechanical or other device. An interception takes place when an employer monitors a telephone call while it is occurring.

The law includes an exception: Employers may monitor telephone calls "in the ordinary course of business." This allows employers to monitor telephone calls by using equipment furnished by the phone company or connected to the phone line—if that equipment is used in the ordinary course of business.

This exception has been construed narrowly by the courts. For example, several cases have found that the monitoring equipment must be an integral part of the telephone system installed by the phone company—not a device the employer subsequently added. And some courts have ruled that to use this exception, employers must have a legitimate business purpose for the monitoring and/or should monitor calls routinely.

Accordingly, not all employee monitoring falls within the business use exception. And this exception covers only call monitoring—not recording. Finally, some state laws do not have a comparable business use exception.

Even if the business use exception doesn't apply, another might: Interceptions are legal if they are carried out with consent. Under federal law, the consent of only one party is necessary. In a few states, all parties must consent. (If your worksite is located in such a state, or if your employees call anyone in such a state, you may be required to obtain consent from all parties.)

Generally speaking, consent can be either implied (where parties are warned that if they participate in a call they agree to be monitored) or expressed (where parties sign a form agreeing to be monitored). Implied consent is administratively easier, but express consent is legally stronger. However, written consent obviously is not feasible for non-employees.

A number of cases have held that, in general, employers must stop monitoring as soon as they determine an employee's phone call is personal. The reason: Listening to the details of a medical or other legitimately confidential conversation could be an intrusion upon seclusion.

In addition, disclosing personal information obtained by telephone monitoring could constitute public disclosure of a private fact. Accordingly, employers should keep confidential any personal information they discover and disclose such information only as necessary to take disciplinary or other corrective action (or to defend any adverse employment action based on it).

E-Mail, Voice Mail And Internet Activities

The review of e-mail, voice mail and Internet activities is subject to the federal Electronic Communications Privacy Act (ECPA) as well as many state laws. The ECPA includes the Wiretap Act.

Under the Wiretap Act, employer liability hinges on whether a message has been intercepted, which depends on *when* a message is acquired. While there is little case law regarding interception for e-mail, voice mail and Internet activity—and what does exist contains apparent inconsistencies—in general, messages are intercepted only if they are acquired *during* transmission.

When is transmission considered completed? That's an open issue. For example, it's not clear if an e-mail transmission is completed when it is sent, or only after it is reviewed by the recipient. Similarly, it's hard to say if a voice mail transmission is considered "complete" when it is left or only after the recipient hears it.

As a result, it's not clear if an e-mail or voice mail message is considered "intercepted" if an employer reviews it in storage, either before or after the recipient reviews it.

A few courts have ruled that an interception takes place if messages are monitored before—but not after—recipients review them. (For example, see *Fraser v. Nationwide Mutual Insurance Co.*, 135 F. Supp. 2d 623 (E.D. Pa. 2001).) Accordingly, the safest approach is to monitor voice and e-mail messages after recipients review them. Similarly, Internet activities should be reviewed only after they are fully completed.

However, even with this strategy, employers may face liability because cases construing the interception requirement as it relates to storage are unclear (to be kind). As a result, employers may need to rely on one of the statutory exceptions to avoid liability. It's unclear if the business use exception applies to e-mail and voice mail, but the consent exception clearly applies.

As with monitoring telephone calls, under federal law, the consent of only one party is required to monitor voice mail and e-mail messages. However, again, a few states require the consent of all parties to the communication.

In addition, some states have specific consent requirements. For example, a new law in Delaware requires employers to notify employees that their electronic communications, voice mail messages and Internet activities may be monitored; employees must acknowledge the notice in writing.

For non-employees, consent is more difficult. Anyone who sends e-mail or voice mail messages to your employees would need to receive notices that their messages may be reviewed, copied, recorded, etc. The legal benefits of providing such notice must be balanced against the business cost.

However, consent is an issue only if there is a prohibited interception. Accordingly, minimizing the risk of prohibited interceptions becomes critical.

Conclusion

Even in difficult times, workplace privacy is not an oxymoron. You must do more than issue policies destroying any reasonable expectations of privacy. You should search/monitor only when you have a legitimate business need.

Moreover, limit searching and monitoring so that you obtain only the information you need—and keep confidential any personal information you may acquire in the process.

---

*See *HR Magazine*, February 2002

Author's note: This article should not be construed as legal advice or as pertaining to specific factual situations.

Jonathan A. Segal, Esq., is a partner in the Employment Services Group of Wolf, Block, Schorr and Solis-Cohen LLP, a Philadelphia-based law firm. His practice concentrates on counseling clients, developing policies and strategic plans, and training managers to avoid litigation and unionization.

From *HR Magazine,* March 2002, pp. 85-86, 89, 91 by Jonathan A. Segal.

UNIT 4

Computers, People, and Social Participation

Unit Selections

18. **Is That a Computer in Your Pants?** Jesse Walker
19. **Do Cheaters Ever Prosper? Just Ask Them**, Peter Wayner
20. **Why Women Avoid Computer Science**, Paul De Palma
21. **Cyber-Stars**, *Black Issues in Higher Education*
22. **The World According to Google**, Steven Levy

Key Points to Consider

- The overview to this unit mentions Alexis de Tocqueville's observation that Americans tend to form civic associations and Robert Putnam's argument that this tendency is declining. Do you think that computing has played any part in the decline? What does Putnam say? What do other scholars say about Putnam's work?
- Howard Rheingold, in "Is That a Computer in Your Pants?" says, "we're entering a world in which the complexity of the devices and the system of interconnecting devices is beyond our capability to easily understand." Is this cause for alarm? Can anything be done about it? What are your suggestions?
- After reading "Why Women Avoid Computer Science," why do you think so few women study computing?

Links: www.dushkin.com/online/
These sites are annotated in the World Wide Web pages.

Adoption Agencies
http://www.amrex.org/

Alliance for Childhood: Computers and Children
http://www.allianceforchildhood.net/projects/computers/index.htm

The Core Rules of Netiquette
http://www.albion.com/netiquette/corerules.html

How the Information Revolution Is Shaping Our Communities
http://www.plannersweb.com/articles/bla118.html

SocioSite: Networks, Groups, and Social Interaction
http://www2.fmg.uva.nl/sociosite/topics/interaction.html

That early and astute observer of American culture, Alexis de Tocqueville (1805–1859), had this to say about the proclivity of Americans to form civic associations:

> Americans of all ages, all conditions, and all dispositions constantly form associations. The Americans make associations to give entertainments, to found seminaries, to build inns, to construct churches, to diffuse books, to send missionaries to the antipodes; in this manner they found hospitals, prisons, and schools. If it is proposed to inculcate some truth or to foster some feeling by the encouragement of a great example, they form a society. Wherever at the head of some new undertaking you see the government in France, or a man of rank in England, in the United States you will be sure to find an association. Nothing, in my opinion is more deserving of our attention than the intellectual and moral associations of America. In democratic countries the science of association is the mother of science; the progress of all the rest depends upon the progress it has made (v. 2, pp. 114–118).

De Tocqueville laid this tendency squarely at the feet of democracy. If all men—we're talking about the first half of the nineteenth century here—are equal before the law, then to do any civic good requires that these equal, but individually powerless, men band together.

A century and a half later, we have the technical means to communicate almost instantly, almost effortlessly across great distances. Yet in 1995, Robert D. Putnam, made the news with an article, later expanded into a book, called "Bowling Alone." He argued that the civil associations de Tocqueville had noticed so long ago were breaking down. Americans were not joining the PTA, the Boy Scouts, the local garden club, or bowling leagues in their former numbers. Putnam discovered that although more people are bowling than ever, participation in leagues is down by 40 percent since 1980. The consequences for a functioning democracy are severe.

Although the articles in this unit do not directly address the idea of civic participation, that question is the necessary glue that holds them together. Do computers assist or detract from civic life? Another French social observer, Emile Durkheim (1858–1917), argued that a vital society must have members who feel a sense of community. Community is easily evident in pre-industrial societies where kinship ties, shared religious belief, and custom, reinforce group identity and shared values. Not so in modern societies, particularly the United States, where a mobile population commutes long distances and retreats each evening to the sanctity and seclusion of their individual homes. Contemporary visitors to the United States are struck by the cultural cafeteria available to Americans. They find a dizzying array of religious beliefs, moral and philosophical perspectives, modes of social interaction, entertainment venues and, now, networked computers. One need only observe a teenager frantically "instant messaging" her friends from a darkened bedroom to know that while computer technology has surely given us great things, it has taken away something as well. The capacity to maintain friendships without face-to-face contact, the ability to construct a computer profile that edits anything not in line with one's interests, seems to push society a steps closer to self-interested individualism.

On the other hand, one can argue that the new communications technologies permit relationships that were never before possible. To cite a large example, the organization moveon.org, organized many thousands of people, in a matter of weeks, entirely over the Internet, to oppose an attack on Iraq in the spring of 2003; or a smaller one, immigration, always a wrenching experience, is less wrenching now since immigrants to the United States can be in daily touch with their families across the globe. Or consider how the virtual bazaar, E-Bay, surely one of the extraordinary aspects of the Internet, puts Americans in touch with Japanese, Latvians, Montenegrans, peoples whom we might never have known. Recall Neil Postman in the first unit: "technology giveth and technology taketh away."

Howard Rheingold has been a technovisionary since the earliest days of the personal computer. An editor of the *Whole Earth*

Catalog, and a host of the Well, one of the earliest and most successful online communities, Rheingold wrote a book on virtual communities in 1993. Now the author of *Smart Mobs: The Next Social Revolution* (Perseus, 2002), he says to the interviewer in "Is That a Computer in Your Pants?" that "we're entering a world in which the complexity of the devices and the system of interconnecting devices is beyond our capability to easily understand." That's part of the downside. The upside is a story of a Kenyan election where poll watchers, fearing that ballots would be tampered with as they were shipped to a central counting place, reported the results electronically from the polling places. Technology giveth and technology taketh away.

Peter Wayner's "Do Cheaters Ever Prosper? Just Ask Them" reports on one of the more curious aspects of social behavior to emerge from the Internet: cheating in the growing world of interactive games. Since a portion of the code for an online game resides on the player's computer, players who are also programmers can examine the code looking for weaknesses. One tactic has been to remove textured walls that hide an opponent's pieces. The opponent thinks he is hiding. The cheater knows exactly where. Game developers are concerned.

As computers have entered nearly every area of American life, critics have been concerned that women and African Americans, underrepresented in science and computing, have been excluded from influencing the shape of the information society. Though women have been present in computing from the beginning—one thinks of Admiral Grace Hopper, leader of the team that developed COBOL, an important programming language, or Ada Lovelace, sometimes called the first programmer—they are a declining minority in computer science. The article, "Why Women Avoid Computer Science," by Paul De Palma adds a novel perspective to the many voices that try to account for this phenomenon.

Social observers have long been concerned about a digital divide along racial lines. "Cyber-Stars" profiles 10 African American leaders and innovators in information technology. Here we meet, among nine other fascinating people, Skip Ellis, Professor of Computer Science at the University of Colorado and the first African American to receive a doctorate in the field.

In a recent *New York Times* article (May 18, 2003), linguist Geoffrey Nunberg says of Google, "You don't get to be a verb unless you're doing something right." So in the long English tradition of nouns that have been transformed into verbs, doing a Google search on, say, "Henry Ford," has become "Googling Henry Ford." The final article in this unit is the story of how Google has emerged as the dominant Internet search engine. According to its author, Steven Levy, Google has been translated into 86 languages and accounts for about half of all Web searches. Yet some worry that Google may damage the skill set of reference librarians. What happens when all the information you need, or think you need, is available without having to leave the house? Try Googling yourself to find out if your virtual presence lines up with your self-concept.

References

Putnam, Robert D. *Bowling Alone: The Collapse and Revival of American Community.* New York: Simon & Schuster, 2000.

Tocqueville, Alexis de. *Democracy in America.* New York: Vintage Books, 1945.

Is That a Computer in Your Pants?

Cyberculture chronicler Howard Rheingold on smart mobs, smart environments, and smart choices in an age of connectivity

Interviewed by Jesse Walker

SINCE 1968, THE *Whole Earth Catalog* has been a valuable sourcebook for freethinkers, do-it-yourselfers, and back-to-the-landers. Its most recent full-fledged catalog, published in 1994, opened by noting that the price of computing "has dropped so far since the first *Whole Earth Catalog* that we have entered the era of desktop everything: desktop publishing, desktop audio, desktop video. Book publishing, radio and television production, and music distribution used to require buildings full of heavy machinery. Communications capabilities once reserved for government or corporate elites now reside in tens of millions of citizens' desktops."

It is a sign of how quickly technology can evolve that those desktops, once the sign of individual liberation, now seem somewhat clunky themselves. Less than a decade after the catalog's then-editor wrote those words, the equivalent computing power can be found not just on desks but in people's pockets. The social implications of that revolution are discussed in *Smart Mobs: The Next Social Revolution* (Perseus, 2002), the most recent book by the man who described the desktop revolution in 1994: Howard Rheingold.

Rheingold has spent more than two decades at the intersection between the cyberculture and the counterculture, including a mid-'80s stint as one of the hosts of the WELL, a *Whole Earth*-sponsored venture that was one of the most successful early online communities. (It still exists today.) The 55-year-old writer has served as editor of the *Whole Earth Review* and of *HotWired* and has written several books, of which the most famous is *The Virtual Community* (1993), a study of the associations people form online.

In *Smart Mobs*, Rheingold observes people communicating via cell phones, pagers, and hand-held computers, explores the new forms of social interaction he sees emerging, and asks what will happen when those technologies become ubiquitous. The book also describes the ongoing effort to add computing power to our environment—the buildings we occupy, the objects we buy, even the clothes we wear—and speculates about what will happen as electronically equipped people interact with this electronically equipped terrain.

Rheingold is no Pollyanna. In his book and his weblog, smartmobs.com, he strikes a careful balance between skepticism and enthusiasm. He's not a determinist either: He recognizes that there are many different ways these technologies could evolve and many different battlegrounds where their social context is being shaped. The book's most interesting investigations center on those political battles and on the question that lurks behind almost all of them: As the line between real space and cyberspace begins to fade, how much power will ordinary people have over the online world?

Rheingold currently lives in Mill Valley, California. Associate Editor Jesse Walker spoke with him in January.

reason: What's the difference between a community and a mob?

Howard Rheingold: The whole notion of "community" is a vast, fuzzy semantic and political swamp. But I think people in communities know each other and have relationships. People in mobs don't necessarily have those relationships.

The same thing is true of a market. People who buy and sell stock together determine collectively the price of those stocks through their transactions. They are engaged together in a collective action. They don't know each other.

reason: What forms of collective behavior are emerging from smart-mob technology?

Rheingold: On the political level, you're seeing peaceful democratic demonstrations like the ones [that brought down President Joseph Estrada] in the Philippines. You're also seeing riots, like the Miss World riots in Nigeria. Not all forms of human cooperation are prosocial. Some of them are antisocial.

In South Korea, Kenya, and the U.S., mobile communications devices helped sway the results of recent elections. In Kenya they feared corruption would enter the process when they shipped the ballot boxes to a central counting place, so poll watchers reported the results directly from the polls instead. In Korea there was a last-minute surge for a candidate who ultimately won that was organized mostly by people using the Internet and SMS [short message service] devices, sending out text messages at the last moment. And in the

U.S. election, Karl Rove, Bush's political strategist, constantly used his Blackberry [handheld Internet device] to coordinate actions by Republican poll workers getting out the vote.

reason: Someone might say, "Well, people get on the phone and organize political action all the time."

Rheingold: A phone tree isn't an ancient form of political organizing, but you have to call every person. One of the reasons why the street demonstrations in the Philippines worked, and the riots in Nigeria worked, is that you can send a text message to people and they can forward it to everyone in their address books. So you can communicate with a very large network very quickly in a way that you simply can't with a telephone.

Also, a lot of people message and use the telephone at the same time. Particularly in business—if you're having a telephone conversation, and someone asks you a question about marketing or engineering, you can get an answer instantaneously from someone who has marketing or engineering information.

Teenagers in Japan and elsewhere use it precisely because you can communicate silently. Your parents or your teachers can't hear you.

reason: That's a more decentralized process than you have with, for example, Karl Rove getting out the vote.

Rheingold: Well, he's coordinating. You have a mixture of hierarchical and decentralized decision making. You've got a widespread group of folks besides the guy giving orders.

We're also seeing other forms of social activity. Hundreds of thousands of young people in Brazil have a group called Blah! that they use to flirt with. You get a screen name, which protects your real identity. You get a profile, which describes who you are. And you can search for profiles and send them messages. They can reply to you through their handle or through their real identity, or they can block communications from you. It's almost entirely about flirting, and it's mostly young people, and it's popular—400,000 people joined it in the first three months it was in operation. They have face-to-face parties with people standing around texting each other, looking around to see if the people who are texting are the ones they're talking to.

So you've got flirting, you've got gaming, you've got riots, you've got elections, you've got political demonstrations. And these are just the first signs of collective action online. I'm not making a big claim about something that exists today. I'm pointing out some early indicators of what may be happening in a future in which millions of people have devices on them that are not just telephones but also computers connected to networks.

reason: In the book you compare smart-mob behavior to the swarm systems observed in ants and other insects.

Rheingold: You need to make an important distinction, in that swarm systems that have been studied in biology and in complex systems consist of relatively unintelligent actors. With humans, of course, we have intelligent actors.

With ants, you have very sophisticated decision making about where to locate the nest and where are the nearest, best sources of food and what are the routes. These are done not by individuals who make decisions with neurosystems but by the emergent decisions of a whole lot of individual actors.

You've seen recently—Steven Johnson wrote very nicely about it in his book *Emergence*—that this kind of behavior goes on in cities. Neighborhoods form not because people make conscious decisions about it but because of the emergent behavior of a lot of people who go to the same place for a certain kind of activity. The stock market, again, is another good example. The price of a stock is not decided by any one person but is an artifact of the aggregate transactions of large numbers of people.

I cite some interesting research with "toy markets" that shows that groups of people can make decisions in an emergent manner better than the individuals in the group. The Hollywood Stock Market is an example. People exchange symbolic money, buying and selling stock on what the box office receipts of Hollywood films that are soon to be released will be. And then the films are released; those stocks that have good box office go up and those that don't go down, so there are winners and losers. It turns out that those markets—those aggregate decisions of everyone who's making an investment—can actually predict what will be box office winners better than the individuals in those groups.

reason: The book is about not just smart mobs, but what happens when smart mobs collide with smart environments—what happens when mobility meets pervasiveness.

Rheingold: I think there are two aspects to smart environments. One is information embedded in places and things. The other is location awareness, so that devices we carry around know where we are. When you combine those two, you get a lot of possibilities.

You can associate information with places by putting, in those places, a device that broadcasts information to nearby devices. More practically, you could do it by simply using a server, so if your device knows where you are and it communicates with a server, you can ask about information that's stored about that place. So, for example, you might want to combine these two and point your device down the street and ask, "Is there a good Chinese restaurant in this direction?" Not just "What does Zagat say about it?" but "What do my friends say about it?"

Or, "I'm new in town. How do I get from where I am in relation to Fifth and Main? And what's the crime rate at Fifth and Main at this time of day?" Or, "I'm about to enter this restaurant. What do the people who've eaten here in the last hour say about the service here?" So there is a lot of information that can be associated with places. There are also questions about who has the right to write that information, as well as to access it.

Then there's the idea that individual objects will have some kind of ambient intelligence—that they'll have sensors in them that have information storage and communication capacity, and little radio circuits. We're now seeing the replacement of bar codes, beginning with the radio frequency ID tag. Gillette has just said it's going to buy a half billion of these. These are little microchips that are inexpensive, getting down to pennies or less than a penny, that you can put on an object. The chips will have information about that object, just as a bar code does, except you can write to this information and read from it using radio devices instead of relying on line of sight.

You could, for example, using this technology, point to a book and find out what *The New York Times* says about it—and also what your book club says about it. You can do that with barcodes today: I reported an experiment on my blog where a friend of mine took a bar code reader and attached it to a hand-held computer. Every object has a story; it's just that citizens and consumers don't have access to what that story is. Soon we're going to have lots of little chips in lots of things, and those chips are going to communicate, and we're going to read information from those chips, and in some cases the chips can read information that we can send to them.

In not too many years, there will be more objects communicating via the Internet than people. We have an environment that's beginning to have ambient awareness. "Intelligent rooms" could have sensors that pick up information you broadcast so that they would know who you are, and what your credit rating is, and what your record with this particular store is.

"The conflict over emerging technologies is whether we'll be active users who shape the medium, as we were with the Internet, or passive consumers who don't have influence over the medium, as we were in the days of one telephone company."

There's also wearable computing, so that it's not the environment that has the ambient awareness but your clothing that can communicate with objects and the environment. So here we have a very complicated situation: Our clothing, the objects we carry, the devices we encounter, and the places we encounter, in the future, will have information associated with them and in some cases the ability to compute.

reason: A lot of this is still in the research stage. We're still talking about that pure model of how things are supposed to work, before you fall into the messiness of how things work in the real world. When I read your book, I kept imagining myself turning on my computerized glasses, looking at an object, and seeing a 404 Error floating in midair.

Rheingold: One of the quotes in the book is that a side effect of this kind of future might be that nothing works and nobody knows why.

It used to be that if your automobile broke, the teenager down the street with the wrench could fix it. Now you have to have sophisticated equipment that can deal with microchips. We're entering a world in which the complexity of the devices and the system of interconnecting devices is beyond our capability to easily understand.

reason: The book mentions Mark Pesce's idea of "techno-animism." And animism is one of the first things I think of when you describe this world where there are spirits in everything, and they're communicating with each other, and you have to go to an expert to mediate between you and them.

On the other hand, Pesce is worried that "widespread popular beliefs that computationally colonized objects are intelligent... could lead to unpleasant unintended consequences." But a lot of people already react to recalcitrant objects as though they were intelligent. I yell at my car when it breaks down whether or not it has microchips in it.

Rheingold: I think this is qualitatively different. There's what used to be known as the "pathetic fallacy" of projecting human emotions onto objects. Here, the projection is facilitated by the object's calling you by name, knowing what the last thing you bought in the store was, knowing what your credit record is. When that happens, you quite naturally assume that it knows more than that. You don't know what it *doesn't* know about you, and therefore the room for that kind of projection is much more vast. It's not just an artifact of the human propensity to anthropomorphize things.

reason: You've pointed out that there are questions about who's going to write the information that's embedded in the environment—whether it will come from the top down or emerge from peer-to-peer communication. Do you think people would stand for any smart environment that tries to direct them instead of the other way around? The recent history of the Internet is a series of business models failing because companies thought they could channel people rather than just being there as tools for them.

Rheingold: There are naive notions of how to use these things in commerce. They're going to fail and get a backlash.

reason: Which of these technologies strike you as useful tools you'd like to have, and with which do you think you'd want to hit the off button as soon as you get a chance?

Rheingold: We already know that spam is a huge downside of online life. If we're going to be spammed on our telephones wherever we go, I think we're going to reject these devices. And it may be, like spam and telemarketing today, an annoyance in life that, no matter how much we personally hate it, our choices aren't going to make it disappear. So that's the hellish side of this.

I do think that giving consumers and citizens information about objects that they might want to purchase or interact with, and places they may want to patronize, gives us power and choice. If I can say, "The service in this place has been really shitty," and thus influence who's going to use it in the future, that's going to give me more power. If I'm able to look at the label of an object and choose whether to purchase it based on my political beliefs, that gives me and other consumers more power. With much of what I'm writing about, there's an upside and a downside, and it's hard to tell which ones are going to prevail. I think it's not *either/or* but *both/and.*

reason: To what extent do you use mobile devices yourself?

Rheingold: I'm not that much of a road warrior, but when I traveled publicizing the book, I carried a Handspring Treo that enables me to download and upload e-mail very easily and quickly to the Sprint network. And it was invaluable. I could get e-mail from a journalist who wanted an interview while I was in a taxicab from the airport and have the interview arranged by the time I got to the hotel. That was very useful to me. It definitely changed my life.

reason: Would you want to wear a computer?

Rheingold: It depends on how much control I have over it, and its price. But yeah, sure. I like to use my MP3 player, I like to use my mobile phone, and there are times when I want to send and receive e-mail on the run. If all that can be combined into something I can wear, then why not?

Again, it depends on how much control I have over it. I don't want to be called all the time-I want to be able to roll it over to voice mail if I need to. I definitely don't want to be spammed that I can get 25 cents off a burger every time I pass a McDonald's. A lot of it's going to depend on what the experience in the environment is of actually using it.

reason: And a lot of that depends on politics.

Rheingold: I think the overall conflict over emerging technologies is going to be whether we'll be active users who shape the medium, as we were with the personal computer and the Internet, or passive consumers who don't have influence over the medium, as we were in the days of three television networks and one telephone company. That's what a lot of these political conflicts over the regulation of new technologies are about.

Another aspect is that vested interests resist technologies that challenge their existing business model.

reason: One of the most interesting political battles you describe is the debate overwireless local area networks, or WiFi.

Rheingold: Telephone companies have paid governments around the world large amounts of money, upwards of $150 billion, for "3G" licenses, to create the "third generation" high-speed data networks to our devices. This is a big, top-down, very expensive infrastructure in which portions of the spectrum are auctioned off to the highest bidders, who have exclusive control of that part of the spectrum for their business purposes.

With WiFi technology, if you install a small card in your PC and another small base station from your Internet connection, you can project wireless Internet access to a small area. If a number of these, coming from the grassroots, link together, then you can have grassroots networks. So we've got broadband Internet access that doesn't rely on this 3G system. And it operates in the unlicensed band, so citizens don't need to have a license, like the 3G companies do, to operate.

So here we've got a conflict between a citizen-operated grassroots broadband system and a telco-operated top-down infrastructure, and the battle is being fought not on the level of technology but on the level of regulation. How is the FCC going to regulate the spectrum?

That is just one of several different emerging technologies that challenge the idea that spectrum should be regulated as property that is exclusively owned. This form of regulation is based on the kind of radio that we had in the 1920s. We now have radio that's much more intelligent in its devices than we had back then, and it's possible that we can treat the spectrum as a commons, as we have the Internet.

reason: What do you mean by a commons?

Rheingold: You don't have to buy a license to own a piece of the Internet. Anyone can send bits on the Internet. No one owns the whole thing. That doesn't mean that you can't have a capitalistic enterprise—it didn't stop Jerry Yang from becoming a billionaire or Google from becoming a billion-dollar business.

It's the difference between the highways and the railroads. You have to be a railroad company to run a train on a railroad, and the schedules are very, very closely coordinated from the top down so the trains don't run into each other. You don't have to own a highway to use it, and people determine how they get to their own destinations.

So part of the electromagnetic spectrum could be opened up to anyone who uses smart devices. The devices play nice with each other, the way routers do on the Internet—your transmitter will check and if this particular frequency is not being used for the next 50 billionths of a second by another device, it'll send its data out on it.

The open spectrum proposal is not that we change the way the entire spectrum is regulated, but that we open up more of the spectrum for experimentation with new devices that would treat it as a commons. So it would still be illegal to transmit on the television stations' frequencies, the emergency frequencies, and others.

"It's a pretty radically American idea: You don't have to rely on some distant institution, whether it's a government or a religion, to give you power and give meaning to your life if you have the tools and the knowledge and the freedom to do it for yourself."

reason: Another battleground you write about is privacy. What issues there are most important to you?

Rheingold: Well, nothing is more important than political liberty. If you don't have that, then the other issues are somewhat moot. Surveillance by people who want to sell you things is annoying. Surveillance by a state that wants to control your behavior is much more important.

People trade in their privacy for two things. One is convenience—it's convenient for Amazon to know things about my purchases, so it can recommend things to me. The other is security—when you go to an airport you submit yourself to a search, because you want to be secure from terrorism. Recently we've seen the state use technology to invade the privacy of citizens to a huge extent. People have accepted this, presumably because they think that they'll be more secure.

If encryption were easy to use and instantiated in devices, then people would have the opportunity to anonymize their transactions. There's definitely a user interface issue, because only the most sophisticated users are going to use anything that's complicated at all. If you had a privacy control that you can switch on and off, that would enable more users to take control.

reason: You also write about peer-to-peer journalism. One aspect you discuss more on your blog than in the book is this phenomenon of "moblogs."

Rheingold: Well, I predicted it in the book, but it hadn't happened yet. It's now happening so much that I'm considering not blogging it anymore.

reason: What's the difference between a moblog and an ordinary weblog?

Rheingold: A weblog is a site where anyone, from their computer, can post to the Web. A moblog is a mobile blog, so you can use your mobile device—a telephone, a video-equipped PDA [personal digital assistant]—to post to the Web. To publish what you witness and what you think from anywhere you are to everyone in the world—that's a big leap. Particularly now that we have the capability of publishing photos as well, and in some cases video.

The Rodney King video showed what happens when the cost of using a video camera drops to the point where you don't have to be a television professional to use one. Soon we'll see something happen in the world that's reported by one or more people from their mobile devices directly to the Internet before you see it on CNN or in *The New York Times*. Individuals have the ability to publicize events in a way that they have not had before, and that will ultimately affect the mass media, just as recently we saw the blogging about the Trent Lott affair having an effect on the political scene.

reason: A lot of the public seems to feel that after the dot-com crash, all technological change suddenly ended. Obviously, that isn't true. But to what extent is what you're writing about being restrained by recent developments in the marketplace?

Rheingold: It's important to note that the same thing happened with electricity and the railroads as well. There was a similar pattern: a world-changing discovery, and a lot of hype about it and utopian expectations and a financial bubble, and then a bust, with a lot of money being lost and a lot of businesses failing. And then, finally, some businesses picking up the pieces—not necessarily the ones that were the pioneers—and becoming very powerful. Ultimately, the changes *were* world-changing. So I think we can mistake the short-term events for the longer-term significance.

I think the financial losses in the high-tech and telecommunications and Internet sectors were so large that it's going to take several years to recover. But that does not mean that either technological progress or social innovation has stopped. Web-logging pretty much emerged as a social phenomenon *after* the Internet crash.

reason: A lot of people still associate the *Whole Earth Catalog* with the 1960s, even though the operation continues to this day. I was trying to think of ways that what you're writing about now is connected to what you were doing with *Whole Earth*, and the first thing that came to mind was the *Catalog*'s credo, "Access to Tools."

Rheingold: Yes. In fact, it goes back a lot further than the '60s. It goes back to Emerson and "Self-Reliance." It's a pretty radically American idea: You don't have to rely on some distant institution, whether it's a government or a religion, to give you power and give meaning to your life if you have the tools and the knowledge and the freedom to do it for yourself.

In the '60s, it was about not relying on the particular culture and government of that time. But the general idea is not relying on *any* particular culture and government, when you have the power to do it yourself.

Do Cheaters Ever Prosper? Just Ask Them

Outwitting a Machine Is One Thing; Bending the Rules Online Is Another

By PETER WAYNER

THE Sims Online is a clean, well-lighted corner of the Internet where people work to build an elaborately decorated, chat-filled virtual world. But if playing by the rules in this realm isn't entertaining enough, there are after-hours joints where rogues and grifters gather to swap schemes for gaming the game and growing rich.

The chatter at **TSOExtreme.com**, for example, is a mix of simple tips for guiding the characters known as Sims and elaborate strategies for earning millions of the online currency known as simoleans. Recently much of the talk has centered on using extra software, known as a bot, to automate the most tiresome clicking so players can rack up hundreds of thousands of simoleans in their sleep.

One of the players engaging in this automated counterfeiting, a 29-year-old financial planner from Texas, said he did so without apology (although he did not want to be identified by name). "I think the bots actually level the playing field for people who have day jobs," he said. "When I play an online game, I can't be the best because there are some college kids out there spending 14 hours a day."

Web sites like TSOExtreme.com are a challenge for the rapidly growing world of interactive games. While breaking the rules or using secret "cheat codes" has always been an accepted, even treasured part of single-player games, new online games match competitors, often strangers, remotely, which changes the dynamic. No one likes to lose unfairly, and those who play by the rules often struggle against schemers who believe that all is fair in love and simulated war.

For their part, many of the cheats say that bending the game's rules is part of the fun. It is only a game, and when it becomes boring it is time to turn to the greater game of beating the system, they argue.

Brian Reynolds, a designer of a new online game, Rise of Nations, likes to joke that he was "the guy who put 'Cheat' on the main menu" when he developed games like Civilization II. A player could use the menu at any time to create new assets like warriors or defenses for a city.

In his new game, however, in which players meet and battle for ratings over the Internet, that option is gone. Mr. Reynolds and his team try to ensure that people who buy the game have a pleasant and balanced experience when battling others to dominate a virtual world. They fear that people would stop playing if those who cheated held all the power.

Haden Blackman, the producer at LucasArts responsible for Star Wars Galaxies, an online game now being tested by 5,000 users, said that preventing cheating was one of the biggest challenges of creating a virtual world.

One lesson the game industry learned the hard way is that dedicated cheats will rewrite software to give themselves an advantage. "There are a lot of great ideas we come up with and skip because there's going to be 1 percent who will abuse them," Mr. Blackman said.

Players reprogram games and insert new instructions to gain an unbeatable edge.

Designers of the new Star Wars game initially planned to let players communicate in strange languages that would be translated by other players' computers, he said. But the developers soon realized that cheats would find a way to break into the hidden dictionary, gaining the ability to speak the various languages and negotiate with aliens from other planets—a skill that would normally develop only over time.

Bots like the ones discussed on TSOExtreme.com are just the beginning. Some players of games with a shooter, like Quake or Counter-Strike, have automated aiming tools that target an opponent more rapidly than the quickest of fingers.

Others reprogram their video cards to hide the elaborate textured walls in a game. All that is left is a wire-frame outline, allowing a player to see through walls and track those hiding behind them.

All of these techniques depend on users' having full control of the software running on their home machines. Adept programmers can rewrite the game or insert new instructions. The other players can either play fair or join the arms race.

The game Rise of Nations challenges a player to take a civilization from stone axes to nuclear weapons. The biggest worry of its designer, Tim Train, is not so much tricks that let players triple their bankroll with a single click, as ones that reveal hidden information or parts of a map.

"We use a simultaneous simulation on each player's machine," he explained. "If your wealth is suddenly increased by 100 times, the other computers notice it and quit."

To prevent people from poking around the computer memory in search of information about the location of hidden objects, the game encrypts all communications and stores data in different places every time users play.

Some software makers are working on more aggressive solutions. Tony Ray, the president of the Houston-based company Even Balance, distributes a free product called Punkbusters that acts as a virus detector by looking for modifications on every player's machine. Game companies are paying for its development in the hope of keeping the games fair. Software installed on every player's machine watches for cheating while periodically filing reports to other players.

"When QuakeWorld came out online, the community was huge and teeming with people," said Mr. Ray, referring to a first-person maze game that was popular in the mid-1990's. "There was serious competition and an enormous amount of online status. Then the cheats showed up, and almost overnight it went from something that was a hugely popular community into something that was a wasteland."

"All of the major developers were saying that they could do nothing to fight cheating because they couldn't control what went on in people's computers," he said. "The whole landscape of online gaming changed when we proved cheating could be fought effectively."

Mr. Ray's job is not easy. Every day he monitors discussion sites where cheats exchange notes and software. If a new tool emerges, he adds it to the list of unacceptable software. The cheats, of course, look for ways to keep their software off his list, and the larger game continues.

Tools like Punkbusters can only detect active reprogramming, not ways in which players abuse loopholes. (Game players often call these "exploits" to distinguish them from outright cheating.)

"Where we run into the gray area is when people do new things in games with the tools we've given them," Mr. Blackman said. "They're just using them in ways that we never expected."

Spencer Armstrong, a game tester in Calgary, Alberta, said he once found that a glitch in a virtual world called Neocron let his shots pass through a tree that blocked return fire. He recounted with a mixture of pride and chagrin that he killed some monsters to run up his score. Only after "taking full advantage" of the situation did he report the bug to the designers of the game, for which he was a pre-release "beta" tester. "During a beta, I play a little fast and loose," he said,.

But outside his circle of close friends, he said, he would never use such a trick. "If you're playing Counter-Strike online competitively against people you haven't met, cheating's wrong," he said. "It's as wrong as blood doping or taking steroids. But if you're playing a bit more for fun, just to explore, and you're playing with the game, then why not cheat?"

Gordon Walton, the executive producer for The Sims Online, said his staff monitors the state of the game, looking for anomalies. They also watch Internet activity and sites like TSO Extreme.com for new techniques for cheating. "If something goofy was going on, we would see it in 2.4 seconds." he said.

This policing, however, is never perfect. "I've never seen more than a tiny fraction of people cheat, but when they do, it can become a tactic," he said. "It's like how everyone can go five miles over the speed limit, because that's how it's enforced. If you leave a cheat long enough, it becomes part of the culture of the game."

Deciding when to step in and reprogram the game is a challenge for designers. Mr. Reynolds, for instance, said it was hard to outlaw a technique that was permitted by the game's logic.

"It may be fair when the game first comes out, but we still have to preserve the game itself," he said. "We'll start to patch it when it destroys the balance of the game."

Some players are still saddened that Electronic Arts, the publisher of The Sims Online, closed a loophole in the game that showered simoleans on anyone who stepped backward immediately after breaking a virtual piñata at an online party.

The worst nightmare for designers are tactics that give players unbeatable power, eliminating the pleasure of watching a game unfold. Even when a technique breaks no rules, balance can sometimes be restored only by banning it. Mr. Armstrong, for instance, was simply exploiting a loophole by shooting through trees. But if everyone did so, the challenge of the game would disappear.

Mr. Blackman said his team would pay extra attention to the economy in Star Wars Galaxies because designers have built in unparalleled freedom for players to create objects and sell them. In theory, this should give players many options and strategies to explore, but it could also lead to players' gaining monopolies. "I'm sure that six months after launch we're going to have plenty of stories," he said.

Sometimes the lines between the players and their game roles blur so that it is difficult to define what is fair. Star Wars Galaxies encourages players to adopt a persona from the "Star Wars" milieu, a world in which not everyone plays by the rules.

Asked how Han Solo, one of his favorite characters, would play, Mr. Blackman laughed and said he "would use any advantage he could get."

"I'm that way," he said. "If you give me an advantage in the game, I'm going to use it. We want to have some things for the power gamer to discover, but there can't be so many that it unbalances the game."

Article 20

Why Women Avoid Computer Science

The numbers prove women embrace the "precision" of mathematics. Could it be the ill-defined nature of computing is what drives them away?

Paul De Palma

Women find careers in computing unattractive. A report from the American Association of University Women says that women account for only 17% of the high school students who take advanced placement exams in computer science and earn only 28% of the undergraduate degrees.[1] This confirms an earlier report that noticed a sharp drop in CS degrees going to women between 1986 and 1994.[2]

Since no one really knows why women avoid computer science—or what to do about it—I feel justified in offering a guess of my own.

As it happens, the literature fairly bubbles over with speculation as to why there are so few young women in computer science courses. We hear about math anxiety, violent computer games, the scarcity of mentors, and a supposed female preference for "relational work".[7] Since no one really knows why women avoid computer science—or what to do about it—I feel justified in offering a guess of my own.

Among the many reasons offered, math anxiety is the most obvious. It is also the least defensible. Commentators never seem to notice that women receive almost half of the undergraduate degrees in mathematics. In fact, they received nearly 40% of them in 1970, well before the women's movement became a mass phenomenon.[5] Not only do young women not avoid mathematics, they embrace it. What if the precision of mathematics, that "most masculine of subjects" in the words of one study,[7] is exactly what has long invited women? The flip side is that the ill-defined nature of computing is what drives them away.

Young men drawn to computer science, engineering, and physics like to tinker. They enjoy taking things apart and putting them back together. They like kits, gadgets, and screwdrivers. They were the boys who set up the audio-visual equipment in high school 30 years ago, and who now man—the choice of gender is deliberate—the school's computer network. They are fascinated with anything that moves, especially if it has wheels or wings, and, crucially, is not alive.[4] The men usually given credit for the microcomputer all started with screwdrivers and soldering irons. Bill Gates and Paul Allen built a Basic interpreter to run on their Altair 8800, a computer kit for hobbyists, in the mid-1970s. Steves Wozniak and Jobs, of Apple fame, built their first machine to dazzle pals in Silicon Valley's Homebrew Computer Club around the same time.

In fact, I claim that microcomputers are responsible for the steep rise in the number of women entering computer science following its introduction, as well as for the steep drop a few years later.[6] In 1971, fewer than 2,400 students received degrees in computer science from a handful of academic departments. By 1986, that number had jumped to nearly 42,000, including almost 15,000 women. It is clear that the dramatic growth of computer science as an academic discipline is due to the microcomputer and, of course, to the extravagant promises that buzz around it. If the number of computer science degrees had continued to grow as it had from 1975 to 1985 (and if the population grew at its average annual rate over the same period), by next year everyone in the U.S. would be the proud holder of one. Lucky for us this didn't happen. The number of recipients began to drop off sharply in 1987, stabilizing by the mid-1990s at about 24,000.

We know why both men and women entered the field through the academic portal in great numbers in the 1980s. The attention paid to the microcomputer led many to believe it was a talismanic object. Why did these numbers drop, and why more sharply for women than for men? For men, the explanation is obvious. Traditional paths to wealth like law, medicine, and business are more certain, and over the long run, far more remunerative, on average, than computing. Further, computing is not a true profession. One need not suffer through a computer science curriculum to enter the field. Finally, computer science is more difficult than many aspiring young millionaires expect. These reasons serve to drive women away as well. And the tinker factor combined to drive them away in greater relative numbers.

Computing has always had an indeterminate feel to it. With its unreadable (and, now nonexistent) manuals, its feature piled upon fabulous feature, our tools are always more complicated than what they're used for. The old programmer's dictum that we use 10% of the features 90% of the time was true long before the first PC. And the manuals from the glory days of the mainframe were, if anything, more opaque than today's commercially written documentation. This has always selected for success those young men—and they were almost always young men—willing to spend endless hours tinkering with software. The microcomputer only exacerbated a process that had long been in place. It simply added hardware tinkering to the software tinkering that had always defined the testosterone-infused conversations among programmers. Perhaps the day will come when young women find things that roll, fly, and plug into an outlet as fascinating as do young men. The nature/nurture debate is an old one, and, at least in the case of toy trucks and ponies with pastel hair, not likely to be settled soon. One day we may find girls playing with trucks and entering computer science in increasingly greater numbers. Until that happy day, however, I have several suggestions to make the field more hospitable. Let's look in a very unlikely place for what young women seem to prefer. Let's look to mathematics itself. Long before law and medicine opened their doors, a significant fraction of undergraduate degrees in mathematics were earned by women. Judging by these numbers, girls and women have always found mathematics attractive. Why not assume mathematicians have been doing something right and have been doing it right for a long time?

My hypothesis, at least as plausible as what I read elsewhere, is this: to make computer science more attractive to women, make it more like mathematics. Computing, despite the layer upon layer of gadgetry that accumulates like sediment at an archeological site, has its basis in mathematics. How do we get to it? First, teach any girl with an aptitude for symbol manipulation how to program. Teach girls, I say, not to search the Web, use a word processor, install an operating system or, God help us, play computer games. Teach girls how to program. To write a program, like solving a math problem, is to discover a pattern with logic. If girls can do mathematics, and they manifestly can, they can program.

Second, when you teach girls how to program, keep things as close to pure logic as possible. Minimize reliance on glitzy software packages, fancy graphical user interfaces, and wildly powerful and complex text editors. This advice is contrary to current practice, even to common sense, but is absolutely correct. These tools form a shell that puts logic at a distance. This is nowhere more clear than with the Linux phenomenon. It is a tinkerer's paradise. It does not surprise me that I've yet to meet a young woman obsessed, as so many young men are, with Linux arcana. To increase the number of women in the field, remove some of the layers. This will not at all harm computer science education and could well have the salutary effect of producing graduates, men as well as women, who can write clear, clean, precise code.

Third, if at all possible, teach computing without microcomputers. Again, this is contrary to received wisdom, but two decades in the field have taught me that microcomputers attract tinkering boys like bees to flowers. Girls, until that glorious day when they begin spending afternoons in the tool aisles at Home Depot, will be driven away. Remove microcomputers and you decrease the distraction from hardware. We are training systems designers, after all; software engineers, not computer technicians.

Fourth, keep the programs short, at least in the early stages. One of the striking features about mathematics education is its reliance on drill. Page through any calculus book and what you will find are thousands upon thousands of nearly identical, comparatively simple problems. Mathematics, to paraphrase a colleague, is the only discipline whose gate is kept by an army of five-minute exercises. Though drill is out of fashion with mathematics reformers, I have long thought it one of the field's charms. Anyone who likes mathematics knows the pleasure of working these problems. They are difficult enough to make one think, but not so difficult as to make one think too much. That is to say, anyone with a reasonable set of gifts can get his or her brain around your garden-variety calculus problem. Since there is something about the determinate nature of mathematics that seems to appeal to girls, I suggest we try to make computing more determinate. Instead of requiring long programming assignments that students must design, code, debug, test, and document, ask students to write many, many small, nearly identical functions. Once they have mastered this skill, they will feel, like students of mathematics, confident about going on to the next level.

Fifth, treat programming languages as notational systems. This means that you should resist the temptation to adopt a new one, no matter how extravagant the promises of its devotees. Remember, the goal here is to try to interest girls in computing. It could well be that Java is the future (as C++ once was, as C once was, as Pascal once was, as, even, Cobol once was), the language of choice for sophisticated systems. Thirteen-year-olds, seventeen-year-olds, or even nineteen-year-olds, don't produce sophisticated systems. However, the way things stand now, they produce simple systems with fabulously complex tools. Remember mathematics. Remember that young women received nearly 40% of the bachelor's degrees without the benefit of feminism. To keep women involved, agree on a programming language appropriate to the task at hand, and don't change it—at least until students have developed a good deal of sophistication.

All of this is speculation, of course. But it is surely no more speculative than exhortations to build girl-friendly computer games[3] or to "prepare tech-savvy teachers".[1] That girls may be drawn to logic more readily than to variations of Mattel's "Barbie Fashion Designer," is counterintuitive. It is certainly out of fashion. Yet a program based on this observation is easy to put together. It requires no grants, no consultants, no expensive outlays for still more equipment. Nor do we have to convince toy manufacturers that women hold up half the sky. We don't even have to reform the high school curriculum. It's odd, I admit, that mathematics, a discipline obsessed with prodigies and timed examinations, would prove so friendly to women. But the numbers are there for anyone to see. Computer science might be looking in all the wrong places.

REFERENCES

1. American Association of University Women. Tech-savvy: Educating girls in the new computer age, 2000; www.aauw.org/2000/techsavvy.html.
2. Camp, T. The incredible shrinking pipeline. *Commun. ACM 40,* 10 (Oct. 1997), 103–110.
3. Gorriz, C., Medina, C. Engaging girls with computers through software games. *Commun ACM 43,* 1 (Jan. 2000), 42–49.
4. McIlwee, J., Robinson, J.G. *Women in Engineering: Gender, Power and Workplace Culture.* State University of New York Press, Albany, 1992.
5. National Center for Educational Statistics. *Digest of Educational Statistics NCES 98-015.* U.S. Government Printing Office, Washington, D.C., 1997.
6. Oechtering, V., Behnke, R. Situations and Advancement Measures in Germany. *Commun. ACM 38,* 1 (Jan. 1995), 75–82.
7. Perlow, L. *Finding Time: How Corporations, Individuals and Families Can Benefit from New Work Practices.* Cornell University Press, Ithaca, NY, 1997.

PAUL DE PALMA (depalma@gonzaga.edu) is an associate professor of mathematics and computer science at Gonzaga University, Spokane, WA.

SPECIAL REPORT

African Americans in Technology

Cyber-stars

Black Issues profiles high achievers in information technology.

Black History Month celebrations long have touted the contributions of African Americans in technology. In this issue, *Black Issues* profiles 10 individuals who are in the process of making history of their own in the arena of information technology. While much of American history documents technological innovation in agriculture and industry, our list of higher education innovators and leaders focuses on the ongoing digital revolution that has been transforming world society and economy over the past several decades.

Our list, while not intended to be a definitive grouping of innovators and leaders, heralds people we call "information technologists." Information technologists hail from many disciplines, which include computer science, information technology administration, school curriculum development, electrical engineering and other fields being transformed by digital technology.

Expanding Horizons

As a well-seasoned veteran of academia, Dr. Clarence Ellis easily could shut his door to students and cloister himself in research. So instead, what is Ellis doing this semester?

Teaching a Computing 101 class to undergraduates who aren't even computing or engineering majors.

"The computer is not just a machine," says Ellis, of the University of Colorado at Boulder. "It can help someone. This class is an important way to reach many students here."

Ellis, 58, divides his course between teaching students how to give instructions to computers and teaching them computer applications. The class enrolls about 160 students.

Since joining Colorado in 1992, he has insisted on periodically teaching the introductory course to encourage students of all ethnicities to expand their horizons. That message wasn't conveyed to him when he was in school, he says.

"Instead, the message at that time was, 'well, you have taken one basic math class and you passed, so you don't need to take any more math. You'll get better grades if you don't stretch yourself,'" Ellis recalls teachers telling him. "People put together an image of what I was supposed to be.

"So I always tell my students to push," he says.

His own initiation to computers was happenstance. As a teenager in the late 1950s, Ellis got a part-time job to help support his family. He guarded an insurance company's computer—this was before microcircuits and it had 2,400 vacuum tubes. Ellis prevented tampering and

PHOTO COURTESY OF THE UNIVERSITY OF COLORADO

Clarence "Skip" Ellis

Title:

Professor of Computer Science and Director of Collaboration Technology Research Group, University of Colorado at Boulder

Education:

Ph.D., Computer Science, University of Illinois; B.S., Math and Physics, Beloit College

vandalism overnight. But working the graveyard shift by himself provided plenty of time to read more than 20 operating manuals. Consequently, he also groomed himself to troubleshoot for his employer.

In 1969, Ellis reportedly became the first African American in the country to earn a doctorate in computer science.

He has worked as a researcher and developer at Bell Telephone Laboratories, IBM, Xerox, Micro-electronics and Computer Technology Corp., Los Alamos Scientific Labs and Argonne National Lab.He has taught at Stanford University, the University of Texas, MIT, Stevens Institute of Technology and in Taiwan. His research spans groupware, coordination theory, office systems, databases, software engineering and workflow systems.

While going out of his way to influence non-computer science majors, Ellis also steers students toward graduate studies in computer science and related fields. In the 1990s, he helped establish the 10-week Summer Multicultural Access to Research Training (SMART) program at the university. The SMART program offers 10 undergraduates internships in science and engineering as well as orientation to life as a graduate student at CU-Boulder.

—*By Lydia Lum*

Advocating Technological Empowerment

If it takes impressive talent to launch a research career in physics, imagine what it takes to switch from that field to computational science research and become a leading national advocate for diversity in the computer science field. Since earning a physics doctorate in 1975 from Stanford University, Dr. Roscoe Giles has carved out a successful career that has blended physics and the science of high performance computing.

A professor in the Electrical and Computer Engineering department at Boston University, Giles conducts computational science research on applications of parallel supercomputers to physics and materials problems. Giles also serves as a team leader for the Education, Outreach and Training Partnership for Advanced Computational Infrastructure (EOTPACI), deputy director of the Boston University Center for Computational Science, and co-director of the Boston University MARINER project. From 1977 to 1983, Giles was an assistant professor of physics at Massachusetts Institute of Technology.

Since the late 1980s, Giles has turned his attention to issues relating to the digital divide. He, along with Dr. Bryant York and others, founded the Institute for African American E-Culture (IAAEC) to bring leading computer scientists, curriculum specialists and other prominent Black educational technologists together to develop innovative digital technology for education and economic empowerment of Black Americans.

"Many of us had been talking for years about how to create an organization to serve interests in the Black community instead of being isolated at our respective institutions," Giles says.

As executive director, Giles raises money and keeps an eye on the research being carried out by a team of IAAEC members who are faculty at various institutions around the nation. The National Science Foundation-funded group's research is largely aimed at educational computing initiatives.

In addition to leading IAAEC, Giles also will be serving as the general chairman of the SC2002 Conference,

PHOTO COURTESY OF BOSTON UNIVERSITY

Roscoe C. Giles

Title:

Professor, Electrical and Computer Engineering, Boston University

Education:

Ph.D., Physics, Stanford University; M.S., Physics, Stanford University; B.A., Physics, University of Chicago

which is higher education's premier supercomputing conference. Giles is the first African American chairman of the annual supercomputing meeting, which will be held in Baltimore in November.

—By Ronald Roach

PHOTO COURTESY OF NORTHWESTERN UNIVERSITY

Louis Gomez

Title:

Associate Professor, Computer Science, Northwestern University

Education:

Ph.D., Cognitive Psychology, University of California at Berkeley; B.A., Psychology, State University of New York at Stony Brook

Urban Innovation

Lofty ideas float abundantly within the halls of academe, but Dr. Louis Gomez takes his lofty ideas directly into Chicago urban schools. Gomez, an associate professor of computer science at Northwestern University, is co-director of the Center for Learning Technologies in Urban Schools (LeTUS). The center, sponsored by the National Science Foundation, is a partnership among Northwestern University, the University of Michigan, Chicago Public Schools and Detroit Public Schools. The program helps provide the latest computing and networking technologies to schools as well as designing science curriculums that are project-based.

"We build curriculums through which students participate," Gomez says. Students may have questions about health issues or about air or water quality or global climate changes. They choose a project, such as global climate changes, and learn more through sets of the latest data. "It's the very same data that professional climate scientists use in their work," Gomez says.

Gomez says LeTUS, in its fourth year, is the achievement he is most proud of. But he also co-directs the Learning Through Collaborative Visualization Project at Northwestern, which helps local schools develop curriculums that connect to other communities. Gomez also helped establish math and science academies at several urban schools, and saw excellent results among students who had participated compared with those who did not.

Gomez, a professor of Learning Sciences at Northwestern, is a longtime member of the Institute for African American E-Culture.

"It's been important for me as a professional researcher to interact with others. I've learned from a lot of powerful and insightful technologists," he says. "I've also been able to point young scholars of color to IAAEC. They get their horizons expanded by seeing a lot of scholars of color doing important cutting-edge work."

As for the digital divide, Gomez says it's more of an idea divide.

"I think that (African Americans) have not had access to powerful uses of day-to-day technology as others have had. But a big part of technology is having access to powerful ideas. The digital divide is grounded in not having powerful ideas that are personally meaningful, being able to do things with technology," he says. When commitments are made to provide technology to schools and communities, Gomez says, there also should be a commitment to training and understanding.

—By Eleanor Lee Yates

High-Tech Mentoring

Years from now, when you're using your cell phone to monitor stock quotes, activate the thermostat in your home from the car, or send e-mail from a chaise lounge on a tropical beach, you'll have Dr. Kevin T. Kornegay and his team of research assistants to thank.

As director of the Cornell Broadband Communications Research Lab, Kornegay's research is helping to revolutionize wireless communications. Last year, he was recognized by Career Communications Group as Black Engineer of the Year, in the higher education category. But, when *Black Issues* asked the associate professor what he hopes his legacy will be, he didn't mention the multimillion dollar research he oversees. Neither did he cite the years he spent at Bell Labs and IBM, nor the growing mass of awards he is collecting. No, the legacy that concerns Kornegay most involves his students.

"I want to have a multiplicative effect," he says. As a graduate student at the University of California at Berkeley, Kornegay recalls being one of only two or three African Americans in the entire nation awarded the doctorate in his field in 1992. Now, he manages 15 graduate students in one of the more diverse research teams at Cornell's engineering school. He will graduate his first African American doctoral candidate this fall, and he has several others working their way through the pipeline.

But producing Black doctorates is only the beginning of Kornegay's ambition. He also hopes his example will inspire his Asian, Latino and White students to receive other African Americans with an open mind.

"The problem is complicated," Kornegay says about widening the engineering pipeline for African Americans. "You have to educate other folks."

Mentorship is Kornegay's way of giving back to those who inspired him. Included in this group are his parents — who imbued him with a respect for education and a strong work ethic — and his uncles Bob and Wade Kornegay, whose achievements as doctorates in engineering and chemistry respectively are noteworthy. Together with his wife, Felicia, the Cornell professor now serves as a role model to his own two sons — Kevin, 9, and Justin, 5 — and to his students.

"I feel that one of my missions is to help dispel these negative images (of African Americans). The way I do that is through my actions, through my level of performance (and) through my accomplishments."

—By Cheryl D. Fields

PHOTO COURTESY OF CORNELL UNIVERSITY

Kevin T. Kornegay

Title:

Associate professor, Electrical Engineering and Computer Science, Cornell University

Education:

Ph.D., Electrical Engineering and Computer Science, University of California at Berkeley; M.S., Electrical Engineering and Computer Science, University of California at Berkeley; B.S., Electrical Engineering, Pratt Institute

Reconfiguring Technology's Landscape

In a field dominated by men, Spelman College associate professor Dr. Andrea W. Lawrence is using her ingenuity to ensure that African American women assume a presence on technology's vast landscape. As president of the Association of Departments of Computer Science/Engineering at Minority Institutions, the Purdue University alumna is a leading player in the national effort to produce more African Americans in technology.

Lawrence initially came to Spelman as an undergraduate in the mid '60s, but left in 1967 to accompany her then-husband to Purdue, where he was pursuing graduate studies. She completed her undergraduate studies there, but eventually returned to Spelman to teach. When she joined the faculty in 1983, she had her master's, but her colleagues persuaded her that in order to have a full career in postsecondary education, she would need a doctorate. So, with the support of her three daughters, she dove in and completed her doctorate in 1993.

"I am the first African American to get a Ph.D. in computer science at Georgia Tech," she says.

Today, Lawrence is chairwoman of the computer science department and is a significant contributor to Spelman's being ranked 41st in *Black Issues*' 2001 edition of the "Top 100" for its production of African American students with baccalaureate degrees in engineering. Its 18 graduates constituted 100 percent of the department's graduating class that year.

"I tell my students that if you concentrate and learn all that you can while you're here, you'll be ready to go to any graduate school or into any career that you want to," she says.

Lawrence's personal research interest is in the field of human computer interaction. She is particularly focused on ways that computer animations can be used to teach computer algorithms. Though she sometimes laments that her teaching and administrative duties leave her little time to pursue research, she never regrets choosing teaching over a career in industry.

"I thought it was important to be a role model and encourage students to follow in my footsteps," she says.

—By Cheryl D. Fields

Andrea W. Lawrence

Title:

Chairwoman, Associate Professor Department of Computer Science, Spelman College

Education:

Ph.D., Computer Science, Georgia Institute of Technology; M.S., Computer Science, Atlanta University; B.S., Mathematics, Purdue University

Community College Advocate

As a community college graduate, Dr. Edward J. Leach knows firsthand the critical role community colleges play in providing minority students opportunities for educational advancement. Since 1999, the New York native has served as an advocate for ensuring that the nation's community colleges expose minorities to digital technology.

Given that more than 40 percent of all Black undergraduates in American higher education are enrolled in community colleges, it falls on Leach to push his organization, arguably one of the most influential groups serving American community colleges, to focus on minority awareness of technology careers and digital divide issues.

"My interest is that minority students learn about the full range of opportunities in high technology. Too often, minorities don't see technology as a field they can pursue," Leach says.

At the League for Innovation, which is based in Mission Viejo, Calif., Leach manages the group's annual Conference on Information Technology (CIT). Averaging about 3,500 attendees, the League for Innovation's CIT is one of the largest conferences devoted to information technology in higher education.

Leach also has had responsibility for managing community college participation in a four-year, $10 million U.S. Department of Education-funded training program that instructs K–12 classroom teachers on using the Internet in the classroom. The program, which is entitled Alliance+, is expected to reach more than 9,000 teachers in the Cleveland, Miami and Phoenix metropolitan areas by the spring of 2003. Cuyahoga Community College, Miami-Dade Community College and Maricopa Community College are providing the teacher training.

—By Ronald Roach

Edward Leach

Title:

Vice President, Technology Programs, League for Innovation in the Community College

Education:

Ph.D., Educational Administration, University of Texas-Austin; M.Ed., Health Education, Miami University; B.S., Secondary Education, Eastern Kentucky University; A.S., General Studies, Genesee Community College

Researching Inclusion

Even as a child, Dr. Valerie Taylor was drawn to math and science. "Math is an objective subject. It doesn't change from year to year like English. One year an English teacher would say my writing was too flowery, another year it was not expressive enough. But each year 2 plus 2 was 4," says Taylor, a nationally known computer science researcher and professor.

Taylor, associate professor in Northwestern University's Electrical and Computer Engineering Department, has won acclaim for her research. A major effort is Project Prophesy, a partnership between Northwestern and Argonne National Laboratory. Her work focuses on analyzing and improving the performance of applications that run on a collection of computers in different geographic locations.

Taylor is also an active member of the Institute for African American E-Culture and is assiduously researching digital divide issues. She is co-principal investigator for an institute project with the National Science Foundation. The project, "New Approaches to Human Capital Development Through Information Technology Research," is looking at some nontraditional ways to teach computer science concepts, such as incorporating hip-hop.

Taylor is accustomed to being among a handful of African Americans at computer science conferences and often being the only woman of color.

"It's been lonely," says Taylor, a native of Chicago. "There's the major issue of isolation, and of often being considered a double minority. You're asked to serve on so many committees and give opinions for being a woman and again for being a minority." Taylor is the only Black female professor in her department. When she first started at Northwestern, she was often mistaken as a secretary. When Taylor attends computer science conferences, she immediately does a "scan" in the meeting hall, waving frantically if she spots another African American woman, who always returns the frantic wave.

Taylor says she doesn't think of herself as a superstar role model, but she does feel it is necessary to give back to her community — both minorities and women — and to show those coming behind her that it can be done.

"It's one thing to dream about a position, but it's good to actually see someone doing it," she says. She adds that it is important to share her excitement for her field with others.

"It's important to tell others that research is not something that one does in isolation. You collaborate with others and share the results you see with other people at conferences. The sharing and collaborations also take place via e-mail and video-conferencing technologies," Taylor says. She is co-chairwoman of the Coalition to Diversify Computing, a joint organization of the Association of Computing Machinery, the Computing Research Association and the Institute of Electrical and Electronic Engineering Computer Society.

Valerie E. Taylor

Title:

Associate Professor, Electrical and Computer Engineering, Northwestern University

Education:

Ph.D., University of California at Berkeley; B.S., M.S., Electrical Engineering, Purdue University

"So much information is conveyed via the Web," Taylor says of bridging the digital divide. "If you have a community that doesn't have access to computers, they don't have access to critical information. But it's not all about technology. Training is just as important as access."

—*By Eleanor Lee Yates*

PHOTO BY SEVANS

Brian K. Smith

Title:

Assistant Professor, Media Arts and Sciences, Massachusetts Institute of Technology

Education:

Ph.D., Learning Sciences, Northwestern University; B.S., Computer Science & Engineering, University of California, Los Angeles

'Making Smart Kids' Smarter

"At the end of the day, the product of good research is good people."

That's what Dr. Brian K. Smith shoots for, working at MIT's Media Lab. "I just want to make smart kids," he says. "Here, we try to figure out how to change human performance. How does all this stuff, this technology, impact the world kids live in?"

At the Media Lab, researchers like Smith, 32, are learning how computational tools capture, analyze and improve the quality of life. For Smith, it's about pioneering research that increases technology access to the social and economic underclass.

He hopes projects like "Image Maps" can improve children's critical thinking. He and his MIT colleagues have developed a camera prototype wired to a satellite receiver and digital compass. The camera lets people, after shooting pictures in a neighborhood near MIT, view images of those same places as they appeared throughout the previous century. This teaches children to think more scientifically about their urban surroundings, Smith says. "The historical images push them to find out what happened to the community and why it changed," he says.

Other projects aren't aimed at a specific age group. Smith has led photography-based discussions among people recently diagnosed with diabetes to help them change their diet and lifestyle. The patients share photos of their meals and their exercise routines and then critique each other. Smith says they nitpick over photos showing ashtrays next to treadmills, or of high-fat dressings drowning the salad greens.

"And sometimes you're trying to change a cultural attitude," Smith says. "If everyone else in the family has always eaten gumbo, and you're diabetic, how are you going to convince the rest of the family that you really shouldn't have that gumbo without offending them?"

After earning his doctorate at Northwestern, Smith in 1997 became the first African American to join MIT's Media Lab as tenure-track faculty. Today, he's still the only African American among the lab of top-tier researchers.

Smith's introduction to computers came at age 9. His father, a Pacific Bell executive, bought the family an Apple II Plus. As he grew up, an intrigued Smith passed many hours dissecting the computer and programming games and graphics.

Even now, Smith candidly says that when he's "tracking technology" in his work, he's often playing a game. "The sense of reality is so amazing when you're playing Nintendo, Game Cube. You have to wonder what these games do to a kid's environment," Smith says.

—By Lydia Lum

Strategic Thinker

Although Hampton University's Debra S. White did not plan a career in higher education information technology administration, her knack for project management and incisive strategic thinking has made for impressive results at the private historically Black university in Hampton, Va. White became the assistant provost for technology at Hampton in January 1999, and in fall 2000 the school was named a "Most Wired Campus" by *Yahoo! Internet Life* magazine. It was one of the first historically Black colleges or universities to achieve the coveted distinction.

The *Yahoo!* recognition, which went to Morehouse College and Tennessee State University at the same time, came more than a year after Hampton had completed an impressive IT makeover that placed wired Internet and cable television connections in the rooms of every student living in campus dormitories. The "drop per pillow" access gave each student high-speed service to the campus network and the Internet.

"I think getting the dormitories wired that year made all the difference with *Yahoo!*," White says.

In addition to fully wiring their dormitories, Hampton ranks among the top HBCUs for instituting online distance education courses and degree programs. The school offers two online degree programs, one in nursing and the other in religious studies. Under White's leadership, Hampton also has joined the exclusive Internet 2 consortium of institutions with links to high performance computing networks, which are the basis for a next generation Internet.

The school has taken a lead in sponsoring IT conferences for the benefit of neighboring schools in the Hampton Roads area in Virginia and the entire HBCU community. Hampton hosted a digital divide conference for HBCUs in fall 2000 and a computer security conference for neighboring Hampton Roads schools in June 2001. This spring, the school will play host to a national conference on computer security issues, which seeks participation from any American higher education institution.

"We feel that as we make strides as a (higher education) IT leader, we have an obligation to give back to others," White says.

She is quick to credit Hampton president Dr. William Harvey for providing her with the opportunity and direction to shape IT administration at the university. White, a history major during her college years at the University of Virginia, literally stumbled into a career in high technology after accidentally colliding with an IBM recruiter on campus. The fortuitous meeting led to an internship, and later, a full-time job with the company after college. White originally had planned to be a high school history teacher.

Working as an IBM marketing representative, White got to work with Harvey because Hampton was one of her clients. The association led to a short-term consulting position at Hampton in the early 1990s, and White even-

Debra S. White

Title:

Assistant Provost for Technology, Hampton University

Education:

M.B.A., The College of William and Mary; B.A., History, University of Virginia

tually left the Hampton Roads area to serve as a chief information officer at a Rhode Island boarding school. Not long after White returned to Hampton Roads in the late 1990s, Harvey persuaded her to become Hampton's first chief information officer with the title of assistant provost for technology.

White also is working on her doctorate in higher education administration from The George Washington University.

—By Ronald Roach

Wired for the Cause

As a youngster growing up in Boston, Dr. Bryant York experienced firsthand the educational benefits of the math and science push by the United States in the aftermath of the 1957 launching of the Soviet satellite Sputnik. One of the few Black junior high and high school students to be enrolled in the prestigious Boston Latin School during the late 1950s, York got the opportunity to take supplementary math courses during summers at the Massachusetts Institute of Technology.

As a professor and research director in the computer science department at Portland State University (PSU) in Oregon, York has not forgotten the impact that the special academic attention had on him. The fact that he grew up poor in a tight-knit family within a supportive Black community has kept him wedded to a strong commitment to helping disadvantaged minorities succeed in math and science.

"I cannot remember when I didn't think that helping people was important," York says.

A co-founder and research director of the Institute for African American E-Culture, York has worked closely with Dr. Roscoe Giles of Boston University, initially as departmental colleagues at BU and as a collaborator in projects to expand African American participation in technology. York has held faculty positions at Boston University and Northeastern University.

At Portland State, York specializes in developing algorithms and codes for computing applications in signal and image processing as well as in crystallography and spectroscopy. He also focuses on using geometric algebra to solve problems in graph theory. York, who is in his first year at Portland State, expects to collaborate with officials in the Portland city school system on developing software tutorial programs in high school mathematics that will work on wireless computing devices.

"PSU has an African American president, Dan Bernstine. This means that there is someone at the top of the institution with more than a passing familiarity with the

Bryant W. York

Title:

Professor, Computer Science, Portland State University

Education:

Ph.D., Computer Science, University of Massachusetts at Amherst; M.S., Management, Sloan School of Management, Massachusetts Institute of Technology; M.S., Computer Science, University of Massachusetts at Amherst; B.A., Mathematics, Brandeis University

issues. PSU also has a very active Graduate School of Education and the nation's oldest continuously active School of Urban Studies and Planning, which provide extensive opportunities for collaboration and connection with national IAAEC projects," he says.

A stint at the National Science Foundation in the early 1990s proved instrumental in getting York to focus on digital divide issues. While he says that the "digital divide is just the most recent manifestation of the economic and educational divides that have existed for years," the issue "began to seriously matter to me back in 1990 while I was at NSF.

"I ran a computer contest at the Benjamin Banneker High School in Washington, D.C., and around the same time I had occasion to visit Thomas Jefferson High School (in Fairfax County, Va.). The difference in facilities was astounding. Thomas Jefferson had a supercomputer, advanced workstations and labs donated by AT&T, Hewlett Packard, IBM and others. Banneker had a small number of archaic PCs," York notes.

York says it's critical to "fight now to develop a generation of people who believe in African American creation and ownership of technology" before low expectations become ingrained in how Blacks see technology.

—By Ronald Roach

THE WORLD ACCORDING TO GOOGLE

What if you had a magic tool that let you find out almost anything in less than a second? Millions of people already have it—and it's changing the way we live.

BY STEVEN LEVY

In a bygone era—say, five years ago—it would have been an occasion to burn shoe leather. A friend clued me in to an eBay item connected with a criminal case I was following. I didn't know who the seller was, and the district attorney on the case didn't know, either. "We're looking into it," he assured me. I checked into it as well. Fifteen minutes later, I had not only the seller's name, I'd discovered that he was a real-estate agent in a small California town. I'd seen a picture of him. I knew which community groups he belonged to, the title of a book he'd written. And what college he had attended. And I found out that the seller had a keen interest in hooking up with younger men—and I'd even read graphic descriptions of what he liked to do with them.

How did I know this? By performing an act done by tens of millions of people every day: typing a query (my quarry's eBay handle, which was the same as his e-mail address) into a blank line on a sparsely decorated Web page. In about the time it takes to sneeze, and for a cost of, oh, zero, his particulars and proclivities were in my hands. And no shoe leather was expended.

Reader, I Googled him.

Internet-search engines have been around for the better part of a decade, but with the emergence of Google, something profound has happened. Because of its seemingly uncanny ability to provide curious minds with the exact information they seek, a dot-com survivor has supercharged the entire category of search, transforming the masses into data-miners and becoming a cultural phenomenon in the process. By a winning combination of smart algorithms, hyperactive Web crawlers and 10,000 silicon-churning computer servers, Google has become a high-tech version of the Oracle of Delphi, positioning everyone a mouseclick away from the answers to the most arcane questions—and delivering simple answers so efficiently that the process becomes addictive. Google cofounder Sergey Brin puts it succinctly: "I'd like to get to a state where people think that if you've Googled something, you've researched it, and otherwise you haven't and that's it." We're almost there now. With virtually no marketing, Google is now the fourth most popular Web site in the world—and the Nos. 1 and 3 sites (AOL, Yahoo) both license Google technology for *their* Web searches. About half of all Web searches in the world are performed with Google, which has been translated into 86 languages. The big reason for the success? *It works.* Not only does Google dramatically speed the process of finding things in the vast storehouse of the Web, but its power encourages people to make searches they previously wouldn't have bothered with. Getting the skinny from Google is so common that the company name has become a verb. The usage has even been anointed by an instantly renowned New Yorker cartoon, where a barfly admits to a friend that "I can't explain it—it's just a funny feeling I'm being Googled."

And when you're Googled, it matters what the results are, since it's the modern version of the Encyclopaedia Britannica, the Yellow Pages and the Social Register, all rolled up in one.

Google's uses are limited only by the imaginations of those who punch in 150 million searches a day. *What* they search for is fascinating: at the reception area at Google, a scrolling, real-time selection of queries (filtered to remove sex-related items) is projected on a bare wall, a temperature probe of what the world wants to know. The company also provides a more methodical analysis with its Google Zeitgeist, posted every week on the site: a top 10 list of rising and falling queries. (Best way to hit the charts? Drop dead. Last month millions posthumously Googled James Coburn and obscure stuntman Merlin Santana.)

Even more interesting is *how* people search. By empowering the masses to make use of the multi-terabit glory of the Web, Google has made supersleuths of us all. Privacy advocates are going crazy at the Pentagon's plan to track citizens' purchases, Web-site visits and phone calls. But as my search for the eBay seller indi-

How Do They Find It So Fast?

In less than half a second, Google will deliver frighteningly accurate information. Here's what happens when you type in a query.

1. **WEB SERVER** Thousands of machines will work on your quest. But when you enter a query on google.com, one computer tracks your search and guides it through the process.

2. **INDEX SERVERS** The query then comes here, a concordance of all the pages on the Web, similar to a book index. The servers look for matches, then determine relevance by complicated rules.

3. **DOCUMENT SERVERS** The matches are sent here, where all the documents on the Web are compressed and stored. "Snippets" of the pages are extracted.

4. **BACK TO YOU** The snippets are sent back to your guide, the Web server, which compiles them into an ordered list of results. Click on the link to go to the matching page.

• **CRAWLING** Every month, Googlebots—special surfing computers—methodically visit all 3 billion (and growing) pages on the Web, grabbing the information to be sorted by the index servers and stored on the document servers. Other bots scan frequently updated sites daily.

• **ADVANCED GOOGLING** Don't stop with simple Web searches. You can also look for images, or scan decades' worth of Internet bulletin-board postings. You can install the Google Toolbar, which puts searching power right on your browser. Type in an address and get a map. Type in a name and state and get a phone number; type in an area code and phone number and get an address.

cates, with Google everybody is Big Brother.

In the singles world, for instance, "Google dating"—running prospective beaus through the search engine—is now standard practice. If the facts about a suitor stack up, then you can not only go on the date with confidence, but you know what to talk about. "If I find out he's a runner, for instance, that's something I know we have in common, and I'll say that I'm a runner, too," says Krissy Goetz, a 24-year-old interactive designer in New York City. The first thing a Google virgin attempts is the often humbling experience of typing one's own name into the query line. The next search is inevitable—a Google dragnet to determine the fate of old flames. A Nobel Prize awaits the theorist who determines a formula that calculates the number of minutes one can use Google before excavating the wreckage of sunken relationships. "It's comforting to know what they've been up to," says Gavin MacDonald, 29, who's checked up on four of his former sweethearts.

For researchers, of course, Google is a dream tool. "I can't imagine writing a nonfiction book without it," says author Steven Johnson. Some even wonder if Google might be too much of a good thing. "I use it myself, every day," says Joe Janes, assistant professor in the information school of the University of Washington. "But I worry about how over reliance on it might affect the skill-set of librarians."

New uses emerge almost as quickly as the typical 0.3 seconds it takes to get Google results. People find long-lost relatives, recall old song lyrics and locate parts for old MGs. College instructors sniffing for plagiarism type in suspiciously accomplished phrases from the papers of otherwise inarticulate students. Computer programmers type in error-code numbers to find out which Windows function crashed their program. Google can even save your life. When Terry Chilton, of Plattsburgh, N.Y., felt a pressure in his chest one morning, he Googled heart attacks, and quickly was directed to a detailed list of symptoms on the American Heart Association site. "I better get my butt to the hospital," he told himself, and within hours he was in life-saving surgery.

Eleven years ago computer scientist David Gelernter wrote of the emergence of "mirror worlds," computer-based reflections of physical reality that can increase our understanding and mastery of the real world. Google is the ultimate mirror world, reflecting the aggregate brilliance of the World Wide Web, on which is stored everything: cookie-bake results, Weblogs, weather reports and the Constitution. And because Google is now the default means of accessing such information, the contents of Google's world matter very much in the real world.

When Judge Richard Posner wrote a book recently to identify the world's leading intellectuals, he used Google hits as a key criterion. When the Chinese government decided that the Web offered its citizenry an overly intimate view of the world outside its borders, what better way to pull down the shades than to block Google? (Within a week the Chinese changed direction; Google was too useful to withhold.) Companies that do business online have become justifiably obsessed with Google's power. "If you drop down on Google, your business can come to a screeching halt," says Greg Boser of WebGuerilla, an Internet consultancy. And if two clashing egos want to see whose Google is bigger, they need only venture to a Web site like GoogleFight to compare results.

Google was the brainchild of two Stanford graduate students who refused to accept the conventional wisdom that Internet searching was either a solved problem or not very interesting. Larry Page was an all-American type (geek variety) whose dad taught computer science in Lansing, Mich. Sergey Brin, with the dark brooding looks of a chess prodigy, emigrated from Russia at the age of 6: his father was a math professor. Brin and Page, who met as 22-year-old doctoral candidates in computer science in 1995, began with an academic research project that morphed into an experiment on Web searching.

Their big idea was something they called PageRank (named after Larry), which took into account not just the title or text on a Web site but the other sites linked to it. "Our intention of doing the ranking properly was that you should get the site you meant to get," says Page. Basically, the system exploited the dizzyingly complex linking network of the Web itself—and the collective intelligence of the millions who surfed the Web—so that when you searched, you could follow in the pathways of others who were interested in that same information.

When you searched for "New York Yankees" on some other engine, the top results might be crowded with sporting goods stores or books on Sparky Lyle. With Backrub (the system's original name), your first hit would be the Official Yankees Home Page. Brin and Page were so confident they could deliver the eureka! result that in addition to the button that elicits search results, they created a cut-to-the-chase button labeled I'M FEELING LUCKY. Take the dare, and if all goes well, you'll go straight to your most relevant destination.

Their system became a cult favorite among Stanfordites, and more computer power was required. Page and Brin would sit on loading docks and wait for new servers to be delivered to the computer-science department. "Pretty soon, we had 10,000 searches a day," says Page. "And we figured, maybe this is really real."

So in 1998 they sought to fund a company. After a 15-minute pitch, Sun Microsystems cofounder Andy Bechtolscheim wrote a $100,000 check on the spot. It was made out to Google, the new name that the founders had chosen ("Googol" is the mathematical term for the number one followed by a hundred zeros). At that point, Brin and Page figured they'd better incorporate, so they could open a bank account in which to deposit the check. Eventually venture-capital firms signed on, and the start-up took space in a Mountain View office park, which was dubbed the Googleplex.

In some ways, the hang-loose atmosphere echoed other self-indulgent bubble operations: massages for employees, dogs running free, a grand piano in the lobby, Jerry Garcia's former chef cooking lunches and dinners in the on-site Google Cafe. But in other respects, the pair gloried in being cheap. They built their own servers, using disk drives that had been discarded as defective but could be revived by a software transplant. They were extremely careful about hiring. And since Brin believed that you didn't have a real business without black ink, they made sure that Google—in defiance of the dot-com ethic—would quickly make a profit.

Making money allows Google to resist another bubble-related pitfall: a premature IPO. "We don't need it," says CEO Eric Schmidt, a former Sun and Novell exec who joined a year ago. "We are doing very well as a private company."

Since it's free to users, how does Google rake in bucks? License fees from places like Yahoo or AOL. Corporate sales—big operations pay as much as a half-million dollars to use Google technology to search their own information. And for as little as $20,000, moderate enterprises can buy Google in a Box, a pizza-size server. But the bulk of the company's revenues (estimated at $100 million this year, and growing at a 100 percent rate) come from the much-maligned category of advertising.

Every Web site insists that its ads provide welcome information, but Google can actually say this with a straight face. "We believe ads have to be relevant to what the user is looking for," says Brin. Advertisers buy words associated with given searches: for a fixed fee (which can reach six figures), they can run campaigns to place a couple of lines on top of the results. And with its AdWords program, Google auctions text-based ads that sit to the right of the results. These "sponsored links" are clearly labeled and limited to eight per page, with no intrusive graphics, banners or pop-ups. "We value our white space on the page very highly," says Google exec Sheryl Sandberg.

Held sacrosanct are the actual search results—they can't be bought. "We take a blood oath on that issue," says Schmidt. But in a small number of cases, Google does mess with the results. It tries to identify and block results from hard-core-porn sites. It has removed certain links that the Church of Scientology contends are in violation of its intellectual-property rights. In its foreign-language versions, Google will follow the local laws, removing, for instance, Holocaust-denial sites. Some people find this censoring worrisome, as they view Google as an infallible reporter of everything on the Web, good and bad.

Google's leaders know that their importance often puts them in risky territory. "Every possible contentious political issue comes up at Google," says Brin. Generally, they go for openness, though they realize that privacy takes a hit when anyone can browse through your life in half a second. Page figures folk will simply adjust: "People are starting to realize, because Google exists, that when you publish something online, it might be associated with you forever."

"Google is a fabulously important central resource, and bears something of a unique responsibility," says Ben Edelman, who co-conducted a Harvard study that revealed 113 objectionable sites missing from foreign-based Google searches. Google agrees, but thinks that the marketplace will take care of the problem. "Every Google query is by choice," says Eric Schmidt. "Our competitors are only a click away."

Indeed, now that Google has revitalized the world of Internet searching, a new wave of slick rivals has emerged. But as of now, AlltheWeb and Teoma have yet to become verbs. And the ultimate competitor, Microsoft, thinks that Google, despite its denials, really wants to be a portal. "The next step in their life cycle is parlaying all the traffic they get into opportunities," says Yusef Medhi, head of Microsoft Network. "And that's where it gets tricky."

Sergey Brin and Larry Page, however, insist that they will maintain their focus. Indeed, Google's main efforts have been in collecting more information to search, and providing new ways to do it. The home page now includes a means to search the Web for images, and there's also a Google dictionary and a Google phone book. If your results are in a foreign language, Google will translate for you. Coming next are special searches for products and quotations.

A recent triumph is Google News, which scours news sites for up-the-the-minute stories, automatically arranging them into a Web page similar to those posted by CNN or Yahoo. Journalism pundits bemoaned how "a computer" could emulate flesh-and-blood editors, but they missed the point. Like all of the company's products, Google News is not about computers making lists, but formulas that extract the combined judgment of human beings posting information to the Internet.

From the office Brin and Page share—a warren crammed with toy cars, kites, hockey sticks and, of course, computer screens dominating their door-on-sawhorse desks—the cofounders dream up even wilder plans. "The ultimate search engine would be smart; it would understand everything in the world," says Page.

"I view Google as a way to augment your brain with the knowledge of the world," says Brin. "It will be included in your brain."

So you have a funny feeling you're being Googled? Get used to it.

UNIT 5

Societal Institutions: Law and Politics

Unit Selections

23. **Bad Documents Can Kill You**, Valli Baldassano and Roy Speed
24. **The Digital Dilemma**, Randall Davis
25. **The Control of Ideas**, George Scialabba
26. **Democracy in an IT-Framed Society**, Åke Grönlund
27. **Should Democracy Online Be Quick, Strong, or Thin?** Joachim Aström
28. **As Goes Software...**, *The Economist*
29. **Governing the Internet**, Zoë Baird

Key Points to Consider

- The overview to this unit mentions that civil institutions were overlooked in the excitement after the collapse of the former Soviet Union. On the Internet find and read Francis Fukuyama's essay, "The End of History." Do you agree with his arguments? Does computing have any role to play in the development of civil institutions?
- Napster and its descendents have been much in the news lately? Do you agree with the recording industry position that downloading music is copyright infringement? Why or why not?
- What parts of the Internet are necessary to regulate? Who should regulate them? Defend your choice.
- At least one state has replaced polling places with mail-in voting. The next step would be to replace mail-in voting with the Internet. How would this affect democracy in the United States?

Links: www.dushkin.com/online/
These sites are annotated in the World Wide Web pages.

ACLU: American Civil Liberties Union
http://www.aclu.org

Information Warfare and U.S. Critical Infrastructure
http://www.twurled-world.com/Infowar/Update3/cover.htm

Issues in Telecommunications and Democracy
http://www.benton.org/publibary/workingpapers/working8.html

Living in the Electronic Village
http://www.rileyis.com/publications/phase1/usa.htm

Patrolling the Empire
http://www.csrp.org/patrol.htm

United States Patent and Trademark Office
http://www.uspto.gov/

World Intellectual Property Organization
http://www.wipo.org/

After the collapse of the former Soviet Union, many Americans believed that democracy and a market economy would develop in short order. Many commentators seemed to have taken a cue from Francis Fukuyama's imposingly entitled essay, "The End of History," that appeared in *The National Interest* in 1989. "What we may be witnessing," he wrote, is "not just the end of the Cold War, or the passing of a particular period of post-war history, but... the universalization of Western liberal democracy as the final form of human government." Fukuyama, deputy director of the State Department's planning staff in the elder Bush administration, hedged a bit. He was careful to argue that the victory of liberal capitalism "has occurred primarily in the realm of ideas or consciousness and is as yet incomplete in the real or material world."

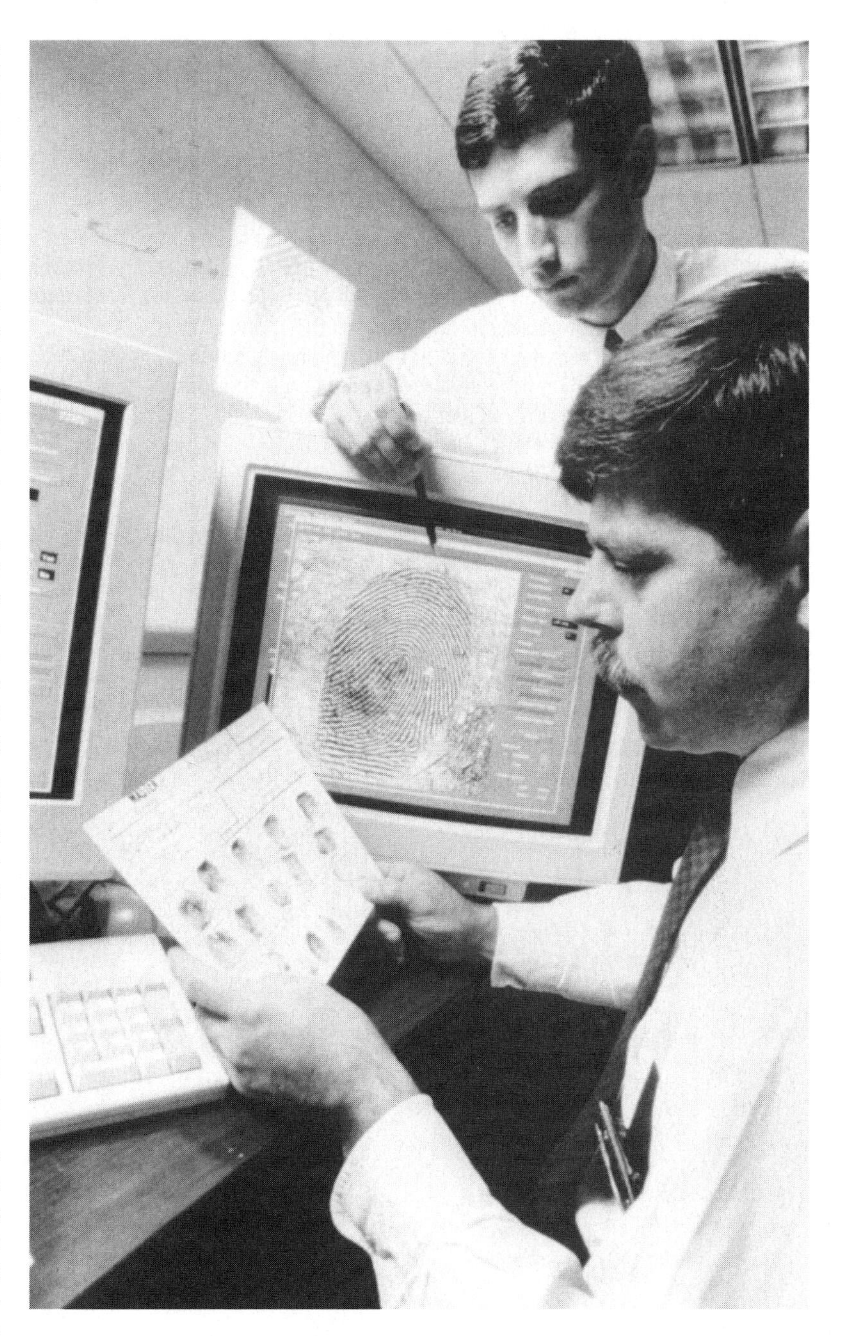

We have grown wiser since those heady times. The events of September 11 showed Americans, in the most brutal fashion, that not everyone shares their values. More importantly, the political and economic chaos that has been so much a part of Russian life for the past decade, has led many commentators to conclude that liberal democracy and a market economy require more than a presence in "the realm of ideas or consciousness." They need, above all else, institutions that govern political and economic relationships. They require mechanisms for business contracts and land use, courts to adjudicate disputes, government agencies to record titles and regulate resources, and not just a mechanism but a tradition of representative government. In a phrase, democracy and a market economy require the institutions of civil society.

The United States and Western Europe have long traditions of civil society, in some cases reaching back hundreds of years. The French sociologist, Emile Durkheim (1858–1917), hoped that as traditional societies gave way to urban industrial societies, rule by contract and law would provide the glue for social cohesion. To a very large extent this has been the case in the United States. The room in which I am writing is part of a house that sits on a small piece of property that belongs to me. I am confident that my title to this property is part of the public record. Were someone to appear on my doorstep with a claim to my property, a procedure exists to adjudicate our dispute. If I do not personally understand the rule, I can hire a lawyer, a specialist in civil procedures, to make my case before an independent judiciary.

But the rapid introduction of information technology over the past decade has proven problematic for the orderly resolution of disputes. It has been difficult for legislators to formulate laws for a set of relationships—those mediated by a computer—that are not well understood. Even if laws are successfully enacted, their existence does not guarantee compliance, especially in the absence of an enforcement mechanism. For instance, several states have passed legislation to restrict unwanted e-mail. Yet, as long as spammers are able to conceal their identities and make use of freely available e-mail accounts, stopping this contemporary plague seems unlikely.

Perhaps just important as law for the maintenance of civil society are institutional procedures, that set of rules and customs that describe the corporate culture of a business, university, or government agency. Institutions have been unable to keep up with the procedural changes that technology has forced upon them. Valli Baldassano and Roy Speed point out some of the consequences in "Bad Documents Can Kill You." More and more frequently, companies are in court trying to defend themselves against their own employees' e-mail. This is not because companies somehow find themselves with a generation of intemperate workers on the payroll. As Speed and Baldassano point out, American employees have been writing incriminating memos for a long time. But with e-mail, anger is more serious. The record is permanent, may be mass-distributed, and might have been hastily and inattentively written.

The mechanisms to resolve my dispute with someone who claims title to my property are ancient, having derived from English Common Law. Digital property changes everything, as Randall Davis notes in "The Digital Dilemma." Digital property may be perfectly copied and widely distributed, as the music industry discovered when Napster appeared on the scene. U.S. intellectual property law has evolved over the past 200 years to balance the interest of society in encouraging the production of intellectual property with its interest in encouraging its diffusion. "The evolving information infrastructure presents a leap in technology that upsets the current balance," says Davis.

George Scialabba, in "The Control of Ideas," takes a darker view. Echoing the most famous political tract of all time, *The Communist Manifesto,* he writes that "A specter is haunting culture: the specter of intellectual-property law." Developments in copyright law, he argues, are shifting the balance toward ownership and away from the public good, far away from what our Constitution's framers had in mind when they wrote: "The Congress shall have Power... to promote the Progress of Science and useful Arts, by securing for limited Times to Authors and Inventors the exclusive Right to their respective writings and Discoveries."

That other arena of civil society, essential because it gives legitimacy to laws enacted by governments, is representative democracy. The ACM is the world's largest and oldest society of computing professionals. In January, 2001, it devoted its flagship journal, *Communications of the ACM,* to the relationship between technology and democracy. Two of the articles are included here, "Democracy in an IT-Framed Society," by Åke Grönlund. and "Should Democracy Online Be Quick, Strong, or Thin?," by Joachim Åström.

The final two articles in this unit are about governance of another kind of institution, the Internet itself. The first, "As Goes Software... " from the English newsweekly, *The Economist,* begins with these ominous words: "Let software, disappear, and life as we know it would break down." To keep it running, the Internet has evolved a governing structure that is akin to a council of elders. *The Economist* argues that governments should support this structure rather than "allowing a small handful of firms to become the not-so-benevolent dictators"

In the final article, "Governing the Internet," Zoë Baird takes a different approach: "A reliance on markets and self-policing has failed to address adequately the important interests of Internet users such as privacy protection, security, and access to diverse content." She says that since the Internet has become mainstream, "mainstream governmental institutions will be expected to step in to protect people from harm and encourage innovation." What shall it be? Normal market mechanisms that work efficiently but have a tendency to monopoly control, governments that have legitimacy but can stifle innovation, or computer professionals who know their creation but may have their own agendas?

Bad Documents Can Kill You

In court, every memo and e-mail is fair game.

By Valli Baldassano and Roy Speed

With increasing frequency, companies that land in court are finding that Exhibit A against them is their own employees' written correspondence. Such evidence may consist of memos, letters, or reports; in more and more cases, the starring role is played by e-mail. Damaging correspondence can come from virtually any employee—even the CEO or the chairman, as in the Microsoft antitrust case: Bill Gates's own e-mail messages, dating as far back as 1992, contradicted his spoken testimony gain and again, leaving his credibility shredded in the eyes of the judge.

"Bad documents" are the corporate lawyer's worst nightmare. They're memos, reports, or e-mail in which employees have been discussing issues related to a particular case and, in the process, committing to writing things that undermine either the lawyer's own theory of the case or the company's credibility. Such documents constitute buried treasure for prosecutors and plaintiffs' attorneys, who now routinely use subpoenas or document requests to cast a wide net, hoping for a rich haul. The government's antitrust investigation of Microsoft may be an extreme example: It's reported that the company turned over to the government close to 30 million documents—mostly e-mail.

Bad documents represent a costly problem, and helping companies prevent their appearance poses an increasingly urgent challenge. This challenge can't be dismissed as merely helping criminals cover their tracks. Litigation is a dirty game, and these days what makes a document "bad" is not that it is incriminating but, rather, that in the hand of a plaintiff's attorney it can be made to *seem* incriminating—regardless of whether any mistakes or wrongdoing actually took place.

The stakes are high. Corporate lawyers faced with bad documents are continually making calculations that run something like this:

Our product was definitely not at fault here, and we can prove it, with reams of product testing all on our side. The problem we'll run into is this memo from a service manager—he was just unhappy with being blamed for a service mishap, but he sounds like he's saying the product is defective. The truth is that he was just letting off a little steam, but the plaintiff's attorney will have a field day with this.

Even worse is a hard copy of the damaging memo containing handwritten notes by the regional manager. In the margin, she writes: "We have to quell this matter, and fast." What she meant was "resolve this misunderstanding"—that is, refocus everyone on our customers' needs and get back to business—but the plaintiff's attorney will claim that her words are evidence of a conspiracy to silence a whistle-blower.

A jury will find this kind of shrill argument a lot more compelling than our test results showing the safety of the product. We don't really have any choice: We have to settle.

An otherwise-defensible argument, in other words, can be rendered untenable by bad documents. And once the word gets out that a case has uncovered a lode of bad documents, it often has the effect of blood in the water: In short order, more suits are filed and the same documents requested. In some cases, companies have abandoned products that took years of research and millions of dollars to develop—not because the products were defective but, rather, because the company's own bad documents mobilized litigants.

Not by Policy Alone

To protect themselves from bad documents, many U.S. companies are taking action, looking for ways to shore up their defenses. In most companies, such efforts are being spearheaded by lawyers, both in-house and outside counsel, and their idea of erecting castle walls is almost always the same: Revise the company's e-mail policy. Such revisions usually boil down to three principal recommendations:

Appropriate use of e-mail. *Be professional,* the guidelines say. *No sexual jokes, please, and no personal use of e-mail—stick to business matters.*

Writing do's and don'ts. *Use correct grammar and punctuation,* the guidelines say, *and, above all, be more careful with what you say. Say what you mean to say, and ask yourself whether you'd enjoy reading what you've written in* The New York Times.

Document retention. Some employees have been found hoarding ancient e-mail, so in the new guidelines excessive saving is verboten. On the other hand, they also warn against selective purging: *If you hear that we're being sued, please don't go purging the files and wiping the backup drives—judges don't like it, and for good reason.*

Now, these are all good recommendations, but are they enough? Do they add up to protection from bad documents?

Such efforts are, for the most part, the result of shallow thinking about the nature of the bad-documents issue. Left to their own devices, lawyers tend to define it as a policy-writing challenge: They exaggerate in their own minds the power of mere words to make a problem go away. A multitude of articles reinforcing this assumption have appeared over the last few years: one lawyer, Michael R. Overly, has written a book that embodies this view, called *E-Policy* (AMACOM). The book's subtitle is revealing: *How to Develop Computer, E-mail, and Internet Guidelines to Protect Your Company and Its Assets.* Note the critical assumption: the belief in the power of policy prescription alone to protect company assets.

Then there's the technology angle: Sensing that their castle walls are riddled with holes, some lawyers are teaming up with information-technology consultants and vendors. These IT folks are eager to define the bad-documents problem—along with abuse of Internet privileges, etc.—as a *software* challenge. What's their silver bullet? They propose software applications designed to ferret out employees who are using company e-mail to swap pornography, or to block all messages containing certain objectionable words. It should come as no surprise that the preface to Overly's *E-Policy* is written by the president of such a firm.

Now, this kind of software is fine, as far as it goes, but how far is that? Could software have detected in Bill Gates' e-mail correspondence his hostile tone when discussing Netscape—and perhaps flagged such words as *anti-competitive?*

Or take the hypothetical example above, where the corporate lawyer decides to settle rather than go to trial, because a trial would showcase his company's bad documents. Could software have prevented this outcome? Could software have determined that the words *quell this matter* would be susceptible to misinterpretation? Could software have suggested the less-inflammatory wording *resolve this misunderstanding?* We suspect that for complex writing choices, software would work about as well as the blundering grammar-checker that comes with your word processor.

What's going on here is probably a version of the old saw: *If the only tool you're comfortable with is a hammer, everything begins to look like a nail.* Lawyers are comfortable with writing policy/guidelines/law, so they view bad documents as a policy-writing challenge. The IT guys are comfortable with computers, so it looks to them like a software challenge.

To sum up: Current efforts may succeed in reducing the amount of pornography-swapping or sexually abusive e-mail crisscrossing company networks, but they won't really prevent employees' producing bad documents of the nonsexual variety, nor will they significantly reduce the kind of legal or regulatory exposure that results from such documents.

Don't Blame E-Mail

The role of e-mail in litigation has received a lot of press in recent years, and journalists in the popular and business presses have just about convinced most of us that 1) the problem is new, and 2) the root cause is a new medium—i.e., e-mail. Wrong on both counts.

E-mail has not brought us a new problem; rather, it has amplified an old one.

American employees have been prolific writers of bad documents for decades: Long before the advent of e-mail, thousands of cases were lost or settled out of court because of bad documents, and they came in the form of old-fashioned, hard-copy memos, letters, or reports, and even hand-scribbled notes. E-mail, in other words, has not brought us a new problem; it has merely amplified an old problem—and for three reasons:

Haste and inattention. With formal memos and letters, we were more guarded. With e-mail, for whatever reason, we tend to let our hair down—with the result that we now routinely commit to writing things that, in hindsight, seem reckless.

High volume. E-mail has increased the likelihood of bad documents due to the sheer volume and proliferation of e-mail messages: They're easier to fire off, for one thing, and any message can be forwarded—perhaps to the wrong party—with a couple of mouse clicks. Other reasons for the high volume: 1) Information once transmitted by phone or fax is now often sent via e-mail: 2) e-mail is steadily encroaching on what used to be the exclusive domain of formal letters and memos. We are even seeing increasing volumes of sensitive customer correspondence moving to e-mail.

Permanence. Contrary to expectations, e-mail has proven to be more durable than hard copy, lingering on forgotten backup drives long after its useful life. (If you have any doubt about this, just recall Bill Gates being forced to read aloud e-mail he wrote in 1992.)

It stands to reason, however, that if bad documents existed before e-mail—and if, even today, bad documents exist in forms other than e-mail—then e-mail cannot be their root cause. So what, in fact, is their cause, and what is the best plan of attack?

First of all: Once bad documents are created, detecting them is difficult and uncertain. Accordingly, the only ap-

The Legacy Of Our Schools

The roots of bad documents are deep, going all the way back to our schooling. The approach to writing promoted in American primary and secondary schools—what we call "writer-centric writing"—leaves all of us prone to creating bad documents.

In American schools and universities, writing is an activity that is fundamentally about self-expression—we learn to view writing primarily as a means of discovering and presenting to the world our thoughts, our feelings, our discoveries. Students come away believing that the true purpose of writing is self-realization (and sometimes self-glorification). Granted, students often must write to prove to teachers how much they know, but even then, the focus is on the writer. In the academic mode, the writer is always paramount, the center of the writing universe. The reader is basically irrelevant to the whole exercise—at most a bystander, a witness, or, in the case of the teacher, a grade-giver.

This focus on the writer, by the way, partly explains why, when we describe a piece of writing as academic in approach, we mean the opposite of inspiring, relevant, or practical—it leaves us (the reader) out of the picture and so leaves us cold.

When we arrive in the business world, it slowly dawns on us that something's wrong—that the way we learned to write in school is of little help in our jobs. The writer-oriented approach, as it turns out, is a poor fit with the demands of business, because in business, writing is all about the readers. An employee writes precisely because she needs to have a specific effect on readers—needs to inform them, move them to act, prevent a wrong action. Consider a simple example:

Suppose my staffers have been showing up late for meetings. To address this situation, I write a memo to them. Implicit in the act of writing is the real-world result that I need—i.e., that they start showing up on time. In fact, what determines the memo's success or failure is whether the desired result actually occurs.

Considerations of "style" or "creativity" are either secondary or altogether beside the point. Here's the thing that businesspeople must take to heart: To write effective business correspondence, you must know—before you write—the specific results and reader responses you are targeting. Then write precisely those things that will produce the desired response or result.

It is quite possible, however, to be on the job for years without having anyone explain this to you. As a result, most of us wander through our business careers with a muddy sense of purpose and the wrong writing equipment—like basketball players wandering onto the court with baseball bats and catchers' mitts, wondering where home plate might be. We know intuitively that something's wrong, but nobody else is complaining; so over time we adjust, we adapt, we do our best. But we're doing the work of business with writing tools that aren't up to the job.

In short, we don't really think before we write; our idea of thinking before we write is staring at a blank computer screen until we think of something to say. The way most Americans write is really the opposite of strategy—a kind of glorified shooting-from-the-hip. The results are the American love affair with e-mail—a shoot-from-the-hip medium—and the occasional bad document.

—V.B. and R.S.

proach with any promise—the only real protection from bad documents—is to *prevent their creation in the first place.* And that means looking at how they're created. As it turns out, bad documents have their roots deep inside each employee's writing habits (see "The Legacy of Our Schools")—the way we Americans write, the way we approach the task of writing itself, and the way we manage documents once they're written.

There is, in other words, no silver bullet. If you want protection from bad documents, you're going to have to change key employee behaviors, a challenge far more daunting than revising e-mail policy or installing software. It is, moreover, a challenge to which most lawyers—even in-house counsel—are unaccustomed.

The Continuing Appeal Of the Superfluous

Over the past several years, we have examined hundreds of bad documents in several different industries, and it is almost always possible to identify the specific remarks that transform a routine piece of correspondence into a bad document. Excise those remarks and—presto!—no bad document.

In addition, employees are betrayed into writing such remarks under two basic conditions:

They have a false sense of security. That is, they are blithely unaware of the sensitivity of their subject, or they nurture illusions about the privacy of their communication. They tend to produce bad documents whenever they lack what you might think of as a healthy, informed paranoia about their business environment.

They are off purpose. That is, when they are *not* in direct pursuit of a tangible business result that would constitute a legitimate reason for writing. All too often, in other words, what transforms an ordinary memo or e-mail into a bad document are things like:

- The offhand or sarcastic remark: "We should include our new seda-

The Usual Suspects

Plaintiffs' lawyers often build a case these days using bad documents to weave a web of inferences. They know from experience that if they can just string together a sufficient quantity of suspicious-sounding items—even if each inference, taken individually, is gossamer—jurors will believe they're looking at a solid case, a smoking gun.

To defend themselves against this practice, employees and corporations must identify precisely the kinds of items that a plaintiff's attorney, when sifting through company correspondence, would find "juicy." Employees must become so familiar with these items that alarm bells sound in their heads whenever they see one—in their own writing or in someone else's. A few examples:

Strong language. Have you used language that—whether you intended it or not—could be inflammatory? Have you used language that implies fault or error, when fault or error has yet to be determined? Part of the problem with inflammatory language is that it doesn't always jump off the page at you—justrecall the hypothetical example near the beginning of this article, in which the phrase *quell this matter* becomes evidence of a conspiracy.

Rumors or speculation. Passing rumors in conversation is bad enough; committing them to writing is foolish—an instant bad document. The same goes for idle speculation: It is critical that in our writing we distinguish *what we know* from *what we think.* Even more dangerous: any kind of speculation about the legal risks or regulatory impact of what you're discussing/doing/considering doing. Legal adversaries will use such speculation to claim that you knew what you were doing and had weighed the consequences.

Commenting on someone else's area of expertise. Suppose you're in marketing and therefore focused on revenues and profits. It's dangerous to hazard an opinion about matters like product safety—e.g., correct use of the product, dosages, expiration dates, etc. The problem: Regardless of what you say—and regardless of whether you have any responsibility or expertise regarding the issue you're commenting on—plaintiffs' lawyers can claim that such remarks show the company weighing decisions about customers' safety based on marketing considerations.

Internal disputes. More and more correspondence represents a single entry—or one voice among many—in an ongoing internal discussion of sensitive corporate issues. E-mail has contributed to the growth of this phenomenon.

More and more teams comprise people in different functions, in different offices, in different time zones, even on different continents; and such circumstances make it virtually impossible to hold frequent face-to-face meetings. Even conference calls can prove difficult to arrange. It may be impossible to convene all members at the same time. Such teams find it tempting to carry on lengthy and complex e-mail "conversations," with each writer cc'ing his remarks to the entire group.

This practice can be exceedingly dangerous if the group is dealing with sensitive issues—working out the company's response to a looming crisis, for example. Employees need to be able to air differing ideas and try different approaches, most of which will prove unworkable and be abandoned. But if a document request turns up such an exchange, even the approaches that were abandoned become "evidence."

—V.B. and R.S.

tive in every 9-year-old's juice box.... "

- The idle speculation: "I wonder whether this would infringe so-and-so's patent.... "
- The angry or resentful outburst: "There is absolutely no communication in this company—NONE. I wouldn't blame the customer for writing us off—all of us—as a bunch of incompetent morons.... "
- The idle comment on someone else's area of expertise—as when a salesperson writes, "We should just change all the expiration dates, extend the product life for another month or so. We'd save millions in expired inventory.... "

We catalog such remarks under the rubric of "the usual suspects" (see sidebar); what they all have in common is that, strictly speaking, they are superfluous. In other words, they are not needed to bring about the specific business results targeted in the correspondence.

Changing Everyday Behavior

Altering deeply ingrained behaviors is, first of all, a challenge that is easy to underestimate. Closely examine any single behavior, and you will likely find that it comprises a rat's nest of beliefs, values, skills, and customs. What we're addressing in this instance, moreover, is not a single behavior but, rather, the complex set of behaviors that we call "writing." You can't uproot and utterly supplant an entire set of such behaviors by having employees watch a video or sit through a briefing.

Second, we know from experience that writing habits in particular are seldom changed without altering managers' duties and accountability. If the desired behaviors are not required and routinely reinforced by managers at all levels, the desired changes simply will not occur.

Now, let's consider the plight of U.S. companies highly vulnerable to litigation or regulatory action—what are their options?

We believe that the leaders of such companies must start by making a difficult determination: whether changing the critical behaviors is worth the expense.

After all, the employee behaviors that need to be changed are deeply entrenched; and if the risk of litigation is relatively small, it may be cheaper, in the long run, to simply take your hits—settle a lawsuit from time to time purely because the plaintiffs got their hands on some of our bad documents.

On the other hand, for some companies litigation is both frequent and potentially devastating, and inaction therefore may not be an option.

Preventing Bad Documents: A Plan of Action

Two elements are critical for companies that are especially vulnerable to bad documents and absolutely must prevent them:

Employee Training. The purpose of the training would be to give employees new approaches to their day-to-day writing tasks. To be successful, the training would have to provide:

- Insight. Employees must see the landscape for what it is: a litigation and regulatory minefield. In addition, they must become conscious of their own writing habits and the ways that an ill-considered writing process can spawn bad documents.
- Policy review. The company guidelines must be not only reviewed but presented in a way that relates directly to employees' day-to-day activities.
- New skills and tools. The training must get beyond writing "tips" and hollow advice (e.g., *Always say what you mean.).* Employees need a new writing process and a new set of tools to work with. The writing toolkit must, in our view, equip employees to do two things: Think before they write (it's not as easy as it sounds) and restrict their writing to what needs to be said to achieve the desired results.
- Opportunities to practice. The training must provide realistic, case-study-type exercises that 1) are specific to the company, and 2) require employees to try out the new tools and approaches.
- Follow-up. A single training session is never adequate to change deeply ingrained behaviors. Several weeks after the initial training, employees must undergo some kind of follow-up session designed to check their progress with the new tools, give additional practice, and move everyone a step closer to proficiency in the new skills.

Managerial reinforcement. Any company that wants to prevent the production of bad documents must redefine its managers' duties to include rigorous enforcement of the tools and approaches promoted in the training. It is not necessary that managers review every single document; it *is* necessary that whenever they are reviewing the work of a subordinate, they reinforce the key principles and tools.

Equally important, when a bad document does arise from a given department, the managers responsible for that department must be held accountable.

In many companies, such accountability would represent a radical departure. Here's a phenomenon we've seen in a number of companies: A manager is cc'd on an ill-considered e-mail exchange, i.e., the participants are discussing sensitive matters, and doing so in a careless fashion, yet the manager does nothing to shut down the discussion. The reason: Shutting down risky discussion—and preventing bad documents—has never been part of the manager's job definition.

What's needed: a radically new approach to writing everyday correspondence.

The most common view, in fact, is the notion that bad documents are unpredictable and unpreventable—an inevitable cost of doing business. But the contrary is true: The causes of bad documents are definitely discoverable, and bad documents themselves are indeed preventable.

Even so, actually preventing them requires a comprehensive strategy and no small measure of commitment. What's more, it requires a radically new approach to writing everyday correspondence—like that memo you drafted this morning. Or the e-mail you fired off just a few minutes ago.

VALLI BALDASSANO is a former assistant U.S. attorney and prosecutor of white-collar crime and healthcare fraud. She is now the director of global compliance for Pharmacia Corp. in Peapack, N.J. ROY SPEED is president of Salient Inc., a Bethel, Conn.-based consultancy that designs solutions to complex business-writing challenges.

THE DIGITAL DILEMMA

How intellectual property laws might embrace the apparently paradoxical goals of motivating individual creation and preserving the ultimate benefits of that creation for the common good.

RANDALL DAVIS

The combination of technologies making up the information infrastructure—information in digital form, computer networks, and the Web—is accompanied by contradictory powers and promises. For intellectual property in particular, it promises more—quantity, quality, access, and markets—while simultaneously imperiling the rewards of those who create and publish it. It is at once a remarkably powerful medium for publishing and distributing information and the world's largest reproduction facility, running unchecked in practice, if not in statute. It is a set of technologies that can improve access to information enormously, yet can inhibit access in ways never before practical.

This set of technologies has arrived in a world in which our existing laws, policies, and practices governing intellectual property depend on subtle, surprisingly complex, and at times conflicting elements of law, public policy, economics, and technology. These elements are in relative balance today but may well be thrown out of balance by the transformations resulting from the information infrastructure.

One core of the problem is illustrated simply. A printed book can be read by one or perhaps two people at once, as long as they're located in the same place as the book. But make the same text available in electronic form, and there is almost no technological limit to the number of people who can access it simultaneously from almost anywhere on earth. At first glance, this is wonderful news for the information consumer and for society; the electronic holdings of libraries (and friends) around the world can be available 24 hours a day, year-round, and would never be checked out. These same advances in technology create new opportunities and new markets for publishers.

There is also a more troublesome side. Publishers and authors wonder how many copies of the work will be sold (or licensed) if networks make possible planetwide access? Their nightmare is that the number is one. How many books (or movies, photographs, or musical pieces) will be created and published online if the entire market might be extinguished by the sale of the first electronic copy?

The consumer nightmare, on the other hand, is that the authors' and publishers' attempt to preserve the traditional marketplace leads to technical and legal protections that sharply reduce access to our common intellectual and cultural heritage—resources long viewed as crucial to democracy and to science.

The information infrastructure thus has the potential to demolish the careful balancing of public good and private interest that has emerged from the evolution of U.S. intellectual property law over the past 200 years. The public good is the betterment of society resulting from the constitutional mandate to promote the "progress of science and the useful arts"; the private interest is served by the time-limited monopoly (a copyright or patent) given to one who has made a contribution to that progress. The challenge is in striking and maintaining the balance, thus offering enough control to motivate authors, inventors, and publishers, but not so much control as to threaten important public policy goals, such as preserving the nation's cultural heritage, providing broad access to information, and promoting education, science, and scholarship. As usual, the devil is in the details, and the past 200 years of intellectual property history have seen a largely successful, albeit evolving, balancing of these details. The evolving information infrastructure presents a leap in technology that upsets the current balance, forcing us to rethink many of our fundamental premises and practices.

The stakes are high, both economically and in social terms. Decisions we make today will determine who benefits from the technology and who has access to what information and on what terms—foundational elements of our future society.

It was in this context that in 1997 the U.S. National Service Foundation, prompted by a recommendation by the Federal Networking Council Advisory Committee, commissioned a study of the issues by the Computer Science and Telecommunications Board of the National Academies. The report, called *The Digital Dilemma: Intellectual Property in the Information Age,* published by the National Academy Press in February 2000, is the focus of this article.

Origins of the Problem

The difficulties we all face today arise primarily from two sources. One is a trio of technological advances that helped produce the infrastructure: the increasing use of digital information; the widespread reach of computer networks; and the creation of the Web. The second is the emergence of computers as a routine part of everyday life. These two developments have fundamentally altered the landscape, and their consequences present significant challenges.

Information in digital form. Information in digital form is orders-of-magnitude easier, faster, and cheaper to reproduce than is information in analog form (for example, hard copy). Digital copies are also perfect, so each one in turn can be the seed for additional perfect copies, quite unlike the situation with traditional media like photocopies.

These properties of digital information are for the most part widely appreciated by those familiar with computers. Somewhat less appreciated is the fact that accessing digital information inevitably means making a copy, even if only an ephemeral one. Such copying is deeply rooted in the way computers work. For example, when you view a Web page, several copies are made automatically, one so the document can be sent from the remote computer to your computer, a second when the document is loaded into memory, and yet another when it is displayed on the screen.

Such copying occurs with all digital information. Use a computer to read a book, look at a picture, watch a movie, or listen to a song, and you inevitably make one or more copies. Contrast this process with the use of traditional media; reading a book does not involve making a copy nor does watching a movie or listening to a song.

This intimate connection between access and copying is significant for intellectual property protection. One essential element of copyright—the right to control reproduction—works as expected in the world of traditional media, where there is an obvious distinction between access and reproduction and where the copyright owner's control of reproduction provides just that—control of reproduction. But in the digital world, where no access is possible except through copying, complete control of copying means control of access as well, a consequence of considerable importance to all stakeholders.

Networks and the Web. Computer networks have radically changed the economics and logistics of information distribution, enabling information to be sent worldwide almost for free and (for items of reasonable size) almost instantaneously. The Web in turn has radically altered the economics and logistics of publication, allowing everyone to be a publisher with worldwide reach. Where reproduction and distribution put information in the hands of those who know they want it, publication makes people aware of the information that is available, a function the Web performs well. The astonishing variety of documents, opinions, articles, and works of all sorts on the Web demonstrates that millions of people worldwide are making use of this capability.

This trio of technological developments—digital information, computer networks, and the Web—are together the source of profound changes in society. Digital information radically changes the economics and character of reproduction; computer networks radically change the economics and character of distribution; and the Web radically changes the economics and character of publication.

For publishers, these developments have opened up new markets and new product opportunities, including online music and books. But the same developments offer advantages to individuals and pirates making and distributing unauthorized copies; the process is orders of magnitude faster, easier, and less expensive than ever before. The important result is that the natural barriers to infringement have eroded significantly. Where unauthorized reproduction and distribution of hardcopy works is limited in part by the difficulty, expense, and loss of quality inherent in the process, with digital information, perfect copies can be made and distributed almost for free. Stakeholders on all sides of the issue wonder whether something can be put in place to restore the balance of forces or whether the world has changed fundamentally and permanently.

Commonplace technology. The second major source of difficulties in the digital dilemma is the routine presence of computers and the Web in work settings, and increasingly in households as well. Technology found only in research laboratories not long ago is now a widely available consumer product. One consequence is that individuals routinely have the means and opportunity to access and copy vast amounts of digital information, including software, text, and audio and video files, but lack a clear picture of what is legal or ethically acceptable. As a result, they are unprepared to deal with the associated intellectual property issues. Corporations dealing with these issues turn to their legal staffs, but individuals are bewildered, if indeed they are aware of the law at all.

A second consequence of the diffusion of the technology into everyday life is that intellectual property law and its enforcement are increasingly concerned with private behavior. Copyright has traditionally been concerned with public actions and their public consequences, such as public performance, public display, and distribution of copies. It has also focused on the behaviors of organizations and individuals whose actions have large-scale public consequences. But with computers now in hundreds of millions of homes worldwide, individuals can do in private what not long ago would have required substantial investment and perhaps criminal intent. As the potential impact of private behavior has grown, so correspondingly has interest in regulating such behavior. This shift in the focus of intellectual property law represents an important consequence of information technology's emergence into everyday life, thus presenting another social and policy challenge in managing the intellectual property balance.

Consequences of Licensing

One of the many problematic issues raised by the digital dilemma is the increasing use of licensing, rather than sale, as the primary mechanism for distributing information. Licensing is in some respects familiar; mass-market software has long been distributed via a (shrink-wrap) license, giving the purchaser a right to use the software but providing no ownership in it. More recently, a variety of digital information has been licensed, including documents, databases, and images.

There are significant differences between selling a work and licensing it. The sale of a physical copy of a work has been the dominant model for transferring intellectual property to the consumer for more than 200 years and involves the complete transfer of ownership rights in a particular copy of the work. Copyright law explicitly anticipates the sale of intellectual property products and, by its "first-sale" rule, gives the purchaser a significant body of rights with the purchased copy.[1] The purchaser is, for example, free to lend, rent, or resell the purchased copy. In that sense, copyright law follows intellectual property products into the marketplace and promotes the continued dissemination of information.

Licenses, by contrast, are contracts, that is, private agreements providing for limited transfer of rights to use an item. They can involve a range of terms and conditions but, unlike copyright law, need not incorporate any public policy considerations beyond some basic limits on what constitutes an enforceable contract. To the extent that digital information is distributed by license, there is no statute, history, or tradition of incorporating such public policy considerations as "fair use."[2]

Licensing can have advantages for all parties; it can provide clarity on terms and conditions of access, as well as increased rights for the institution beyond those provided under copyright, including the ability to make unlimited copies for local use. Licensing may also increase the options for making information available. For example, a license may grant time-limited access to some part of a book or report, perhaps for far less than the purchase price for the entire work.

But there are also concerns about the effect licensing may have on public access. Consider libraries as the archetypal example. In the print world, a library's failure to renew a subscription or buy an updated version of a book has no effect on the availability to patrons of earlier volumes or editions. In the world of licensed information, however, ending a subscription to an electronic publication may mean the end of access to earlier volumes or editions as well. While some libraries and publishers have worked to negotiate licenses that preserve fair use and other public-access features, concerns remain about the use of a mechanism lacking any of the built-in protections for public access embodied in a copyright law.

Questions also arise about the interaction of licenses and copyright. For example, copyright law today gives owners of copies of computer software the privilege to make backup copies. Can this privilege be taken away by a shrink-wrap license? Can a license term prohibit disclosing flaws to other potential users? These and related questions are far from being resolved.

If licensing becomes the dominant means of distributing information in mass markets, additional concerns arise for works considered part of our common intellectual and social heritage. One could imagine a world in which novels, poems, and paintings are available only (or mostly) by license rather than sale. The consequences for public access of such a world are far from clear.

Finally, the trend toward licensing means that increasing amounts of information are delivered as *experiences,* rather than as artifacts. This is not entirely unfamiliar; where books are information artifacts, first-run movies are information experiences. We have lived with both for some time, but the difference matters. Buy a book and you own it forever; pay for access to a digital book and when the period of service is over you often retain nothing.

Responses to the Dilemma

There are a variety of actions that can be taken in response to the challenges posed by this dilemma. I focus here on four: technological protection mechanisms, innovative business models, taking a broader perspective on the problem, and rethinking the nature of copyright.

Technological solutions. The key technical problem in large-scale management of digital information is determining how to provide access without giving up all control. A variety of clever schemes have been proposed, many relying on a combination of encryption and rights-management software. Encryption encodes information so it can be accessed only with the appropriate key; rights-management software enables fine-grain control of access, specifying such things as the number of accesses permitted and whether the material may be printed.

A common scenario for using encryption involves making it both machine-specific and persistent. Encryption can be made machine-specific by incorporating into the encryption process some reliable property of the decryption/playback device. For a computer, for example, the serial number of the hard drive or CPU might be used. Then, even if both the file and encryption key are passed on to others, the information remains inaccessible because it cannot be decrypted on machines with different identifiers.

But what if the original purchaser decrypts the information and passes it on to others? Persistent encryption tries to prevent this from happening by narrowing as much as possible the window of opportunity during which the decrypted information is available, even to an authorized user. In this approach, information is decrypted just in time, that is, just before it is used, making it available only as briefly as possible, and then only in small chunks at once. It is never stored, even temporarily.

Rights management involves providing some indication of the rights the consumer has purchased; this information is either encrypted along with the content itself or possibly maintained on a separate "rights server" accessed over the Web. Software on the user's machine then controls access to the information, consulting the rights listing to determine whether a requested action is permitted.

Technological solutions can be useful but are limited in a number of important ways. One constraint arises from the need for consumer devices to be simple and fast. In some cases, this fundamental need precludes the use of industrial-strength encryption, which, though nearly impossible to crack, may be too slow for some consumer uses. However, the less-powerful encryption systems used in commercial products (such as the content-scrambling system used to encrypt DVDs) have been cracked.

Second, anchoring content to a specific machine raises an interesting problem for consumers: What happens when you upgrade your computer (or other playback device)? Must you repurchase everything you bought previously?

Finally, there is substantial difficulty in attempting to provide end-to-end protection within a general-purpose computer. PCs have been successful to a significant degree because they have open architectures; that is, components of the machine (such as the hard drive and the video card) are accessible to the consumer. As long as the machine is designed this way, decrypted information can be intercepted and captured as it passes from one place to another inside the machine. Hardware and software designers could make such steps progressively more difficult, but the effort they would have to expend, and the consequential costs for all involved, would be substantial.

Business models. In general, although technology can play a useful role as a deterrent to unauthorized copying, it is far from a panacea. Consider, then, a second possibility: the use of innovative business models. By selecting an appropriate business model, a rights holder can at times significantly influence the pressure for and degree of illegal commercial copying and unauthorized reproduction.

Several general principles offer insight into the sorts of business models that can help. One principle suggests making the product cheaper and easier to buy than to steal. The point is to reduce the motivation to deal with unauthorized sources from the outset. Music provides an example; single tracks can be bought online for 99 cents. But why pay even a dollar for something you might be able to get for free? Because, even with peer-to-peer programs (like Napster and Gnutella), the music isn't really free; there's an investment of time and effort in finding and downloading it. With the informal, all-volunteer effort at the heart of all the file-sharing schemes, the difficulty of finding what you want may be substantial, and the time required to download (from an overloaded personal computer in a dorm room somewhere) may be significant.[3] Would you pay a dollar to avoid the hassle? Quite likely. Hence, even beyond the obvious issues of ethics and legality, the answer to "Why pay?" is: for service, reliability, and speed.

A second general principle suggests reconceptualizing the basic product. As noted, the digital music business may be primarily a service business, rather than a product business. As the value in the digitized music itself becomes increasingly difficult to protect (all digital information is difficult to protect without losing control of it), the value may reside in providing speed, reliability, and ease of access, rather than in artifacts like CDs or tapes.

A third principle is illustrated by writer Stephen King, whose publication *The Plant* appeared online in installments beginning mid-2000 with unrestricted downloading of the installments. King warned, however, that if too few people actually paid for their downloads, the installments would stop coming. This is intellectual property approached not as law, but as economics (pay or it dies) and as sociology ("no stealing from the blind newsboy," in King's elegant description).[4]

These general principles suggest that thinking about the digital information business in innovative ways leads to a number of nontraditional business models. Importantly, each of these models creates an environment in which there is significantly less need for intellectual property protection:

Give away the product; make money from an auxiliary service. The Linux operating system, for example, is given away, yet a number of companies are in the business of providing service, consulting, customization, and extensions to the organizations using it.

Give away the product; sell upgrades. Many antivirus vendors make available free, fully functional versions of the programs on their Web sites.

They give them away in order to sell subscriptions to the regular updates they add to their antivirus databases.

Give away one piece that promotes another. Adobe gives away its Acrobat Reader software to popularize the Acrobat PDF format and to create a market for all its other programs that create PDF files.

Offer extreme customization. Custom CDs with a particular customer's selection of audio tracks are likely to be a less appealing target for reproduction.

Offer a mass-market product at a low price and high volume, along with frequent improvements. Many software products fit in this category. Keeping the price low reduces the pressure for piracy, while constant improvement means the damage from unauthorized reproduction is time-limited.

None of these models solves the problem completely, but each one can sharply reduce the need for intellectual property enforcement.

There is also a more general point here about the relative power of law and business models: Although legal prohibitions against copying are useful against large-scale pirates, they are unlikely to be nearly as effective against individual infringers, where detection and enforcement are problematic. Where such private behavior is concerned, business models may offer a far more effective means of dealing with intellectual property issues.

Multiple perspectives. The problems arising from the interaction of intellectual property and the information infrastructure need to be considered in a context encompassing not only law, technology, and markets, but economics more generally, as well as psychology and public policy.

This multiplicity of views is important in three ways. First, each of them brings a fundamentally different approach and mindset to the problem. As all of them are relevant, there is power in considering each different conception of the problem. Second, some disagreements arise because the positions are grounded in different perspectives (such as law, rather than economics) and are thus, in effect, asking (and answering) different questions. Finally, being aware of the multiplicity of perspectives may open additional routes for dealing with the issues; not every problem needs to be legislated into submission.

Is copy still the right concept? One final response to the digital dilemma asks this fundamental question about intellectual property. All of the preceding discussion accepts a fundamental perspective underlying copyright, namely, copying as a foundational legal and conceptual notion. As the very name of the law indicates, the right to control reproduction is central to copyright. Deciding whether a work has been copied has, as a result, been a fundamental issue underlying much of copyright history and analysis.

But is the notion of copy still an appropriate conceptual framework in the age of digital information? Two reasons suggest it might not be. One, as discussed earlier, is that legitimate use of a digital work *requires* making a copy. Hence, noting that a copy has been made tells far less about the legitimacy of the behavior than it does in the hardcopy world, where there are few legitimate rationales for copying an entire work.

A second is that, because copying is so bound up with the way computers work, controlling the act of copying, in the view of some legal scholars, provides unexpectedly broad powers, considerably beyond those intended by the copyright law. In the world of physical works, once a work is published, the rights holder cannot in any pragmatic sense control access to the copies distributed. Social institutions (such as bookstores and libraries) and individuals with copies enable any motivated reader to gain access to the information in the work.

But when access requires reproduction, the right to control reproduction is the right to control access, even to an individual copy already distributed. Authors would not, of course, routinely deny access to their published digital works. But because access requires reproduction, control of reproduction provides control of access to individual published copies, a right not conceived as part of copyright, and hence not to be embraced lightly, whether or not it's routinely exercised.

Considering that control of reproduction is a means, not the goal, can we find some other mechanism more tightly connected to the goal of motivating individual contributions to progress in science and the arts, whether in the digital or analog world? Finding such a mechanism is not easy, but one suggestion may help promote serious consideration of the issue.

It may be useful to start not by asking whether a copy has been made, but by considering what the law is attempting to achieve—ensuring progress in the arts and sciences. We should therefore ask instead whether a use being made of a work is substantially destructive of a common means of achieving that goal, namely, providing incentive to authors. This approach is similar in overall spirit to the concept of fair use, which requires consideration of the effect on the market for the work or on the value of the work. But it is somewhat broader in scope, as incentive arises for authors in more than the marketplace alone, coming as well, for example, from the ability to control the time, place, and manner of publication.

This view would not conflict with all of the other traditional exclusive rights in copyright. Creation of derivative works, distribution, public performance, and display of the work can all be conceived of and protected on grounds independent of whether a copy is made. They also affect incentive, whether through economic effects in the marketplace or through other factors, and hence would be consistent with an incentive-based analysis.

Any such substantial change in the legal framework would also, of course, bring problems. Therefore, there would have to be a substantial period of familiarization, as well as a means of dealing with the tension between trying to make such a law easier to follow (by drawing a sharp line defining what constitutes incentive-destroying use) and keeping the criteria more general (as is the case for fair use), allowing the law to address unanticipated situations in the future. Nevertheless, the discussion and examination of what constitutes a well-grounded model of intellectual property protection in the digital world may be well worth the effort.

Looking ahead

The development and deployment of the information infrastructure presents a variety of challenges, ranging from the pragmatics of enforcing laws that can be casually broken by individuals (in private, inexpensively, and almost undetectably), to the possibility and perhaps the need to rethink some of the foundational concepts underlying these laws. Yet, from its origins in the patent laws of Venice in the 1400s through to modern times, intellectual property law has evolved and changed in response to such challenges. What is likely to happen this time? Several things.

To some degree, society will simply adjust to the new reality and carry on in familiar ways. Recall how software vendors gave up on the awkward technical mechanisms used in the 1980s to defeat piracy (such as distributing their products on disks that could not be copied in the ordinary way) and continued to do business and prosper in a world where there is nontrivial piracy. So it is likely to be with the distribution of digital content. Customers will grow increasingly used to subscriptions to online information, and authors and publishers will continue to do their work in the presence of some unauthorized reproduction.

But as the turmoil in the music, publishing, and movie industries suggests, the upheaval created by new technology may mean that accommodation is not enough. New business models will need to be explored and tested. New approaches to intellectual property issues will need to be founded on more than law and technology, embracing as well an understanding of the economics of information, sociology, and psychology. Intellectual property itself may need to be reconceptualized to some degree, in recognition of the changes we now face.

The issues are difficult but inescapable. We are all unavoidably engaged in an experiment that tests our ingenuity and resourcefulness in finding ways to accomplish the apparently paradoxical goals of motivating individual creation while still reserving the ultimate benefits of that creation for the common good. And we need to do so in a world where replication, distribution, and publication are astonishingly easier and less expensive than they have ever been. These issues are as important as they are difficult; the decisions we make today will shape foundational elements of our future society.

Notes

1. The first sale rule is contained in Section 109 of the Copyright Act, saying, in part: "... the owner of a particular copy [of a copyrighted work]... is entitled, without the authority of the copyright owner, to sell or otherwise dispose of the possession of that copy...." It's called the first-sale rule, because the rights of the copyright owner over a particular copy of the work are extinguished by the first sale of that copy.
2. Fair use is a legal principle enabling certain uses of copyrighted material, even in the absence of permission. Among the most familiar examples are the short quotes used by one writer when commenting on the work of another, as in, say, book reviews, position papers, and satires.
3. Looking for a song by Neil Young and can't find it? Try looking for "Niel Young" instead.
4. At press time, the experiment had been suspended for a variety of interesting reasons; see Mr. King's explanation at www. stephenking. com/sk_120400_2.html.

RANDALL DAVIS (davis@ai.mit.edu) is a professor in the computer science department at MIT in Cambridge, MA.

Article 25

The Control of Ideas

BY GEORGE SCIALABBA

The Future of Ideas: The Fate of the Commons in a Connected World By Lawrence Lessig. Random House, 353 pages, $30.00

Copyrights and Copywrongs: The Rise of Intellectual Property and How It Threatens Creativity By Siva Vaidhyanathan. New York University Press, 243 Pages, $27.95

A SPECTER IS HAUNTING CULTURE: the specter of intellectual-property law. Soon every embodiment, however emphemeral, of thought or imagination may be defined as a "product," its every use commercially controlled. Thanks to digital technology, as Lawrence Lessig pointed out in his *Code and Other Laws of Cyberspace* (1999), a book is potentially no longer just a book. An online publisher, for example, will be able to specify

> whether you could read the book once or one hundred times; whether you could cut and paste from it or simply read it without copying; whether you could send it as an attached document to a friend or simply keep it on your machine; whether you could delete it or not; whether you could use it in another work, for another purpose, or not; whether you could simply have it on your shelf or have it and use it as well.

Similar restrictions will apply to compact discs, videos, Web sites, databases, software applications, and anything else that is encoded or transmitted digitally. All of them will be packaged with programs that can monitor, and then either charge for or block, every imaginable use.

Why is this "propertization" of culture disturbing? One reason is its possible effect on equality. The present unmetered World Wide Web is analogous to the public library and broadcasting systems, which at least in principle foster social equality by making cultural resources available on equal terms to the rich and nonrich. Another reason is its effect on community. To adapt Cass Sunstein's perspective in *Republic.com,* increasingly individualized consumption packages may well increase cultural fragmentation.

In his new book, *The Future of Ideas,* Lessig emphasizes another reason: the likely ill effects on innovation. Whatever other harm the new law of intellectual property may do, he warns, it will probably also chill the remarkable creativity associated with the pre-commercial Internet. Up to now, new ways of connecting to the Net, communicating on the Net, and perhaps most important, distributing art, ideas, and information across the Net have been devised at an amazing rate. By and large, this was not done for profit.

Consider the "architecture" of the Internet. The GNU/Linux operating system (the world's fastest-growing and a serious rival to Unix), the Apache server (two-thirds of all servers on the Web), the Perl programming language, the BIND (Berkeley Internet Name Domain) system, the "sendmail" program (which runs on 75 percent of all servers), and the protocols of the World Wide Web—"these projects," Lessig writes, "together constitute the soul of the Internet." They *are* the revolution. All of them were developed as, and remain, "open code" projects. That is, the code in which they are written is unowned or its governed by a "General Public License," a permissive form of copyright that allows anyone to modify the code, provided he or she makes those modifications available free to everyone else. The code that enables the Internet is thus common property. It is, to use a traditional term that Lessig adapts to cyberspace with extraordinary rigor and originality, a "commons."

A commons is a resource that is available to everyone (or everyone in some community) without permission. The term will be familiar to many readers from Garrett Hardin's well-known argument about the "tragedy of the commons." To take Hardin's example: If a pasture is held in common, the benefits of adding to one's herd will accrue to oneself, while the costs will be shared. The result is overgrazing and a ruined pasture. The solution is exclusive property rights.

This little parable has played a large part in forming contemporary intuitions about political economy. The belief that private control almost invariably produces the most efficient use of scarce resources is part of the common sense of market societies and is regularly invoked in order to oppose state regulation or public ownership. But as Lessig makes clear, this maxim does not apply straightforwardly to intellectual resources—a point that media studies professor Siva Vaidhyanathan also makes in *Copyrights and Copywrongs.*

Pasture is what economists call a "rivalrous" resource. One persons' (or cow's) consumption leaves less for others. Culture is a nonrivalrous resource. One person's consumption leaves no less for others. Rivalrous resources can be depleted; nonrivalrous resources cannot. From the point of view of efficiency, it follows that different kinds of property rights should govern the two kinds of resources. In Lessig's formulation:

> If the resource is rivalrous, then a system of control is needed to assure that the resource is not depleted—which means the system must assure that the resource is both produced and not overused. If the resource is nonrivalrous, then a system of control is needed simply to assure that the resource is created.... Once it is created, there is no danger that the resource will be depleted. By definition, a nonrivalrous resource cannot be used up.

With a nonrivalrous resource, one can have a commons, without the tragedy. In *Code* and in *The Future of Ideas,* Lessig shows at great length that the precommercial Internet was the site of much rapid and fruitful innovation precisely because it was a commons. And he shows at even greater length that the evolution of intellectual-property law—driven by corporate leviathans and their lawyer-gnomes, and articulated by free-market ideologues on the judicial bench—is drastically changing the open character of the Internet, enclosing the commons.

WHAT IS THE CHARACTER OF the Internet, and what does it have to do with innovation? "How the Internet was designed," Lessig claims, "intimately affected the freedoms it has enabled.... And arguably no principle of network architecture has been more important to the success of the Internet than this single principle of network design—e2e." The term means "end-to-end." Between the edges, or ends, of the network (that is, individual users) was a simple, neutral data-transport system that would run whatever new applications were programmed in at the ends, no matter who owned the wires and machines in the middle. This meant that anyone could invent and distribute new applications or modify existing ones. And a great many people—scruffy graduate students, lowly coders, bored engineers, and scientists diddling around on company time—did. GNU/Linux, Apache, the Internet and Web protocols, and so on, were collective achievements.

This end-to-end "architecture of freedom" guaranteed progress but not profits. So, large, vertically integrated companies are moving to substitute an architecture of control, breaking up end-to-end by "layering onto the original code layer of the Internet new technologies that facilitate greater discrimination, and hence control, over the content and applications that can run on the Net." Microsoft has used its control over Windows' source code to prevent Windows users from switching to non-Microsoft Internet browsers, like Netscape Navigator. AOL Time Warner hopes to combine its vast resources of broadband cable pipe, network access, and content in ways that will handicap competitors and box in customers. Cable companies that provide Internet access artificially limit "video streaming," since streamed video is a potential competitor of cable programming. Freelancers compiled wonderfully comprehensive new archives of popular music that stimulated much musical experimentation among people without access to expensive equipment. But lawyers for the recording industry have pretty much choked off such unfettered innovation.

Besides these strategies for heading off novel technical uses of digital media, there are also powerful new surveillance techniques for clamping down on even the most casual uses of content. Intellectual-property advocates "obsess about the ability for content to be 'stolen,'" Lessig notes, "but we must also keep in view the potential for use to be more perfectly controlled." For example, computer programs called "bots" scan the Web for copyrighted content and report back to their corporate masters.

> The pattern here is extremely common. Copyright holders vaguely allege copyright violations; a hosting site, fearing liability and seeking safe harbor, immediately shuts down the site. The examples could be multiplied thousands of times over, and only then would you begin to have a sense of the regime of control that is slowly emerging over content posted by ordinary individuals in cyberspace. Yahoo!, MSN, and AOL have whole departments devoted to the task of taking down "copyrighted" content from any Web site, however popular, simply because the copyright holder demands it. [Bots] find this content; ISPs [Internet service providers] are ordered to remove it; fearing liability, and encouraged by a federal law that gives them immunity if they remove the content quickly, they move quickly to take down the content.

Filmmakers are also hard hit. Evocation by allusion is common to all art. But numerous movies have been held up because the director made passing use of something that someone had, however implausibly, copyrighted. Every image, every melody, every brand name, "every piece of artwork, any piece of furniture or sculpture, has to be cleared before you can use it," a director tells Lessig. Every shot has to go through the studio's legal department. Independent filmmakers, with no studio behind them, have to self-censor or take their chances. "The cost," one of them complains, "is creativity. Suddenly the world you're trying to create is completely generic and void of the elements you would normally [make use of]." As Lessig comments: "This is not a picture of copyrights imperfectly protected; this is a picture of copyright control out of control."

Lessig and Vaidhyanathan tell many such stories, depressingly similar, about the cable-TV, music, film, publishing, and software industries. In each case, new modes of creation and distribution enabled by the Internet threaten the market share of big players. The behemoths respond by "locking up" their products with encryption software, requiring users to sign away even traditionally protected rights of "fair use," using their ownership or source code or of supply-and-distribution networks to marginalize potential competitors, or simply threatening newcomers with ruinously expensive lawsuits. Only federal regulation can preserve the open environment that elicited such remarkable innovation in the recent past. But it won't happen. The courts—where most federal judges are now appointees of Ronald Reagan or the two George Bushes—forget to balance private claims against the public interest and instead give the behemoths what they want. Legislators, intensively lobbied and campaign-funded, also cave in.

This shrinking of the public domain is not at all what the nation's founders had in mind. Constitutionally speaking, intellectual property is not like other property. Section 8 of Article I reads: "The Congress shall have Power... to promote the Progress of Science and useful Arts, by securing for limited Times to Authors and Inventors the exclusive Right to their respective Writings and Discoveries." It is clear, as Lessig and Vaidhyanathan show, that the founders did not intend to give creators (much less their corporate employers) unlimited ownership rights. Unlimited exclusive control, they recognized, would stifle progress. The purpose of copyrights and patents is to promote innovations; the proper goal of copyright and patent law is to strike a balance between incentive and access, between rewarding achievement and facilitating more achievement.

Besides, being sensible persons and not Chicago School doctrinaires, the founders understood that "Science and useful Arts" are to some extent a gift economy. Gratitude, the pleasure of discovery, the impulse to self-expression, and devotion to a common enterprise motivate creators quite as much as lucre. Of course, artists need to make a living, and even to get rich. Lessig, who clerked for Richard Posner and Antonin Scalia, is not an anarchocommunist. But the real point is to keep the tune flowing, the conversation alive, the gift in motion. Poets, jazz musicians, filmmakers, physicists, and coders know this. It's not their fault (and it's not primarily for their benefit) that the balance has been lost—that, as Lessig laments, "the ability to propertize culture in America is [now] essentially unlimited... even though the plain text of the Constitution speaks volumes against such expansive control."

In *Copyrights and Copywrongs*, Siva Vaidhyanathan covers much of the same ground as *The Future of Ideas* but pays more attention to history and sociology and less to technology and legal theory. Three chapters on the history of copyright in literature, film, and music (this last with fascinating material on blues and rap) are framed by two analytical chapters, one surveying the common-law roots and constitutional meanings of copyright, the other assessing the likely cultural consequences of the revolution in intellectual-property law. Smoothly written and equable in tone, it makes a valuable supplement to Lessig's brilliant but slightly hectic exposition.

"A REPUBLIC, IF YOU CAN KEEP IT," Benjamin Franklin is said to have answered someone in the crowd outside Independence Hall who asked what the deliberations inside had produced. We've done an indifferent job, as Christopher Lasch, Walter Karp, Robert Wiebe, and others have reminded us. An important feature of that republic was a culture of innovation made possible by laws that found a reasonable balance between commerce and creativity. This feature, like the culture of deliberation that briefly flourished in the early Republic, is being eroded by the pressures of competition and concentration. Lessig himself, as skeptical as Franklin, doubts that these pressures will be successfully resisted in the end. But at least, thanks to *Code* and *The Future of Ideas*, Vaidhyanathan's *Copyrights and Copywrongs*, Sunstein's *Republic.com*, Seth Shulman's *Owning the Future*, and a few other farsighted works, we need not be herded altogether passively into the global cyber-playpen.

GEORGE SCIALABBA, *reviews books for* The Boston Globe, The Washington Post, *and other publications.*

DEMOCRACY IN AN IT-FRAMED SOCIETY

Interest in the use of computers for improving a democracy widely considered decayed seems to be increasing with the growing use of the Internet. Indeed, a recent AltaVista search for "electronic democracy" yielded well over 5,000 pages. Much of this material discusses projects trying to make an impact on democratic practices.

Åke Grönlund, Guest Editor

Electronic democracy, sometimes teledemocracy or digital democracy, are terms often used synonymously to refer to the use of information and communications technologies (ICTs) to connect politicians and citizens by means of information, voting, polling, or discussion.

This implicit definition seems widespread; people often refer to e-democracy as something you can be "for" or "against"[2]. Since no one living in democratic countries is against democracy (with the exception of marginal groups), then it must be the "e" people find objectionable. E-democracy is generally seen as a tool for abandoning the representative democratic system for one with more direct citizen input (sometimes referred to as "quick democracy;" see Åström's article in this section).* Arguments against e-democracy are similar to those against direct democracy, such as the risk of populism, lower-level political discourse, loss of deliberation, creating an unclear role of politicians, and instability of democratic institutions, among others. Additional arguments specific to the electronic medium include issues of security and privacy.

The articles in this special section* present a more inclusive view of e-democracy. The argument is that the role of the electronic medium in the democratic system extends far beyond electronic town hall meetings and polling. The use of ICT permeates most activities related to societal planning, governance, and political organization, including organization in the civil society, which means using ICT also has implications for working democracy in representative systems. Therefore, to understand the role of ICT in the working process of the democratic system, e-democracy research should be framed in a context encompassing all aspects of the system.

One requirement for the system—besides formal rule by the people—is the ability to make things happen; it needs to be both effective and efficient. Democracy needs good citizens *and* good institutions. From this perspective, democracy can be illustrated as a large business occupying thousands of professionals of different specialties working in different fields of numerous processes concerned with passing proposals from the stage of ideas to the stage of operation. This includes activities of research, planning, implementation, administration, evaluation, decision making, propaganda, communication, and many other issues of which public debate is only a small part. We can see democracy as a connected set of activities making up a whole, much like we do in the business area. Electronic government is then parallel to business administration with the important difference of having a democratic key signature. As such, it is not possible to be against e-democracy since that would mean abandoning several well-established uses of ICT in many of these activities.

The narrow definition of e-democracy makes democracy an option—not a defining part—of the core business of government. The wide definition turns the concepts the other way around with e-democracy encompassing e-government. The articles in this special section* argue that a broader definition of e-democracy is necessary for understanding the full implications of ICT use. A more encompassing definition would also help make the field more relevant to the debate on the decreasing vitality of democracy and more useful for those trying to achieve changes in the practices of the formal democracy. There are two principal reasons for this claim:

First, studying a narrowly defined e-democracy leads to looking at online voting, discussion, and information projects. In fact, governments and citizens are practicing far more interesting uses of computers, and these practices should be studied from a democratic perspective.

Whenever information technology enters a new field of practice, the debate quickly focuses on how ICT tools can support some activity. Not surprisingly, we have recently seen a number of reports on computer support for voting[4], for supporting professional politicians[6,7], and the like. Moreover, we have seen the field of *community informatics*[3,5] emerge, focusing on virtual groups in civil society.

While computer support for individuals and groups are important, e-democracy studies must move toward a more systematic and comprehensive view of the democratic system, focusing on issues concerning the entire production chain; business procedures, knowledge management, cooperation, and so on.

Voting, professional politics, and social processes in civil society are key elements to the democratic system. However, this trio is not enough. There are more processes that are equally important, maybe even more so. I refer to the everyday administrative processes regarding investigations and proposals over which political debates rage and from which information to citizens is distributed piecemeal via politicians and media. One important feature of these processes is the fact they are already saturated with IT; decision-support systems, simulation tools, visualization tools, ERP systems, systems for economy planning and follow-up, data-mining tools, and so on. The student of working democracy would be well advised to start with the basic daily importance of IT.

Second, ICT is much more than a tool. We live in what Manuel Castells calls a culture of "real virtuality;... a system in which reality itself (that is, people's material/symbolic existence) is entirely captured, fully immersed in a virtual image setting, in the world of make-believe, in which appearances are not just on the screen through which experience is communicated, but they become the experience.... [T]he medium has become so comprehensive, so diversified, so malleable that it absorbs in the same multimedia text the whole of human experience, past, present, and future"[1].

This also means the actors in the democratic system will have to play by the rules of the medium. Castells calls this "informational politics"; if politicians want to reach people, they "must process their projects and strategies through a similar technological medium" regardless of the contents of their political message and ideals. This framing of politics in the media space "impacts not only elections, but political organization, decision-making, and governance, ultimately modifying the nature of the relationship between state and society."

Though the Internet is still not the predominant medium for politics, its importance increases by the day.

There are light-years between this view of ICT as a medium permeating most of our activities and the view of e-democracy as something you can be "for" or "against." As a practitioner in any field pertaining to the democratic system, you can't be against a medium that so intrusively and persistently frames all your activities.

Though the Internet is still not the predominant medium for politics, its importance increases by the day. Therefore, important research tasks include examining the many ways in which ICT frames politics. The articles here give some ideas about the issues to cover. They consider three basic nodes—formal politics, the administration, and the civil society—and some of the many processes in which they work and are linked together.

Formal Politics

An important part of any organization is the client-organization encounter. In business this is often called "the moment of truth." It is researched for the purpose of helping personnel to better serve the organization's mission. Paradoxically, such an encounter in the public sector, which is supposed to act for its citizens, is often referred to as "delivery of information." Anttiroiko reviews the series of European Commission's initiatives conceived to bring European governments into e-governments and finds a view of citizenship as service recipients rather than active participants. He finds democracy at the margin of a basically techno-economic agenda.

Ågren examines another part of the EU initiatives in the ICT field—the commission's directives and the ensuing national legislation on privacy protection. He finds the directives so strong that in practice they would prohibit any public political debate online.

Together these articles paint a picture of the EU in practice as strongly against more participatory forms of democracy, focusing on citizens as efficient workers and service users rather than people participating in societal decision-making. In terms of the political models Åström provides, the EU's efforts offer a very "thin" view of democracy.

There is only a tiny stream of research and development work on the micro societal dialogue, which treats the encounter as an important part of the meeting between society and the citizen. One such stream is represented by Becker who brings 20 years of teledemocratic experiments to the table. Becker considers current initiatives regarding the use of IT for enhancing democracy. His findings exhibit a number of positive results from methods to enhance deliberation, and he is hopeful that "strong," deliberative methods will become standard tools in everyday democracy.

Administration

Decision-making processes are central to democracy because they should work in a democratic way, not just produce decisions. Decision-making processes are found at numerous levels, with different objectives, preconditions, and procedural traditions.

Decision-making processes concerning government activities have infrastructure dimensions such as public equal access and durability. This is true not only for roads and railroads, but also for government services.

Decision processes typically stretch over considerable time and they involve several steps from inception to realization, such as planning, financing, environmental screening, implementation, service provision, control, and evaluation. Most of these processes are administrative and are supported by various ICT tools.

A common feature of these processes is an increasing level of complexity due to more intricate legislation (for example, international), more complicated causal relations (for example, environment effects) and so on. Thus, there is a need for support. ICT may help because it can extract and visualize certain aspects of a material and assumptions and values can be represented in built-in evaluation models.

Built-in decision models affect people's ability to share and understand the premises on which decisions are made. These models can be made explicit, or they can be concealed. Such technology has the opportunity to become a rhetorical tool in the hands of politicians as well as a tool for democratic enlightenment and opportunity for exerting influence over decisionmaking processes on the part of citizens. Work in this area is limited to very few people within the IT field. Indeed, the field of e-democracy could contribute by widening the audience.

Another aspect of such powerful tools and techniques that modern public servants have at their disposal is they strengthen the administrators' position toward the politicians. They tend to know better than their political counterparts about the real world of the politician's constituency. Informed citizens approach the public servants directly. Politicians themselves also rely more and more on the expertise, insights, and analytical power of the bureaucracy that are enhanced by ICT developments. In this way important intermediary roles for public servants are evolving. Snellen uses geographic information systems to exemplify this change, and contends it's time for a new political theory incorporating these new roles.

Watson and Mundy couple e-government and e-democracy focusing on making democracy part of daily operations. Democracy is not just views or opinions, but also a view of where the money goes. They discuss efficiency and effectiveness as two complementary aspects of making democracy work, and they present a strategy for implementation.

La Porte, Demchak, and Friis examine national-level, public agency Web sites in 192 countries for transparency, interactivity, and openness in order to understand the social history of government Web use. Though still in the early days of this social phenomenon, the path technology takes will last for many years to come. This ongoing research inspects the choices made in the evolution of government Web use.

Civil Society

The knowledge about how people live is crucial for politicians. In the early days of democracy, political agitators traveled to factories because that was where the new voters were located. They talked to them, listened to them, and thus learned about their concerns and how they could best be reached with political arguments.

Today's parallel to the yard outside the factory gates includes virtual societies in various forms; not just the ones designed for political discussions, but all kinds of like-minded groups. The Web has become a professional and social meeting place for many citizens. These forums are their medium of expression. This is where social processes pertaining to formal democracy are formed. Learning about how they work and how people talk and think in and about this medium is crucial for anyone concerned with the revitalization of formal democracy.

Schuler discusses civic culture as the fundament of democracy. He claims community networks are important examples of institutions with the potential to meet critical democratic demands. Seattle Community Network is such an example. Schuler also considers the roles of technology and calls for computer professionals to consider their roles in developing democratic technology. He argues computer science should be considered an embedded practice rather than an instrumental discipline.

Taylor and Burt compare Web sites of voluntary organizations to parliamentary ones on some key democratic values. Taylor and Burt find parliamentary Web sites are not engaging citizens in order to reinvigorate democracy through the development of active forms of citizenship. Voluntary sector bodies, however, are using Web sites to stimulate active citizenship in new and exciting ways. Indeed, the authors see a development where voluntary sector democracy will increase in importance at the expense of parliaments.

We hope these articles exemplify the variety involved in the "framing of politics in the electronic medium," as Castells would say. We predict many important changes in the functioning of the democratic systems due to the ongoing transformation of processes into the framework of the electronic medium. Research on e-democracy could fill an important role in this transformation by engaging in a comprehensive agenda for studying the role of ICT in this change.

References

1. Castells, M. *The Rise of the Network Society.* Blackwell Publishers, Malden, MA, 1996.
2. Dutton, W. H., Elberse, A., and Hale, M. A case study of a netizen's guide to elections. *Commun. ACM 43,* 12 (Dec. 1999), 48–54.
3. Gurstein, M. *Community Informatics: Enabling Communities with Information and Communications Technologies.* Idea Group Publishing, 2000.
4. Larsen, K. I. Voting technology. *Commun. ACM 42,* 12 (Dec. 1999), 55–57.
5. Schuler, D. *New Community Networks: Wired for Change.* Addison-Wesley, Reading, MA, 1996.
6. Schwabe, G. *E-Councils—Systems, Experiences, Perspectives.* DEXA 2000, Database and Expert Systems Applications.
7. Watson, R. T., Akselsen, S., Evjemo, B., and Aarsaether, N. Teledemocracy in local government. *Commun. ACM 42,* 12 (Dec 1999), 58–63.

***Editor's note:** This is one of several articles that appeared in a special section in *Communications of the ACM,* January 2001/Vol. 44. No.1.

Åke Grönlund (gron@informatik.umu.se) is the head of Research Education in the Department of Informatics and Director of the Center for Studies of IT in the Public Sector at Umeå University, in Umeå, Sweden; www. informatik.umu.se/~gron.

Should Democracy Online Be Quick, Strong, or Thin?

The concept of democracy is essential to the debate on electronic democracy. While it may seem quite straightforward, there is in fact a number of varying definitions of democracy. Though the semantic meaning of the word—government by the people—is undisputed, there are great diversities in interpretations of who should be regarded as the people and how they technically should govern.

JOACHIM ÅSTRÖM

In order to outline a basic framework, three models representing three different democratic ideals are presented here, each providing different views of the techniques and institutional settings assumed to make the principles work in practice[6,8].

The literature contains innumerable classifications, categorizations, typologies, and models describing variations of democracy: radical democracy, liberal democracy, participatory democracy, elitist democracy, protective democracy, pluralistic democracy, to mention a few (for examples, see[5,6,8]). The conceptual richness of the literature gives reason to try to find a few broad categories that simplify the picture. The three models used here—*quick, strong,* and *thin* democracy—are based on Premfors'[10] complementary to Barber's[2] strong and thin categories. These models are rooted in traditional democratic discourse and are useful as a link between democratic theory in a deeper sense and its electronic manifestations. Of course, the brief discussion here does not attempt to cover every aspect of the democratic discourse, but will hopefully function as a framework for the articles in this section. Table 1 summarizes some key aspects of democracy that differentiate the three models.

Quick democracy. One common point of view in the debate on e-democracy is the recommendation of citizens' direct participation in political decision-making. In this view, all citizens are assumed to have at least the same amount of wisdom as the elite. Thus, it is of utmost importance that the will of the majority is allowed to directly influence decisions in all areas of society. The representative model is seen as a practical necessity in some situations, but is generally regarded as a necessary evil that could and should be avoided in different ways.

Use of information and communication technology (ICT) is seen as one such way. One of the major obstacles for direct citizen participation in decision-making is a technical one: frequent manual public referendums would require loads of staff during an extended period of time, amounting to huge costs. ICT has been brought forward as a technical remedy to this problem[4].

Radical proponents of this model see ICT as the decisive means by which direct democracy Athenian style can be implemented in today's society. In their proposed model professional politicians and political parties become more or less redundant. Instead, a new kind of public rule will emerge. Through computer networks, individuals' views and opinions can be solicited, registered, stored, and communicated, so direct democracy can be implemented not only at a local level but nationally and even internationally. Representative democracy is then substituted by independent cybercitizens who act in a responsible manner at the electronic agora, without any politician acting as an intermediary and guardian[7].

Less radical proponents do not want to abolish the representative system altogether, but combine it—*revitalize it*—with direct elements. Some envision a type of direct democracy in which there is still a party-based government chosen by elections. This government would put

Table 1. Central dimensions of democracy

	Quick democracy	Strong democracy	Thin democracy
Aim	Power to the people	Consensus	Efficiency/Choice
Ground for legitimacy	Principle of majority	Public debate	Accountability
Citizens' role	Decision-maker	Opinion former	Customer
Mandate of the elected	Bound	Interactive	Open
ICT use focusing	Decisions	Discussion	Information

Source: Åström 1999

important bills and other political decisions to popular votes, just as it does with legislative votes under representative democracy[4]. Others suggest a more frequent use of advisory opinion polls, by way of ICT, making sure the parliament really knows what the people want.

The most important **participatory activity** for many citizens has been casting a vote into the ballot box.

Strong democracy. The most important participatory activity for many citizens has been casting a vote into the ballot box. In recent years, however, more attention has been given to public debate as a political tool. According to the strong view of democracy, real democracy is more than the sum of its parts. Political decisions are considered legitimate if and only if they are made through certain procedural circumstances. The source of legitimacy is not the predetermined will of individuals, but rather the process of its formation—deliberation.

Just as quick democracy, strong democracy wants, and indeed requires, active citizens. Real democracy is realized only to the extent that ordinary people are given opportunities to carry on a dialogue about, and act on, matters of common interest. Unlike quick democracy that wants to increase the speed of decision-making processes, strong democracy wants to slow them down by involving people in discussion and deliberation processes, something that can be achieved to a large extent in various electronic forums[2].

Proponents of strong democracy are often positive to an increased use of direct democratic elements. Unlike the quick interpretation of democracy, however, this is combined with a certain amount of skepticism toward the raw public opinion. It is an illusion to believe that qualified standpoints in complex societal issues are automatically "out there" and can easily be caught in polls or referendas in accordance with the principle of majority. Quick democracy is seen as resting on a misinterpretation of the nature of government by the people[9]. Voting and polling should be deliberative, and citizens informed by information, discussion, and debate.

In the strong model of democracy participation is seen not only as a means to giving people power, but also as providing education leading to increased understanding about society. Today, much attention is paid to the benefits of horizontal communication among citizens (see Doug Schuler's article, "Computer Professionals and the Next Culture of Democracy," in *Communications of the ACM*, January 2001): when people discuss societal issues, a platform is created for respect, confidence, tolerance, and openness. These are the crucial ingredients of a strong democracy.

Thin democracy. Unlike the other two models, the thin model does not consider it important to increase the level of citizen participation. This is because the ordinary citizen is perceived as uninterested in politics and unqualified to participate. Instead, the basic idea is to have the elite competing for the citizens' votes. Elections are about choosing leaders based on a general account of their programs. The elite must then have sufficient room to maneuver, to revise and detail their political programs. The ground for legitimacy is the accountability of the elite—that the public in free elections can tell who they want to govern their common affairs.

Thin democracy derives from a utilitarian or protective conception of democracy[8]. While there is no need for general participation, there is a strong claim to information about entitlements to public services by all citizens. This leads to another information strategy than suggested by the other two models. Since citizens are seen as consumers, it is not necessary to provide them with information on which collective decisions are based, not beforehand, not afterward. Instead public information can be restricted to public services. Proponents of thin democracy are often skeptical of the view that democracy demands transparence, that "the houses of power be a house of glass"[12]. The visibility element may improve but also distort behavior. For instance, visibility distorts when it imposes "image selling" to the detriment of responsible behavior. Furthermore, visibility can well enhance, if not create, conflict to the degree that removal from visibility is the most practiced and practical way of lessening tensions.

There are at least three ways in which ICT use can help implement this model of democracy. First, political organizations can use ICT to gather support and disseminate information. Online communications are an inexpensive means of reaching many people and targeting particular segments of the population, making these networks well-suited to contemporary political activity[11]. Second, ICTs can support the elected representatives and improve their leadership; they can access experts, information from their home base, from their workplace, and their constituents. Third, the citizen can be strengthened in the role as customer to public service and ICTs can add value to public services by enhancing customer inquiry and feedback facilities[3].

REFERENCES

1. Åström, J. Digital demokrati? IdÈer och strategier i lokal IT-politik. *SOU* 117 (1999). Fritzes, Stockholm, Sweden.
2. Barber, B. *Strong Democracy.* University of California Press, Berkeley, CA, 1984.
3. Bellamy, C. and Taylor, J.A. *Governing in the Information Age.* Open University Press, Buckingham, UK, 1998.
4. Budge, I. *The New Challenge of Direct Democracy.* Polity Press, Cambridge, UK, 1996.
5. Gutman, A. *Democracy. A Companion to Contemporary Political Philosophy.* R.E. Goodin, R.P. Philip, Eds. Blackwell Publishers Ltd., Oxford, UK, 1993.
6. Held, D. *Models of Democracy.* Polity Press, Cambridge, UK, 1987.
7. Ilshammar, L. Demokr@i. Det elektroniska folkstyrets möligheter och problem. *SOU* 56 (1997). Fritzes, Stockhom, Sweden.
8. Macpherson, C.B. *The Life and Times of Liberal Democracy.* Oxford University Press, Oxford, UK, 1977.
9. Petersson, O. Politikens möjligheter. Har folkstyrelsen någon framtid? SNS förlag, Stockholm, Sweden, 1996.
10. Premfors, R. (2000) Den starka demokratin. Atlas, Stockholm, Sweden, 2000.
11. Rash, W. *Politics on the Nets.* W. H. Freeman, New York, NY, 2000.
12. Sartori, G. *The Theory of Democracy Revisited.* Chatham House, Chatham, NJ, 1987.

Joachim Åström (joakim.astrom@sam.oru.se) is a Ph.D. student in political science at Örebro University, Sweden.

As goes software...

...so goes business—and, perhaps, even society itself

LET software disappear, and life as we know it would break down, at least in developed countries. It controls most of the objects which surround us: computers, of course, but also telephones, cars, toys, TVs, much of our transport system, and so on. Yet if the vision of web services comes to pass, today's dependence on software will appear slight. Life in the cloud will mean that much of what we do, as *homo oeconomicus* at least, will be automated, from restaurant reservations to car purchases, from share trades to entire business deals.

All this is at least some years off, and may not happen at all. But the prospect raises some interesting questions. Who will write all the code needed for these services? What needs to be done to ensure that it is reliable and secure? And, last but not least, is there a way to prevent a few dominant companies or governments from controlling the cloud? Conveniently, the Internet and the institutions it has spawned may hold some answers.

Laments about a "software crisis" are almost as old as the industry itself. There are never enough skilled programmers to satisfy the demand for high-quality code. But in the years ahead this chronic imbalance could turn into a veritable "software gap", as an American presidential advisory group made up of leading computer scientists put it in a 1999 report. "This situation", the researchers wrote, "threatens to inhibit the progress of the current boom in information technology."

The group is even more concerned about the current fragility of software. Even much-tested commercial varieties are often riddled with bugs, lack security, do not perform well and are difficult to upgrade. This was a bore when most software was confined to isolated devices and networks, but it becomes a serious problem in the world of web services. Software delivered online has to be able to withstand the onslaught of millions of users, and is at risk of security attacks from myriad sources.

Whereas these technical issues have been discussed for some time, the social and political aspects have only recently come to the surface. As code increasingly penetrates daily life, it becomes de facto law that regulates behaviour, argues Lawrence Lessig, a Stanford law professor, in his book "Code and Other Laws of Cyberspace" (Basic Books, 1999). For example, code needs to be compatible with our ideals of privacy and free speech. Another pressing issue is open standards. The continuing antitrust trial against Microsoft has shown that the world needs common technical rules that are not controlled by a single company (or indeed a government). Such rules can provide a level playing field for competition. But they must not be too strict, because that would stifle innovation and diversity.

The other main regulatory issue is less obvious: it concerns directories, the digital equivalent of telephone books. Even more than open standards, they will hold the cloud together. Some directories will tell users where to find web services and what they offer; others will keep track of available hardware; and yet others will list not only the identity of users, but also where they are and whether they are online at that moment.

The reason why these directories might need to be regulated is that they are subject to strong networking effects: the more data they contain and the more users they have, the more valuable they become and the more data and users they will attract. Sometimes it will even make sense to have a single directory, as it does for the domain-name system (DNS), the current address book of the Internet. Competing domain-name systems would probably balkanise cyberspace.

Whoever controls such directories will wield potentially enormous power. If a company owned, for example, the directory for web services, it could try to make its own electronic offerings more accessible than those of its competitors. The continuing controversy about the Internet Corporation for Assigned Names and Numbers (ICANN), the body that administers the DNS, is the clearest example so far of how difficult it can be to regulate these directories.

There are other simmering disputes, too, such as whether and when AOL Time Warner should open its dominant instant-messaging (IM) system and extend it to other providers. The point about IM, a cross between a telephone call and e-mail, is that it keeps track of whether users are currently online and, in the future, will also be able to monitor where they are. This is important information for providers of smart web services. That is why the Federal Communications Commission (FCC) made its approval of the AOL/Time Warner merger contingent on the new company's promise to open up its IM system once it includes video services.

Microsoft had heavily lobbied the FCC, telling the agency that for IM to live up to its promise it must share the features of "openness and interoperability that characterise both the public telephone network and the Internet". It will be interesting to see whether Microsoft will apply the same philosophy to its own recently announced directory-like services, intended to become building blocks of the .NET world.

Luckily, the Internet is already helping to solve some of these dilemmas. Its very structure, for instance, has caused the software gap to narrow. Programmers no longer have to live in America or other developed countries, but can work from anywhere on the globe. In the future, there will increasingly be a global market for software development, just as one already exists for the manufacturing of electronics. The fast-growing software industry in India is only the beginning.

Moreover, the Internet allows for massive testing and peer review, boosting the quality of code, in particular through open-source projects. The more people look at a program, the more likely it is that mistakes will be spotted. "Given enough eyeballs, all bugs are shallow," writes Eric Raymond, another leading thinker of the open-source movement, in his influential book "The Cathedral & the Bazaar" (O'Reilly, 1999).

Finally, it is the Internet's institutions—such as the Internet Engineering Task Force (IETF)—that offer a possible solution to the regulatory issues. These consensus-building bodies are not just a good mechanism to develop robust and flexible open standards; their decision-making processes could also be applied to other issues, such as the regulation of directories. These communities are guided by respected members, known as "elders" or "benevolent dictators" (for open-source projects), who have gained their status because of the quality of their contributions.

Most of these elders are technical and social engineers who work for academic institutions or other not-for-profit organisations. Governments would do well to provide economic support for these elders instead of regulating directly, argues Paul Romer, an economics professor at Stanford University: "This would be money far better spent than on antitrust actions or agencies like the FCC."

This may be the Internet's most crucial effect on the software industry: that it has made it possible for groups akin to scientific communities, rather than market forces alone, to lay the groundwork of the digital world. That seems to be a far sounder solution than allowing a small handful of firms to become the not-so-benevolent dictators of the cloud.

From *The Economist,* April 14, 2001, pp. 25-26.

Governing the Internet

Engaging Government, Business, and Nonprofits

Zoë Baird

The rapid growth of the Internet has led to a worldwide crisis of governance. In the early years of Internet development, the prevailing view was that government should stay out of Internet governance; market forces and self-regulation would suffice to create order and enforce standards of behavior. But this view has proven inadequate as the Internet has become mainstream. A reliance on markets and self-policing has failed to address adequately the important interests of Internet users such as privacy protection, security, and access to diverse content. And as the number of users has grown worldwide, so have calls for protection of these important public and consumer interests. It is time we accept this emerging reality and recognize the need for a significant role for government on key Internet policy issues.

To do so without stifling innovation will require government to operate in unfamiliar ways, sharing power with experts in the information technology (IT) community, with business, and with nonprofit organizations. The first-mover advantage exists in policymaking as well as in business, and some commercial interests are moving as fast as they can to define Internet rules to their benefit without regard for the public interest. To achieve an Internet that reflects a commitment to public good as well as to commercial interests, we have to create more pluralistic models for Internet governance, models in which governments, industry, and nonprofit organizations craft policy—balancing each other and working together in transparent processes that earn the public's trust.

Many of the initial Internet oversight bodies emphasized self-regulation, bottom-up control, decentralization, and privatization, reflecting a conviction that government would never "get it" or move fast enough to keep pace with technological change. Often, engineers set the standards and industry set the consumer models largely outside of the public eye. As one Internet innovator, John Perry Barlow, wrote in his "Declaration of the Independence of Cyberspace," "Governments of the Industrial World, you weary giants of flesh and steel... On behalf of the future, I ask you of the past to leave us alone.... You do not know our culture, our ethics, or the unwritten codes that already provide our society more order than could be obtained by any of your impositions."

The loose and creative work of cyberspace pioneers served the Internet superbly as it was being formed and into its early maturation. But now some previously vaunted notions of efficient, private, speedy self-governance are failing to meet expectations. Tensions have arisen over such issues as whether a country has jurisdiction over Internet activities originating in other countries, whether regulation of content such as hate speech and pornography is appropriate, how different privacy protections should apply, and who gets space on prime virtual real estate such as dot-com. In addition, post–September 11 concerns about security in a networked world call into question the wisdom of keeping government off to the shoulder of the information superhighway.

A NEW MODEL OF GOVERNANCE

The reality is that government participation in regulating the Internet is necessary. Given the new economic and geopolitical environment, finding the right balance between an open, networked system and the security of a more closed environment requires significant participation by government. Although governments do not all share the same values, they are the only institutions that can provide stability and a place for debate over what public values need to be protected. These issues are significant policy questions that require democratic resolution, not just technical matters that can be left to experts. As Stanford University Law School Professor Lawrence Lessig has argued, in the digital age software code is law because software developers can shape the Internet's technical architecture in ways that guide or restrict users' experiences.

Indeed, despite some wariness, the American public indicates a clear preference for government involvement. In a study conducted by the Markle Foundation and Greenberg Quinlan Rosner Research in 2001 (prior to September 11), respondents said by a two-to-one margin that "the government should develop rules to protect people when they are on the Internet, even if it requires some regulation of the Internet." Thus the goal should no longer be keeping government out of cyberspace, but finding a way to make governmental oversight and intervention as speedy, agile, and technologically savvy as the medium demands.

The borderless nature of the Internet makes effective Internet governance even more challenging. Establishing the proper role for government inevitably means discerning the parts to be played by different countries and also the multilateral organizations they have formed. International forums on IT will play a critical role in writing the rules of the game for the next phase of world economic, political, and cultural history. However, to be legitimate, global governance forums will also need improved democratic processes.

International institutions engaged in Internet governance will have to confront three significant challenges if they are to achieve legitimacy: increasing participation by developing countries, providing access to nonprofit organizations, and ensuring democratic accountability.

Developing countries face some major barriers to participation. A recent study conducted under the auspices of the Digital Opportunity Task Force of the G-8 group of highly industrialized nations found that developing countries often lack the financial and human resources necessary to take part effectively in important venues. Moreover, complicated policy processes and decision-making arrangements leave poorer countries at a disadvantage within individual institutions. The multiplicity of institutions addressing IT policy also makes it hard for developing nations to contribute. These barriers are further raised by the intrinsic complexity of new technologies, by the difficulty of keeping pace with industry and consumer economic priorities, by a dearth of effective models for inclusive policymaking, and by the lack of financial resources for experts and travel.

If left unaddressed, this situation can devolve into a downward spiral in which stakeholders who feel shut out either obstruct or ignore IT policy efforts. A major obstacle to the success of governance institutions will exist as long as developing countries feel they do not have the expertise or the resources to understand whether the actions of these bodies are in their interest—and thus will often prefer to block action rather than accede to initiatives.

Barriers also exist to the participation of nonprofit organizations in global Internet governance. Principally, these barriers arise because of a lack of recognition that Internet policy issues need to be decided in governance institutions that involve representation not only from governments and businesses, but also from broader constituencies representing the public interest. As public protests surrounding meetings of the World Trade Organization (WTO), the International Monetary Fund, and the World Bank have made clear, economic globalization and accelerating technological change raise significant public policy questions. The debates over global governance that arose in those venues are now also taking place in the IT world, where questions about participation, accountability, and transparency are becoming increasingly urgent. Nonprofits can contribute to the governance process by developing, articulating, and synthesizing noncommercial views, and also by providing leadership, resources, and public-spiritedness.

The voices of developing nations and civil society need to be heard, and they must be able to participate with equal dignity in global Internet governance if they are to successfully influence Internet policies or, if not, at least accept those policies as legitimate. All three sectors—government, business, and nonprofit—from both developing and developed countries need to have seats at the table when Internet policy is made. Democratic governments provide public accountability and possess enforcement and oversight capabilities; the private sector offers technological expertise and a driving culture of innovation; and nonprofit organizations, which are less bureaucratic than governments and less commercially motivated than businesses, provide their own expertise and inspire confidence through their focus on the public interest. No single institution or sector is equipped to handle the task on its own.

Finally, Internet governance structures must usher in improved openness and accountability. Nontraditional bodies (such as the Internet Corporation for Assigned Names and Numbers [ICANN], the World Wide Web Consortium, or TRUSTe) that engage in Internet regulation and oversight have arisen in recent years, but their decision-making processes are too often both inaccessible and unaccountable to those most affected.

Ultimately, achieving transparency and accountability is in an institution's own self-interest. Establishing clearly the scope of authority of a governance organization and the rationale for its actions increases its effectiveness and bolsters its credibility.

I THINK ICANN

The current debates about ICANN are a harbinger of future dilemmas of Internet governance. ICANN remains the frontier institution and the test case for global governance in the IT sector.

The U.S. government created ICANN in 1998 as a private, nonprofit corporation to regulate the Internet's unique identifier systems, including the domain name system (DNS). This may sound like an arcane topic, but the

DNS is vital to the Internet's operation. It is an instructive example of the kind of seemingly technical issues that have major economic and policy implications needing to be addressed through effective governance models. For example, whoever controls the DNS will determine what new suffixes, such as "com" or "org" (known as top-level domain names, or TLDs), can come after the "dot" in Internet addresses. ICANN is also slated to take control of the root-server system, the authoritative database of all TLDs and the means by which individual computers are able to "find" Web sites or Internet addresses. In the words of ICANN's Committee on Evolution and Reform, "ICANN serves as the global Internet community's open policy-making forum" for these general-purpose TLDs and therefore offers "dispute resolution, business models, and mechanisms for local community participation and policymaking."

When ICANN recently chose new TLDs, however, it never explained or documented its decision-making process. Representative Edward Markey (D-Mass.) of the House Telecommunications and Internet Subcommittee complained, "Events at the Vatican are shrouded in less mystery than how ICANN chooses new domain names."

Although ICANN was created by the U.S. government, no government official from any country has a seat on the organization's board; governments play, at best, only an advisory role. Recognizing the wide spectrum of groups with a stake in the Internet, ICANN has created a decentralized structure of supporting organizations, advisory committees, working groups, and task forces from which it aims to distill agreement about the Internet's future direction. It was also called on to involve ordinary users in its work in an unprecedented manner. In 2000 ICANN held direct elections for almost half its board of directors, theoretically allowing anyone in the world with an e-mail address to vote. As the first election of its kind, it was not particularly successful because it had severely limited resources and because there was little consideration of what constituted a legitimate constituency or adequate representation. In fact, the ICANN election demonstrated the impossibility of securing genuinely global representation through direct elections. But, importantly, it did succeed in establishing that there are public policy implications of ICANN decisions and that adequate representation of the public interest is needed.

In February 2002, ICANN's own president, Stuart Lynn, joined the chorus of critics who complained that the organization was not sufficiently open or accountable to the vast global public it serves. Lynn declared that ICANN was overburdened with process, lacked necessary funding and participation from crucial stakeholders, and was in danger of failing its mission if it kept to its present course. Lynn proposed shrinking the size of the ICANN board, increasing its authority, and scrapping direct elections in favor of government representatives—prompting longtime ICANN critic Professor Michael Froomkin to gibe, "It is strange that ICANN, which was created to save the Internet from governments, is now turning to governments to save it from the Internet." The review process following Lynn's proposal—including congressional hearings, the ICANN Committee on Evolution and Reform, and the actions of the board itself—illustrates the challenges in moving toward a more accountable governance structure that will represent all stakeholders. The process to date has moved slowly, produced thin results, and emphasizes the need for greater attention to the course of the transition to better Internet governance.

ICANN's credibility as a global manager of critical parts of the Internet's infrastructure depends on the board's ability to ensure that all the various private and public interests are represented. Government involvement is one step toward providing public-interest representation but is insufficient on its own. Only with truly broad representation on its board—including nonprofit organizations—can ICANN adequately address the crisis of legitimacy that plagues it. As most observers would agree, ICANN, in spite of being organized as a private, nonprofit corporation, still performs "public trust" functions. If ICANN is not to become a governmental entity, then it must implement a better system of decision-making and must not abandon the goal of ensuring public representation.

Furthermore, ICANN must take steps to bolster transparency and accountability. These steps should include some kind of public oversight by politically accountable officials; development of due-process principles and clear, publicly available procedures for the resolution of complaints; public disclosure of its funding sources and budgets; staff and board members who are held accountable to a clear set of professional norms and standards; open meetings; and documentation of the rationale for ICANN's policy decisions and actions.

These challenges were recognized in the amended September 2002 memorandum of understanding (MOU) between the U.S. Department of Commerce and ICANN. The MOU extends ICANN's mandate for one year and provides for heightened scrutiny of its accountability, transparency, and responsiveness to Internet stakeholders. Over the next year, ICANN will need to show substantial progress if it is to gain the confidence of the Internet community and warrant its continued role in IT governance.

THE ROAD AHEAD

Any organization that attempts to make global IT policy must encourage worldwide public participation. Some international policymaking bodies have begun trying to engage broader constituencies. The World Intellectual Property Organization, for example, has assisted stakeholders that have limited or no means of participation, providing them with training, information, equipment, and support.

The WTO helps promote developing-country participation in governance through regular training sessions on trade policy in Geneva; technical cooperation activities, including seminars and workshops in various countries; and Trade Reference Centers for more than 75 poor countries, which provide trade ministries with the IT required to access the WTO Internet site and other trade-related sites, including electronic databases. Whereas there was little possibility for direct public involvement in WTO proceedings prior to the 1999 Seattle protests, today the organization is trying to broaden participation through explicit outreach to individuals, including more transparency and more information posted on the Web. In addition, interested parties may now submit comments to the WTO.

These developments are a welcome start, yet much remains to be done. Take TRUSTe, a nonprofit entity substituting for government in certifying Web sites' privacy policies. When Yahoo abruptly changed its privacy preferences for customers without their consent, TRUSTe allowed Yahoo to continue to carry its "trustmark" without being held accountable to users who relied on the seal's integrity.

In contrast, under the safe-harbor provisions negotiated between the United States and the European Union, the self-regulation of corporations will be backed by the enforcement powers of governments. These safe-harbor provisions were drafted to bridge the gap between divergent U.S. and European approaches to privacy protection.

It is too soon to tell which system, that exemplified by TRUSTe or one based on the safe-harbor provisions, will be most effective. The bottom line, however, is clear: increasing the perceived legitimacy of international governance institutions and regimes demands greater accountability and transparency.

The Internet has become part of the mainstream, and therefore mainstream governmental institutions will be expected to step in to protect people from harm and encourage innovation. But government cannot do this alone without the know-how and creativity of both the business world and civil society. A pluralistic and broad-based model is needed. It will be difficult to create the norms and institutions required for different sectors to work together in equal partnership, yet experiments such as the G-8 Digital Opportunity Task Force and the UN Information and Communications Technologies Task Force already show promise. Both were set up by governments but are led by a mix of government, business, and nonprofit organizations from the developed and developing worlds.

Making fair and effective public policy in our networked society is an enormous challenge, and one that will not be overcome simply by recognizing the inherent complexities of the process. The road ahead may not be easy, but keeping the global public interest at the forefront will steer Internet governance in the right direction.

ZOË BAIRD is President of the Markle Foundation.

UNIT 6

Risk and Security

Unit Selections

30. **Homeland Insecurity**, Charles C. Mann
31. **Are You the Weak Link?** Kevin D. Mitnick
32. **Code Red for the Web**, Carolyn Meinel
33. **Networking the Infrastructure**, Wade Roush
34. **Will Spyware Work?** Kevin Hogan
35. **The Shock of the Old**, Edward Tenner
36. **Data Extinction**, Claire Tristram

Key Points to Consider

- The overview to this unit mentions Michael Crichton's latest novel, *Prey.* The physicist Freeman Dyson reviews this novel in the February 13, 2002 issue of *The New York Review of Books* (http://www.nybooks.com/articles/16053) Do you agree with what he has to say about the threats that technology holds for us?
- Kevin Mitnick, author of "Are You the Weak Link?" and a convicted computer criminal, is now a computer security consultant. Can you imagine a bank robber going to work for the banking industry? How about a car thief consulting for the police department? Do these examples say anything about the way we view white-collar crime in general and computer crime in particular? Explain.
- Use the Internet to find out more about Robert Tappan Morris, mentioned in the overview to this unit. His family history is interesting. Why?
- Do you feel safe giving your credit card number to merchants over the Web? Find out how (or if) your number is protected from criminals who might traffic between you and the merchant?

Links: www.dushkin.com/online/
These sites are annotated in the World Wide Web pages.

AntiOnline: Hacking and Hackers
http://www.antionline.com/index.php

Copyright & Trademark Information for the IEEE Computer Society
http://computer.org/copyright.htm

Electonic Privacy Information Center (EPIC)
http://epic.org

Internet Privacy Coalition
http://www.epic.org/crypto/

Center for Democracy and Technology
http://www.cdt.org/crypto/

Survive Spyware
http://www.cnet.com/internet/0-3761-8-3217791-1.html

An Electronic Pearl Harbor? Not Likely
http://www.nap.edu/issues/15.1/smith.htm

If literature and film are any guide, we in the United States and Western Europe have tangled feelings about technology. On the one hand, we embrace each technical marvel that enters the market place. On the other, a world in which machines threaten humanity is a cultural staple. Currently, Michael Crichton's latest novel, *Prey,* is frightening us with killer robots that evolved by natural selection to inhabit bodies, snatch souls, and take over the world. As I write this overview, teenagers around the country are lining up to watch the handsome couple from *The Matrix,* Neo and Trinity, once again take on our creations run amuck.

As it happens, we have good reason to worry about technology, especially computer technology, but the risks are more prosaic than machines that farm humans for their energy. They include privacy intrusions, software that cannot be made error-free, and deliberate sabotage. We even have reason to fear that much of our cultural heritage, now digitized, will be inaccessible when the software used to encode it becomes obsolete. These are issues that concern practicing computer scientists and engineers. The *Communications of the ACM,* the leading journal in the field, has run a column in recent years called "Inside Risks," dedicated to exploring the unintended consequences of computing. Another ACM journal, *Software Engineering Notes,* devotes a large part of each issue to chronicling software failures. The author of "The Shock of the Old," Edward Tenner, is also the author of a distressing chronicle of technical mishaps: *Why Things Bite Back: Technology and Revenge of Unintended Consequences* (Vintage, 1997).

With the attacks of September 11, computer security, always a troublesome issue, has been receiving a great deal of attention. The lead article in this unit, "Homeland Insecurity," is a long and fascinating profile of Bruce Schneier, once a prominent writer on cryptography. His Applied Cryptography (Wiley, 1996) is a standard reference. Schneier is now the owner of a computer security firm that brings a commonsense, low-tech approach to computer crime. He believes that current approaches to network security, emphasizing technical cure-alls, are, at best, wrong. Some will even make us less safe. A story from the automobile industry illustrates the problem. In the 1990s, manufacturers began to make the ignitions of expensive cars hard to hot-wire and so more difficult to steal. The technical fix worked. It has reduced the likelihood that a car will be stolen from a parking lot. It seems also to have contributed to the invention of carjacking, a more dangerous crime.

The first article in the unit portrays a reformed technologist. The second is by his one-time opposite turned business competitor. Kevin Mitnick is a reformed computer criminal, now offering computer security advice. He is also a hacker of legendary standing. Mitnick argues that while companies are spending more and more on sophisticated technologies to guard their systems, they have "neglected the weakest link: employees." He calls the art of teasing passwords from employees "social engineering." Mitnick makes the case that intrusions through an old-fashioned con are as dangerous as the attacks of technically sophisticated hackers.

Ever since a Cornell graduate student, Robert Tappan Morris, released a worm onto the fledgling Internet in 1988, computer experts and users alike have been aware of computer network vulnerability. In "Code Red for the Web," Carolyn Meinel tells the story of the Code Red worm, "a self-replicating, self-contained" program, that infected more than 359,000 servers within 14 hours of its release in 2001. Meinel, herself, is becoming an increasingly common type in the world of hacking, an insider working for the good guys. She runs an interesting Web site for hackers (www.happyhacker.org) that offers this advice from someone who calls himself "Agent Steal," and who claims to be writing from an unnamed federal prison: "Let me tell you what this all means. You're going to get busted, lose everything you own, not get out on bail, snitch on your enemies, get even more time than you expected, and have to put up with a bunch of idiots in prison. Sounds fun? Keep hacking." Good advice, of course.

The next three articles, all drawn from a special issue of Technology Review, following the September 11, 2001, terrorist attacks, are about how we might prepare ourselves for another. "Networking the Infrastructure," by Wade Roush takes a technical approach, arguing that "The key lies in developing and deploying technologies that will tie infrastructure components together into a system that's far smarter and more self-aware than anything we have today." Built to withstand nuclear warfare, the Internet is the ideal for an interconnected, redundant infrastructure.

Both Kevin Hogan in "Will Spyware Work?" and Edward Tenner in "The Shock of the Old" take a more skeptical view of the role of computer technology in protecting us from terrorism. Hogan begins with the fundamental question that is still being asked, 2 years after the attacks. How is it, with the vast resources and global reach of the American intelligence agencies, that the government was not warned about the plot? The answer, according to Hogan, is partly due to a flaw in the system: "Security and intelligence experts agree that the mass of information generated [by intelligence technology] every day around the world far outstrips the capacity of present-day technologies to process it." We have already mentioned Edward Tenner, author of "The Shock of the Old." Here he argues that while American authorities were "on high alert, not only for accidental failures of vital systems but for cyberattacks," the terrorists who did arrive used methods that "were surprisingly low tech."

The final article in the unit, "Data Extinction," also from *Technology Review,* points out a problem that everyone who owns a computer has encountered but which is receiving very little attention in our rush to digitize cultural resources. Digital documents, from photographs to recorded music to written work, are inaccessible when the devices used to create them become obsolete. This problem, so easy to state, is surprisingly difficult to solve.

SPECIAL REPORT

HOMELAND INSECURITY

A top expert says America's approach to protecting itself will only make matters worse. Forget "foolproof" technology—we need systems designed to fail smartly.

- *To stop the rampant theft of expensive cars, manufacturers in the 1990s began to make ignitions very difficult to hot-wire. This reduced the likelihood that cars would be stolen from parking lots—but apparently contributed to the sudden appearance of a new and more dangerous crime, carjacking.*
- *After a vote against management Vivendi Universal announced earlier this year that its electronic shareholder-voting system, which it had adopted to tabulate votes efficiently and securely, had been broken into by hackers. Because the new system eliminated the old paper ballots, recounting the votes—or even independently verifying that the attack had occurred—was impossible.*
- *To help merchants verify and protect the identity of their customers, marketing firms and financial institutions have created large computerized databases of personal information: Social Security numbers, credit-card numbers, telephone numbers, home addresses, and the like. With these databases being increasingly interconnected by means of the Internet, they have become irresistible targets for criminals. From 1995 to 2000 the incidence of identity theft tripled.*

BY CHARLES C. MANN

As was often the case, Bruce Schneier was thinking about a really terrible idea. We were driving around the suburban-industrial wasteland south of San Francisco, on our way to a corporate presentation, while Schneier looked for something to eat not purveyed by a chain restaurant. This was important to Schneier, who in addition to being America's best-known ex-cryptographer is a food writer for an alternative newspaper in Minneapolis, where he lives. Initially he had been sure that in the crazy ethnic salad of Silicon Valley it would be impossible not to find someplace of culinary interest—a Libyan burger stop, a Hmong bagelry, a Szechuan taco stand. But as the rented car swept toward the vast, amoeboid office complex that was our destination, his faith slowly crumbled. Bowing to reality, he parked in front of a nondescript sandwich shop, disappointment evident on his face.

Schneier is a slight, busy man with a dark, full, closely cropped beard. Until a few years ago he was best known as a prominent creator of codes and ciphers; his book *Applied Cryptography* (1993) is a classic in the field. But despite his success he virtually abandoned cryptography in 1999 and co-founded a company named Counterpane Internet Security. Counterpane has spent considerable sums on advanced engineering, but at heart the company is dedicated to bringing one of the oldest forms of policing—the cop on the beat—to the digital realm. Aided by high-tech sensors, human guards at Counterpane patrol computer networks, helping corporations and governments to keep their secrets secret. In a world that is both ever more interconnected and full of malice, this is a task of considerable difficulty and great importance. It is also what Schneier long believed cryptography would do—which brings us back to his terrible idea.

"Pornography!" he exclaimed. If the rise of the Internet has shown anything, it is that huge numbers of middle-class, middle-management types like to look at dirty pictures on computer screens. A good way to steal the corporate or government secrets these middle managers are privy to, Schneier said, would be to set up a pornographic Web site. The Web site would be free, but visitors would have to register to download the naughty bits. Registration would involve creating a password—and here Schneier's deep-set blue eyes widened mischievously.

People have trouble with passwords. The idea is to have a random string of letters, numbers, and symbols that is easy to remember. Alas, random strings are by their nature hard to remember, so people use bad but easy-to-remember passwords, such as "hello" and "password." (A survey last year of 1,200 British office workers found that almost half chose their own name, the name of a pet, or that of a family member as a password; others based their passwords on the names Darth Vader and Homer Simpson.) Moreover, computer users can't keep different passwords straight, so they use the same bad passwords for all their accounts.

Many of his corporate porn surfers, Schneier predicted, would use for the dirty Web site the same password they used at work. Not only that, many users would surf to the porn site on the fast Internet connection at the office. The operators of Schneier's nefarious site would thus learn that, say, "Joesmith," who accessed the Web site from Anybusiness.com, used the password "JoeS." By trying to log on at Anybusiness.com as "Joesmith," they could learn whether "JoeS" was also the password into Joesmith's corporate account. Often it would be.

The way people think about security, especially security on computer networks, is almost always wrong. All too often planners seek cures, magic bullets to make problems vanish. Most of the security measures envisioned after September 11 will be ineffective—and some will even make Americans less safe than they would be without them.

"In six months you'd be able to break into Fortune 500 companies and government agencies all over the world," Schneier said, chewing his nondescript meal. "It would work! It would work—that's the awful thing."

During the 1990s Schneier was a field marshal in the disheveled army of computer geeks, mathematicians, civil-liberties activists, and libertarian wackos that—in a series of bitter lawsuits that came to be known as the Crypto Wars—asserted the right of the U.S. citizenry to use the cryptographic equivalent of kryptonite: ciphers so powerful they cannot be broken by any government, no matter how long and hard it tries. Like his fellows, he believed that "strong crypto," as these ciphers are known, would forever guarantee the privacy and security of information—something that in the Information Age would be vital to people's lives. "It is insufficient to protect ourselves with laws" he wrote in *Applied Cryptography*. "We need to protect ourselves with mathematics."

Schneier's side won the battle as the nineties came to a close. But by that time he had realized that he was fighting the wrong war. Crypto was not enough to guarantee privacy and security. Failures occurred all the time—which was what Schneier's terrible idea demonstrated. No matter what kind of technological safeguards an organization uses, its secrets will never be safe while its employees are sending their passwords, however unwittingly, to pornographers—or to anyone else outside the organization.

The Parable of the Dirty Web Site illustrates part of what became the thesis of Schneier's most recent book, *Secrets and Lies* (2000): The way people think about security, especially security on computer networks, is almost always wrong. All too often planners seek technological cure-alls, when such security measures at best limit risks to acceptable levels. In particular, the consequences of going wrong—and all these systems go wrong sometimes—are rarely considered. For these reasons Schneier believes that most of the security measures envisioned after September 11 will be ineffective, and that some will make Americans *less* safe.

It is now a year since the World Trade Center was destroyed. Legislators, the law-enforcement community, and the Bush Administration are embroiled in an essential debate over the measures necessary to prevent future attacks. To armor-plate the nation's security they increasingly look to the most powerful technology available: retina, iris, and fingerprint scanners; "smart" driver's licenses and visas that incorporate anti-counterfeiting chips; digital surveillance of public places with face-recognition software; huge centralized databases that use data-mining routines to sniff out hidden terrorists. Some of these measures have already been mandated by Congress, and others are in the pipeline. State and local agencies around the nation are adopting their own schemes. More mandates and more schemes will surely follow.

Schneier is hardly against technology—he's the sort of person who immediately cases public areas for outlets to recharge the batteries in his laptop, phone, and other electronic prostheses. "But if you think technology can solve your security problems," he says, "then you don't understand the problems and you don't understand the technology." Indeed, he regards the national push for a high-tech salve for security anxieties as a reprise of his own early and erroneous beliefs about the transforming power of strong crypto. The new technologies have enormous capacities, but their advocates have not realized that the most critical aspect of a security measure is not how well it works but how well it fails.

The Crypto Wars

If mathematicians from the 1970s were suddenly transported through time to the present, they would be happily surprised by developments such as the proofs to Kepler's conjecture (proposed in 1611, confirmed in 1998) and to Fermat's last theorem (1637, 1994). But they would be absolutely astonished by the RSA Conference, the world's biggest trade show for cryptographers. Sponsored by the cryptography firm RSA Security, the conferences are attended by as many as 10,000 cryptographers, computer scientists, network managers, and digital-security professionals. What would amaze past mathematicians is not just the number of conferences but that they exist at all.

Cryptology is a specialized branch of mathematics with some computer science thrown in. As recently as the 1970s there were no cryptology courses in university mathematics or computer-science departments; nor were there crypto textbooks, crypto journals, or crypto software. There was no private crypto industry, let alone venture-capitalized crypto start-ups giving away key rings at trade shows (*crypto key* rings—techno-humor). Cryptography, the practice of cryptology, was the province of a tiny cadre of obsessed amateurs, the National Security Agency, and the NSA's counterparts abroad. Now it is a multibillion-dollar field with applications in almost every commercial arena.

As one of the people who helped to bring this change about, Schneier is always invited to speak at RSA conferences. Every time, the room is too small, and overflow crowds, eager to hear their favorite guru, force the session into a larger venue, which is what happened when I saw him speak at an RSA conference in San Francisco's Moscone Center last year. There was applause from the hundreds of seated cryptophiles when Schneier mounted the stage, and more applause from the throng standing in the aisles and exits when he apologized for the lack of seating capacity. He was there to talk about the state of computer security, he said. It was as bad as ever, maybe getting worse.

In the past security officers were usually terse ex-military types who wore holsters and brush cuts. But as computers have become both attackers' chief targets and their chief weapons, a new generation of security professionals has emerged, drawn from the ranks of engineering and computer science. Many of the new guys look like people the old guard would have wanted to arrest, and Schneier is no exception. Although he is a co-founder of a successful company, he sometimes wears scuffed black shoes and pants with a wavering press line; he gathers his thinning hair into a straggly ponytail. Ties, for the most part, are not an issue. Schneier's style marks him as a true nerd—someone who knows the potential, both good and bad, of technology, which in our technocentric era is an asset.

Schneier was raised in Brooklyn. He got a B.S. in physics from the University of Rochester in 1985 and an M.S. in computer science from American University two years later. Until 1991, he worked for the Department of Defense, where he did things he won't discuss. Lots of kids are intrigued by codes and ciphers, but Schneier was surely one of the few to ask his father, a lawyer and a judge, to write secret messages for him to analyze. On his first visit to a voting booth, with his mother, he tried to figure out how she could cheat and vote twice. He didn't actually want her to vote twice—he just wanted, as he says, to "game the system."

Unsurprisingly, someone so interested in figuring out the secrets of manipulating the system fell in love with the systems for manipulating secrets. Schneier's childhood years, as it happened, were a good time to become intrigued by cryptography—the best time in history, in fact. In 1976 two researchers at Stanford University invented an entirely new type of encryption, public-key encryption, which abruptly woke up the entire field.

Public-key encryption is complicated in detail but simple in outline. All ciphers employ mathematical procedures called algorithms to transform messages from their original form into an unreadable jumble. (Cryptographers work with ciphers and not codes, which are spy-movie-style lists of prearranged substitutes for letters, words, or phrases—"meet at the theater" for "attack at nightfall.") Most ciphers use secret keys: mathematical values that plug into the algorithm. Breaking a cipher means figuring out the key. In a kind of mathematical sleight of hand, public-key encryption encodes messages with keys that can be published openly and decodes them with different keys that stay secret and are effectively impossible to break using today's technology. (A more complete explanation of public-key encryption is on *The Atlantic*'s Web site, www.theatlantic.com.)

WHY THE MAGINOT LINE FAILED

In fact, the Maginot Line, the chain of fortifications on France's border with Germany, was indicative neither of despair about defeating Germany nor of thought mired in the past. It was instead evidence of faith that technology could substitute for manpower. It was a forerunner of the strategic bomber, the guided missile, and the "smart bomb." The same faith led to France's building tanks with thicker armor and bigger guns than German tanks had, deploying immensely larger quantities of mobile big guns, and above all committing to maintain a continuous line—that is, advancing or retreating in such coordination as to prevent an enemy from establishing a salient from which it could cut off a French unit from supplies and reinforcements. (Today, military strategists call this "force protection.") But having machines do the work of men and putting emphasis on minimal loss of life carried a price in slowed-down reaction times and lessened initiative for battlefield commanders.

—Ernest R. May, *Strange Victory: Hitler's Conquest of France* (2000)

The best-known public-key algorithm is the RSA algorithm, whose name comes from the initials of the three mathematicians who invented it. RSA keys are created by manipulating big prime numbers. If the private decoding RSA key is properly chosen, guessing it necessarily involves factoring a very large number into its constituent primes, something for which no mathematician has ever devised an adequate shortcut. Even if demented government agents spent a trillion dollars on custom factoring computers, Schneier has estimated, the sun would likely go nova before they cracked a message enciphered with a public key of sufficient length.

Schneier and other technophiles grasped early how important computer networks would become to daily life. They also understood that those networks were dreadfully insecure. Strong crypto, in their view, was an answer of almost magical efficacy. Even federal officials believed that strong crypto would Change Everything Forever—except they thought the change would be for

The Worm in the Machine

Buffer overflows (sometimes called *stack smashing*) are the most common form of security vulnerability in the last ten years. They're also the easiest to exploit; more attacks are the result of buffer overflows than any other problem...

Computers store everything, programs and data, in memory. If the computer asks a user for an 8-character password and receives a 200-character password, those extra characters may overwrite some other area in memory. (They're not supposed to—that's the bug.) If it is just the right area of memory, and we overwrite it with just the right characters, we can change a "deny connection" instruction to an "allow access" command or even get our own code executed.

The Morris worm is probably the most famous overflow-bug exploit. It exploited a buffer overflow in the UNIX fingerd program. It's supposed to be a benign program, returning the identity of a user to whomever asks. This program accepted as input a variable that is supposed to contain the identity of the user. Unfortunately, the fingerd program never limited the size of the input. Input larger than 512 bytes overflowed the buffer, and Morris wrote a specific large input that allowed his rogue program to [install and run] itself... Over 6,000 servers crashed as a result; at the time [in 1988] that was about 10 percent of the Internet.

Skilled programming can prevent this kind of attack. The program can truncate the password at 8 characters, so those extra 192 characters never get written into memory anywhere... The problem is that with any piece of modern, large, complex code, there are just too many places where buffer overflows are possible... It's very difficult to guarantee that there are no overflow problems, even if you take the time to check. The larger and more complex the code is, the more likely the attack.

Windows 2000 has somewhere between 35 and 60 million lines of code, and no one outside the programming team has ever seen them.

—Bruce Schneier, *Secrets and Lies: Digital Security in a Networked World* (2000)

the worse. Strong encryption "jeopardizes the public safety and national security of this country," Louis Freeh, then the director of the (famously computer-challenged) Federal Bureau of Investigation, told Congress in 1995. "Drug cartels, terrorists, and kidnappers will use telephones and other communications media with impunity knowing that their conversations are immune" from wiretaps.

The Crypto Wars erupted in 1991, when Washington attempted to limit the spread of strong crypto. Schneier testified before Congress against restrictions on encryption, campaigned for crypto freedom on the Internet, co-wrote an influential report on the technical snarls awaiting federal plans to control cryptographic protocols, and rallied 75,000 crypto fans to the cause in his free monthly e-mail newsletter, *Crypto-Gram* (www.counterpane.com/crypto-gram.html). Most important, he wrote *Applied Cryptography*, the first-ever comprehensive guide to the practice of cryptology.

Washington lost the wars in 1999, when an appellate court ruled that restrictions on cryptography were illegal, because crypto algorithms were a form of speech and thus covered by the First Amendment. After the ruling the FBI and the NSA more or less surrendered. In the sudden silence the dazed combatants surveyed the battleground. Crypto had become widely available, and it had indeed fallen into unsavory hands. But the results were different from what either side had expected.

As the crypto aficionados had envisioned, software companies inserted crypto into their products. On the "Tools" menu in Microsoft Outlook, for example, "encrypt" is an option. And encryption became big business, as part of the infrastructure for e-commerce—it is the little padlock that appears in the corner of Net suffers' browsers when they buy books at Amazon.com, signifying that credit-card numbers are being enciphered. But encryption is rarely used by the citizenry it was supposed to protect and empower. Cryptophiles, Schneier among them, had been so enraptured by the possibilities of uncrackable ciphers that they forgot they were living in a world in which people can't program VCRs. Inescapably, an encrypted message is harder to send than an unencrypted one, if only because of the effort involved in using all the extra software. So few people use encryption software that most companies have stopped selling it to individuals.

Among the few who do use crypto are human-rights activists living under dictatorships. But, just as the FBI feared, terrorists, child pornographers, and the Mafia use it too. Yet crypto has not protected any of them. As an example, Schneier points to the case of Nicodemo Scarfo, who the FBI believed was being groomed to take over a gambling operation in New Jersey. Agents surreptitiously searched his office in 1999 and discovered that he was that rarity, a gangster nerd. On his computer was the long-awaited nightmare for law enforcement: a crucial document scrambled by strong encryption software. Rather than sit by, the FBI installed a "keystroke logger" on Scarfo's machine. The logger recorded the decrypting key—or, more precisely, the passphrase Scarfo used to generate that key—as he typed it in, and gained access to his incriminating files. Scarfo pleaded guilty to charges of running an illegal gambling business on February 28 of this year.

Schneier was not surprised by this demonstration of the impotence of cryptography. Just after the Crypto Wars ended, he had begun writing a follow-up to *Applied Cryptography*. But this time Schneier, a fluent writer, was blocked—he couldn't make himself extol strong crypto as a security panacea. As Schneier put it in *Secrets and Lies*, the very different book he eventually did write, he had been portraying cryptography—in his speeches, in his congressional testimony, in *Applied Cryptography*—as "a kind of magic security dust that [people] could sprinkle over their software and make it secure." It was not. Nothing could be. Humiliatingly, Schneier discovered that, as a friend wrote him, "the world was full of bad security systems designed by people who read *Applied Cryptography*."

In retrospect he says, "Crypto solved the wrong problem." Ciphers scramble messages and documents, preventing them from being read while, say, they are transmitted on the Internet. But the strongest crypto is gossamer protection if malevolent people have access to the computers on the other end. Encrypting transactions on the Internet, the Purdue computer scientist Eugene Spafford has remarked, "is the equivalent of arranging an armored car to deliver credit-card information from someone living in a cardboard box to someone living on a park bench."

To effectively seize control of Scarfo's computer, FBI agents had to break into his office and physically alter his machine. Such black-bag jobs are ever less necessary, because the rise of networks and the Internet means that computers can be controlled remotely, without their operators' knowledge. Huge computer databases may be useful, but they also become tempting targets for criminals and terrorists. So do home computers, even if they are connected only intermittently to the Web. Hackers look for vulnerable machines, using software that scans thousands of Net connections at once. This vulnerability, Schneier came to think, is the real security issue.

With this realization he closed Counterpane Systems, his five-person crypto-consulting company in Chicago, in 1999. He revamped it and reopened immediately in Silicon Valley with a new name, Counterpane Internet Security, and a new idea—one that relied on old-fashioned methods. Counterpane would still keep data secret. But the lessons of the Crypto Wars had given Schneier a different vision of how to do that—a vision that has considerable relevance for a nation attempting to prevent terrorist crimes.

Where Schneier had sought one overarching technical fix, hard experience had taught him the quest was illusory. Indeed, yielding to the American penchant for all-in-one high-tech solutions can make us *less* safe—especially when it leads to enormous databases full of confidential information. Secrecy is important, of course, but it is also a trap. The more secrets necessary to a security system, the more vulnerable it becomes.

To forestall attacks, security systems need to be small-scale, redundant, and compartmentalized. Rather than large, sweeping programs, they should be carefully crafted mosaics, each piece aimed at a specific weakness. The federal government and the airlines are spending millions of dollars, Schneier points out, on systems that screen every passenger to keep knives and weapons out of planes. But what matters most is keeping dangerous passengers out of airline cockpits, which can be accomplished by reinforcing the door. Similarly, it is seldom necessary to gather large amounts of additional information, because in modern societies people leave wide audit trails. The problem is sifting through the already existing mountain of data. Calls for heavy monitoring and record-keeping are thus usually a mistake. ("Broad surveillance is a mark of bad security," Schneier wrote in a recent *Crypto-Gram*.)

To halt attacks once they start, security measures must avoid being subject to single points of failure. Computer networks are particularly vulnerable: once hackers bypass the firewall, the whole system is often open for exploitation. Because every security measure in every system can be broken or gotten around, failure must be incorporated into the design. No single failure should compromise the normal functioning of the entire system or, worse, add to the gravity of the initial breach. Finally, and most important, decisions need to be made by people at close range—and the responsibility needs to be given explicitly to people, not computers.

The moral, Schneier came to believe, is that security measures are characterized less by their success than by their manner of failure. All security systems eventually miscarry in one way or another. But when this happens to the good ones, they stretch and sag before breaking, each component failure leaving the whole as unaffected as possible.

Unfortunately, there is little evidence that these principles are playing any role in the debate in the Administration, Congress, and the media about how to protect the nation. Indeed, in the argument over policy and principle almost no one seems to be paying attention to the practicalities of security—a lapse that Schneier, like other security professionals, finds as incomprehensible as it is dangerous.

Stealing Your Thumb

A couple of months after September 11, I flew from Seattle to Los Angeles to meet Schneier. As I was checking in at Sea-Tac Airport, someone ran through the metal detector and disappeared onto the little subway that runs among the terminals. Although the authorities quickly identified the miscreant, a concession stand worker, they still had to empty all the terminals and re-screen everyone in the airport, including passengers who had already boarded planes. Masses of unhappy passengers stretched back hundreds of feet from the checkpoints. Planes by the dozen sat waiting at the gates. I called Schneier on a cell phone to report my delay. I had to shout over the noise of all the other people on their cell phones making similar calls. "What a mess" Schneier said. "The problem with airport security, you know, is that it fails badly."

For a moment I couldn't make sense of this gnomic utterance. Then I realized he meant that when something goes wrong with security, the system should recover well. In Seattle a single slip-up shut down the entire airport, which delayed flights across the nation. Sea-Tac, Schneier told me on the phone, had no adequate way to contain the damage from a breakdown—such as a button installed near the x-ray machines to stop the subway, so that idiots who bolt from checkpoints cannot disappear into another terminal. The shutdown would inconvenience subway riders, but not as much as being forced to go through security again after a wait of several hours. An even better idea would be to place the x-ray machines at the departure gates, as some are in Europe, in order to scan each group of passengers closely and minimize inconvenience to the whole airport if a risk is detected—or if a machine or a guard fails.

Schneier was in Los Angeles for two reasons. He was to speak to ICANN, the Internet Corporation for Assigned Names and Numbers, which controls the "domain name system" of Internet addresses. It is Schneier's belief that attacks on the address database are the best means of taking down the Internet. He also wanted to review Ginza Sushi-Ko, perhaps the nation's most exclusive restaurant, for the food column he writes with his wife, Karen Cooper.

The government has been calling for a new security infrastructure: iris, retina, and fingerprint scanners; hand-geometry assayers; face-recognition software; smart cards with custom identification chips. Their use may on the whole make Americans less safe, because many of these tools fail badly—they're "brittle," in engineering jargon.

Minutes after my delayed arrival Schneier had with characteristic celerity packed himself and me into a taxi. The restaurant was in a shopping mall in Beverly Hills that was disguised to look like a collection of nineteenth-century Italian villas. By the time Schneier strode into the tiny lobby, he had picked up the thread of our airport discussion. Failing badly, he told me, was something he had been forced to spend time thinking about.

In his technophilic exuberance he had been seduced by the promise of public-key encryption. But ultimately Schneier observed that even strong crypto fails badly. When something bypasses it, as the keystroke logger did with Nicodemo Scarfo's encryption, it provides no protection at all. The moral, Schneier came to believe, is that security measures are characterized less by their manner of success than by their manner of failure. All security systems eventually miscarry. But when this happens to the good ones, they stretch and sag before breaking, each component failure leaving the whole as unaffected as possible. Engineers call such failure-tolerant systems "ductile." One way to capture much of what Schneier told me is to say that he believes that when possible, security schemes should be designed to maximize ductility, whereas they often maximize strength.

Since September 11 the government has been calling for a new security infrastructure—one that employs advanced technology to protect the citizenry and track down malefactors. Already the USA PATRIOT Act, which Congress passed in October, mandates the establishment of a "cross-agency, cross-platform electronic system… to confirm the identity" of visa applicants, along with a "highly secure network" for financial-crime data and "secure information sharing systems" to link other, previously separate databases. Pending legislation demands that the Attorney General employ "technology including, but not limited to, electronic fingerprinting, face recognition, and retinal scan technology." The proposed Department of Homeland Security is intended to oversee a "national research and development enterprise for homeland security comparable in emphasis and scope to that which has supported the national security community for more than fifty years"—a domestic version of the high-tech R&D juggernaut that produced stealth bombers, smart weapons, and anti-missile defense.

Iris, retina, and fingerprint scanners; hand-geometry assayers; remote video-network surveillance; face-recognition software; smart cards with custom identification chips; decompressive baggage checkers that vacuum-extract minute chemical samples from inside suitcases; tiny radio implants beneath the skin that continually broadcast people's identification codes; pulsed fast-neutron analysis of shipping containers ("so precise," according to one manufacturer, "it can determine within inches the location of the concealed target"); a vast national network of interconnected databases—the list goes on and on. In the first five months after the terrorist attacks the Pentagon liaison office that works with technology companies received more than 12,000 proposals for high-tech security measures. Credit-card companies expertly manage credit risks with advanced information-sorting algorithms, Larry Ellison, the head of Oracle, the world's biggest database firm, told *The New York Times* in April; "We should be managing security risks in exactly the same way." To "win the war on terrorism," a former deputy undersecretary of commerce, David J. Rothkopf, explained in the May/June issue of *Foreign Policy*, the nation will need "regiments of geeks"—"pocket-protector brigades" who "will provide the software, systems, and analytical resources" to "close the gaps Mohammed Atta and his associates revealed."

Such ideas have provoked the ire of civil-liberties groups, which fear that governments, corporations, and

Gummi Fingers

Tsutomu Matsumoto, a Japanese cryptographer, recently decided to look at biometric fingerprint devices. These are security systems that attempt to identify people based on their fingerprint. For years the companies selling these devices have claimed that they are very secure, and that it is almost impossible to fool them into accepting a fake finger as genuine. Matsumoto, along with his students at the Yokohama National University, showed that they can be reliably fooled with a little ingenuity and $10 worth of household supplies.

Matsumoto uses gelatin, the stuff that Gummi Bears are made out of. First he takes a live finger and makes a plastic mold. (He uses a free-molding plastic used to make plastic molds, and is sold at hobby shops.)Then he pours liquid gelatin into the mold and lets it harden. (The gelatin comes in solid sheets, and is used to make jellied meats, soups, and candies, and is sold in grocery stores.)This gelatin fake finger fools fingerprint detectors about 80% of the time...

There's both a specific and a general moral to take away from this result. Matsumoto is not a professional fake-finger scientist; he's a mathematician. He didn't use expensive equipment or a specialized laboratory. He used $10 of ingredients you could buy, and whipped up his gummy fingers in the equivalent of a home kitchen. And he defeated eleven different commercial fingerprint readers, with both optical and capacitive sensors, and some with "live finger detection" features... If he could do this, then any semiprofessional can almost certainly do much more.

—Bruce Schneier, *Crypto-Gram*, May 15, 2002

the police will misuse the new technology. Schneier's concerns are more basic. In his view, these measures can be useful, but their large-scale application will have little effect against terrorism. Worse, their use may make Americans less safe, because many of these tools fail badly—they're "brittle," in engineering jargon. Meanwhile, simple, effective, ductile measures are being overlooked or even rejected.

The distinction between ductile and brittle security dates back, Schneier has argued, to the nineteenth-century linguist and cryptographer Auguste Kerckhoffs, who set down what is now known as Kerckhoffs's principle. In good crypto systems, Kerckhoffs wrote, "the system should not depend on secrecy, and it should be able to fall into the enemy's hands without disadvantage." In other words, it should permit people to keep messages secret even if outsiders find out exactly how the encryption algorithm works.

At first blush this idea seems ludicrous. But contemporary cryptography follows Kerckhoffs's principle closely. The algorithms—the scrambling methods—are openly revealed; the only secret is the key. Indeed, Schneier says, Kerckhoffs's principle applies beyond codes and ciphers to security systems in general: every secret creates a potential failure point. Secrecy, in other words, is a prime cause of brittleness—and therefore something likely to make a system prone to catastrophic collapse. Conversely, openness provides ductility.

From this can be drawn several corollaries. One is that plans to add new layers of secrecy to security systems should automatically be hewed with suspicion. Another is that security systems that utterly depend on keeping secrets tend not to work very well. Alas, airport security is among these. Procedures for screening passengers, for examining luggage, for allowing people on the tarmac, for entering the cockpit, for running the autopilot software—all must be concealed, and all seriously compromise the system if they become known. As a result, Schneier wrote in the May issue of *Crypto-Gram*, brittleness "is an inherent property of airline security."

Few of the new airport-security proposals address this problem. Instead, Schneier told me in Los Angeles, they address problems that don't exist. "The idea that to stop bombings cars have to park three hundred feet away from the terminal, but meanwhile they can drop off passengers right up front like they always have..." He laughed. "The only ideas I've heard that make any sense are reinforcing the cockpit door and getting the passengers to fight back." Both measures test well against Kerckhoffs's principle: knowing ahead of time that law-abiding passengers may forcefully resist a hijacking en masse, for example, doesn't help hijackers to fend off their assault. Both are small-scale, compartmentalized measures that make the system more ductile, because no matter how hijackers get aboard, beefed-up doors and resistant passengers will make it harder for them to fly into a nuclear plant. And neither measure has any adverse effect on civil liberties.

Evaluations of a security proposal's merits, in Schneier's view, should not be much different from the ordinary cost-benefit calculations we make in daily life. The first question to ask of any new security proposal is, What problem does it solve? The second: What problems does it cause, especially when it fails?

Failure comes in many kinds, but two of the more important are simple failure (the security measure is ineffective) and what might be called subtractive failure (the security measure makes people less secure than before). An example of simple failure is face-recognition technology. In basic terms, face-recognition devices photograph people; break down their features into "facial building elements"; convert these into numbers that, like fingerprints, uniquely identify individuals; and compare the results with those stored in a database. If someone's facial score matches that of a criminal in the database, the person is detained. Since September 11 face-recognition technology has been placed in an increasing number of public spaces: airports, beaches, nightlife districts. Even visitors to the Statue of Liberty now have their faces scanned.

Face-recognition software could be useful. If an airline employee has to type in an identifying number to enter a secure area, for example, it can help to confirm that someone claiming to be that specific employee is indeed that person. But it cannot pick random terrorists out of the mob in an airline terminal. That much-larger-scale task requires comparing many sets of features with the many other sets of features in a database of people on a "watch list." Identix, of Minnesota, one of the largest face-recognition-technology companies, contends that in independent tests its FaceIt software has a success rate of 99.32 percent—that is, when the software matches a passenger's face with a face on a list of terrorists, it is mistaken only 0.68 percent of the time. Assume for the moment that this claim is credible; assume, too, that good pictures of suspected terrorists are readily available. About 25 million passengers used Boston's Logan Airport in 2001. Had face-recognition software been used on 25 million faces, it would have wrongly picked out just 0.68 percent of them—but that would have been enough, given the large number of passengers, to flag as many as 170,000 innocent people as terrorists. With almost 500 false alarms a day, the face-recognition system would quickly become something to ignore.

The potential for subtractive failure, different and more troublesome, is raised by recent calls to deploy biometric identification tools across the nation. Biometrics—"the only way to prevent identity fraud," according to the former senator Alan K. Simpson, of Wyoming—identifies people by precisely measuring their physical characteristics and matching them up against a database. The photographs on driver's licenses are an early example, but engineers have developed many high-tech alternatives, some of them already mentioned: fingerprint readers, voiceprint recorders, retina or iris scanners, face-recognition devices, hand-geometry assayers, even signature-geometry analyzers, which register pen pressure and writing speed as well as the appearance of a signature.

Appealingly, biometrics lets people be their own ID cards—no more passwords to forget! Unhappily, biometric measures are often implemented poorly. This past spring three reporters at C'T, a German digital-culture magazine, tested a face-recognition system, an iris scanner, and nine fingerprint readers. All proved easy to outsmart. Even at the highest security setting, Cognitec's FaceVACS-Logon could be fooled by showing the sensor a short digital movie of someone known to the system—the president of a company, say—on a laptop screen. To beat Panasonic's Authenticam iris scanner, the German journalists photographed an authorized user, took the photo and created a detailed, life-size image of his eyes, cut out the pupils, and held the image up before their faces like a mask. The scanner read the iris, detected the presence of a human pupil—and accepted the imposture. Many of the fingerprint readers could be tricked simply by breathing on them, reactivating the last user's fingerprint. Beating the more sophisticated Identix Bio-Touch fingerprint reader required a trip to a hobby shop. The journalists used graphite powder to dust the latent fingerprint—the kind left on glass—of a previous, authorized user; picked up the image on adhesive tape; and pressed the tape on the reader. The Identix reader, too, was fooled. Not all biometric devices are so poorly put together, of course. But all of them fail badly.

"Okay, somebody steals your thumbprint," Schneier says. "Because we've centralized all the functions, the thief can tap your credit, open your medical records, start your car, any number of things. Now what do you do? With a credit card, the bank can issue you a new card with a new number. But this is your *thumb*—you can't get a new one."

Consider the legislation introduced in May by Congressmen Jim Moran and Tom Davis, both of Virginia, that would mandate biometric data chips in driver's licenses—a sweeping, nationwide data-collection program, in essence. (Senator Dick Durbin, of Illinois, is proposing measures to force states to use a "single identifying designation unique to the individual on all driver's licenses"; President George W. Bush has already signed into law a requirement for biometric student visas.) Although Moran and Davis tied their proposal to the need for tighter security after last year's attacks, they also contended that the nation could combat fraud by using smart licenses with bank, credit, and Social Security cards, and for voter registration and airport identification. Maybe so, Schneier says. "But think about screw-ups, because the system will screw up."

Smart cards that store non-biometric data have been routinely cracked in the past, often with inexpensive oscilloscope-like devices that detect and interpret the timing and power fluctuations as the chip operates. An even cheaper method, announced in May by two Cambridge security researchers, requires only a bright light, a standard microscope, and duct tape. Biometric ID cards are equally vulnerable. Indeed, as a recent National Research Council study points out, the extra security supposedly provided by biometric ID cards will raise the economic incentive to counterfeit or steal them, with potentially disastrous consequences to the victims. "Okay, somebody steals your thumbprint," Schneier says. "Because we've centralized all the functions, the thief can tap your credit, open your medical records, start your car, any number of things. Now what do you do? With a credit card, the bank can issue you a new card with a new number. But this is your *thumb*—you can't get a new one."

The consequences of identity fraud might be offset if biometric licenses and visas helped to prevent terrorism. Yet smart cards would not have stopped the terrorists who attacked the World Trade Center and the Pentagon. According to the FBI, all the hijackers seem to have been who they said they were; their intentions, not their identities, were the issue. Each entered the country with a valid visa, and each had a photo ID in his real name (some obtained their IDs fraudulently, but the fakes correctly identified them). "What problem is being solved here?" Schneier asks.

Good security is built in overlapping, cross-checking layers, to slow down attacks; it reacts limberly to the unexpected. Its most important components are almost always human. "Governments have been relying on intelligent, trained guards for centuries," Schneier says. "They spot people doing bad things and then use laws to arrest them. All in all, I have to say, it's not a bad system."

THE HUMAN TOUCH

One of the first times I met with Schneier was at the Cato Institute, a libertarian think tank in Washington, D.C., that had asked him to speak about security. Afterward I wondered how the Cato people had reacted to the speech. Libertarians love cryptography, because they believe that it will let people keep their secrets forever, no matter what a government wants. To them, Schneier was a kind of hero, someone who fought the good fight. As a cryptographer, he had tremendous street cred: he had developed some of the world's coolest ciphers, including the first rigorous encryption algorithm ever published in a best-selling novel (*Cryptonomicon*, by Neal Stephenson) and the encryption for the "virtual box tops" on Kellogg's cereals (children type a code from the box top into a Web site to win prizes), and had been one of the finalists in the competition to write algorithms for the federal government's new encryption standard, which it adopted last year. Now, in the nicest possible way, he had just told the libertarians the bad news: he still loved cryptography for the intellectual challenge, but it was not all that relevant to protecting the privacy and security of real people.

In security terms, he explained, cryptography is classed as a protective countermeasure. No such measure can foil every attack, and all attacks must still be both detected and responded to. This is particularly true for digital security, and Schneier spent most of his speech evoking the staggering insecurity of networked computers. Countless numbers are broken into every year, including machines in people's homes. Taking over computers is simple with the right tools, because software is so often misconfigured or flawed. In the first five months of this year, for example, Microsoft released five "critical" security patches for Internet Explorer, each intended to rectify lapses in the original code.

HOW INSURANCE IMPROVES SECURITY

Eventually, the insurance industry will subsume the computer security industry. Not that insurance companies will start marketing security products, but rather that the kind of firewall you use—along with the kind of authentication scheme you use, the kind of operating system you use, and the kind of network monitoring scheme you use—will be strongly influenced by the constraints of insurance.

Consider security, and safety, in the real world. Businesses don't install building alarms because it makes them feel safer; they do it because they get a reduction in their insurance rates. Building-owners don't install sprinkler systems out of affection for their tenants, but because building codes and insurance policies demand it. Deciding what kind of theft and fire prevention equipment to install are risk management decisions, and the risk taker of last resort is the insurance industry...

Businesses achieve security through insurance. They take the risks they are not willing to accept themselves, bundle them up, and pay someone else to make them go away. If a warehouse is insured properly, the owner really doesn't care if it burns down or not. If he does care, he's underinsured...

What will happen when the CFO looks at his premium and realizes that it will go down 50% if he gets rid of all his insecure Windows operating systems and replaces them with a secure version of Linux? The choice of which operating system to use will no longer be 100% technical. Microsoft, and other companies with shoddy security, will start losing sales because companies don't want to pay the insurance premiums. In this vision of the future, how secure a product is becomes a real, measurable, feature that companies are willing to pay for... because it saves them money in the long run.

—Bruce Schneier, *Crypto-Gram*, March 15, 2001

Computer crime statistics are notoriously sketchy, but the best of a bad lot come from an annual survey of corporations and other institutions by the FBI and the Computer Security Institute, a research and training organization in San Francisco. In the most recent survey, released in April, 90 percent of the respondents had detected one or more computer-security breaches within the previous twelve months—a figure that Schneier calls "almost certainly an underestimate." His own experience suggests that a typical corporate network suffers a serious security breach four to six times a year—more often if the network is especially large or its operator is politically controversial.

Luckily for the victims, this digital mayhem is mostly wreaked not by the master hackers depicted in Hollywood techno-thrillers but by "script kiddies"—youths who know just enough about computers to download and run automated break-in programs. Twenty-four hours a day, seven days a week, script kiddies poke and prod at computer networks, searching for any of the thousands of known security vulnerabilities that administrators have not yet patched. A typical corporate network, Schneier says, is hit by such doorknob-rattling several times an hour. The great majority of these attacks achieve nothing, but eventually any existing security holes will be found and exploited. "It's very hard to communicate how bad the situation is," Schneier says, "because it doesn't correspond to our normal intuition of the world. To a first approximation, bank vaults are secure. Most of them don't get broken into, because it takes real skill. Computers are the opposite. Most of them get broken into all the time, and it takes practically no skill." Indeed, as automated cracking software improves, it takes ever less knowledge to mount ever more sophisticated attacks.

Given the pervasive insecurity of networked computers, it is striking that nearly every proposal for "homeland security" entails the creation of large national databases. The Moran-Davis proposal, like other biometric schemes, envisions storing smart-card information in one such database; the USA PATRIOT Act effectively creates another; the proposed Department of Homeland Security would "fuse and analyze" information from more than a hundred agencies, and would "merge under one roof" scores or hundreds of previously separate databases. (A representative of the new department told me no one had a real idea of the number. "It's a lot," he said.) Better coordination of data could have obvious utility, as was made clear by recent headlines about the failure of the FBI and the CIA to communicate. But carefully linking selected fields of data is different from creating huge national repositories of information about the citizenry, as is being proposed. Larry Ellison, the CEO of Oracle, has dismissed cautions about such databases as whiny cavils that don't take into account the existence of murderous adversaries. But murderous adversaries are exactly why we should ensure that new security measures actually make American life safer.

Any new database must be protected, which automatically entails a new layer of secrecy. As Kerckhoffs's principle suggests, the new secrecy introduces a new failure point. Government information is now scattered through scores of databases; however inadvertently, it has been compartmentalized—a basic security practice. (Following this practice, tourists divide their money between their wallets and hidden pouches; pickpockets are less likely to steal it all.) Many new proposals would change that. An example is Attorney General John Ashcroft's plan, announced in June, to fingerprint and photograph foreign visitors "who fall into categories of elevated national security concern" when they enter the United States ("approximately 100,000" will be tracked this way in the first year). The fingerprints and photographs will be compared with those of "known or suspected terrorists" and "wanted criminals." Alas, no such database of terrorist fingerprints and photographs exists. Most terrorists are outside the country, and thus hard to fingerprint, and latent fingerprints rarely survive bomb blasts. The databases of "wanted criminals" in Ashcroft's plan seem to be those maintained by the FBI and the Immigration and Naturalization Service. But using them for this purpose would presumably involve merging computer networks in these two agencies with the visa procedure in the State Department—a security nightmare, because no one entity will fully control access to the system.

Equivalents of the big, centralized databases under discussion already exist in the private sector: corporate warehouses of customer information, especially credit-card numbers. The record there is not reassuring. "Millions upon millions of credit-card numbers have been stolen from computer networks," Schneier says. So many, in fact, that Schneier believes that everyone reading this article "has, in his or her wallet right now, a credit card with a number that has been stolen," even if no criminal has yet used it. Number thieves, many of whom operate out of the former Soviet Union, sell them in bulk: $1,000 for 5,000 credit-card numbers, or twenty cents apiece. In a way, the sheer volume of theft is fortunate: so many numbers are floating around that the odds are small that any one will be heavily used by bad guys.

Large-scale federal databases would undergo similar assaults. The prospect is worrying, given the government's long-standing reputation for poor information security. Since September 11 at least forty government networks have been publicly cracked by typographically challenged vandals with names like "CriminalS," "S4t4n1c SOuls," "cr1m3 Org4n1z4dO," and "Discordian Dodgers." Summing up the problem, a House subcommittee last November awarded federal agencies a collective computer-security grade of F. According to representatives of Oracle, the federal government has been talking with the company about employing its software for the new central databases. But judging from the past, involving the private sector will not greatly improve security. In March, CERT/CC, a computer-security watchdog based at Carnegie Mellon University, warned of thirty-eight vulnerabilities in Oracle's database software. Meanwhile, a centerpiece of the company's international advertising is the claim that its software is "unbreakable." Other software vendors fare no better: CERT/CC issues a constant stream of vulnerability warnings about every major software firm.

Schneier, like most security experts I spoke to, does not oppose consolidating and modernizing federal databases per se. To avoid creating vast new opportunities for adversaries, the overhaul should be incremental and small-scale. Even so, it would need to be planned with extreme care—something that shows little sign of happening.

One key to the success of digital revamping will be a little-mentioned, even prosaic feature: training the users not

Remember Pearl Harbor

> Surprise, when it happens to a government, is likely to be a complicated, diffuse, bureaucratic thing... It includes gaps in intelligence, but also intelligence that, like a string of pearls too precious to wear, is too sensitive to give to those who need it. It includes the alarm that fails to work, but also the alarm that has gone off so often it has been disconnected. It includes the unalert watchman, but also the one who knows he'll be chewed out by his superior if he gets higher authority out of bed. It includes the contingencies that occur to no one, but also those that everyone assumes somebody else is taking care of. It includes straightforward procrastination, but also decisions protracted by internal disagreement. It includes, in addition, the inability of individual human beings to rise to the occasion until they are sure it *is* the occasion—which is usually too late. (Unlike movies, real life provides no musical background to tip us off to the climax.) Finally, as at Pearl Harbor, surprise may include some measure of genuine novelty introduced by the enemy, and possibly some sheer bad luck.
>
> The results, at Pearl Harbor, were sudden, concentrated, and dramatic. The failure, however, was cumulative, widespread, and rather drearily familiar. This is why surprise, when it happens to a government, cannot be described just in terms of startled people. Whether at Pearl Harbor or at the Berlin Wall, surprise is everything involved in a government's (or in an alliance's) failure to anticipate effectively.
>
> —Foreword by Thomas C. Schelling to *Pearl Harbor: Warning and Decision* (1962) by Roberta Wohlstetter

to circumvent secure systems. The federal government already has several computer networks—INTELINK, SIPRNET, and NIPRNET among them—that are fully encrypted, accessible only from secure rooms and buildings, and never connected to the Internet. Yet despite their lack of Net access the secure networks have been infected by e-mail perils such as the Melissa and I Love You viruses, probably because some official checked e-mail on a laptop, got infected, and then plugged the same laptop into the classified network. Because secure networks are unavoidably harder to work with, people are frequently tempted to bypass them—one reason that researchers at weapons labs sometimes transfer their files to insecure but more convenient machines.

Schneier has long argued that the best way to improve the very bad situation in computer security is to change software licenses. If software is blatantly unsafe, owners have no such recourse, because it is licensed rather than bought, and the licenses forbid litigation. It is unclear whether the licenses can legally do this (courts currently disagree), but as a practical matter it is next to impossible to win a lawsuit against a software firm. If some big software companies lose product-liability suits, Schneier believes, their confreres will begin to take security seriously.

Computer networks are difficult to keep secure in part because they have so many functions, each of which must be accounted for. For that reason Schneier and other experts tend to favor narrowly focused security measures—more of them physical than digital—that target a few precisely identified problems. For air travel, along with reinforcing cockpit doors and teaching passengers to fight back, examples include armed uniformed—*not* plainclothes—guards on select flights; "dead-man" switches that in the event of a pilot's incapacitation force planes to land by autopilot at the nearest airport; positive bag matching (ensuring that luggage does not get on a plane unless its owner also boards); and separate decompression facilities that detonate any altitude bombs in cargo before takeoff. None of these is completely effective; bag matching, for instance, would not stop suicide bombers. But all are well tested, known to at least impede hijackers, not intrusive to passengers, and unlikely to make planes less secure if they fail.

"The trick is to remember that technology can't save you," Schneier says. "We know this in our own lives. For real safety we park on nice streets where people notice if somebody smashes the window. Or we park in garages, where somebody watches the car. In both cases people are the essential security element. You always build the system around people."

It is impossible to guard all potential targets, because anything and everything can be subject to attack. Palestinian suicide bombers have shown this by murdering at random the occupants of pool halls and hotel meeting rooms. Horrible as these incidents are, they do not risk the lives of thousands of people, as would attacks on critical parts of the national infrastructure: nuclear-power plants, hydroelectric dams, reservoirs, gas and chemical facilities. Here a classic defense is available: tall fences and armed guards. Yet this past spring the Bush Administration cut by 93 percent the funds requested by the Energy Department to bolster security for nuclear weapons and waste; it denied completely the funds requested by the Army Corps of Engineers for guarding 200 reservoirs, dams, and canals, leaving fourteen large public-works projects with no budget for protection. A recommendation by the American Association of Port Authorities that the nation spend a total of $700 million to inspect and control ship cargo (today less than two percent of container traffic is inspected) has so far resulted in grants of just $92 million. In all three proposals most of the money would have been spent on guards and fences.

The most important element of any security measure, Schneier argues, is people, not technology—and the people need to be at the scene. Recall the German journalists who fooled the fingerprint readers and iris scanners.

None of their tricks would have worked if a reasonably attentive guard had been watching. Conversely, legitimate employees with bandaged fingers or scratched corneas will never make it through security unless a guard at the scene is authorized to overrule the machinery. Giving guards increased authority provides more opportunities for abuse, Schneier says, so the guards must be supervised carefully. But a system with more people who have more responsibility "is more robust," he observed in the June *Crypto-Gram*, "and the best way to make things work. (The U.S. Marine Corps understands this principle; it's the heart of their chain of command rules.)"

"The trick is to remember that technology can't save you," Schneier says. "We know this in our own lives. We realize that there's no magic anti-burglary dust we can sprinkle on our cars to prevent them from being stolen. We know that car alarms don't offer much protection. The Club at best makes burglars steal the car next to you. For real safety we park on nice streets where people notice if somebody smashes the window. Or we park in garages, where somebody watches the car. In both cases people are the essential security element. You always build the system around people."

Looking for Trouble

After meeting Schneier at the Cato Institute, I drove with him to the Washington command post of Counterpane Internet Security. It was the first time in many months that he had visited either of his company's two operating centers (the other is in Silicon Valley). His absence had been due not to inattentiveness but to his determination to avoid the classic high-tech mistake of involving the alpha geek in day-to-day management. Besides, he lives in Minneapolis, and the company headquarters are in Cupertino, California. (Why Minneapolis? I asked. "My wife lives there," he said. "It seemed polite.") With his partner, Tom Rowley, supervising day-to-day operations, Schneier constantly travels in Counterpane's behalf, explaining how the company manages computer security for hundreds of large and medium-sized companies. It does this mainly by installing human beings.

The command post was nondescript even by the bland architectural standards of exurban office complexes. Gaining access was like a pop quiz in security: How would the operations center recognize and admit its boss, who was there only once or twice a year? In this country requests for identification are commonly answered with a driver's license. A few years ago Schneier devoted considerable effort to persuading the State of Illinois to issue him a driver's license that showed no picture, signature, or Social Security number. But Schneier's license serves as identification just as well as a license showing a picture and a signature—which is to say, not all that well. With or without a picture, with or without a biometric chip, licenses cannot be more than state-issued cards with people's names on them: good enough for social purposes, but never enough to assure identification when it is important. Authentication, Schneier says, involves something a person knows (a password or a PIN, say), has (a physical token, such as a driver's license or an ID bracelet), or is (biometric data). Security systems should use at least two of these; the Counterpane center employs all three. At the front door Schneier typed in a PIN and waved an iButton on his key chain at a sensor (iButtons, made by Dallas Semiconductor, are programmable chips embedded in stainless-steel discs about the size and shape of a camera battery). We entered a waiting room, where Schneier completed the identification trinity by placing his palm on a hand-geometry reader.

Beyond the waiting room, after a purposely long corridor studded with cameras, was a conference room with many electrical outlets, some of which Schneier commandeered for his cell phone, laptop, BlackBerry, and battery packs. One side of the room was a dark glass wall. Schneier flicked a switch, shifting the light and theatrically revealing the scene behind the glass. It was a Luddite nightmare: an auditorium-like space full of desks, each with two computer monitors; all the desks faced a wall of high-resolution screens. One displayed streams of data from the "sentry" machines that Counterpane installs in its clients' networks. Another displayed images from the video cameras scattered around both this command post and the one in Silicon Valley.

On a visual level the gadgetry overwhelmed the people sitting at the desks and watching over the data. Nonetheless, the people were the most important part of the operation. Networks record so much data about their usage that overwhelmed managers frequently turn off most of the logging programs and ignore the others. Among Counterpane's primary functions is to help companies make sense of the data they already have. "We turn the logs back on and monitor them," Schneier says. Counterpane researchers developed software to measure activity on client networks, but no software by itself can determine whether an unusual signal is a meaningless blip or an indication of trouble. That was the job of the people at the desks.

Highly trained and well paid, these people brought to the task a quality not yet found in any technology: human judgment, which is at the heart of most good security. Human beings do make mistakes, of course. But they can recover from failure in ways that machines and software cannot. The well-trained mind is ductile. It can understand surprises and overcome them. It fails well.

When I asked Schneier why Counterpane had such Darth Vaderish command centers, he laughed and said it helped to reassure potential clients that the company had mastered the technology. I asked if clients ever inquired how Counterpane trains the guards and analysts in the command centers. "Not often," he said, although that training is in fact the center of the whole system. Mixing long stretches of inactivity with short bursts of frenzy, the work rhythm of the Counterpane guards would have been familiar to police officers and firefighters everywhere. As I watched the guards, they were slurping soft drinks, listening to techno-death metal, and waiting for something to go wrong. They were in a protected space, looking out at a dangerous world. Sentries around Neolithic campfires did the same thing. Nothing better has been discovered since. Thinking otherwise, in Schneier's view, is a really terrible idea.

FURTHER READING

For clear primers on modern cryptography and on network security, it is hard to do better than Bruce Schneier's *Applied Cryptography* (1993) and *Secrets and Lies* (2000), respectively; these books (especially the latter) render technological arcana comprehensible to even the willfully Luddite.

The consensus classic in the field of cryptology remains ***The Codebreakers: The Story of Secret Writing*** (1967), by David Kahn. Kahn spent four years working on a book that sought, in his words, "to cover the entire history of cryptology." (That is in fact a modest description of a 1,200-page book that begins with a chapter called "The First 3,000 Years" and closes, twenty-five chapters later, with "Messages From Outer Space.") All subsequent chroniclers of cryptography unavoidably stand on Kahn's shoulders. But *The Codebreakers* nearly died aborning: reportedly, the Pentagon tried to suppress its publication; only after Kahn agreed to delete three passages was the book finally published. Kahn issued a new edition of the book in 1996, bringing his history nearly up to the century's end. Two of the most relevant books on the subject of homeland security, both published in 1998, were also the most prescient. ***Terrorism and America: A Commonsense Strategy for a Democratic Society,*** by Philip B. Heymann, and ***America's Achilles' Heel: Nuclear, Biological, and Chemical Terrorism and Covert Attack***, by Richard A. Falkenrath, Robert D. Newman, and Bradley A. Thayer, warned of the imminent danger of a major terrorist attack on American soil.

Although the proposed Department of Homeland Security was hastily thrown together, the idea for such an entity had circulated within the government for years. Some of the proposals can be found in the excellent compilation of disparate reports that the U.S. Senate Committee on Foreign Relations put together last fall, when it was preparing for hearings on the subject of national security. The compilation is called ***Strategies for Homeland Defense*** and is available on the Internet at purl.access. gpo.gov/GPO/LPS15541.

Charles C. Mann, an Atlantic *correspondent, has written for the magazine since 1984. He is at work on a book based on his March 2002* Atlantic *cover story, "1491."*

From *The Atlantic Monthly,* September 2002, pp. 81-83, 86-88, 90, 92-96.

BEST PRACTICE

Are You the Weak Link?

A legendary hacker reveals your company's greatest vulnerability and the steps you can take to stop sabotage.

by Kevin D. Mitnick

Companies are more security conscious than ever, lavishing attention on sophisticated technologies and physical defenses to safeguard their intellectual capital. But they've neglected the weakest link: their employees. It's these frontline and midlevel workers who intruders increasingly target and who unwittingly give away the keys to the kingdom.

I know, because I used to be a hacker. I discovered how easy it was to dupe employees into giving me their companies' most sensitive information—user names, passwords, account and dial-up numbers—and use it to hack into the heart of their networks. My cleverness landed me in federal prison for five years. But since my release in 2000, I've worked to help businesses and government shore up their defenses. Here's what I tell them.

The Sinister Art of Persuasion

The greatest misconception about security is that a computer is the hacker's most dangerous tool. Not so. It's the phone. As security technologies improve, attackers are resorting to old-fashioned con games to get what they want. Why pound on the heavily defended corporate firewall when it's easier to just trick the assistant who answers the phone into revealing his boss's password?

Attackers who talk their way into a company's "secure" systems are skilled at exploiting basic human nature to manipulate their unwary targets. That's why I call them social engineers. (The term was first used by early phone hackers to describe deceiving phone company employees into revealing proprietary information.)

Drawing on 50 years of behavioral science research, Arizona State University psychology professor Robert Cialdini argues that persuasion works by appealing to a few fundamental facets of human nature: the desire to be liked, to reciprocate, to follow others' lead, to follow through on public commitments, to acquire things in scarce supply, and to defer to authority. I'd add to this list that most people are reflexively trusting and give others the benefit of the doubt—traits that make the social engineer's job all the easier.

The message must come from the top that every employee is vulnerable to the social-engineering threat, and every employee is part of the security team.

Being aware of how persuasion works is the basis for erecting defenses against these attackers, as I'll show. But first, consider this fictional account—a composite of real cases—of a social engineer who installs a keystroke logger (a type of computer wiretap) into a senior executive's computer.

The phone rings in HR at a large publishing house in New York.

"Human resources. This is Sarah."

"Hi, Sarah. This is George in the parking garage. We've had a problem with the parking access cards—some new employees are complaining they're not working. So we need to reprogram the cards for the new hires that have started within the past 30 days. How can I get hold of the newbies?"

"I can check our new-hire list and call you back. What's your phone number?"

"Well, I'm just heading out on break. Can I call you back in half an hour or so?"

"Sure."

When "George" calls Sarah back, she produces the names and numbers of two recent hires, and she volunteers that one is the new VP, and the other is Clark Miller, an administrative assistant in finance. Bingo, George's next call, around six o'clock that evening, is to Clark.

"Finance. Clark speaking."

"I'm glad I found somebody working late. Listen, this is Ron Vitarro I'm the VP of the book division. I don't think we've been introduced. Welcome to the company."

"Oh. Thank you."

"Clark, I'm at a conference in Los Angeles, and I've got a crisis. I know you're busy, but help me out, and I'll personally show you around the division."

"Of course. What can I do?"

"Go up to my office. There's a manuscript I need. Do you know where my office is?"

"No."

"It's the corner office on the 15th floor—room 1502. I'll call you there in a few minutes. When you get to the office, you'll need to press the call-forward button on the phone so my call won't go directly to my voice mail."

"Okay. I'm on my way now."

Ten minutes later, Clark is in Ron Vitarro's office, has canceled Ron's call forwarding, and is waiting when the phone rings. Our social engineer, posing as Ron, tells him to launch Internet Explorer on Ron's computer, type in www.geocities.com/ron_vitarro/manuscript.exe, and hit Return.

A dialog box appears, and the imposter tells Clark to click Open instead of Save. The computer appears to start downloading a manuscript, but then the screen goes blank. When Clark reports that something seems to be wrong, the caller plays along.

"Oh, *no*. Not *again*. I've been having a problem downloading from that Web site, but I thought it was fixed. Well, okay. Don't worry. I'll figure out another way to get the file later."

Then he asks Clark to restart the computer so Ron can be sure it is working properly. He talks Clark through the steps for rebooting. When the computer is running again, he thanks Clark warmly and hangs up. Clark returns to his desk, pleased that he's made this good contact with a VP.

Of course, Clark doesn't know he's been duped by a clever social engineer, and he has just helped a hacker install spy ware on the VP's computer. The new software would record Vitarro's every keystroke—e-mail, passwords, Web sites visited—along with screen shots, and e-mail them to the hacker's anonymous, free mailbox in Ukraine.

Like most such scams, this one required limited technical expertise (disguising spy ware as a manuscript) and a little planning. The hacker had to gather certain information in advance—Vitarro's office location, the times that he would be out, and so forth. But details of this sort are easily discovered with tactics no more complicated than getting the list of new employees.

Using techniques like these, social engineers can gain control of a company's computer and telephone systems, convince security guards and other workers that they're employees, hijack senior executives' cell- and home-phone voice mail, and access a company's complete customer list, financials, and product development plans. And that's just the beginning.

Most companies have virtually no defenses against social engineers. But every company should take a few simple steps to mitigate this glaring weakness.

What You Can Do

The message must come from the top that every employee is vulnerable to the social-engineering threat, and every employee is part of the security team. This is not a job the "security guys" in facilities and IT can do alone.

It's crucial that you alert people at all levels about the nature of the threat, the consequences of social-engineering break-ins, and the security policies in place. If you don't have a policy that specifically addresses social-engineering tactics, develop one. It should cover rules governing computer and voice-mail passwords, how to handle suspicious callers, the need to challenge unidentified visitors, and so on.

Whatever form it takes, your education program should raise (and maintain) awareness and motivate the workforce to care about information security. It should reinforce the company's written policy by describing how to recognize and foil a social-engineering attack. And, because people are quick to tune out old, too-familiar messages, it must provide novel and continuing reminders.

Approaches may include role-playing exercises, e-mail and voice-mail reminders, and security columns in the company newsletter and on the intranet. You could also rank security awareness on employee performance reports and annual reviews. And you could even try gimmicks like fortune cookies in the cafeteria that contain security messages. (A fortune might advise, "Never use your child's birth date as a password!")

Finally, as every manager knows, no amount of training and policy making will work if employees don't take responsibility for the problem. The key to getting people to buy in to any effort is to appeal to their self-interest. Rewards for good security behavior (and sanctions for disregarding policy) are important. Above all, though, employees must appreciate that social-engineering attacks can threaten them individually, as well as damage the organization. Companies, for instance, keep private information about every employee, from social security numbers to direct-deposit account numbers, that social engineers may be eager to get their hands on.

Many security approaches to threats from social engineering are common sense, but not every vulnerability is obvious. A security firm that specializes in probing for weaknesses and shoring up defenses can help. Security consultants can conduct penetration tests using the same techniques that enemies will use to steal or destroy your valuable information. The experience of being probed this way can be alarming, which is just the point.

***Kevin D. Mitnick** is cofounder of Defensive Thinking, a Los Angeles-based information security firm, and is coauthor with William L. Simon of* The Art of Deception *(John Wiley & Sons, 2002), from which this article is adapted.*

Code Red for the web

Could the Internet crash? This summer's Code Red attacks could foreshadow destructive cyberwarfare between hacker groups or between governments

BY CAROLYN MEINEL

"Imagine a cold that kills. It spreads rapidly and indiscriminately through droplets in the air, and you think you're absolutely healthy until you begin to sneeze. Your only protection is complete, impossible isolation."

AMERICAN HACKERS are being enlisted to help fight the U.S. government's cyberwars.

Jane Jorgensen, principal scientist at Information Extraction & Transport in Arlington, Va., which researches Internet epidemiology for the Defense Advanced Research Projects Agency, isn't describing the latest flu outbreak but an affliction that affects the Web. One such computer disease emerged this past July and August, and it has computer security researchers more worried about the integrity of the Internet than ever before. The consternation was caused by Code Red, a Web worm, an electronic ailment akin to computerized snakebite. Code Red infects Microsoft Internet Information Servers (IIS). Whereas home computers typically use other systems, many of the most popular Web sites run on IIS. In two lightning-fast strikes, Code Red managed to infiltrate hundreds of thousands of IIS servers in only a few hours, slowing the Internet's operations. Although Code Red's effects have waned, patching the security holes in the estimated six million Microsoft IIS Web servers worldwide and repairing the damage inflicted by the worm have cost billions of dollars.

What really disturbs system administrators and other experts, however, is the idea that Code Red may be a harbinger of more virulent Internet plagues. In the past, Web defacements were perpetrated by people breaking into sites individually—the cyberwarfare equivalent of dropping propaganda leaflets on targets. But computer researchers dread the arrival of better-designed automated attack worms that could degrade or even demolish the World Wide Web.

Further, some researchers worry that Code Red was merely a test of the type of computer programs that any government could use to crash the Internet in times of war. This past spring's online skirmishes over the U.S. spy plane incident with China emphasize the dangers. Full-scale cyberwarfare could cause untold damage to the industrialized world [see box, "What Happens if the Internet Crashes?"]. These secret assaults could even enlist your PC as a pawn, making it a "zombie" that participates in the next round of computerized carnage.

Save for the scales on which these computer assaults are waged, individual hacking and governmental cyberwarfare are essentially two sides of the same electronically disruptive coin. Unfortunately, it's hard to tell the difference between them until it's too late.

More than 395,000 servers were infected with the CODE RED WORM in less than 14 HOURS.

Often popularly lumped in with viruses, Code Red and some similar pests such as Melissa and SirCam are more accurately called worms in the hacker lexicon. Mimicking the actions of its biological namesake, a software virus must incorporate itself into another program to run and replicate. A computer worm differs

What Happens if the Internet Crashes

WHAT WOULD BE the consequences if the Internet failed in the face of a hacking onslaught? They would be far worse than not being able to make bids on eBay—potentially affecting product manufacturing and deliveries, bank transactions, telephony and more. Should it occur five years from now, the results could be a lot more severe.

Today many businesses use the World Wide Web to order parts and arrange shipments. A collapse of the system would interrupt just-in-time manufacturing, in which components reach the production line within a day or two of being used, to save on inventory costs. Many retail stores also rely on the Web to keep their shelves stocked. Within days, they could start to empty.

By then you may not be able to use your checkbook or ATM card either, as many banks are using the Internet instead of dedicated lines to save money. Other economic institutions such as Wall Street are said to be more susceptible to hackers corrupting trading data than to a shutdown of the system. The latter eventuality would be met by closing down the market.

Whereas most phones would still work if the Web went down today, experts say that may change a few years from now. Internet telephony started as a way for geek hobbyists to get free long-distance phone calls. Now, however, many calls that originate from an ordinary phone travel part of the way over the public Internet.

Meanwhile unclassified communications of the U.S. Armed Services go through NIPRNET (Non-Secure Internet Protocol Router Network), which uses public Internet communications. The Department of Defense is now "immensely dependent" on NIPRNET, according to Greggory Peck, a senior security engineer for FC Business Systems in Springfield, Va., which provides computer services to the federal government.

Many people ask whether airliners might start falling out of the sky if the World Wide Web crashes. The Federal Aviation Administration's air-traffic control system is sufficiently antiquated that it is in no danger of being held hostage to the Internet.

—C.M.

in that it is a self-replicating, self-contained program. Worms frequently are far more infectious than viruses. The Code Red worm is especially dangerous because it conducted what are called distributed denial of service (DDoS) attacks, which overwhelm Internet computers with a deluge of junk communications.

During its July peak, Code Red menaced the Web by consuming its bandwidth, or data-transmission capacity. "In cyberwarfare, bandwidth is a weapon," says Greggory Peck, a senior security engineer for FC Business Systems in Springfield, Va., which works to defend U.S. government clients against computer crime. In a DDoS attack, a control computer commands many zombies to throw garbage traffic at a victim in an attempt to use up all available bandwidth. This kind of assault first made the news last year when DDoS attacks laid low Yahoo, eBay and other dot-coms.

The earlier DDoS incidents mustered just hundreds to, at most, thousands of zombies. That's because attackers had to break into each prospective zombie by hand. Code Red, being a worm, spreads automatically—and exponentially. This feature provides it with hundreds of times more zombies and hence hundreds of times more power to saturate all available Internet bandwidth rapidly.

The initial outbreak of Code Red contagion was not much more than a case of the sniffles. In the five days after it appeared on July 12, it reached only about 20,000 out of the estimated half a million susceptible IIS computer servers. It wasn't until five days afterward that Ryan Permeh and Marc Maiffret of eEye Digital Security in Aliso Viejo, Calif., a supplier of security software for Microsoft servers, discovered the worm and alerted the world to its existence.

WEB WATCHER David Moore monitored the rapid spread of Code Red.

On July 19 the worm reemerged in a more venomous form. "More than 359,000 servers were infected with the Code Red worm in less than 14 hours," says David Moore, senior technical manager at the Cooperative Association for Internet Data Analysis in La Jolla, Calif., a government- and industry-supported organization that surveys and maps the Net's server population. The traffic jam generated by so many computers attempting to co-opt other machines began to overload the capacity of the Internet. By midafternoon, the Internet Storm Center at incidents.org—the computer security industry's watchdog for Internet health—was reporting "orange alert" status. This is one step below its most dire condition, red alert, which signals a breakdown.

Then, at midnight, all Code Red zombies quit searching for new victims. Instead they all focused on flooding one of the servers that hosts the White House Web site with junk connections, threatening its shutdown. "The White House essentially turned off one of its two DNS servers, saying that any requests to whitehouse.gov should be rerouted to the other server," says Jimmy Kuo, a Network Associates McAfee fellow who assisted the White House in finding a solution. Basically, the system administrators dumped all communications addressed to the compromised server. As it turned out, Code Red couldn't cope with the altered Internet protocol address and waged war on the inactive site. "The public didn't notice anything, because any requests went to the other server," Kuo says.

By the close of July 20, all existing Code Red zombies went into a pre-

Code Red internet worms

CODE RED is an Internet worm that infects unprotected Microsoft Internet Information Servers (IIS), on which many popular Web sites run. During the summer, the worm's secret assaults turned IIS computers into "zombies" that conducted what is called a distributed denial of service attack on the White House Web site, attempting to overwhelm it by flooding it with garbage communications. More effective worms have the potential to saturate the Web's data-transmission capacity, possibly disabling the Internet.

THE ATTACK OF CODE RED

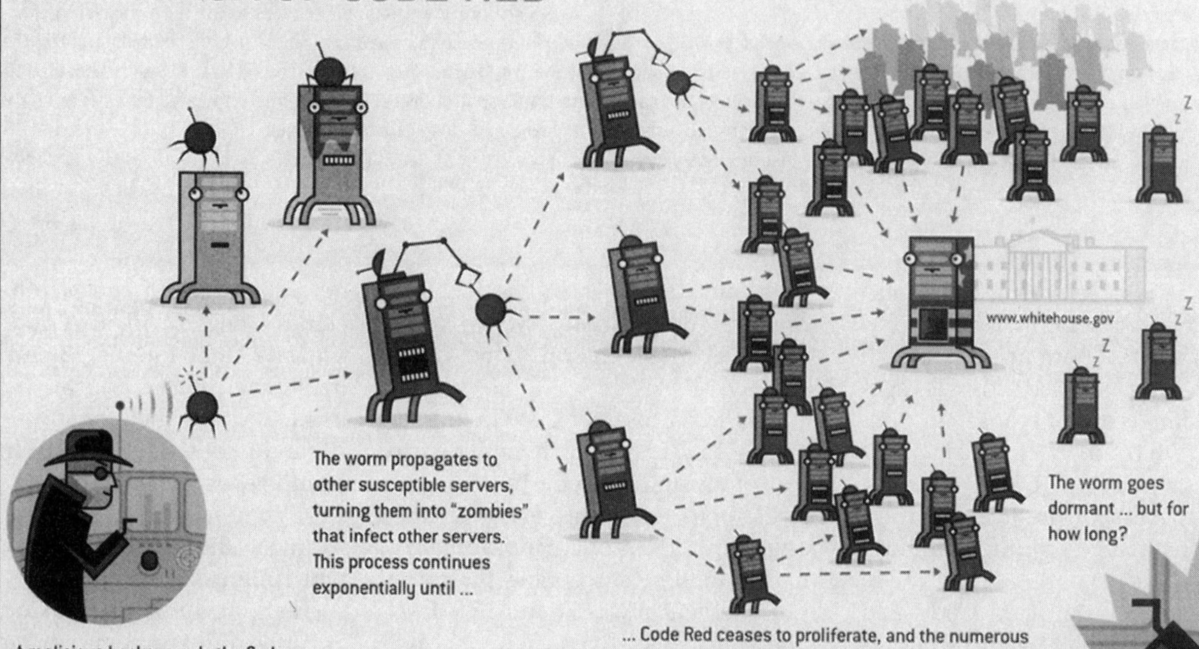

INTERNET PROTOCOL ADDRESSES INFECTED BY CODE RED

RAPID RISE—During a 12-hour period on July 19, 2001, the number of Internet protocol addresses compromised by the first large-scale assault of the Code Red worm surged from around 16,000 to about 280,000. After its initial spread, Code Red went dormant. Soon thereafter, however, a reinfection caused another, smaller outbreak. Experts estimate that the worm's attacks and the following Code Red II outburst will cost several billion dollars to rectify.

programmed eternal sleep. As the worms lodge only in each computer's RAM memory, which is purged when the machine shuts down, all it took was a reboot to eradicate their remnants. Case closed.

Or was it? A few days later analysts at eEye revealed that if someone were to release a new copy of Code Red at any time between the first through the 19th day of any month (the trigger dates coded in by the original hacker), the infection would take off again.

Over the next 10 days computer security volunteers worked to notify Microsoft IIS users of the vulnerability of their servers. On July 29 the White House held a press conference to implore people to protect their IIS servers against Code Red's attacks. "The mass traffic associated with this worm's propagation could degrade the functioning of the Internet," warned Ronald L. Dick, director of the FBI's National Infrastructure Protection Center. By the next day Code Red was all over the news.

The second coming of Code Red was, as expected, weaker than the first. On August 1, it infected approximately 175,000 servers—nearly all those susceptible and about half the total of the previous episode. A slower infection rate and fewer vulnerable servers held Internet disruptions to a minimum. After a while, the second attack subsided.

But that was not the end. Yet another worm was unleashed on August 4 using the same break-in method as Code Red. The new worm, dubbed Code Red II, installed a backdoor allowing a master hacker to direct the activities of victim computers at will. The worm degraded intranets with "arm storms" (floods of Ethernet packets) and hunted for new victims. In short order, Code Red II disabled parts of the Web-based e-mail provider Hotmail, several cable and digital subscriberline (DSL) Internet providers and part of the Associated Press news distribution system. As time passed, Code Red II managed to infect many corporate and college intranets. Halfway through August, Code Red II disabled some Hong Kong government internal servers. The most common victim computers were personal Web servers run by Windows 2000 Professional. This rash of disruptions prompted incidents.org to again declare an orange alert. Experts estimate that 500,000 internal servers were compromised.

In mid-August, Computer Economics, a security research company, said that Code Red had cost $2 billion in damage. By the time it is fully purged from the Internet, the computer attack will probably rank among the most expensive in history. Nearly $9 billion was spent to fight last year's LoveLetter virus, and 1999's Melissa worm assault cost $1 billion to repair.

Code Red II installed a backdoor allowing a MASTER HACKER to direct victim computers at will.

Of course, Code Red isn't the only worm out there. Some of them are aimed at home computers. A worm called W32/Leaves, for example, permits a remote attacker to control infected PCs in a coordinated fashion, enabling synchronized waves of attacks. (Although Code Red II allows this possibility as well, it lacks the coding that enables remote control.) The Computer Emergency Response Team, a federally funded watchdog organization at Carnegie Mellon University, has received reports of more than 23,000 W32/Leaves zombies. The current total is unknown, but as W32/Leaves continues to propagate, the infected population will probably grow significantly. In July, Britain's Scotland Yard charged an unidentified 24-year-old man with creating W32/Leaves.

"Almost any computer, operating system or software you may buy contains weaknesses that the manufacturer knows lets hackers break in," says Larry Leibrock, a leading researcher in computer forensics and associate dean for technology of the business school of the University of Texas at Austin. Future "federal regulation could require that vendors take the initiative to contact customers and help them upgrade their products to fix security flaws," he continues. "Today, however, it is up to each consumer to hunt down and fix the many ways hackers and cyberwarriors exploit to abuse their computers."

World Cyberwars

BEYOND THE THREAT posed by malicious hacker programs is the danger of Internet attacks conducted in a concerted fashion by top computer talent spurred to act by international events. The cyberbattles that broke out over the collision of a Chinese fighter plane that collided with a U.S. Navy EP-3E spy plane this past April give a hint of how such a conflict might play out.

According to accounts in the press, the hacker exchanges began when negotiations for the release of American hostages stalled. On April 9 and 10, attackers defaced two Chinese Web sites with slurs, insults and even threats of nuclear war. During the following week, American hackers hit dozens more Chinese sites. Those supporting China responded by disfiguring one obscure U.S. Navy Web site. China, however, held a weapon in reserve. In late March the National Infrastructure Protection Center had warned of a new worm on the loose: the 1i0n Worm. Lion, the hacker who founded the hacker group H.U.C. (Honkers Union of China), has taken credit for writing it. Unlike the initial Code Red's preprogrammed zombies, 1i0n's zombies accept new commands from a central computer. Also, 1i0n infects Linux computers, which means it can masquerade as

What Can Be Done to Defend the Web?

AS POGO the comic-strip character said, "We have met the enemy and he is us." One of the weakest links in protecting the Internet is the home PC user. Cybernetic worms—self-replicating hacker software that can wreak havoc on Internet operations—can turn personal computers into "zombies," or slave agents that help to destroy other computer operations. Of particular concern are worms that can conduct effectively targeted distributed denial of service (DDoS) attacks, in which zombie computers deluge a Web site with useless communications.

Computer professionals are being asked to get the word out to home users to check for zombies. "That's because our worst Internet nightmare is the grandma who uses her DSL [high-bandwidth-capacity digital subscriber line that is always connected] to shop on eBay," says Greggory Peck of FC Business Systems, which provides computer services to the federal government. High bandwidth means that a home zombie can pump lots of junk into the Internet, swamping targeted Web sites.

You may think your home computer is safe from assault because it runs automatic virus updates or because you registered your software and receive vendor e-mails about product upgrades. Guess again. Few vendors feel obligated to help users keep hackers out. That's why it's important for home users to install firewalls.

Complicating the safety issue, most new PCs will soon by running the Windows XP operating system, which enables "raw sockets." Sockets are software constructions that generate the packets (the smallest data-transmission units) that transfer information across networks. With raw sockets technology, packets can be crafted in an arbitrary manner even if that violates safeguarding protocols. Raw sockets, for example, enabled the 1i0n worm to hide on Linux servers by forging Internet addresses. They also allow hackers to create malformed packets that will crash a receiving computer.

Beyond the home PC, another approach to defending the Web is to arrest more computer criminals. Nowadays, though, dangerous attackers may operate through a chain of compromised computers, with one or more being located across national borders. To obtain evidence in these cases requires cooperation among the law-enforcement agencies of two or more countries.

International pursuit of computer criminals would be made easier by adoption of the "Convention on Cyber-crime" now under consideration by the 44 nations of the Council of Europe, which includes the U.S., Canada and Japan. Part of the treaty would also criminalize possession or creation of computer crime instructions or programs except for the authorized testing or protection of a computer system. (The text of the Cyber-crime Treaty is available at conventions.coe.int/treaty/EN/projets/cybercrime.htm)

These restraints are controversial, though. At least 35 lobby groups, including the Electronic Frontier Foundation and the Global Internet Liberty Campaign, oppose the treaty because they believe it would restrict freedom of speech and invade personal privacy. It's hard to find antidotes to viruses and worms if researchers cannot study copies of them on their computers.

Another solution is to require that Internet servers be secure. For example, the U.S. Federal Trade Commission proposed a regulation in July that requires financial service companies to guard their networks against "anticipated threats." This is only a small step in the right direction.—*C.M.*

any computer on the Net. This property makes it hard to track down infected servers.

Meanwhile pro-U.S. hack attacks escalated. The official Chinese publication, *People's Daily*, reported that "by the end of April over 600 Chinese Web sites had come under fire." In contrast, Chinese hackers had hit only three U.S. sites during the same period.

In the next few days the Chinese hacker groups H.U.C., Redcrack, China Net Force, China Tianyu and Redhackers assaulted a dozen American Web sites with slogans such as "Attack anti-Chinese arrogance!" On the first of May several DDoS strikes were initiated. Over the next week Chinese hackers took credit for wrecking about 1,000 additional American Web sites.

On May 7 China acknowledged its responsibility for the DDoS attacks and called for peace in a *People's Daily* news story. It ran: "The Chinese hackers were also urged to call off all irrational actions and turn their enthusiasm into strength to build up the country and safeguard world peace."

U.S. law-enforcement agencies, the White House and U.S. hacker organizations never objected to the American side of this cyberconflict, although the FBI's infrastructure center had warned of "the potential for increased hacker activity directed at U.S. systems."

How to Wage Covert Cyberwarfare

IN VIEW OF the spy-plane episode, some commentators have wondered whether the U.S. Federal government encouraged American hackers to become agents of cyberwar. After all, the U.S. has worked with private groups to wage covert warfare before, as in the Iran/Contra scandal. And links between the two communities have been reported. It's difficult, however, to say exactly how strong the connection between hackers and the government might be. Clearly, the murky world of hacking doesn't often lend itself to certainty. And because it is the policy of the U.S. National Security Agency and various Defense Department cyberwarfare organizations not to comment on Web security matters, these relationships cannot be confirmed. Still, the indications are at least suggestive.

Consider the history of Fred Villella, now an independent computer consultant. According to numerous press reports and his own statements, Villella took part in counterterrorism activities in the 1970s. In 1996 he hired hackers of the Dis Org Crew to help him conduct training sessions on the hacker threat for federal agencies. This gang also helps to staff the world's largest annual hacker convention, Def Con.

Erik Ginorio (known to the hacker world as Bronc Buster) publicly took credit for defacing a Chinese government Web site on human rights in October 1998. This act is illegal under U.S. law. Not only was Ginorio not prosecuted, he says Villella offered him a job. Villella could not be reached for comment.

In another hacker-government connection, Secure Computing in San Jose, Calif., became a sponsor of Def Con in 1996. According to its 10-K reports to the U.S. Securities and Exchange Commission, Secure Computing was created at the direction of the National Security Agency, the supersecret code-breaking and surveillance arm of the U.S. government. Two years after that, Secure Computing hired the owner of Def Con, Jeff Moss. Several former Villella instructors also staffed and managed Def Con.

Questionable things happen at Def Cons. At the 1999 Def Con, for example, the Cult of the Dead Cow, a hacker gang headquartered in Lubbock, Tex., put on a mediagenic show to promote its Back Orifice 2000 break-in program. Gang members extolled the benefits of "hacking to change the world," claiming that eight-year-olds could use this program to break into Windows servers.

Meanwhile Pieter Zatko, a Boston-area hacker-entrepreneur and a member of the gang, was onstage promoting a software plug-in for sale that increased the power of Back Orifice 2000. According to the Cult's Web site, Back Orifice 2000 was downloaded 128,776 times in the following weeks. On February 15, 2000, President Bill Clinton honored Zatko for his efforts by inviting him to the White House Meeting on Internet Security. Afterward Zatko remained with a small group to chat with the president.

Every year Def Con holds a "Meet the Feds" panel. At its 2000 meeting, Arthur L. Money, former U.S. assistant secretary of defense for command, control, communications and intelligence, told the crowd, "If you are extremely talented and you are wondering what you'd like to do with the rest of your life—join us and help us educate our people [government personnel]."

In 1997 Moss launched the Black Hat Briefings. In hacker lingo, a black hat is a computer criminal. Theoretically, these meetings are intended to train people in computer security. They bear considerable similarity to Def Con, however, only with a $1,000 price tag per attendee. Their talks often appear to be more tutorials in how to commit crime than defend against it. For example, at one session attendees learned about "Evidence-Eliminator," billed as being able to "defeat the exact same forensic software as used by the U.S. Secret Service, Customs Department and Los Angeles Police Department."

Get enough zombies attacking enough targets, and the ENTIRE INTERNET could become unusable.

It should be noted that the U.S. government does have a formal means to wage cyberwar. On October 1, 2000, the U.S. Space Command took charge of the Computer Network Attack mission for the Department of Defense. In addition, the U.S. Air Force runs its Information Warfare Center research group, located in San Antonio.

Given these resources, why would the U.S. and China encourage cybermilitias? "It's very simple. If you have an unofficial army, you can disclaim them at any time," says Mark A. Ludwig, author of *The Little Black Book of Computer Viruses* and the upcoming *The Little Black Book of Internet Viruses.* "If your military guys are doing it and you are traced back, the egg's on your face."

Wherever it came from, the Code Red assault was just a taste of what a concerted cyberwar could become. "I think we can agree that it was not an attempt at cyberwar. The worm was far too noisy and easily detected to be much more than graffiti/vandalism and a proof-of-concept," says Harlan Carvey, an independent computer security consultant based in Virginia.

NET VIROLOGIST Mark A. Ludwig writes about computer viruses and worms.

Stuart Staniford, president of Silicon Defense in Eureka, Calif., notes, however, that if the zombie computers "had a long target list and a control mechanism to allow dynamic retargeting, [they] could have DDoSed [servers] used to map addresses to contact information, the ones used to distribute patches, the ones belonging to companies that analyze worms or distribute incident response information. Code Red illustrates that it's not much harder for a worm to get *all* the vulnerable systems than it is to get some of them. It just has to spread fast enough."

Code Red already offers deadly leverage for nefarious operators, according to Marc Maiffret, who bills himself as "chief hacking officer" of eEye: "The way the [Code Red] worm is written, it could allow online vandals to build a list of infected systems and later take control of them."

Get enough zombies attacking enough targets, and the entire Internet could become unusable. Even the normal mechanisms for repairing it—downloads of instructions and programs to fix zombies and the ability to shut off rogue network elements—could become unworkable. In addition, hackers constantly publicize new ways to break into computers that could be used by new worms. A determined attacker could throw one devastating worm after another into the Internet, hitting the system every time it struggled back and eventually overpowering it.

"We know how [crashing the Internet] can be done right," says Richard E. Smith, a researcher with Secure Computing and author of the newly published book *Authentication.* "What I've found particularly disquieting is how little public fuss there's been [about Code Red]. The general press has spun the story as being an unsuccessful attack on the White House as opposed to being a successful attack on several hundred thousand servers: 'Ha, ha, we dodged the bullet!' A cynic might say this demonstrates how 'intrusion tolerant' IIS is—the sites are all penetrated but aren't disrupted enough to upset the owners or generate much press comment. The rest of us are waiting for the other shoe to drop."

MORE TO EXPLORE

The Computer Emergency Response Team's Guide to Home Network Security: **www.cert.org/tech_tips/home_networks.htm**

The Internet Storm Center: **www.incidents.org**

The National Infrastructure Protection Center: **www.nipc.gov**

The Cooperative Association for Internet Data Analysis: **www.caida.org**

Microsoft Windows NT, 2000 and XP security information: **www.ntbugtraq.org**

Free security test for home computers: **grc.com** and **security2.norton.com/us/home.asp**

Microsoft Windows NT, 2000 and XP information: **www.microsoft.com/technet/treeview/default.asp?url=/technet/itsolutions/security/current.asp**

CAROLYN MEINEL writes frequently about computer security. Based in Sandia Park, N.M., she is the author of *The Happy Hacker* and *Überhacker! How to Break into Computers.* Meinel's upcoming book *War in Cyberspace*, examines Internet warfare. Her Web site, happyhacker.org, is a resource for home computer users.

Networking the Infrastructure

The technology of redundancy could lead to smarter cities, designed to alert us of danger.

By Wade Roush

It's a gray late-September Sunday in San Francisco, a few weeks after the carnage at the World Trade Center, and my dog and I are walking along the beach near the Golden Gate Bridge. The huge structure seems graceful, spare and absolutely immovable. Yet with a brain steeped in movie special effects and, now, the all-too-real TV images of September 11, I can't help imagining the scene if a 767 were to rocket down out of the clouds, decapitating one of the bridge's towers or snapping the main suspension cables. I can see wires recoiling in slow motion, the main span sagging and shearing apart, cars and trucks and pedestrians plunging into the bay 67 meters below.

How many people are imagining similar horrors in their own cities, where the skylines remain unscathed? Ever since the seemingly invincible Twin Towers disappeared in a cloud of dust, Americans have been spooked about the danger to the national infrastructure. Naturally, we're wondering if anything can be done to harden skyscrapers against suicide attacks. But we're also reexamining our entire technological fabric—buildings and bridges and tunnels, stadiums and train stations and shopping malls, water supplies and the electrical grid, computer and telephone networks, roads and railways—and asking how it can be made more resistant to the predations of terrorists. "We have to start envisioning, and preparing for, worst-case scenarios," says Nancy Greene, president of the American Civil Defense Association, a Starke, FL-based nonprofit organization dedicated to preparing the population for natural and unnatural disasters. "People are finally starting to wake up, but unfortunately it takes this sort of action to make it happen."

The good news, say Greene and other experts paid to think about such things, is that there is little call for catastrophism. The country's sheer size and the distributed nature of many aspects of the infrastructure—from roads to centers of commerce to communications—limit the amount of disruption any single terrorist group could cause. But that kind of resilience is weak in other interconnected systems such as the power grid and our water system and even missing entirely from the structural framework of buildings and cities. If engineers could beef up those interconnections already in existence and introduce them where they're nonexistent, we could limit the damage from an attack even further.

The key lies in developing and deploying technologies that will tie infrastructure components together into a system that's far smarter and more self-aware than anything we have today. Engineers, security consultants and authorities on counterterrorism are working hard to weave together the threads of this technological fabric, which will be pervaded by instruments that can sense harmful chemicals in a reservoir, relay critical data about a damaged building's structural integrity to rescue workers, help map escape routes or streamline the flow of electricity in a crisis. These high-tech networks—joined with simulation tools, enhanced communications channels and safer building designs—could go a long way toward creating an "intelligent city," where danger can be pinpointed and emergency response directed with precision.

THE POWER OF DIVERSITY

The template for this new, more secure infrastructure—already replete with interconnected redundancy and a kind of intelligence—is the Internet. Its underlying packet-switching protocol allows data blocks such as e-mail messages to be chopped up, scattered through the network via whatever pathways are open, and reassembled by the addressee. The destruction of one or even several routes may slow down data but doesn't prevent it from reaching its final destination. "The Internet was designed to survive nuclear war, so it will automatically route around disruptions. That's a good model for thinking about some of the other things like electricity and the 911 system," says James An-

The Intelligent City

In a scenario proposed by MIT researchers, a centralized Web-based information system receives real-time data from sensors embedded in surrounding buildings. In an emergency, such as a fire, the monitoring station employs computer models to initiate the best response. It then uses the Web to notify the hospital, fire department and other emergency personnel. The location of rescue workers is tracked by wearable computers linked to a global positioning system. Another message is relayed to a traffic signal to redirect drivers away from the disaster.

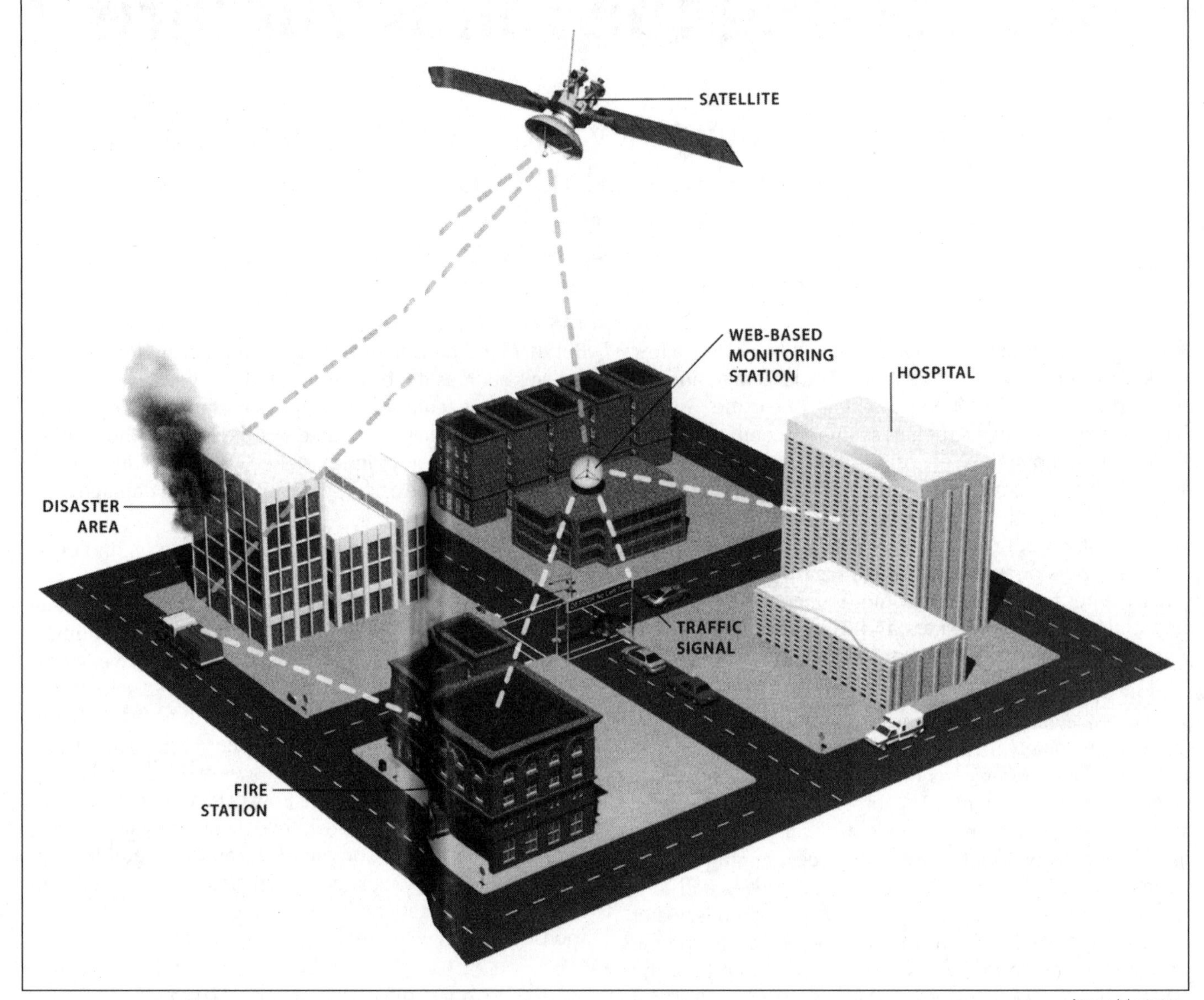

JOHN MACNEIL

drew Lewis, a senior fellow and director of technology policy at the Center for Strategic and International Studies in Washington, DC.

The nation's water supplies already share some of the Internet's hardiness. Rare is the city that depends on a single source for its water. New York City, for instance, draws water from 19 reservoirs and three lakes in upstate New York via an interconnected network of tunnels and aqueducts. If terrorists were to blow up one aqueduct, the others would still flow. If they were to dump biological agents such as botulinum toxin into one reservoir, it could theoretically be cut off from the system until purified.

But much more could be done to keep drinking water safe. For example, "We could instrument our reservoirs [to detect contaminants] very cost effectively and very quickly," suggests Roger McCarthy, chairman of Menlo Park, CA-based Exponent Failure Analysis Associates, which consults with industry and government on disaster response and readiness. In fact, the U.S. Environmental Protection Agency was granted $2.5 million in federal funding this year for research on bioterrorism, including the development of new technology for detecting biological agents in water. And researchers at Sandia National Laboratories in Albuquerque, NM, are already field-testing

Partnerships to Improve Critical Infrastructures			
INFRASTRUCTURE	FEDERAL AGENCY	PRIVATE INDUSTRY	PURPOSE OF PARTNERSHIP
Banking and finance	Department of the Treasury	Financial Services Information Sharing and Analysis Center	Provide members with early warnings about cyberattacks, such as the 1999 Melissa virus
Electric power	Department of Energy	North American Electric Reliability Council	Train utility employees to recognize and report suspected acts of physical or electronic sabotage
Emergency services			
>Fire and rescue	Federal Emergency Management Agency	National Fire Academy	Research fire-related threats, consult with and collect data from fire departments and publish information
>Law enforcement	Department of Justice, Federal Bureau of Investigation	National Communications System	Provide access to time-sensitive warnings of attacks on computing and communications infrastructure
>Public health	Department of Health and Human Services	To be determined	To be determined
Information technology	Department of Commerce	Information Technology Association of America	Build an online network for exchanging information about electronic threats and countermeasures
Telecommunications	Department of Commerce	National Coordinating Center for Telecommunications	Create and share electronic "event tickets" that contain information about vulnerabilities, threats, and outages
Oil and gas	Department of Energy	National Petroleum Council	Create an information-sharing and analysis center
Transportation			
>Surface	Department of Transportation	Association of American Railroads	Set up an industry information-sharing and analysis center
>Air	Department of Transportation	To be determined	To be determined
Water	Environmental Protection Agency	Association of Metropolitan Water	Build an Internet-accessible center to broadcast alerts and information on vulnerabilities and crisis response

tiny electronic sensors that can be lowered into reservoirs or underground wells to sniff for toxic chemicals. The sensors contain "chemiresistor" chips that measure changes in electrical resistance caused by volatile organic compounds; this data flows to collection stations where scientists can analyze the electrical signatures produced by the different compounds, identifying contaminants without having to transport actual water samples to the lab. The data can also be transmitted wirelessly to Web servers that would help spread the information to water safety officials around the country.

Ensuring that such information would get to the people who can use it is a key part of efforts to shore up the infrastructure. And as one of eight areas singled out by the federal government's Critical Infrastructure Protection program—launched by President Bill Clinton in 1998 amid growing concerns about chemical, biological and computer-based attacks—(see above) the nation's public water supplies will soon be linked to an Internet-accessible information-sharing and analysis center. Water utilities will pay a fee to join the exchange and use it to access and distribute data about contaminants found in the water supply as well as obtain intelligence reports from agencies monitoring terrorist threats.

The Washington, DC-based Association of Metropolitan Water Agencies, in charge of implementing the system, is patterning it after similar centers already operating in banking and finance and information technology. Other information-sharing systems are planned for transportation, telecommunications, emergency services, electric power and oil and gas distribution—all with the goal of giving government and private industry timely information about events disruptive to operations. "We've got to figure out how to get effective cooperation between local, state, federal and private organizations," says Randy Larsen, director of the ANSER Institute for Homeland Security, a nonprofit research organization in Arlington, VA, that consults with the government on national security issues. The centers, he says, mark a good start in that direction.

Cooperation and information sharing aren't all that's needed, however. Major parts of the infrastructure must be modernized so they can absorb and respond to disruptions more quickly and flexibly, observers say. The electrical grid, for example, needs new computerized controls to ensure that stresses on the system—whether in the form of a deliberate attack or simply a high-demand summer day—don't lead to widespread outages.

The problem isn't a lack of interconnections. While some power industry critics are calling for the construction of new transmission lines to add redundancy to the network, most regions of the nation already have several alternative paths for getting power from point A to point B. The real difficulty lies in controlling the flow of electricity. Today's power systems can't smoothly siphon electricity from overloaded lines to those with unused capacity, nor do they have any way of damping sudden disturbances such as voltage surges or selecting the best transmission path around a local outage. In short, as Lewis explains, the grid lacks the Internet's inherent resilience: "If part of the grid goes down, the rest of the system doesn't figure out how to route around it." And in an emergency, that means engineers must scramble to reroute power manually, either from a control center or by making manual adjustments to transformers in the field. "It's a dumb, antiquated system with no real architecture, so of course it's vulnerable to local attack," says McCarthy.

But here, too, help is on the way. Companies such as Siemens, ABB and Mitsubishi Electric are already testing new "power electronics" devices that can help automate the flow of electricity and smooth out unwanted fluctuations. One sophisticated switch, known as a gate turnoff thyristor, can detect lightning-speed spikes in power voltage and turn itself on and off fast enough to tame them and let controllers redirect excess power. Using these new power processors, which are being tested on key transmission lines that send power from upstate New York to Manhattan, engineers will be able to shunt power from one line to another at the touch of a button *(see "A Smarter Power Grid," TR July/August 2001)*. In emergency situations, the new devices should help grid managers switch seamlessly between primary and backup generating stations and transmission lines, minimizing the effects of attacks on individual facilities.

BUILDING THE I-CITY

Beefing up the interconnections of a city's utilities will go a long way toward making urban areas more resilient in the face of disaster. But what about strengthening the interconnections of the city itself? The same kind of redundancy and diversity found in the Internet, the water system and the power grid could be incorporated into city buildings and structures. Connecting those components electronically and then monitoring them could provide emergency-response crews with critical and timely information about any damage.

The system begins on the structural level with the buildings themselves. Additional support elements and secondary evacuation routes could help ensure that an event that compromises part of a structure doesn't lead to a catastrophic loss of life. Oral Buyukozturk, a professor in the MIT Department of Civil and Environmental Engineering, calls this principle "the technology of redundancy." Backup systems "should be incorporated into structures such that failure cannot be reached in one step," he explains. "Rather, it should take several steps."

While additional technologies such as stronger fireproofing might have delayed the accordion-like collapse of the World Trade Center towers, no one is suggesting that they could have prevented it. But the fact that few people escaped from offices above the stricken floors suggests that the airplane impacts did cut off most of the emergency stairwells in one step. And that, say Buyukozturk and others, brings the adequacy of tall-building evacuation systems into question. "We need better fire prevention methods and materials and better evacuation plans for tall buildings," Buyukozturk says. "The stairway should only be the first level of evacuation. The second level should perhaps be a special vertical tunnel or elevator, maybe installed in a tube made of a material such as reinforced concrete that is less affected by heat." Buyukozturk points to the pressurized service tunnel between the two railway tunnels under the English Channel as a working example. Thanks to the escape route the service tunnel provided, a November 1996 train-car fire that raged for nearly nine hours in one of the railway tunnels—causing considerable structural damage—killed no one.

When it comes to saving lives and stemming chaos in an emergency, it's also crucial that infrastructure managers are able to act intelligently. To do that, they need information. A growing number of engineers and city planners say the kind of intelligence exemplified by power electronics and the information-sharing and analysis centers should be woven through a structure's framework.

Researchers at Xerox's Palo Alto Research Center, for example, are proposing that legions of tiny, wirelessly interconnected sensors literally be mixed into building materials to provide a continuous report on a structure's physical state. "If you have sensors that are dirt-cheap and untethered—meaning they operate either on batteries or on passive energy that can be beamed to them—they could be blended into building materials such as concrete or brick," explains Feng Zhao, principal scientist of Xerox's Collaborative Sensemaking Project. "If each 'smart brick' has embedded sensors wirelessly communicating with other bricks, then during an emergency they can detect the extent of the damage."

Suppose a terrorist bomb blows a hole in a wall made from smart bricks or other networked materials. Some sensors would be knocked out of commission. But data collected from those that remained could allow structural engineers to quickly determine how big the hole is and how much stress has been placed on the remaining structure, explains Zhao. Even the demise of sensors could provide valuable information. "If these sensors are self-locating and part of the structure collapses, then as these bricks fall they are going to record and transmit their displacement," Zhao adds. "Maybe you can reconstruct their trajectories to see exactly how the building collapsed and where people might be trapped, and you can actually send rescue workers to the right place. That could be really useful."

Under more typical conditions, such sensor networks could be used to monitor the vibrations of passing vehicles or even footsteps, giving them obvious applications in the worlds of surveillance and military intelligence, which explains why Zhao's group is partly funded by the U.S. Defense Advanced Research Projects Agency. But Xerox's current prototype sensors range from a little larger than a quarter to the size of a shoebox, not quite small enough to incorporate into building materials. Zhao predicts it will take five to 10 years to make the hardware tiny enough and cheap enough—and suitably beef up the needed communications and data analysis software—to realize his vision. Nevertheless, he says his telephone has been "ringing off the hook" since September 11. "A lot of people think our sensor technology is right at the middle of making sure our cities are safer."

Indeed, such technologies could readily be adapted to monitor entire cities and coordinate disaster response, says Franz-Josef Ulm, a colleague of Buyukozturk in MIT's civil and environmental engineering department. "For about two years we've been discussing the concept of the 'I-City,' where basically you use monitoring and simulation of the physical state of the infrastructure—tunnels, bridges, buildings and so forth—to solve questions of the operations of the city," says Ulm (see *"The Intelligent City"*).

One small test of the I-City idea is occurring on the MIT campus, where Ulm's students are wiring a flagpole with sensors that will monitor its temperature and movements caused by wind. The data will be sent to a server computer that displays the stats in real time on the Web. Meanwhile, simulation software will use the data to predict how much time remains until the flagpole fails from structural fatigue.

If these same kinds of sensors were sprinkled throughout a building's architecture, they could transmit the information upward from individual structures to the city monitoring station to a national antiterrorism or disaster center. They could even be used to coordinate law enforcement and military responses. "How will we even know we are under attack in the 21st century?" asks the ANSER Institute's Larsen. "If you have an airplane crash in Chicago and the 911 system goes out in Sarasota and you have a big petroleum fire in Houston, are these just random acts? One of the things we need is a national command center, so we know an attack is going on, and that sort of real-time information is going to be very important."

A MEASURED RESPONSE

Because it's so difficult to know where terrorists will strike next, there is a natural impulse to retrofit as many components of the infrastructure as quickly as possible. But the resulting expense could be both crushing and ultimately futile, since terrorists might simply select targets that haven't yet been hardened. Most experts are therefore recommending a measured, planned approach to infrastructure protection, starting with a realistic look at threats and vulnerabilities. "We can't guard against every contingency, and there's no point in trying to do so," says policy analyst Peter Chalk, a specialist in national security and international terrorism issues at the Rand Corporation in Arlington, VA.

One prediction security experts can make is that the next attack probably won't resemble the last one. Thanks to heightened airport security and passenger awareness, for example, it's hard to imagine another attack using hijacked planes succeeding. "The plane as a delivery vehicle [for destructive energy] has been substantially abrogated just because of recent history," opines Exponent's McCarthy. But that doesn't mean landmarks like the Golden Gate Bridge are out of peril; indeed, notes McCarthy, there's a real threat to bridges and other structures in coastal cities from ships laden with explosive materials such as petrochemicals.

Foreseeing true threats and responding appropriately will require a new kind of thinking and a sustained sense of urgency, McCarthy and other experts say. As the immediate trauma of September 11 fades, there's a strong and understandable temptation to return to business as usual. But those who design, build and maintain the infrastructure are realizing that they must now make planning for the worst a part of their everyday work.

From *Technology Review,* December 2001, pp. 39-42 by Wade Roush.

Will Spyware Work?

Despite the most sophisticated intelligence-gathering technologies in the world, the United States failed to discover a band of terrorists that plotted within its borders. Will we miss them next time?

Kevin Hogan

As the United States tries to grapple with the new realities of war and terrorism, questions for its intelligence community keep coming: How could something like September 11 occur without plans being detected? Who was tracking the activities of suspected terrorists inside the country? How were they even here in the first place? What happened to those high-tech, Big Brother-type surveillance tools like the notorious global-communications eavesdropping network Echelon, or Carnivore, the FBI's Internet snoopware, that were supposed to sniff out criminal activity?

For several decades, electronic systems have been quietly put in place to intercept satellite communications, tap phone calls, monitor e-mail and Web traffic and then turn this massive flow of information into intelligence reports for U.S. leaders and investigative aids for law enforcement. Yet despite the $30 billion invested in them, and all the secrecy afforded them, government information technologies still could not connect the proverbial dots of the World Trade Center plot. "Obviously, there were intelligence failures on a number of levels," says Barry Posen, a defense policy analyst with MIT's Center for International Studies.

Now that it is apparent that these supposedly all-seeing government systems are not all-knowing, how can we ascertain that they work at all? While the technologies to intercept and capture any and every communication conjure images of an Orwellian omniscience (see "Big Brother Logs On," TR September 2001), many experts say the ability to derive useful knowledge from all that data is still far from plausible. Even as the processing times get faster and the software gets smarter, the process of turning raw data into assured intelligence is far from perfect. If the goal is capturing, listening to and then actually sussing every single electronic communication in the United States, "In practical terms, we're not even close," says Gary McGraw, CTO at Cigital, a Dulles, VA-based network security software vendor.

It doesn't seem to be for lack of trying, however. Today, the U.S. intelligence community comprises more than a dozen major agencies, including the CIA, FBI and the National Security Agency. Within these bodies, there are dozens more departments, such as the CIA's directorate of science and technology, that specifically develop information technologies to aid in the practice of knowing what other people don't want them to know.

Now that it is apparent that these surveillance systems are not so all-knowing, how can we ascertain that they work at all?

While the agencies theoretically cooperate, especially since September 11, there is no centralized information system to compare and contrast data collected among them. Critics claim that this bureaucratic and technical fragmentation is one reason terrorists were able to hatch their plan under the government's radar.

It is far from the only one. Even if intelligence agencies seamlessly integrate their knowledge, the tools available to them now and for the foreseeable future do not appear up to the task of providing the early warning needed to thwart terrorist plots. "My first reaction is not necessarily a question of why didn't these tools work, but how hard it would have been to discover this in the first place," says Sayan Chakraborty, vice president of engineering at Sigaba, a San Mateo, CA-based company specializing in e-mail encryption.

HEARING WITHOUT LISTENING

Despite its most recent, catastrophic lapses, the United States has a long and distinguished history of successfully using advanced information-gathering and analysis tools against its enemies. The Signals Intelligence Section, the

Tapping into What Is Typed

Carnivore intercepts and copies all data packets sent through a specific hub that match prescribed settings, such as source, destination, e-mail address and keywords that appear in subject headers. The data are then reconstructed and displayed in either pen mode, which limits the view to address information, or full mode, which shows the entire contents.

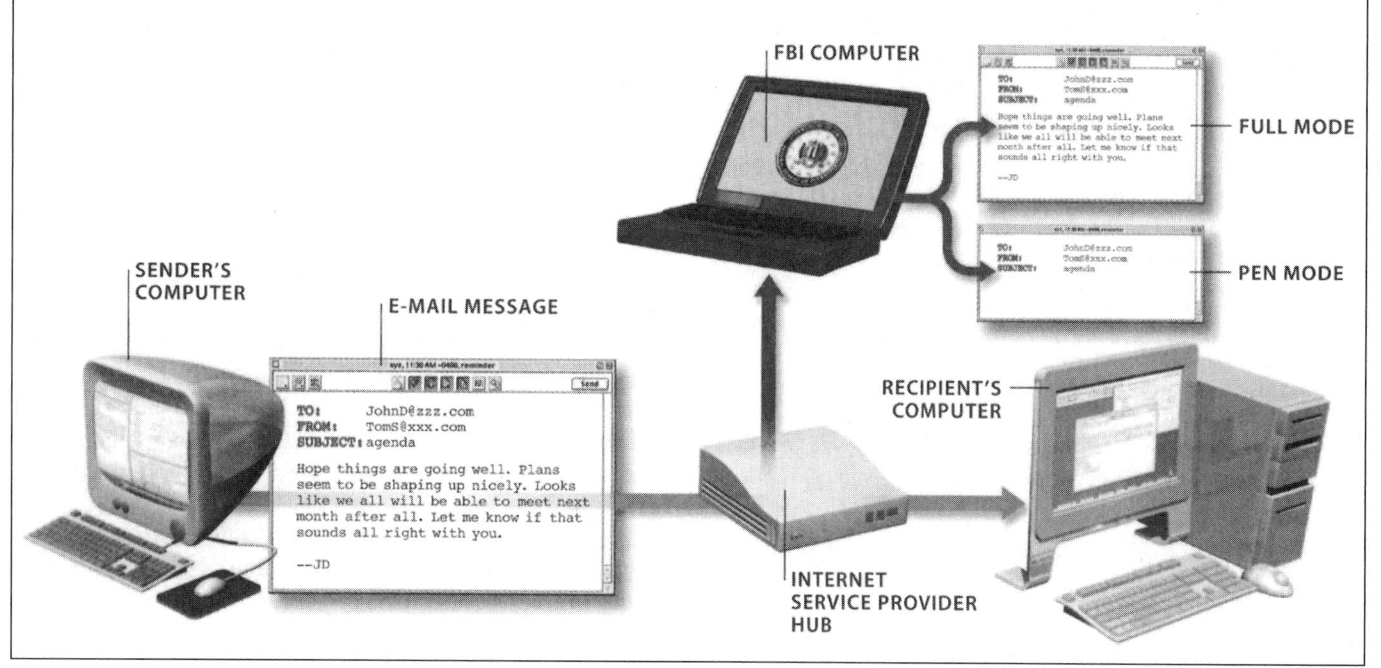

SLIM FILMS

forerunner of today's National Security Agency, came into being in World War II, when the United States broke the Japanese military code known as Purple and discovered plans to invade Midway Island. The NSA's early forays in cryptography contributed to the development of the first supercomputers and other information technologies. In his book *The Wizards of Langley: Inside the CIA's Directorate of Science and Technology*, National Security Archive senior fellow Jeffrey T. Richelson published more than 40 declassified documents that trace the CIA's exploitation of science and technology for the purposes of intelligence gathering. "From the early 1950s to the present, technology has played an essential part in analysis," he says.

Even the most advanced spying technology can be stymied by countermeasures that are embarrassingly primitive.

The granddaddy of today's governmental electronic surveillance is Echelon, the National Security Agency's infamous, yet officially unacknowledged, global surveillance network. Said to be the most comprehensive and sophisticated signals intelligence setup in existence, Echelon reportedly has the capability to monitor every communication transmitted by satellite outside of U.S. borders—by some counts, three billion telephone calls, email messages, faxes and broadcasts daily. Technically, Echelon technology could monitor domestic communications too, though that is prohibited under U.S. law.

According to a European Parliament report released in September, Echelon collects information through a complex web of radio antennae at listening stations across the planet. Other sources claim that one listening station in particular, at Menwith Hill in England, operated by U.S. and British intelligence services, is placed in the most convenient spot to tap transatlantic communications cables as well. Investigations cited by the American Civil Liberties Union and others report that Echelon rakes these immense volumes of data through "dictionary" software that operates on a vast computer network hosted by intelligence agencies from five countries—the United States, Britain, Australia, Canada and New Zealand. The dictionary program flags messages containing any of a set of predetermined keywords, such as "bomb" or "President Bush." The words are rumored to be changed on a regular basis.

How the actual process of data sifting works remains a mystery. National security restrictions prohibit anyone from speaking publicly about the program. Quips one source who has followed the technology, "Anyone who knows about it won't talk about it, and anyone who talks about it doesn't really know about it." Some experts suspect, however, that Echelon's data processing is based on a variety of technologies in use in the commercial world today, including speech recognition and word pattern finding. "Word pattern recognition is nothing new," says Winn Schwartau, a security consultant in Seminole, FL, and the author of *Information Warfare and Cybershock*. "We've been using that sort of stuff for years. But if you look at how advanced the searching abilities for the average person have become, I can only imagine the type of stuff that government security agencies have in operation."

According to Schwartau and others, the ability to sort through billions of messages and divine anything useful encompasses a number of techniques. Speech recognition systems and optical character readers convert spoken words (from phone conversations) and printed text (as from intercepted faxes) into catalogued and searchable digital data. Language translation software turns many of the world's spoken tongues into the English that the U.S. intelligence community prefers. Data-mining software searches volumes of data and establishes relationships among them by finding similarities and patterns.

Echelon has supposedly been using techniques like these to churn data into knowledge about foreign governments, corporations and even specific individuals since the 1970s. Subjects of surveillance are reported to have even included the likes of Princess Diana, whose work eliminating land mines ran counter to U.S. policy. And in the months leading up to September 11, 2001, according to reports from the German newspaper *Frankfurter Allgemeine Zeitung*, snippets produced by Echelon intimated that "a big operation" was in place by terrorists seeking to destroy "American targets." Other information collected may in hindsight be pieced together to divine a much clearer picture of the operation. Unfortunately, things did not come together in time to warn of the attacks.

WATCH WHAT YOU TYPE

Another government snooping technology that has been the subject of controversy since long before September 11 is Carnivore. Comprising a set of programs in development by the FBI since 1996, Carnivore is devised to intercept data traffic sent over the Internet to assist federal authorities in criminal investigation. According to the FBI, Carnivore is installed only with the cooperation of an Internet service provider and after obtaining appropriate judicial approval to track e-mail, instant messages and Web search trails. And the system inspects only those communications that are legally authorized for interception.

That, at least, is the theory. Civil liberties organizations such as the ACLU, the Electronic Frontier Foundation and the Electronic Privacy Information Center worry Carnivore could be used to monitor much more than that.

To counter that suspicion, the U.S. Department of Justice hired Chicago-based IIT Research Institute to perform the only testing of Carnivore permitted outside government agencies. According to IIT's report, published last December, Carnivore works much like the commercial network diagnostic programs—called "sniffers"—that are used to monitor corporate networks, and runs on nothing more than an average personal computer.

After securing the proper warrants, the FBI will approach an Internet service provider to attach a Carnivore-loaded PC to its internal cabling. When plugged into a hub, the collection computer sees all data packets going by. It then copies only those packets that match settings prescribed by the FBI and approved by court order. Agents can view the captured packets in two different modes. In so-called pen mode, the system displays only information that identifies the sender and the intended recipient—numerical Internet addresses and e-mail names—and subject lines. In "full mode," the agent can access not just this address information but also the entire contents of the message.

Once Carnivore has been installed at the Internet service provider, it is controlled remotely, according to the IIT report. The collection computer is connected to an analog voice line installed specifically for the particular tap. The intercepted data are stored on a two-gigabyte disk, which is then taken back to FBI laboratories for analysis. The data packets—broken bits of e-mail messages, Web pages and any other form of data sent across the Internet—can then be rebuilt and reviewed.

While Echelon and Carnivore are the most infamous intelligence collection tools, they are not the only ones, however. Government skunk works are constantly cooking up new tools to assist in covert surveillance operations. These include other quasi-legendary projects like Tempest, the code word for a number of surveillance technologies that can capture data displayed on computer screens by picking up electromagnetic emissions from the internal electron beams that create the images.

Every once in a while, the intelligence community opens its cloak to show off some of its tricks. Last March, for example, Larry Fairchild, director of the CIA's office of advanced information technology, brought a group of reporters into the basement of the agency's headquarters in Langley, VA. There, he demonstrated two programs deemed safe for public consumption: Fluent and Oasis.

Fluent performs computer searches of documents written in different languages. An analyst types in a query in English, just as if he or she were using a garden-variety search engine like Google. The software fishes out relevant documents in a number of foreign languages—including Russian, Chinese, Portuguese, Serbo-Croatian, Korean and Ukrainian—and then translates them into English.

Oasis converts audio signals from television and radio broadcasts, such as those from Qatar-based al-Jazeera, into text. It distinguishes accents, whether the speaker is male or female, and whether one voice is different from another of the same gender. The software then generates a transcript of those transmissions, identifying which voice uttered which statements. While Oasis can today comprehend only English-language programs, the CIA is developing versions that work in Chinese and Arabic, among other languages. Oasis can reportedly process and analyze a half-hour broadcast in as little as 10 minutes, as opposed to the 90 minutes that the task typically takes for an analyst working without the software.

FUTURE FUTILITY

Assuming all this impressive high-tech wizardry is fully operational, how could a band of terrorists, including many already suspected as such, operate within U.S. borders for years and still escape detection—undoubtedly making phone calls and exchanging e-mail with coconspirators all the while? The answers, unfortunately, don't provide a basis for optimism about the ability of these systems to offer much protection in the new war against terrorism.

First, security and intelligence experts agree that the mass of information generated every day around the world far outstrips the capacity of present-day technologies to process it. "You're talking about incredible mountains of information, and trying to find that needle," says McGraw.

Intelligence agency leaders themselves have admitted their vulnerabilities. "We're behind the curve in keeping up with the global telecommunications revolution," National Security Agency director Michael Hayden told CBS's *60 Minutes* in a rare public admission last February. In testimony to Congress days after the attacks on the World Trade Center and Pentagon, Attorney General John Ashcroft warned that terrorists still have the "competitive advantage" when it comes to domestic espionage, and that "we are sending our troops into the modern field of battle with antique weapons."

Then there is the matter of encryption technologies that can turn even intercepted communications into gobbledygook. "The odds are nigh on impossible that the NSA or anybody else is going to be able to break" an encrypted message, says security expert and author Schwartau. Another technology that Osama bin Laden s minions reportedly used falls under the rubric of steganography: cloaking one type of data file within another. It is possible, for example, to hide a text file with attack plans within a bit-mapped photo of Britney Spears. Just try to filter down the number of those images flying around the Internet.

And even the most advanced spying technology can be stymied by embarrassingly primitive countermeasures. Conspirators can go the old-fashioned route of disguising their activities by using simple ciphers that substitute letters for numbers or other letters; Thomas Jefferson used such codes in his international communiques as George Washington's secretary of state. Cigital's McGraw says this would be the easiest way to avoid detection: "To use a crude example: maybe the terrorists substituted the word 'banana' for 'bomb' and 'orange' for 'World Trade Center.' Do you flag every unusual pattern with random associations?"

Beyond the pure technology issues lies the question of how these tools can be used in a way that is compatible with an open and democratic society. Even in the rally-round-the-flag mood following the attacks, many U.S. citizens expressed concern about the government's expanding authority to snoop on their movements and communications. Organizations like the Electronic Frontier Foundation are highly vigilant about governmental attempts to expand the use of surveillance technologies such as Carnivore. "We really have no sense beyond a few basics they decided to reveal about how they use these tools," says Lee Tien, senior staff attorney for the organization. "They just want us to accept that they need them, without explaining why or how."

And while technologies like Carnivore have proved useful in investigations of specific individuals, they could be abused when directed at wider groups. People can quickly become "suspects" on no more evidence than an e-mail received or a Web site visited.

In the end, computer-based surveillance technologies may be best employed after the fact, says John Pike, director of GlobalSecurity.org, a Web-based military and intelligence policy group headquartered in Alexandria, VA. He notes that Carnivore, in particular, "was very effective in tracking down" and arresting former FBI agent and Soviet spy Robert Hanssen. "It also helped dramatically after the bombing to track down these terrorists' activities. It helped them detain at least 400 to 500 other people as suspects." According to Pike, U.S. citizens are going to have to become comfortable with such mass arrests if this type of technology is going to be used.

Even if the obstacles of bureaucracy, societal resistance and technical limitations were all to be surmounted, there's no assurance that high-tech spyware would ever provide the kind of security that people now crave. Will these technologies help recognize the danger next time? Even the most sophisticated intelligence paraphernalia still can't guarantee success when pitted against the malevolent combination of human ingenuity and capacity for evil.

The Shock of the Old

Our focus on new technology, as both the source of our vulnerabilities and the answer to our problems, can go too far.

By Edward Tenner

On September 11, when terrorists forcibly diverted two airline flights into the twin towers of the World Trade Center and a third plowed into the Pentagon, stunned surprise and inconsolable grief could be our only initial response. Then came an apprehension that will long be with us: how many other terrorist cells are still out there, and will we be able to find them in time?

But to many of those who have followed the scientific and technical side of warfare and terrorism, there was yet another jolt. It was comparable to the horror of the military analysts in December 1941 who had been expecting a Japanese preemptive strike in the Philippines or elsewhere in Asia, but not at Pearl Harbor. Assumptions were fatally wrong. Things were not supposed to be this way. We faced an old nightmare, not the futuristic dystopia of information warfare and massive chemical or biological attack that we had dreaded.

In the 1990s, as advanced systems triumphed in the Gulf War and the Nasdaq index began to soar, conflict was supposed to be going high tech. In December 1995, for example, a dozen Marine Corps generals and colonels, including the commandant, General Charles Krulak, visited the World Trade Center. They were studying how to master information overload by observing some of the top traders of the New York Mercantile Exchange practicing simulated commodity activity. Later, they conducted simulated combat exercises with 15 traders at advanced workstations on Governor's Island off the southern tip of Manhattan. How could the images on those 69-centimeter monitors have warned them that less than six years later, the Twin Towers would become the battleground of a domestically launched air war?

Of course we feared attacks from the Middle East and elsewhere in the late 1990s. But the bad guys, we thought, were getting online, just like us. As the year 2000 approached, military and civilian authorities were on high alert, not only for accidental failures of vital systems but for cyberattacks using the date change as a smoke screen. Yet the nation's pipelines and electrical grids survived the new year without incident. Even the powerful anti-U.S. emotions of the Kosovo war produced no serious assault on the U.S. infrastructure. Only too late did we realize what a cataclysm had been in preparation.

Our tragic mistake was not that we pursued the new. It was that we neglected the old. And it's a pattern that could have troubling implications if we don't recognize its applicability to other key parts of our technological culture.

In the case of the September 11 attacks, as journalists soon realized, the terrorists' methods were surprisingly low tech. In fact, the technologies involved had been established for a generation—30 years, plus or minus five.

While the building design was tested to withstand a hit from a 707 jet, the Boeing 747, with its immense fuel loads, was already in service by 1969. The terrorists also apparently needed no sophisticated knowledge of automatic pilots and global positioning satellites. They had simply, and all too well, learned the classic principles of flying.

The immediate goal of the hijackers was also a 1970s concept: stunning the world with photogenic violence, as at the 1972 Munich Olympics. Thanks to satellite feeds, cheap color televisions and the Internet, these images could now have a more rapid and vivid impact, but the principle was old hat. So was the idea, dating at least from the time of the Ho Chi Minh sandal—carved by resourceful Viet Cong soldiers from rubber tire segments—that the improvised technologies of poor countries and peoples might humiliate the West. The terrorists understood all too well this neglected feature of technology: with enough determination, practice and time, mature and even seemingly outdated tactics and devices can be reborn.

What can halt future attacks? The events showed the limits of communications monitoring and satellite surveillance. The question remains whether more ambitious programs like the FBI's troubled Carnivore e-mail-sniffing technology or facial recognition software will unearth new data on terrorist activity, or simply compound the familiar problem of information overload and produce an illusion of control. The frequent false alarms from even the simplest home security systems are already a plague for the police.

We obviously need to think more about protection from both newer and older forms of attack. One common feature of both is reliance on personal networks. The terrorist cells' apparent methods of recruiting from the same regions, clans and families, and moving frequently from base to base, make them difficult to infiltrate conventionally—but they also reveal patterns to experienced analysts, making more targeted technical surveillance possible. We don't need another decimal place of accuracy from computational social-science studies but a better intuitive understanding of the terrorists and their civilian neighbors. At the same time, the tacit knowledge possessed by the most effective police officers and detectives deserves more respect. One of our great challenges will be to formalize and teach these elusive skills to security screeners at airports and elsewhere.

THE SHOCK OF THE OLD IS NOT LIMITED TO BREACHES OF NATIONAL SECURITY. MANY PROFESSIONS ARE LOSING THEIR TECHNOLOGICAL BALANCE.

But the shock of the old is not limited to breaches of national security. The civil engineer and historian Henry Petroski, in his book *Engineers of Dreams: Great Bridge Builders and the Spanning of America*, points to a 30-year cycle in which a new generation of professionals forgets the hard-won lessons of its predecessors' errors. Indeed, there are signs that many professions have started to lose their technological balance. Many U.S. medical residents, for example, are no longer highly skilled in using a stethoscope to interpret body sounds. The demands of training physicians for tomorrow's biotechnology may be in conflict with the best preparation for hands-on contact with today's patients. Doctors obviously need to know the latest science, but both educational trends and the pressures of managed care make it harder for them to read facial expressions alongside lab reports.

What makes a good lawyer, too, is not just access to databases of legislation and decisions but intuitive knowledge of clients and clients' environments. That's why most lawyers still avoid representing themselves despite all the new tools at their disposal. They're paying not for formal information but for tacit knowledge.

Librarians tell me that students often spend much more time finding certain information on the Web than they would have needed using standard printed reference books. Internet skills are indispensable—in fact, they too are not taught enough—but so is the ability to access the vast body of essential knowledge that has not been and may never be available in an electronic format. The high cost of both electronic and paper information, not to mention terminals and printers, challenges librarians, but most of them recognize that each mode has irreplaceable advantages.

In fact, engineering itself is not just the application of mathematical equations but a subtle balance of aesthetics, economics and science in which culture counts as much as calculation. Computer-assisted design can accelerate execution of ideas but can never replace the insight that comes from immersion in the traditions of building. It was the cultural resonance of towers and polygons, used by brilliant designers, that made the targets of September 11 such powerful icons, not simply their acres of usable space.

Just as the Nasdaq's collapse well before September 11 was a symptom of an economy out of balance, so this infinitely greater catastrophe reminds us to seek a new equilibrium between virtual reality and the real kind, between pixels and iron and concrete, flesh and blood. As Dan Rather told his viewers during the ordeal, "This is not a graphic."

Edward Tenner is a visiting researcher in the Princeton University Department of English and author of Why Things Bite Back: Technology and the Revenge of Unintended Consequences (*Vintage Books*).

DATA EXTINCTION

ALL RECORD OF OUR ELECTRONIC AGE COULD BE ERASED—UNLESS WE LISTEN TO THE NEW DIGITAL PRESERVATIONISTS.

Claire Tristram

IN 1988 KEITH FEINSTEIN BOUGHT A STAR WARS arcade game for his college dorm room. Besides keeping him in beer and pizza money for the next four years, it also launched him on a personal journey that has lasted into the present: he now owns more than 900 vintage video arcade games, which he exhibits in a traveling show known as Videotopia. "People cry," says Feinstein, who is now 34, and who remembers a childhood complete with the earliest Pong console and an Atari 2600 he loved. "They can walk into an exhibit with hundreds of machines, and in all that incredible cacophony, they run right to their game. These games were a part of our lives. They were our first interactive media." Some of Feinstein's lovingly preserved devices are probably the last working models on the planet—the only machines where the 20-year-old software behind these games can come alive on the hardware it was meant for.

"WE KNOW HOW TO KEEP PAPER INTACT **FOR HUNDREDS OF YEARS. BUT DIGITAL INFORMATION IS ALL IN CODE. WITHOUT ACCESS** TO THAT CODE, IT'S LOST."

Just about the time Feinstein bought his first arcade game, Abby Smith was completing a PhD in medieval Russian history at Harvard University. She was troubled, though, that only a handful of writings from before the 14th century—mostly liturgical documents—had survived the tumult of Russian history. How much had been irretrievably lost? How much of her own time was going to be lost to the future? Something about those questions struck Smith as far more interesting than the work she was doing, so she threw over Russian history to specialize instead in library science. For the past two decades, Smith has helped the U.S. Library of Congress in its task of preserving history. At first she occupied herself with such tasks as saving Lincoln's original Gettysburg address from deterioration, but as our culture has grown more digital, Smith has in turn become ever more focused on solving the problem of preserving digital artifacts. She is currently director of programs at the Council on Library and Information Resources, a Washington, DC, nonprofit organization that's helping the Library of Congress draft a proposal asking legislators to fund research on a long-term solution. "The layman's view is that digital information is more secure, when in fact it's far more ephemeral," she says. "We know how to keep paper intact for hundreds of years. But digital information is all in code. Without access to that code, it's lost."

Smith and Feinstein are working opposite ends of the same problem: how to preserve digital things—data, software and the electronics needed to read them—as they age. Paper documents last for hundreds of years, but more and more of what matters to us is digitally produced, and we can't guarantee that any of it will be usable 100, or 10, or even five years from now. Feinstein's contribution toward staving off digital obsolescence is to scour flea markets for old circuit boards that might have the chips he needs to repair old games; he is obsessed with keeping every game in his collection working. Smith's approach is to develop a plan for preserving culture itself; she is obsessed with guaranteeing, for example, that 300 years from now, people will be able to read files that locate nuclear-waste sites. Both are faced with the knowledge that current methods for preserving digital things work poorly, even in the short term.

Just how bad is the problem? Examples of digital things lost forever abound, some personal in scale, some global. Software patents that can be infringed freely because the original software no longer works, preventing the patent holders from proving prior art. Land use and natural-resource inventories for the State of New York compiled in the late 1960s that can't be accessed because the customized software needed to open the files no longer exists. NASA satellite data from the 1970s that might have helped us understand global warming, were they not unreadable today.

But far worse is yet to come. "Once you begin to understand what's going on at a more technical level," says Smith, "you realize that what's lost could be catastrophic." We can count on paper documents to last 500 years or longer, barring fire, flood or acts of God. But digital things, be they documents, photographs or video, are all created in a language meant for a specific piece of hardware; and neither computer languages nor machines age well. The amount of material at risk is exploding: the volume of business-related e-mail is expected to rise from 2.6 trillion messages per year in 2001 to 5.9 trillion by 2005, according to IDC, an information technology analysis firm. Maybe most of those messages deserve to be rendered unreadable, but critical documents and correspondence from government and private institutions are in just as much danger of digital obsolescence as spam.

Then there are databases, and software, and images, all of which are in a constant state of change: JPEG, for example, the standard many digital-camera users rely on to store family photos, is already in the process of being outmoded by JPEG 2000, a higher-quality compression standard. "Unless we do something drastic," says Margaret Hedstrom, professor of information at the University of Michigan's School of Information, "in one or two or five years it's going to be very difficult for people to look back and see the photos they took."

Proposed solutions include *migration*, which consists of updating or sometimes entirely rewriting old files to run on new hardware; *emulation*, a way of mimicking older hardware so that old software and files don't have to be rewritten in order to run on new machines; and more recently, *encapsulation*, a way of wrapping an electronic document in a digital envelope that explains, in simple terms, how to re-create the software, hardware or operating systems needed to decode what's inside.

All three solutions, however, have the same sticky problem: the fixes themselves are time-bound, able to work only for several years, or perhaps a few decades, before another fix needs to be made. They also require us to act now to preserve what we think might be important to the future. "We have the problem of how to preserve digital media—hard enough to solve—and we have the additional, impossible responsibility of deciding what to save," says Smith. "Nothing will be preserved by accident."

A newly proposed solution, ironically enough, might make use of a very old technology: paper itself. Not to preserve all the digital documents we are creating in hard copy, but rather to preserve the specifications for a decoding mechanism—a kind of "universal computer" defined by a few hundred lines of software code—that will allow the documents to be deciphered in the future. Archived on paper and across the Internet, the mechanism would be guaranteed to survive for centuries. Proponents of such an approach say it will make it possible to preserve *everything*—a complete record of humanity. Maybe then history can finally stop repeating itself.

WHAT'S SO HARD ABOUT DIGITAL PRESERVATION?

The naive view of digital preservation is that it's merely a question of moving things periodically onto new storage media, of making sure you copy your files from eight-inch floppy disks to five-and-a-quarter, to three-and-a-half, to CD, and on to the next thing before the old format fades away completely. But moving bits is easy. The problem is that the decoding programs that translate the bits are usually junk within five years, while the languages and operating systems they use are in a state of constant change.

Every piece of software, and every data file, is at its heart written to instruct a given piece of hardware to perform certain tasks. In other words, it is written in the language of a machine, not of humans. Whenever you create a digital thing, be it a document, a database, a program, an image or a piece of music, it is stored in a form that you can't read. "It's like it was written in invisible ink," says Jeff Rothenberg, a researcher at Rand, a think tank in Santa Monica, CA. "As soon as it's stored it disappears from human eyes, and you need the right resources to render it visible again, just like invisible ink needs some sort of solvent to be read." Yet rebuilding old hardware or keeping it around forever to interpret nearly extinct software or formats is economically prohibitive: when shippers dropped one of Feinstein's vintage arcade games, shattering it, its original manufacturer calculated the insurance costs to restore the cabinet alone at $150,000, while making new chips for the game—from dies that no longer exist—would have cost millions.

Software companies confront the problem of digital preservation every day as they update their code, making sure it works with the latest hardware and operating systems, while at the same time ensuring that customers can access old files for a reasonable amount of time. But without some sort of digital resuscitation, every application—from the original binary codes written in the 1940s to WordPerfect to the latest million-dollar database application—eventually stops working, and every data file eventually becomes unreadable. *Every* application and *every* file.

The evolution of operating systems—the programs that allow other programs to run—provides yet another challenge. As Microsoft improves Windows, for example, it introduces new guidelines for programmers, known as application programming interfaces every few months,

Digital-Preservation Proposals

TECHNIQUE	DESCRIPTION	PROS	CONS
Migration	Periodically convert digital data to next-generation formats	Data are "fresh" and instantly accessible	Copies degrade from generation to generation
Emulation	Write software mimicking older hard-ware or software, tricking old programs into thinking they are running on their original platforms	Datat don't need to be altered	Mimicking is seldom perfect; chains of emulators eventually break down
Encapsulation	Encase digital data in physical and software "wrappers," showing future users how to reconstruct them	Details of interpreting data are never separated from the data themselves	Must build new wrappers for every new format and software release; works poorly for nontextual data
Universal virtual computer	Archive paper copies of specifications for a simple, software-defined decoding machine; save all data in a format readable by the machine	Paper lasts for centuries; machine is not tied to specific hardware or software	Difficult to distill specifications into a brief paper document

adding some features and taking others away. In each new release, some interfaces are "deprecated," meaning that programmers are advised to stop using them in the software they write. But what does that mean for programs written before the change? Most programs that use deprecated features will work for a while but they access the underlying architecture in a less direct way than the newer interfaces do, and the program is likely to run more slowly. How long before it stops? Most people actively trying to keep old files and applications operational say that five years is pushing it. "Interfaces change continually," says one Windows developer. "It's like asking how often the beach changes shape. Sometimes big storms come and nothing looks the same.

But when programs are painstakingly rewritten to conform to new operating-system guidelines, they eventually become unable to access files created by their own precursors. "I frankly don't expect to have a version of Quicken in 10 years that will be able to read my tax files from today," says Gordon Bell, who led the development of some of the first minicomputers as vice president of research and development at Digital Equipment, and who now works as a senior researcher at Microsoft's Bay Area Research Center. "Especially anything that is database oriented, with a lot of complexity in the data structure, is difficult to move from one generation to the next."

MIGRATION: DIGITAL TRANSPLANT OPERATIONS

One of the most common methods for preserving digital information is migration, where the bits in a file or program are altered to make them readable by new hardware and operating systems. It's what happens when you open an old document, such as a Microsoft Word 95 file, with a new iteration of the same software, say Microsoft Office 2001. The drawbacks? Each file needs to be opened, converted and saved individually, a process that grows impossibly large when you consider a librarian's or archivist's initiative to save as much of the historical record as possible. And eventually even the most meticulous of software companies stops supporting old versions of its products. If a file has not been migrated before that time, it's digital gibberish.

Worse, each time a file is migrated, some information is irreversibly lost. "Imagine someone saying, 'Okay, the way we're going to preserve Rembrandt is that five years from now we're going to have another artist come in and copy his paintings, and then we'll throw away the original,' says Rand's Rothenberg. "And so on after another five years. The notion is laughable with art, because you know that every time you copy, you corrupt. It's the same with computers."

"EMULATION DOESN'T PRESERVE, IT JUST MIMICS. IT'S LIKE THAT GUY WHO **RESHOT PSYCHO: YOU RECOGNIZE SOMETHING OF THE ORIGINAL, BUT** MOSTLY YOU NOTICE HOW DIFFERENT IT IS FROM THE ORIGINAL."

Migrating text files is hard enough; migrating application software is even more so. Indeed, the term "migrating" is a misnomer, since it often means throwing out the old program and writing an entirely new one in a new programming language, a process that programmers prefer to call "porting." The new program may look the same on the monitor, but underneath it is new. No matter how carefully software engineers have worked to simulate the old program, every line of code is different, with new bugs and new idiosyncrasies.

In any case, it's rarely the goal of the new program to simulate the old one exactly; it's far more common for programmers to want to improve upon the past. That's a goal that keeps computer science advancing at an exponential rate, and it probably also explains why the technical problem of preserving the past has received so little attention from those who helped create the problem in the first place.

"Computer scientists are in a profession where there is virtually no need for historical information," says Abby Smith. "They don't need information from the 1650s or the 1940s. They are used to things superseding what came before. For those in the humanities, there is no such notion. They work by accumulation, not replacement."

EMULATION: DIGITAL CPR

An even purer example of the problems associated with preserving digital objects is seen in the widespread attempt to keep arcade games like Joust and Asteroids playable today. Feinstein is keeping old games alive by preserving the machines that run them, but many others are trying a different means: hacks are importing the games onto today's PCs.

Such hacks use a technique called emulation, creating a program that simulates the registers (storage locations in the central processing unit) and behaviors of the old machine, and which can fool old games into thinking they are being run on old hardware. Emulation has the advantage of keeping the original bits of a given file or program intact, warts and all. "In porting, it's difficult to capture the bugs and idiosyncrasies of the original," says Jeff Vavasour, chief technical officer of Emeryville, CA-based Digital Eclipse, which is currently writing software to revive the original Joust and other arcade classics. "In games, that's important. So we don't port. We use emulation instead."

Indeed, emulation has been proposed as a way to keep not just games but everything else digital alive. It has its own drawbacks, however. "Emulation doesn't preserve, it just mimics," says Feinstein. "The timing will be all wrong. Or the sound will be off.... It's like the guy who reshot the film *Psycho* using Hitchcock's shot book. You recognize something of the original, but mostly you recognize how different it is from the original."

Looking for hard evidence to support claims like Vavasour's, that emulation is better at preserving digital content's original look and feel, Hedstrom and his colleague Cliff Lampeso at the University of Michigan recently organized one of the first studies to compare migrated and emulated versions of the same software. Subjects first spent an hour learning the maze game Chuckie Egg on its original platform, the BBC Micro, a microcomputer popular in Britain in the mid-1980s. They then played the game twice more on modern PCs, once with a version that had been migrated into a modern computer language and again with the original BBC Micro code running inside an emulator. Hedstrom and Lampeso found no statistically significant difference in the way the subjects rated the performance of the two versions. Says Hedstrom, "It was not apparent that emulation did a better job."

Nonetheless, some computer scientists have suggested "chains" of emulators as a temporary solution to the problem of digital obsolescence: as each generation of hardware grows obsolete, it will be replaced by a layer of emulation software. But it's an idea that has others shaking their heads. "It's extremely dangerous to talk about emulation as a solution," says David Bearman, president of Archives and Museum Informatics, a consulting group that works with business and government entities, helping them preserve digital files. "It gives an excuse to managers and governments around the world to put off doing things that really need to be done right now."

ENCAPSULATION: DIGITAL CRYONICS

Neither migration nor emulation, then, offers a satisfactory long-term way to wrest digital bits from what Shakespeare called "the wrackfull siege of batt'ring days' The only real way to keep digital things alive for the duration, many believe, is to lift them out of this inexorable march of digital progress—but to leave signposts that will tell future generations how to reconstruct what has passed.

Consortia of libraries and archivists worldwide are working on a solution called encapsulation: a way to group digital objects together with descriptive "wrappers" containing instructions for decoding their bits in the future. A wrapper would include both a physical outer layer, similar to the jacket of a floppy disk, imprinted with human-readable text describing the encapsulated content and how to use it, and a digital inner layer containing the specifications for the software, operating system and hardware needed to read the object itself. A Microsoft Word document, for example, might be packaged with instructions for re-creating Word, Windows and perhaps even an emulated version of a Wintel PC. For text documents, at least, encapsulation seems likely to be a viable method for long-term preservation, especially once international standards bodies agree on a uniform system for building wrappers. But if the documents being preserved contain more than simple text, encapsulation seems less likely to succeed: there are simply too many new software releases, compression schemes and hardware formats each year to describe all of them through encapsulation.

"The pagination is off even when you open a last generation Word document," observes Steve Gilheany, senior systems engineer at Archive Builders, a Manhattan Beach, CA-based records-management consulting group that has assisted the city of Los Angeles in its digital-document preservation. "Imagine then what happens when you try to open it in a hundred years or try to access a digital object more complicated than pages of text."

Gilheany's proposed solution is simpler, borrowing the concept behind that archetypal decryption key, the Rosetta stone. He recommends archiving critical files in at least three formats: The first would be a standard raster or bit-map format, where there is a one-to-one correspondence between how coordinates are stored and how they are displayed, without the kind of compression used today for large files like JPEG images. The second would be the file's native format, whatever it happens to be, to simplify any future modifications. The third would be a "vector-based" format storing each letter, symbol or image in the form of a mathematical description of its shape on the page; Adobe Systems' Portable Document Format is one example. In theory, each version could be used to decode the others. Gilheany has spent eight years assisting the Los Angeles city government in converting its original infrastructure documents into raster and PDF files, and in the absence of a better solution, most government agencies and others with critical archival needs are taking a similar approach.

Encapsulation and conversion, though, require foresight; as Smith notes, anything that isn't expressly encapsulated or converted will surely disappear. These solutions also aren't particularly long lived, at least compared with things like stone hieroglyphs or even paper. "Some researchers predict very long lifetimes for some types of media," says Raymond Lorie, a research fellow at IBM's Almaden Research Center in San Jose, CA. "But if a medium is good for *N* years, what do we do for *N*-plus-one years? Whatever *N* is, the problem does not go away."

THE UNIVERSAL VIRTUAL COMPUTER

Proponents of emulation and encapsulation are thinking the wrong way, Lorie believes. Packaging complex data with the software needed to read it is too complicated, he thinks, and saving data in simple formats and trusting that someone a century hence will still be able to decode them is too risky. Instead, he's building a universal decoding machine—a primitive program that would begin working behind the scenes to preserve a digital thing as soon as it was created—and proposing that it be promulgated so widely that it would become an inextricable part of our culture, like copies of the Bible or the U.S. Constitution. This program would be written in a simple machine language; it could be used to unlock files and to run application software even after the formats in which the files are stored grow obsolete; and most important, it wouldn't require any particular foresight about which things should be saved.

Lorie believes that this program, which he calls the universal virtual computer, should be constructed independently of any existing hardware or software, so that it is independent, too, of time. It would simulate the same basic architecture that every computer has had since the beginning: memory, a sequence of registers, and rules for how to move information among them. Computer users could create and save digital files using the application software of their choice; when a digital file was saved, though, it would also be backed up in a file that could be read by the universal computer. When someone wanted to read the file in the future, only a single emulation layer—between the universal virtual computer and the computer of that time—would be needed to access it.

"Ray's suggested universal virtual computer is a good idea," comments Rand's Rothenberg. In fact, he says it's one possible version of a concept he has been developing himself, something called the "emulation virtual machine." Rothenberg's machine would be a universal platform for emulating obsolete computers, which could then run obsolete software to render obsolete digital objects. Lorie's solution, Rothenberg says, is similar in spirit but "far less general."

ARCHIVED ON PAPER, THE PLANS FOR A UNIVERSAL DECODING **MACHINE WOULD SURVIVE FOR CENTURIES, ALLOWING US TO SAVE** MILLIONS OF DOCUMENTS AROUND THE WORLD.

Lorie, however, believes in keeping things simple—so simple, in fact, that he wants to fit the specifications for his universal computer into only 10 to 20 pages of text, which could be distributed via the Web and copied out on paper everywhere, assuring their survival. "Saving one single paper document allows us to save millions of documents around the world," he says.

Will it work? Last September Lorie demonstrated his approach at the National Library of the Netherlands, successfully translating a PDF version of a scientific paper on drug research into his universal format. The reconstruction not only kept the look of the original's fonts and formatting, it also created "metadata" to clue in future users about its content.

In addition to text files, Lorie's approach could also be used to save today's digital photographs, sound and video files, and software applications for future generations; the content or software need only be described and saved in a way that is compatible with the universal computer. But he believes that the ability to decode today's data files will be far more valuable than the ability to run old software. Imagine, for example, being able to view data not just with today's visualization tools but in ways that won't be invented for another hundred years. "It's not just that you want to save the document," he explains. "You want to make the data within the document available to whatever new programs we may have in the future."

UNAWAKENED DEMAND

Boiling down the specifications for the universal virtual computer into a handful of pages poses technical problems that Lorie believes can be solved. But will they be? Like everything else involving information technology, they won't be until there is enough demand to pay for the development work. By that time, however, many digital things may be past the point of resuscitation. Lorie is the only researcher at IBM with funding to study the universal virtual computer. "I wish I could say I have 20 people working on the problem, but I don't," he says.

Robert Morris, director of the Almaden lab and Lorie's boss, doesn't equivocate. "It's unfortunate, but the reason there's not a huge amount of activity is because there isn't a lot of money in it." he says. "At the moment there are not a lot of people clamoring to solve this problem."

That may change as computer users realize how much has already evaporated. In October 2001 Brewster Kahle, the man behind a project known as the Internet Archive, put up a Web site known as the Wayback Machine, a way for people to search the archive's collection of 10 billion Web pages it had crawled over the previous five years. With 1997-era Web pages in his archive, Kahle is already grappling with preservation questions. Many of the pages suffer from broken links and half-missing text, and whole classes of items—those protected by passwords or payments, for example—aren't archived at all. "We don't know how much we've lost," he says.

Like global warming, the problem of digital preservation is so big that it's hard to grasp. But when a million people are using the Wayback Machine and not finding the digital files they're searching for? Then the problem starts to become real.

"People count on libraries to archive human creativity," Abby Smith says. "It's important for people to know, though, that libraries are at a loss about how to solve this problem." When computer users are saving documents or images, they don't think twice about making them accessible to future generations, she says. "They need to."

UNIT 7

International Perspectives and Issues

Unit Selections

37. **Immigration and the Global IT Workforce**, Lawrence A. West and Walter A. Bogumil
38. **Wiring the Wilderness in Alaska and the Yukon**, Seymour E. Goodman, James B. Gottstein, and Diane S. Goodman
39. **The Quiet Revolution**, Suelette Dreyfus
40. **Dot Com for Dictators**, Shanthi Kalathil
41. **ACM's Computing Professionals Face New Challenges**, Ben Shneiderman

Key Points to Consider

- The article "Immigration and the Global IT Work Force" talks about a shortage of technical workers. The government statistics cited come from 1998. Has the situation changed since then? What is the current occupational outlook for tech workers?
- Use the Internet to examine the arguments for H1-B visas to the United States. What is your position on granting temporary visas to technical workers?
- The writers of the article "Wiring the Wilderness in Alaska and the Yukon," say, "so far it is not bringing wholesale prosperity to any village we could find." Is this surprising to you? Why or why not?
- It is often argued that information technologies have the potential to democratize politically oppressive regimes. Do you agree? Use the information in "The Quiet Revolution" and "Dot Com for Dictators" in formulating your answer.

Links: www.dushkin.com/online/
These sites are annotated in the World Wide Web pages.

Encryption in the Service of Human Rights
http://www.aaas.org/spp/dspp/cstc/briefing/crypto/dinah.htm

Information Revolution and World Politics Project
http://www.ceip.org/files/projects/irwp/irwp_descrip.ASP

National Security in the Information Age
http://www.terrorism.com/documents/devostthesis.html

Satellite Imagery in Court
http://www.crowsey.com/spacearticle.htm

For the past several years, we have been hearing a great deal about a global economy, the exchange of goods and services and, though to a lesser degree, labor across national boundaries. Yet human beings have been trading across long distances for centuries. The discovery of Viking artifacts in Baghdad and seashells in the Mississippi Valley are two of many, many examples. The beginnings of capitalism in the fifteenth century accelerated an existing process. But when most commentators speak of globalization, they refer to the increasingly interdependent trade since World War II[1] and, especially, the phenomena we have witnessed since the collapse of the former Soviet Union: the global availability of the Internet and satellite communications. Without the new information technologies, the global marketplace would be unthinkable. These make it possible to withdraw money from our bank accounts using ATM machines in central Turkey, make cell phones calls from nearly anywhere on the planet, or check our e-mail from a terminal located in an Internet café in Katmandu. They also make it possible for businesses to transfer funds around the world and, if you are in the computer business, to employ talented, and inexpensive, software engineers in growing high-tech centers like Bangalore, India.

During the high-water mark of the 90s information technology expansion, the computer industry conducted an intense lobbying campaign to grant temporary visas to foreign workers. "In 1998, FOR THE SECOND CONSECUTIVE YEAR, THE [sic] U.S quota of 65,000 H-1B visas for temporary (1–6 years) employment of foreign workers with technical skills was exhausted before the end of the fiscal year," according to Lawrence A. West and Walter A. Bogumil in, "Immigration and the Global IT Workforce." Though things have cooled off since then, the issue of importing workers for the tech sector is still an important one. The salaries for software engineers in developing nations are less than a quarter of what their American counterparts receive. The incentive to emigrate is a strong one. In so doing, emigrating engineers deprive their own countries of skills—often developed at public expense—and may, in the long run, result in "a pervasive gap in the wealth-creating potential between nations of the world."

The phenomenon of globetrotting tech workers is only one of many consequences of a global economy held together by information technology. Substantial populations across the world are beyond the reach of the Internet, increasing the disparity between the rich and the poor. It is seldom economically feasible for an Internet service provider to set up a connection in a remote village. As a result, according to "Wiring the Wilderness in Alaska and the Yukon," "it is doubtful if one-hundredth of 1 percent of people in such villages worldwide are minimally regular Internet users." This compares to 10 percent to 70 percent of the urban populations in some of the developed countries. Perhaps this is not fatal. Though the authors find that some communities in Alaska and the Yukon are connected through satellite links, "so far it is not bringing wholesale prosperity to any village we could find."

Not all international consequences of computer technology are economic. One of the most exciting developments in computer science over the past few years is strong cryptography, the art of enciphering messages. For practical purposes, freely available cryptographic software can produce unbreakable codes. Governments, including our own, have worried about this for a decade. Whatever you might think about making wiretap-proof software available to criminals in the United States, it is being put to good use in countries with repressive governments. Suelette Dreyfus in "The Quiet Revolution" describes how Dr. Patrick Ball, of the American Association for the Advancement of Science is training human rights workers to use software that lets them encrypt findings about government abuse in order to protect their sources.

Authoritarian governments find themselves in a fix, according to "Dot Com for Dictators." Either they choose to shun the Internet with its ability to enable communication among dissidents and so languish economically, or jump on the information superhighway and look for ways to control it. Some regimes are using sophisticated censorship software to stay ahead of their wired opponents. Still others—Singapore is the best example—show that a country can have a tightly controlled political system and at the same time make effective use of information technology. While almost half of Singapore's citizens are Internet users, the ruling party still has a firm grasp on political power. In fact, there is some evidence that its tightly controlled nature, as well as its size, has contributed to the government's ability to allow computers for everything from marriage license applications to questions about genetic counseling to occur online.

No discussion of the international consequences of computer technology is complete without mentioning movies, TV programs, and recorded music. The United States exports over 60 billion dollars worth each year. Alarmed at the influence that U.S. cultural products are having on national cultures, many governments have adopted quotas like those in Canada where 60 percent of broadcast time is set aside for Canadian programming. Although such efforts may be undermined by developments like satellite broadcasting and Internet transmission of video, digital technology cuts two ways. Digital video cameras and editing software are reducing the costs of making films and TV programs, allowing overseas producers to compete with Hollywood.

According to Ben Schneiderman, writing in February 2002, computing professionals are in a "position to take a leadership role in responding to the challenges brought on by last fall's terror attacks." Some of these are international in nature. In "ACM's Computing Professionals Face New Challenges," he recommends that ACM encourage development of a computing infrastructure in all countries. This, he argues, would broaden "participation in information and communication technologies," and reduce computing inequities among nations.

1. Merrett, Christopher D. "The Future of Rural Communities in a Global Economy." Retrieved 5/28/03 from: http://www.uiowa.edu/ifdebook/features/perspectives/merrett.shtml

IMMIGRATION AND THE GLOBAL IT WORKFORCE

Competing for IT talent in a global labor market.

Lawrence A. West and Walter A. Bogumil

IN 1998, FOR THE SECOND CONSECUTIVE YEAR, THE U.S. quota of 65,000 H-1B visas for temporary (1–6 years) employment of foreign workers with technical skills was exhausted before the end of the fiscal year. Leaders form many technology industries conducted a vigorous lobbying campaign in 1998 that resulted in legislation raising the quota to 115,000 for fiscal years 1999 and 2000, but in 2000 even the expanded quota was used up six months into the year. Legislation was subsequently passed in 2000 to expand the quota to 195,000 for the following three years.

The demand for IT professionals in the U.S. is occurring at the same time that other developed countries are experiencing similar shortages and when developing countries need their IT workers to support infrastructure creation, new industrial efforts, and government programs. Meanwhile, the ability of the U.S. to attract foreign workers reflects an unprecedented mobility in the worldwide IT labor force giving rise to "labor liquidity" in which individual workers can seek out demand and demand can seek out available workers. The result of this situation is a worldwide market for IT professionals in which government policies reinforce or hinder the competitiveness of a country's firms and economy. Countries are competing with each other for a scarce and valuable resource in much the same way they have previously competed for gold, timber, or oil. In stead of competing with armies and navies, though, nations in this modern contest for economic prosperity are competing with visa quotas, working conditions, salaries and benefits, and opportunities to work with cutting-edge technologies and business environments.

The IT Labor Shortage

Most bewildering is the government's reluctance to give strong preference to applicants with advanced training, despite the benefits they bring to the economy and the great demand for skilled workers.

GARY BECKER[2]
1992 Nobel Laureate in Economics

By early 1998 the shortage of qualified IT workers in the U.S. had become a matter of considerable concern. The Department of Commerce's Bureau of labor Statistics (BLS) reported that computer scientists, computer engineers, and systems analysts would be three of the fastest-growing occupations through the year 2006. Projections of demand for computer programmers are also high, though not as high as for the preceding classifications. The Office of Technology Policy analyzed the BLS data and reached the conclusion that there would be nearly 138,000 new jobs per year in these core IT occupational clusters through 2006[11]. In a separate 1998 study, the Information Technology Association of

America (ITAA) found that nearly 10% of all U.S. IT positions were unfilled in that year[5]. The total of 346,000 vacancies occurred at roughly similar rates throughout the country, regardless of organization size, and across various organizational types.

Further, remedial actions are not keeping up with demand. While enrollment in bachelor-level programs in computer science is increasing, total graduations in computer science and management information systems at the bachelor's and master's levels remain at less than half of the new annual demand and don't begin to address the backlog[12].

A number of organizations, including the American Engineering Association and the U.S. Office of Management and Budget, have criticized the methodologies of these studies[3, 7]. In response, the National Science Foundation funded a study by the Computing Research Association that found: "... the data are inadequate to ascertain what mismatch there is, if any, between national supply and demand" but "the preponderance of evidence suggests that there is a shortage of IT workers, or at least a tight labor market"[3, p. 10].

The tight IT labor market is not unique to the U.S. A recent Microsoft study found that Western Europe has a current shortage of 850,000 IT sector jobs[a] with the shortage expected to grow to 1.7 million by 2003[9]. Germany alone is reported to have a shortage of between 75,000 and 80,000 IT professionals[b] and other European Union (EU) countries report shortages of varying severity. Canadian researchers report that a 1998 shortage of 20,000 IT professionals will grow to nearly half a million by 2010[1], spurred in part by internal demand and partly by an exodus of IT talent to higher pay in the U.S. Meanwhile, parts of Latin American face a shortage of IT professionals driven by infrastructure development needs, need e-commerce projects, improved banking services, new demands by multinational firms, and an outflow of IT talent, often to the U.S. India, long a supplier of knowledge workers to the rest of the world, is now facing its own IT work force crunch as new e-commerce opportunities and a thriving offshore software development industry create increased domestic demand for IT professionals.

Economic Implications of an IT Work Force Shortage

The annual labour of every nation is the fund which originally supplies it with all the necessaries and conveniences of life which it annually consumes....

Adam Smith
The Wealth of Nations

The size of any shortage tells only part of the story. From 1990 to 1998 the growth in the IT sector of the U.S. economy has been modest at 2% but statistics show that the effect of IT as a driver of economic growth has more than doubled over the same period[10]. Further, overall economic growth has been impressive with gross domestic product (GDP) increasing by 48% over this period (6% per year). Additionally, overall investment in IT equipment (including telephone equipment) grew from 3% annually in the 1960s to 45% by 1996. Falling prices in the IT sector have also been credited with reducing the U.S. annual inflation rate in the mid-1990s by one percent. Finally, growth in IT industries and IT positions in other industries has created a number of high-paying jobs with average wages for IT position sat $46,000 per year compared to $28,000 for the 1996 private-sector economy.

The economic impact of IT internationally varies greatly. One report indicates the industrialized countries of Western Europe have lost $105.74 billion in GDP since 1998 due to a shortage in technology workers, with similar losses expected annually in the near term[9]. Taiwan's approximately $30 billion/year computer industry has had difficulty filling technical positions for several years and Singapore's continued development has been significantly constrained by difficulty filling an estimated 11% per year growth in IT staffing requirements. In India, a centuries-old history of scholarship and a rich system of educational institutions has given rise to a burgeoning software industry, much of it devoted to satisfying the needs of Europe and the U.S. Recent growth in this important sector is now being constrained by a shortage of IT professionals, created in part by an exodus of some of the nation's best programmers to the U.S., Europe, and elsewhere. As more countries begin to compete in this industry the missing technicians may be the difference between maintaining a current level of competitiveness and pushing forward ahead of the competition.

Salary is one of the most obvious elements of competitiveness in any labor market and is key in the present instance as well, especially when comparing developed and developing countries.

Less-developed countries face different consequences of a shortage. Some countries have nurtured educational, social, and economic infrastructures for decades and are poised to see their economies fully participate in the world economy, just as the requirements for participation have changed. Shortages of IT workers in some Latin American countries, for example, are constraining the countries' ability to upgrade their banking infrastructures at a time when electronic banking, e-commerce, and participation in a global financial network are keys to financial effectiveness. In the least-developed countries, a shortage of IT talent means that foreign contractors must bring their own technologists with them. These countries also suffer from a lack of workers in the government sector during a time when infrastructure management is critical. Those workers who don't leave the country completely are much more likely to choose positions with multinational or other private-sector firms.

Every Man's Interest

The whole of the advantages and disadvantages of the different employments of labour and stock must, in the same neighbourhood, be either perfectly equal or continually tending to equality. ....very man's interest would prompt him to seek the advantageous, and to shun the disadvantageous employment.

ADAM SMITH
The Wealth of Nations

In the modern labor market IT-literate workers have an unprecedented ability to learn of opportunities in distant markets and to pursue them. As a result, the average IT worker's "neighborhood" is global in scope resulting in an international competition for scarce IT professionals. The diverse and interlocking elements that define "advantageous employment" for domestic and immigrant workers alike, and how these elements become instruments in the competition for IT labor, are explored here.

Salary is one of the most obvious elements of competitiveness in any labor market and is key in the present instance as well, especially when comparing developed and developing countries. Whereas a new college graduate in MIS or computer science might expect a starting salary between $35,000 and $50,000 in certain U.S. labor markets, their counterparts in many developing countries will be lucky to see a quarter of that amount. Even adjusting for differences in cost of living, it is often easier for single (usually male) immigrant IT professionals to live comfortably, save money, and support a family in the U.S. than in their home countries.

Opportunity for professional growth is another element of the competition between nations for IT labor. Many IT workers understand that their resume is their most important asset and seek out positions where they can work with modern or leading-edge technologies. While many countries offer opportunities to work in emerging areas, the U.S. is the undisputed leader in the sheer number and variety of IT jobs working with resume-enhancing technologies. This situation is fueled by a number of factors, some of which are themselves elements of the competition for IT labor.

Consider, for example, the confluence in the U.S. of 270 million people, a computer-literate work force, a computer-literate public, an effective telecommunications infrastructure, venture capital, research universities, companies and governments with established IT infrastructures, median household income at approximately 40 times the cost of a personal computer; and a government willing to support immigration programs for critical skills. These factors embody the essence of Porter's diamond model for an innovation-driven economy[8] and create the demand for new IT technology while at the same time fueling the supply. The question that faces policymakers in other countries is where their nation has room to improve their competitiveness by attracting or retaining skilled IT talent.

Australia, for example, has a literate and affluent population, but lacks the market size and concentration of investment capital to compete with the U.S. in providing IT employment opportunities. As a result, there are some 5,000 Australians working in Silicon Valley despite a shortage of over 30,000 IT professionals at home. Some Latin American and European countries suffer because of their limited telecommunications infrastructures. While countries like Chile have modern systems with competitive telecommunications pricing and Internet access, others have government-run telephone companies with service levels that don't support modern e-commerce development. In some countries dedicated Internet connections are not available and all telephone calls, including Internet connectivity, are priced by the duration of the connection. A complaint in some African countries is that the phone system is so unreliable no e-commerce or interorganizational system development is feasible.

Quality of life is another element of the competition between nations for IT talent. Those countries with large existing immigrant populations provide a natural social support system for new arrivals and thus are more competitive than more xenophobic nations. Conversely, many countries have been the beneficiaries of talented professionals leaving troubled areas such as Colombia, the Balkans, the Middle East, and South Africa in large numbers.

A different competitive arena involves the welcoming mechanisms for prospective workers. Consider, for example, three aspects of U.S. policy that affect this area. First, the U.S. has raised the volume of temporary professional work visas twice in as many years as demand has increased. In contrast, the original German proposal to create 20,000 five-year technology positions for foreign workers faced serious public and political opposition[6]. Second, U.S. law also allows professional workers on H-1B visas to apply for permanent residence while in the U.S. In contrast, Germany's new program forbids permanent immigration and Germany has publicly announced it is not a "country of immigration." Other countries have varying support for permanent immigration by their guest workers. Great Britain has a relatively high proportion of immigrant citizens compared to other European countries and Canada's laws are also liberal in supporting permanent immigration[4]. Finally, U.S. law explicitly provides for families of foreign technology workers to accompany their sponsor under several visa and immigration programs. In contrast, the German program was originally designed to specifically prohibit entry of family members.

The U.S. and Germany aren't the only countries with programs to attract foreign technology workers. Canada, Japan, and even India have all taken recent steps to facilitate the entry of foreign professional workers, especially IT specialists. Australia and New Zealand recruit foreign professionals, including those from the U.S., by promoting the natural beauty of their countries and the relaxed lifestyles. Australia is also considering easing the immigration process for IT specialists and has already relaxed its rules for foreign students who wish to remain to work. Other countries are taking steps to address the outflow of companies and talented individuals. Britain has recognized that a recent tax change is penalizing independent contractors and is considering revising the law. Ireland, a modern success story in the cultivation and support of a technology-based economy, has developed a program that gives Irish passports to first- and second-generation descendents of Irish emigrants who wish to return home.

Conclusion

Prosperity depends on creating a business environment, along with supporting institutions, that enable the nation to productively use and upgrade its inputs.

MICHAEL E. PORTER[8]
The Competitive Advantage of Nations

With worldwide competition for IT professionals and unprecedented mobility in the IT work force it seems that the best method for attracting or retaining IT workers involves the development of an overall program of economic, social, and technical opportunity. India and China, for example, seem to be experiencing a reverse brain drain as experienced IT professionals return home to take leadership roles in new ventures. Increased domestic demand, fueled by a combination of new domestic software needs, increased Internet connectivity, new e-commerce ventures, and local software shops developing for foreign customers, are all attracting experienced managers and entrepreneurs back home and providing rewarding employment for local entry-level technologists. Costa Rica has parlayed political stability, a growing educational infrastructure, and an aggressive program to recruit foreign firms such as Intel into an unemployment rate less than 5% and wage and job opportunities that tend to keep talented citizens at home. Trinidad and Tobago has created a foreign investment zone aimed at high-tech industries and has eliminated import duties on computer equipment in an attempt to both increase foreign investment and to encourage a generation of domestic computer users.

Unfortunately, these and similar programs do not affect the overall supply of IT workers. As long as IT professionals remain mobile and world demand and market circumstances give some nations advantages in recruiting IT professionals, the disadvantaged nations will come up short. When the consequence is a spiraling deterioration in the ability of these countries to develop modern economies then the result will be a pervasive gap in the wealth-creating potential between nations of the world.

Do countries have options? Yes. But any program to address local work force shortages must address a multitude of the factors that constitute the advantages and disadvantages of employment in any particular place. In the final analysis, each country has the natural advantage stemming from the reluctance of most people to leave home, family, and the comfort of familiar surroundings. We have seen, though, that disparity in opportunities has served to overcome this tendency toward inertia for informed IT professionals. Countries wishing to retain these skills at home will need, first of all, to address these disparities.

NOTES

a. The IT sector was much more broadly defined in this study and includes computer-literate clerical workers.
b. The German figures are for IT-specific professions such as programmers, analysts, computer scientists, and so forth.

REFERENCES

1. A crisis that won't go away. *Computing Canada 25*, 8 (Feb. 26, 1999), 8.
2. Becker, G. Give me your yearning high-skilled professionals. *Business-Week* Apr. 24, 2000), 30.
3. Freeman, P. and Aspray, W. *The Supply of Information Technology Workers in the U.S.* Computing Research Association, Washington, DC, 1999.
4. Have we lost our minds? *Education Review* 1, 2 (July/August 1999); www.caut.ca/English/Publications/Review/9907_lostminds/page1.htm.
5. *Help Wanted: A Call for Collaborative Action for the New Millennium.* Information Technology Association of America

(ITAA) and Virginia Polytechnic Institute and State University, Arlington, VA, January 12, 1998.

6. Martin, P. Germany: Green Cards? City of Frankfurt Main Office of Multicultural Affairs; www.stadt-frankfurt.de/amka/english/informations/usuk_informations_text.htm, 2000.
7. Matloff, N. Critique of the Department of Commerce report entitled "America's New Deficit, The Shortage of Information Technology Workers." American Engineering Association, Inc.; www.aea.org/news/doc_critique.htm.
8. Porter, M. *The Competitive Advantage of Nations.* The Free Press, NY, 1998.
9. Rhoads, C. Germany faces storm over tech staffing—Labor groups are enraged by proposal to import badly needed workers. *Wall Street Journal* (Mar. 7, 2000), A23.
10. U.S. Department of Commerce, Secretariat on Electronic Commerce. *The Emerging Digital Economy.* U.S. Department of Commerce, Washington, D.C., April 1998.
11. U.S. Department of Commerce, Office of Technology Policy. *America's New Deficit.* U.S. Department of Commerce, Washington, D.C., January 1998.
12. U.S. Department of Education. *Digest of Educational Statistics 1997.* U.S. Department of Education, Washington, D.C., 1997.

Lawrence A. West (lwest@bus.ucf.edu) is an assistant professor of MIS at the University of Central Florida in Orlando, FL.

Walter A. Bogumil (wbogumil@bus.ucf.edu) is an associate professor of Management at the University of Central Florida in Orlando, FL.

From *Communications of the ACM*, July 2001, pp. 34-38.

Wiring the Wilderness in Alaska and the Yukon

Breaking down the partitions that divide the digital world.

Seymour E. Goodman, James B. Gottstein, and Diane S. Goodman

The Internet's global spread has been so extensive and rapid—almost 200 countries have been connected during the last dozen years—that the Net is beginning to be noticed for its absence as well as for its presence. Access is not yet as universal as many believe it could and should be. As a consequence of these shortfalls, the world is being partitioned into information age "haves" and "have-nots," called a "digital divide."

A digital divide may be defined as "a substantial asymmetry in the distribution and effective use of information and communication resources between two or more populations"[9]. There are a number of divides even if only the Internet is considered, with distinctions between populations based on urbanization, nationality, geographic isolation, gender, income, education, language, occupation, and ethnicity. Multiple distinctions make for stark gaps. Thus, poor, semiliterate, ethnic minorities in small, isolated rural villages, in the world's poorest countries are not as likely, by probabilities that differ by orders of magnitude, to be frequent or sophisticated users as are people not characterized by any of these traits. It is doubtful if one-hundredth of 1% of the people in such villages worldwide are minimally regular Internet users, easily qualifying as a "substantial asymmetry" against the 10%–70% of the urban populations of some of the most wired nations. Since there are millions of villages scattered around the world, wiring them, as well as bridging other digital divides, is attracting the attention of many governments and international organizations[1, 4, 5, 7, 8].

So if costs are high and the villagers cannot pay, who does? Directly or indirectly, the answer is going to have to be government or international organizations such as the World Bank.

Is the time ripe for dramatic progress? The decreases in costs and increases in technological choices that characterize both computing and telecommunications technologies, including the means to overcome once insurmountable geographic difficulties, should enable much to be done.

What would qualify as successfully solving this problem? A modest answer might consist of providing access, at a cost affordable with disposable incomes, to the village population of at least a large region within a country. Bandwidth would have to be at least adequate for comfortably visiting most Web sites. Another answer might also require a respectable segment of this population—10% is substantial by global averages—to actually use the Internet.

Access

Satellite and other wireless technologies have progressed to the point where it is not too difficult in theory to provide reasonable physical access to even the most isolated villages. The key question is: Who pays?

The answer: Not the villagers. With few exceptions (mostly villages with natural resources that can be exploited for extraction or tourism), the great majority of remote villages barely get by as subsistence agricultural, fishing, or crafts communities. Technological advances aside, it still costs far more to bring adequate bandwidth to a user in a village of 150 people in, say, Chile's Tierra del Fuego, Siberia, or to the mountains of Bhutan, than to almost anybody else on the planet. Paying the real costs of access is just not within their individual or community means.

So if costs are high and the villagers cannot pay, who does? Directly or indirectly, the answer is going to have to be government or international organizations such as the World Bank. Thus far, for most of the world's villages, the answer is "nobody," and that answer is not going to change anytime soon. There are too many people in too many villages in too many countries. Even in nations such as Nepal or Uganda, where their governments give the problem some positive attention, they are simply financially and otherwise incapable of doing much for such large fractions of their populations[3].

Has this divide been bridged anywhere? Are there places where this digital divide exists in all its dimensions, but where it is not so overwhelming in scale, and where national or local governments are rich enough and well enough disposed toward this problem, that efforts could realistically be made to deal with it? We went looking for such solutions in May and June 2000 in Alaska and Canada's Yukon Territory.

Except for a few places that can be counted on one's fingers, these northern expanses are populated by villages or towns of less than 10,000 people. The great majority of the villages have less than 500 people, so are minimally (often not at all) connected by roads to anywhere, import far more than they export, and are settled mostly by Native Alaskans or people of Canada's First Nations. There are few year-around, cash-economy jobs, and many of these (postmaster, school staff, and maintaining a dirt airstrip, to name a few) are government positions. Wealthy national/state/territory governments have professed commitments to getting more people connected and to subsidizing the small, and mostly poor, indigenous peoples. Some of this has already been done through the provision of basic telephony. So, if there is going to be an existence of proof that the village digital divide can be bridged somewhere, it is likely to be here.

Indeed, both countries have supplied the Internet to most of the villages above the Anchorage-Whitehorse latitudes, including the 12 we randomly visited. Both have done so through subsidies. Alaska has generously funded school facilities in its villages, and the Internet comes into almost every school via 56Kbs–128Kbs satellite links. These are up to 90% subsidized by the E-Rate legislation passed by the U.S. Congress in 1996 to update its Universal Services Fund, which is designed to bring affordable telecommunications to all of its citizens and administered by the Federal Communications Commission. A similar subsidy to the village health clinics is also in the preliminary stages of implementation as part of new telemedicine efforts. In addition, a few dozen village governments have time-limited access to the Internet via an 800-number, dial-up supported by the Department of the Interior; all of the 227 Recognized Tribal Organizations in Alaska are expected to have such access within a year.

The Canadian Yukon Territorial government (YTG) has adopted a policy of subsidizing Internet access to its more remote communities so that the cost of a dial-up connection is the same as in its capital, Whitehorse. Currently, the local ISP's serving these remote communities pay the lesser of 20% of the bandwidth costs or 30% of their gross receipts. This means that ISPs have been paying for 20% of the bandwidth costs for serving these communities. A major infrastructure upgrade to bring more bandwidth into these communities is being undertaken by the YTG. It is trying to gain approval through its regulatory commission of a contribution fund, whereby all utility customers contribute through their rates to pay for the increased village bandwidth.

The American/Alaskan connections are rigidly restricted ("stove-piped"), with as many as three to five separate pipes into a single village. For example, only students and teachers for school purposes, while physically on the school grounds, may use the E-Rate links. That leaves the links unused or underutilized for perhaps as much as 70% of their total annual capacity, producing undesired side effects in that a child cannot use the Internet outside of school hours and the summer, and has to stop using it once he or she graduates. If others want to use the Internet, they have to get their own equipment and pay 7–12 cents/minute for an often poor, long-distance dial-up connection—something few can afford. There is not enough potential market for a private ISP to set up in these high-cost villages to serve the other citizens, particularly as the stove-piped subsidies have eliminated some of the large customer groups. A few villages are better off because of peculiar circumstances such as relatively cheap microwave phone access to a nearby town. McGrath, a village of 430 people in central Alaska, is unusual in that it supports its own ISP set up by the local electric power company. But in most places, the net result has been the establishment of a new digital divide within each village—one that separates students and government people from parents, senior citizens, and everyone else.

The Canadian/YT arrangements are much less discriminating. They subsidize connections to whole villages. So, for example, a 56Kbs link to Old Crow north of the Arctic Circle is 80% paid for by the YTG and used by the entire village. YKNet, an ISP two-thirds owned by the nonprofit Yukon Net Operating Society and one-third by the Whitehorse phone company, pays the other 20%. YKNet then is able to provide any citizen 120 hours/month of Internet access via local dial-up modems for $24.95 (Canadian), which is well within the disposable income of most families or small businesses. As of early June 2000, YKNet served about a dozen villages and towns. At least four additional ISPs provided comparable services to other places in northwestern Canada.

So Alaska and the Yukon have established the necessary access criteria we've defined, although the Alaskan solutions have opened up a digital divide of their own within most villages. There is great dissatisfaction in the villages as well as within the Alaskan state government about this stovepiping. Strenuous efforts are currently under way to remove, modify, or reinterpret these restrictions, which were developed for the rest of the U.S., where circumstances are very different.

Beyond Access

But what about the more difficult usage conditions for closing the village digital divide? Are user levels up to at least 10%, and is use effective in that most people "can find relevant content, know-how to use the technologies to satisfy their own needs, and are engaged and represented in the policy process"?[9]

The 10% level is easily satisfied in Alaska since at least 20% of the populations of almost all villages consist of school-age children and their teachers. There are over 800 Internet subscriptions among the 10,000 villagers in the Yukon. Most of these are to homes, and it is common for two or more members of a family to use the same account. So the Yukon also meets this threshold.

As to finding relevant content, Alaska/Yukon villagers start with an enormous advantage over the vast majority of villagers worldwide in that almost all are native speakers of English, literacy is above 90%, and they have disposable incomes in U.S./Canadian dollars. (More typical of villages worldwide are now literacy rates in languages hardly favored, or even known, in cyberspace. Between high costs, no telecommunications, no convertible currency, and literacy disadvantages, the Internet is often a nonstarter for these people.) Not surprisingly, this is reflected in the use of the Net for educational, entertainment, and shopping purposes among young people. For example, some of the most popular Web pursuits that we observed during our visits were concerned with snowmobiles and North American sports. There is a seasonal element to Internet use, with the heaviest home use coming at the end of the long, dark winters.

In making arguments for closing the village digital divide, the economic values of information and contacts on the Net are often cited. Farmers will be able to find better prices for their produce, fishermen can find timely data on weather and fish runs, native artists will lower transaction costs and eliminate middlemen, and so forth. Some of this happens[6], but so far it is not bringing wholesale prosperity to any village we could find, and much of it is embryonic.

Other important needs that might be satisfied with the aid of the Internet relate to health and education. Virtually every Alaskan village has a clinic staffed by at least a health aide, who has less training than a registered nurse. Telemedicine has significant potential, especially to enable villagers to be seen by a doctor in a reasonable amount of time and with considerably less expense, and there have been some interesting experiments and demonstrations[8]. Educational use is supposed to be included in the curriculum of every school. We found actual use varies considerably from school to school, and is dependent on the staffs' interests and knowledge. There would seem to be a natural market for distance education, but so far this has not developed.

Government is important to the economies and welfare of all of the villages, often providing the largest sources of money and jobs. The Internet has the potential to increase, change, and improve the ways in which the communities and their citizens deal with government. It also provides new opportunities for native governments to deal with each other. These possibilities are just beginning to be explored.

There has been at least one significant example of regional political activism using the Net. A large herd of about 150,000 Porcupine River caribou migrates between northern Yukon Territory and northeastern Alaska. Many people in both Canada and the U.S. are concerned that the herd is endangered by oil exploration and future extraction possibilities. This has become a common cause between the native governments in the area against the oil companies. The issue has obtained some prominence on the Internet and has facilitated political action among the native governments of the indigenous inhabitants on both sides of the border.

It also doesn't hurt to keep in mind that new technologies and content may come with unintended and undesirable side effects. When satellite television first came to approximately 250 people in Huslia in the late 1970s, community life in the village reportedly shut down for two years.

Of the dozen villages we visited, the one that seemed to be dong best at making something of the Internet for itself was Old Crow, with about 270 people (90% native) in the Canadian Yukon. Computing and the Internet are used extensively by the native government organizations. In fact, the village is in the final stages of constructing a large, modern public building fully wired with provision for about 40 computers. The people who will actually use it designed the interior. It was the most impressive IT-related facility we have ever seen in a poor, remote part of the world that has been put there by and for the local population. Computers are used in Old Crow's school, although access to the Internet is not stovepiped as it is in Alaska. Old crow is home to approximately 80 computers, with at least 10% of its population connected to the Internet. The more knowledgeable people in town and the YKNet ISP try to provide an informal but fairly effective help service to the user community[2].

One of the most glaring problems we observed in all of the villages we visited was slow movement up the learning curve for the local populations. There was considerable receptivity to and curiosity about the Internet. Almost all the users we met spoke well of their experiences and of a desire for more frequent and extensive use. But most people, especially in the smaller villages, were struggling with basic applications and often complained of slow connections. They didn't have people available who could help them, either in person or online, except perhaps with only minimal technical aid. Having even one knowledgeable, enthusiastic, local "guru" can make a significant difference in making the Internet more rapidly and effectively utilized.

ALASKA AND NORTHERN CANADA have demonstrated that where there is the political will to provide Internet access in poor, small, remote villages, it is possible to do so. A few other wired countries (Finland and

Sweden, among others) may be making similar progress, although with more homogeneous populations.

While it is premature at best to say the Internet will remake village communities, its acceptance so far shows promise that it will prove to be a valued addition to the variety and quality of life. Assuming some cost impediments will be overcome, we might conjecture that the fractions of the populations that well use the Net are comparable to those of the parent countries.

REFERENCES

1. Department of Commerce. Falling through the net: Defining the digital divide. NTIA, Washington, D.C. (July 1999).
2. Freedman, D. Cold comfort. Forbes ASAP; www.forbes.com/asap/00/0529/174.htm.
3. Goodman, S., Kelly, T., Minges, M., and Press, L. Computing at the top of the world. *Comm. ACM 43,* 11 (Nov. 2000), 23.
4. Internet Society. Internet Society applauds G-8 charter on global information society. Statement of July 25, 2000.
5. Markoff, J. It takes a World Wide Web to raise a village. *New York Times* (August 7, 2000), C1, C5.
6. Paulin, J. Internet becomes second nature after three years in Unalaska. *Alaska J. Commerce* (July 23, 2000), 20.
7. Press, L. A client-centered networking project in rural India. *On The Internet 5,* 2 (Jan./Feb. 1999), 36–38.
8. Thompson, G.N., et al., Public Meeting, Regulatory Commission of Alask. State of Alaska (November 3, 1999), Anchorage, AK.
9. Wilson, E.J. II, Closing the digital divide: An initial review. Draft report for the Internet Policy Institute, Washington DC (Apr. 24, 2000).

SEYMOUR GOODMAN (goodman@cc.gatech.edu) is a professor of International Affairs and Computing, Georgia Institute of Technology, Atlanta, GA.

JAMES GOTTSTEIN (gotts@touchngo.com) is CEO of Touch N' Go Systems, Anchorage, AK.

DIANE GOODMAN (gooddee@mindspring.com) served as project research assistant.

The quiet **revolution**

From Guatemala to Kosovo, human rights groups have taken a page out of a spy thriller by learning the art of encryption

SUELETTE DREYFUS

A quiet revolution is creeping through human rights groups around the world. Don't expect to see noisy marches through the streets of Guatemala or angry protests in Kosovo, though both places are hotspots in the transformation. The revolution is running through electronic ether and human grey matter.

Computer technology, and particularly cryptography software (which uses secret codes to transform data into a stream of seemingly random characters), is subtly changing the balance of power between repressive governments and the human rights groups that watch them. From Cambodia to El Salvador, grassroots human rights organizations are embracing software that allows them to track government abuses and then hide their data in order to protect sources.

A driving force in this revolution is Dr. Patrick Ball, deputy director of the science and human rights program at the American Association for the Advancement of Science (AAAS). For the past nine years, Ball has been discreetly travelling in the wake of wars and insurrections to train human rights workers in the science of information gathering. He has shaped and protected databases in places such as El Salvador, Guatemala, Haiti, Ethiopia, Albania, Kosovo and South Africa, among others.

Crucial testimony under lock and key

When Ball first began this training in the early 1990s, most human rights workers were technophobes. Technology, used for so long as a tool of spying by repressive governments, was clearly the enemy. Every project was tough work, as Ball tried to convince people in the field to adopt increasingly cheap computer software as a means of deftly turning the tables on governments. About three years ago however, the climate began to change.

"Human rights groups are beginning to recognize the tremendous analytic power large-scale data brings to us and you simply cannot do that without technology," says Ball. While visiting groups in Cambodia who were learning to use this technology, I was struck by the enormous piles of paper on every desk. It could take two weeks to extract one simple figure, such as how many rapes were reported in Cambodia in a month.

Cheap computers and, more importantly, easy-to-use software programmes are changing that, says Ball. Database, spreadsheet, word processing and communications programmes have made it possible for even small organizations to track abuses with scientific rigour.

This analytic precision makes a powerful weapon. It also makes a logical target for political opponents. Witnesses often risk life and limb when they come forward to report an abuse committed by the government. As a result, "human rights groups are using cryptography in the field to secure databases, investigations, field reports and witness identities—all data that might put somebody's security or liberty at risk," Ball says.

In fact, encryption played a key role in breaking the silence born from 36 years of terror and civil war in Guatemala, which killed more than 100,000 people, most of them Mayan Indians. Until recently, most Guatemalans would have been shocked by the fact that the following testimony was publicly documented: "My sister went shopping in Rabinal, but when she got to the hamlet of Plan de Sanchez the army was already there. There they grabbed her and raped her in a house. There were fifteen girls raped and then they were riddled with bullets. Afterwards, they were buried by the people in a clandestine cemetery."

New flashpoints in the crypto-wars

This personal account, from a report by AAAS and the International Center for Human Rights Research (CIIDH) in Guatemala City, was one of many given by witnesses who wanted their names kept secret for fear of retribution. The CIIDH and several partner organizations gathered more than 5,000 testimonies between 1994 and 1995.

THE TRUTH ABOUT HAITI

The revolution in human rights work isn't just about securing data, it's also about uncovering and analyzing the right information. A case in point is Haiti's Truth Commission, which has worked with Dr. Ball since 1995. After conducting about 5,500 interviews, the commission documented more than 18,000 reported human rights abuses before analyzing the data to determine the truth about what happened in Haiti under military rule, specifically in 1993–94.

"When we took a list of all the people who were killed and made a graph of it, we saw that political murders bunched up in a couple of different points in time," says Ball. When the team timelined the data against other events, they discovered a surge in human rights abuses at the same time as a U.S. troop carrier entered the waters around the island—a possible first step to military intervention.

"What was interesting is that a lot of apologists for the Haitian regime had argued that this violence in the streets was just nationalist fever—that it was really the fault of the U.S. by threatening to intervene. But over time, you see the same fights all over the country implying a kind of co-ordination of those who were committing the terror," says Ball. "You also wouldn't expect detention by state authorities to increase at the same time as extortion by paramilitary organizations."

The most logical conclusion, says Ball, was that Haitian paramilitary groups created state-sanctioned terror in the streets to intimidate and dissuade Haitian society from calling for U.S. intervention and the restoration of President Aristide.

CIIDH was one of the first human rights groups in the world to secure its database by using PGP, now the most popular cryptography software in the field. Workers smuggled laptop computers and solar panels into remote mountain areas where they spent months scouring the region by foot and mule to gather testimony from people forced to hide from the military. They systematically burnt every paper trace of their work and encrypted the data before sending it back to the capital for analysis. They later emailed PGP-encrypted copies of the material overseas to a safe back-up site.

Guatemala remains one of the best examples of how a human rights community embraced technology, according to Ball. They continue to use security software to protect the identities of witnesses as well as the integrity of the data—to ensure that political opponents don't sneak into databases to corrupt the information and discredit the group's work.

The bulk of intelligence activities does not involve. . . sleuthings but careful analyses and judgments of openly available data.

R. G. H. Siu,
American philosopher (1917–1999)

Nevertheless, "some groups choose not to use cryptography because hiding their work would make the government consider them a national security threat," says Ball. "I don't really think that any of the human rights groups is a security threat. They may embarrass certain military or police officials who have committed atrocities, but all the groups I know are dedicated to their country's democratization and civil liberties."

Throughout the 1990s, the U.S. government and activists fought a political war over the right to use and to share strong cryptography with the rest of the world—a war that Ball says has now finished in the U.S. "At the end of the day," he says, "the U.S. government decided the economic and civil liberty costs of regulating crypto were greater than the rather shrill claims made by law enforcement and national security officials," who maintained that the tools would assist criminals and terrorists.

While he has not seen any crypto-wars waged in the countries where he has worked, there are still places that either control the use of cryptography or are hoping to do so in the future. According to Ball, "the war front in the fight for widespread human rights access to crypto is currently in North Korea, Iran, Vietnam—and the UK." To avoid this battle, many groups don't admit to using encryption. Why advertise the fact that a computer screen of seemingly random characters can be transformed into witness reports of killing and torture?

The report, *State Violence in Guatemala, 1960–96: A quantitative reflection,* can be found at: http://hrdata.aaas.org/ciidh

---

AUSTRALIAN JOURNALIST AND AUTHOR OF *UNDERGROUND—TALES OF HACKING, MADNESS AND OBSESSION ON THE ELECTRONIC FRONTIER* (RANDOM HOUSE, 1997)

Dot Com for Dictators

Tales of cyberdissidents fighting government censors feed the conventional wisdom about the Internet's role as a powerful tool against tyranny. But if democracy advocates want to spur meaningful change, they must also recognize the Net's ability to change authoritarian regimes from within. As nations such as China embrace the Web to streamline government and boost economic growth, they also create opportunities for greater transparency, accountability, and freedom.

By Shanthi Kalathil

Call it Authoritarianism 2.0: Forced to choose between jumping on the information superhighway or languishing on the unwired byways of technology, many authoritarian regimes are choosing to go along for the Internet ride. In addition to helping autocratic rulers compete in the global economy, the Internet and other information and communication technologies (ICTs) can streamline authoritarian states and help them govern more effectively—attractive options for many leaders. In some of these countries, reform-minded officials are even using the Internet to increase transparency, reduce corruption, and make government more responsive to citizens.

But hardheaded autocrats aren't suddenly soliciting e-mail advice from dissenters. Controlling information has always been a cornerstone of authoritarian rule, and leaders are naturally suspicious of the Web. Public Internet access could expose large swaths of a population to forbidden information and images or galvanize grass-roots opposition, as has already happened in many countries where Internet users are growing in number and challenging oppressive governments. As a result, authoritarian regimes are deploying sophisticated censorship schemes to stay one step ahead of online dissidents.

Such instances of technological one-upmanship have created the appearance of an Internet arms race pitting would-be revolutionaries and democracy-hungry publics against states determined to block, censor, and monitor citizens. Indeed, anecdotes about empowered cyberdissidents, amplified by faith in the democratic nature of the technology, have helped spread the notion that the Internet ineluctably thwarts authoritarian regimes. Little surprise, then, that human rights advocates and press freedom organizations publicly condemn crackdowns on the Internet as violating technology's democratizing manifest destiny.

But technological censorship and its evasion, while relevant to any discussion of political freedom, represent only one part of a larger developmental puzzle. Even if

China

Leader: Hu Jintao

Total Population: 1.3 billion

Number of internet Users: 26.5 million

Freedom House Rating: Not free

The Official Line: The speed and scope of [information flows] have created a borderless information space around the world... the melding of the traditional economy and information technology will provide the engine for the development of the economy and society in the 21st century."—*Jiang Zemin, former chief of the Chinese Communist Party*

Reality Check: Despite leaders' glowing rhetoric, China blocks thousands of Web pages within its borders, encourages self-censorship among users, and blankets its domestic information technology industry with conflicting regulations. The country has also embarked on a comprehensive e-government program designed to maximize bureaucratic efficiency and discourage corruption.

the Internet does not necessarily contribute to the downfall of authoritarianism, the Web does help transform authoritarianism's modern expression. Although other programs censor and spread propaganda, e-government initiatives that reshape bureaucracy, dispense education and health information, and increase direct communication between officials and the public actually improve the quality of life for citizens and boost transparency. Understanding these distinct effects of technology is crucial for those interested in using the Internet effectively to increase political liberalization and improve governance in closed societies. Efforts by outside governments and activists to champion hackers and cyberheroes in authoritarian states may win headlines, but the more mundane task of supporting e-government programs is just as likely—if not more so—to foster lasting reform.

DIALING UP FOR DOLLARS

Historically, authoritarian states in developing countries provided economic benefits and stability in return for the right to rule. Authoritarian and semiauthoritarian regimes such as China, Malaysia, and Singapore have already thrown government weight behind domestic information technology industries that stimulate the local economy. Malaysia has long promoted its Multimedia Super Corridor as a haven for technology companies—complete with tax perks and hands-off censorship policies for investors. Vietnam, while struggling with economic reforms, nonetheless aims to develop a local "knowledge economy" based on a tech-savvy population of programmers. Even authoritarian regimes such as Myanmar (Burma) that are relatively wary of all forms of ICT often emphasize wiring those key industries that generate hard currency, such as tourism.

On the other hand, some authoritarian countries have significantly less incentive to promote Internet access within their borders. Isolated by an embargo and fearful of widespread Internet use, Cuba has chosen to restrict entrepreneurship and greater competition in its tiny Internet industry. Economic use of the Internet in Cuba has followed the country's general pattern of separating its external and domestic sectors, and thus the majority of Internet use occurs in the tourist and export-oriented industries. Also shunned by many foreign investors and governments for its shoddy human rights record, Myanmar has been slow to open to information technology development. A 1996 decree makes possession of even an unregistered telephone (much less a computer) illegal and punishable by imprisonment—a regulation the government has made good on over the years.

Yet, if cash-strapped authoritarian states wish to tap the global economy, they will face growing pressure to permit private investment and market-led development within Internet sectors. Prodded by the Association of Southeast Asian Nations (ASEAN), Myanmar is starting to liberalize its draconian ICT laws and invite technological investment from friendly neighbors. Institutions like the World Bank and the International Monetary Fund now encourage deregulating the telecommunications sector and opening it to investment, while entities like the World Trade Organization (WTO) require certain reforms in return for membership. China, for example, had to agree to foreign telecommunications investment to join the WTO. Such reforms can, in turn, reduce state influence in key economic sectors and promote local growth in domestic Internet industries.

Authoritarian states also use ICTs like the Internet to promote larger development goals. The state-supported All China Women's Federation (ACWF), for instance, helps rural women get accurate, up-to-date health information online through local organizations that have Internet access. Via its Web site, the ACWF also offers women anonymous counseling on issues such as rape and spousal abuse. In Cuba, where mass Web access remains restricted, authorities have been pursuing online health initiatives. The Ministry of Public Health's Infomed, one of Cuba's oldest networks, connects medical centers nationwide and uses e-mail lists to disseminate health alerts. Egypt, a semiauthoritarian country that has not attempted to censor the Internet, is developing technology-access community centers to promote rural education.

STREAMLINING THE STATE

In countries that embrace ICT development, authoritarianism is no longer solely the domain of creaky bureaucracies and aging dictators. By implementing e-government policies—such as wiring key industries and federal departments—states can guide Internet development to serve their own goals. As a result, authoritarian states are shedding years of inefficiency and waste, paring down unwieldy bureaucracies, and consolidating central authority through more efficient communication with remote provinces. Such advancements are seemingly antithetical to democratization, but expanding government Internet programs can also make regimes more transparent and allow citizens to directly express their concerns about government performance.

The semiauthoritarian country of Singapore, in particular, has led the world in revamping its bureaucracy and changing the way government interacts with citizens. Singapore's ICT sector is one of the world's most dynamic, and the city-state boasts sky-high Internet penetration rates, with an estimated 2.1 million citizens online out of a total population of 4.5 million. Singapore's crown Internet jewel is its eCitizen program, which smoothly integrates services from several government departments and packages them in a user-friendly way. Just about any action requiring interaction with the government can be performed online, and the list is constantly expanding.

Myanmar (Burma)

Leader: Than Shwe

Total Population: 42.2 million

Number of Internet Users: 500

Freedom House Rating: Not free

The Official Line: A 1996 decree promotes "the emergence of a modern developed state through computer science" but forbids the unanauthorized use of computers or computer networks.

Reality Check: Myanmar severely restricts freedom of speech and of the press, and Internet use in the country is minimal, limited primarily to elites. Harsh punishments deter the public from seeking clandestine access.

Under the eCitizen site's "Get Married" subheading, for instance, visitors can file notice for either a civil or Muslim marriage, scan a roster of justices of the peace, find out about pre- and post-marriage counseling programs, and even obtain a list of hospitals providing genetic counseling. By using the Internet to enhance government responsivenes s and quality of life, Singapore's ruling party has turned the Internet into an asset that increases citizens' satisfaction with their government.

Singapore, of course, is something of a special case—it has a tiny population of just 4.5 million and is hardly a full-blown authoritarian state. Opposition parties, for example, participate in regular elections that are held at constitutionally mandated intervals. But they face other obstacles.

As the U.S. State Department's 2001 human rights report delicately puts it, "Government leaders historically have utilized court proceedings, in particular defamation suits, against political opponents and critics.... Both this practice and consistent awards in favor of government plaintiffs have raised questions about the relationship between the Government and the judiciary and led to a perception that the judiciary reflects the views of the executive in politically sensitive cases." Moreover, as the report goes on to note, "The Constitution provides for freedom of speech and expression but permits official restrictions on these rights, and in practice the Government significantly restricts freedom of speech and of the press." Web sites, for instance, that the government considers political must be registered with the authorities. The established media, which is connected to the government and espouses uncritical views, has a strong Internet presence. Since most civil society groups tend to have some connection to the ruling People's Action Party (PAP), they too use the Internet in government-approved ways. When a handful of independent groups used the Internet to provide a platform for criticism of the PAP, the party responded with new regulations. Many of these independent sites quickly shuttered operations rather than risk the continual regulatory ire of the PAP. The government's grip on power is generally aided by use of ICTs, which help modernize government operations and open communication channels between the government and the public. Civil society organizations' use of the Internet, on the other hand, has not yet proved a potent challenge to the PAP's mixture of official regulations and unspoken inducements to damp politically threatening speech.

Small and capable states such as Singapore can generally reap the benefits of e-government technology more quickly than large states with unwieldy bureaucracies. Nonetheless, across the board, many authoritarian regimes moved early and forcefully on e-government plans. In Egypt, the most politically significant Internet use takes place not among opposition groups but within the government itself. During the last two decades, Egypt computerized regional governments and then connected them through a national network. The country now has a central government Web site, and about 500 other government entities are online. In April 2001, Egypt announced an e-government initiative to provide civil services and promote intragovernmental collaboration using a technological infrastructure provided by Microsoft.

Egypt

Leader: Hosni Mubarak

Total Population: 70.7 million

Number of Internet Users: 560,000

Freedom House Rating: Not free

The Official Line: "The technology that portrays itself to be global, needs to be truly so not only in terms of reach, but more importantly in terms of equal access and mutual benefit.... These new technologies need to be geared towards the advancement of the developing world."—*President Hosni Mubarak*

Reality Check: Egypt is one of the few countries in the Middle East to forgo a coordinated Internet censorship scheme, while heavily promoting the use of Internet technology for development. However, recent arrests of Internet users indicate the government remains sensitive to dissenting opinion online.

China, which uses the term "informatization" to describe the incorporation of ICTs into all spheres of life—political, economic, and social—is developing a particularly ambitious e-government plan. In addition to implementing a comprehensive project called Government Online to make services and information available to the public, individual Chinese ministries are partnering with private companies to eliminate corruption. By using online procurement auctions, ministries can eliminate layers of middlemen, along with traditional opportunities for graft. In major cities, municipal Web sites not only provide helpful local information but also solicit feedback on projects, such as large-scale construction work. These initiatives have yet to reach poverty-stricken interior provinces, but even government officials there are beginning to think creatively about Internet kiosks and basic Internet training.

E-government provides the citizens of authoritarian regimes with important benefits. True, such programs can also help strengthen authoritarian states, particularly if they augment central authority. Some governments may also be interested only in the facade of improved governance. Yet cynical power calculations are not the sole reason officials in these countries pursue e-government initiatives. Internal reformers may attempt to use such measures as a basis for political liberalization, if not outright democratization. In China, for instance, midlevel officials have expressed the desire to use the Internet to increase government transparency and bolster accountability.

LESS CONTROL IS MORE

For all their power in creating the architecture for national Internet development, many authoritarian regimes have realized that adapting to the information age means relinquishing a measure of control. Savvy leaders understand they simply cannot dominate every facet of the Internet and rarely erect foolproof fire walls. Indeed, countries such as Malaysia and China allow a freer information environment online than they do in traditional print and broadcast media. Many employ measures of "soft control" to shape the boundaries of Internet use.

Cuba

Leader: Fidel Castro

Total Population: 11.2 million

Number of Internet Users: 60,000

Freedom House Rating: Not free

The Official Line: The Ministry of Computing and Communications' mission is "to prompt, facilitate and organize the massive use of information, communication, electronics and automation technology services and products to satisfy the expectations of all spheres of society."

Reality Check: The Cuban government restricts popular use of the Internet to individuals and organizations that are supportive of the regime. In the future, the general public is likely to gain access only to preapproved Internet sites.

Regimes often promote self-censorship—a task easily accomplished in an authoritarian atmosphere—rather than official censorship, access restrictions, and other forms of overt control. Such governments also encourage private Internet companies to filter content or police users. Moreover, years of ideological conditioning and the threat of punitive action keep citizens from crossing the boundaries of politically acceptable Internet use, making it easy for authorities to sustain an environment where comprehensive censorship is unnecessary.

Iran

Leader: Mohammad Khatami

Total Population: 66.6 million

Number of internet Users: 250,000

Freedom House Rating: Not free

The Official Line: Iranian state radio has announced that "steps have been taken so that the entire population can use Internet services around the country."

Reality Check: Internet service providers have multiplied recently, but so have regulations. A commission dominated by religious hard-liners (and some intelligence officials) has recently been set up to monitor news Web sites deemed illegal.

Authoritarian countries seeking to encourage domestic Internet industries can also present a wide array of politically unthreatening, domestically generated content that satisfies the demands of most Internet users, whose basic online needs often mirror those of residents in advanced industrialized democracies. Want to e-mail a friend, get news on a favorite sports team, or check local weather? It's easy to do in China without ever having to use proxy servers to access government-blocked Web pages. China's own private and state-owned Internet companies have generated a staggering body of information—all in Mandarin Chinese, using the People's Republic's own simplified characters—that falls largely within the boundaries of the country's harsh content restrictions. Whether via rules stipulating that all online news must flow from official sources or by making examples of those who transgress regulations, China's government has created a domestic Internet for domestic consumption.

The concept that subtler forms of ideological influence might prove effective has extended to many propaganda departments as well. In authoritarian countries where the government has taken an active interest in the Internet, the official newspaper is generally one of the first government organs to establish an online presence, which may be substantially more engaging and inviting than stodgy print counterparts. In Vietnam, the Communist Party's official *Nhan Dan* newspaper was among the first government bodies to go online in 1999. China's *People's Daily* Web edition provides not only the official take on news but a snazzy English site with links to, among other things, Chinese government white papers. The Chinese-language version features a popular chat room, called the Strong Country Forum, where users can and do debate issues related to national security, international relations, and China's global role. Unsurprisingly, such discussions feature a distinctively nationalistic tinge. These forums can provide the government with a subtler means of ideological control than the blunt instrument of official rhetoric.

REWIRING REGIMES

These rarefied forms of ideological control did not evolve overnight. Many governments have shaped Internet policy by imitating each others' policies and techniques. In China, where both domestic and foreign observers are examining the Internet's impact, officials have long sought to emulate Singapore's success in neutralizing the Web as a medium for political opposition. Authoritarian countries in the Middle East, such as the United Arab Emirates, also look to Singapore's successful e-government and e-commerce programs. For its part, China is formally advising Cuba on ICT policies and has sent Chinese Information Industry Minister Wu Jichuan to Cuba to explore joint projects. Even in Myanmar, where Internet access is tightly controlled, the government is borrowing technology strategies (or at least tech-friendly lingo) from authoritarian neighbors in ASEAN.

The Internet may be empowering autocrats, but it is also forcing them to reassess, adapt, and, in some cases, make critical changes. True, e-government programs can streamline the state, extend the central government's reach, and increase citizen support, but they also represent a hidden opportunity for political liberalization. It is a mistake to discount them simply because they come from within authoritarian governments themselves. Yet many Western policymakers and activists tend to regard autocratic moves toward e-government as mere window dressing, focusing instead on using technology to strengthen popular opposition movements. The latter approach deals with means—such as anticensorship techniques—instead of the presumably desirable ends of increased openness.

Heightened political reform and more responsive governance require not only combating censorship but also promoting Internet use that tangibly benefits citizens of authoritarian regimes while increasing government transparency. Approaches currently under consideration by the U.S. Congress, such as unblocking Web sites or offering anonymizing software to citizens in authoritarian nations, will commit large sums of money to fixing only one small piece of the greater liberalization puzzle. Rather than treating the Internet as an innately liberating tool that, if unleashed in closed societies, will release a tide of opposition sentiment, policymakers should identify and support specific actions and Internet policies that are likely to promote openness in authoritarian countries. This approach should not preclude the opportunity to combat censorship. However, since countless nongovernmental organizations, private companies, and individuals are already working toward that goal, government-funded Western support should also help reformers within authoritarian regimes use technology to make government accountable and transparent—reformers who may not attract the media attention that dissidents and human rights campaigners command.

[Want to Know More?]

This article draws on research from Shanthi Kalathil and Taylor C. Boas's ***Open Networks, Closed Regimes: The Impact of the Internet on Authoritarian Rule*** (Washington: Carnegie Endowment for International Peace, 2003).

For an assessment of the Internet's ability to promote freedom globally, see Michael J. Mazarr's, ed., ***Information Technology and World Politics*** (New York: Palgrave, 2002). Another first-rate analysis of the Internet's democratizing impact in the developing world is ***Launching Into Cyberspace: Internet Development and Politics in Five World Regions*** (Boulder: Lynne Rienner, 2002) by Marcus Franda. For more on the challenges to the conventional wisdom surrounding the Web, read Andrew L. Shapiro's ***"Think Again: The Internet"*** (FOREIGN POLICY, Summer 1999).

Several sources provide excellent country- and region-specific case studies of the Internet's impact on authoritarian rule. For analysis on the Middle East, including Iraq and Syria, see Benjamin Goldstein's report **"The Internet in the Mideast and North Africa: Free Expression and Censorship"** (New York: Human Rights Watch, 1999), available on the Human Rights Watch Web site, and Jon Alterman's **"The Middle East's Information Revolution"** (*Current History*, Vol. 99, January 2000). Two of the best works on the much-studied intersection of globalization, commercialization, and the Internet in China are ***After the Propaganda State: Media, Politics, and "Thought Work" in Reformed China*** (Stanford: Stanford University Press, 1999) by Daniel C. Lynch and **"You've Got Dissent! Chinese Dissident Use of the Internet and Beijing's Counter-Strategies"** (Santa Monica: RAND, 2002) by Michael Chase and James Mulvenon. See also Kalathil's **"China's Dot-Communism"** (FOREIGN POLICY, January/February 2001). In **"The Weakest Links"** (FOREIGN POLICY, November/December 2002), Tobie Saad, Stanley D. Brunn, and Jeff House map the world based on nations' global Internet linkages.

Many human rights and press freedom organizations monitor Internet censorship in authoritarian countries. Some of the best studies include Reporters sans Frontieres' **"Enemies of the Internet,"** as well as the Committee to Protect Journalists' annual ***Attacks on the Press*** (New York: Committee to Protect Journalists, 2002). Both are available on those organizations' Web sites.

For links to relevant Web sites, access to the *FP* Archive, and a comprehensive index of related FOREIGN POLICY articles, go to www.foreignpolicy.com.

Aid organizations are beginning to get the message: The United States Agency for International Development (USAID), for example, has committed more than $39 million over five years to promote e-government, e-commerce, and ICT diffusion in Egypt. At present, however, there is little coordination or information sharing between various agencies and groups in the United States, much less internationally. Apart from USAID, other arms of the U.S. government are pursuing their own Internet-based initiatives, while recent anticensorship measures proposed in Congress by Republican Rep. Christopher Cox of California, among others, take no notice of these activities. If an Office of Global Internet Freedom (as suggested in proposed U.S. legislation) is to be established, it should have as its mandate not merely unjamming Web sites but also coordinating various government efforts to better achieve democratic reform.

Once strong-arm regimes open the door to technology, they may find it difficult to return to a culture of bureaucratic secrecy, unscrupulous abuse of power, and unaccountability. Using technology to illuminate murky government processes and craft better public services may not automatically lead to more politically liberal atmospheres, but these moves are helping to spur more government oversight—or at least create the expectation of it. authoritarian governments may not enter the information age with reform in mind, but it can be a welcome result.

Shanthi Kalathil is an associate at the Carnegie Endowment for International Peace. She is coauthor, with Taylor C. Boas, of Open Networks, Closed Regimes: The Impact of the Internet of Authoritarian Rule *(Washington: Carnegie Endowment for International Peace, 2003.)*

ACM's Computing Professionals Face New Challenges

Technologists can make a difference on so many critical fronts.

Ben Shneiderman

The ACM community is in a position to take a leadership role in responding to the challenges brought by last fall's terror attacks. Some of us have already been contacted to contribute designs for improving security at airports, verifying identity at check-in, or redesigning cockpits to give more options to pilots and ground controllers. Others will be asked to redesign systems that trace financial transactions across international borders or examine email patterns among loosely affiliated groups. These efforts win the broadest support when our decisions about how to pursue safety and security are coupled with a strong defense of civil liberties and privacy.

Computing professionals can help provide insights for policymakers to enrich their options, while striving to avoid the trap of making unnecessary tradeoffs that sacrifice too many of our valued liberties.

I hope the ACM community will show inspirational and international leadership by stepping forward in this time of international transformation. It can do more than respond to requests for help; it can initiate innovative computing-related efforts to serve the needs of citizens in developed and developing nations. ACM members have relevant expertise that could be focused to develop socio-technical systems that prevent terrorism, cope more effectively with attacks, and eliminate the circumstances that breed support for terrorist movements. Some efforts will have immediate payoffs; others are longer-term investments in transforming infrastructures at home and abroad.

Computing professionals can help provide insights for policymakers to enrich their options, while striving to avoid the trap of making unnecessary tradeoffs that sacrifice too many of our valued liberties. We can also promote clear goal statements with measurable criteria so that we can gauge improvement and understand costs. Finally, while promoting sociotechnical solutions, we need to recognize the importance of human participation and responsibility in any system, and to be wary of unrealistic claims by technology promoters.

I propose four challenges:

1. Prevent future terrorism. Initiate internal discussion about how information and communication technologies can contribute to public safety by preventing terrorism while preserving the values of open societies. ACM should join other professional societies (for example, IEEE, AAAS, and IFIP) already discussing the pros and cons of national identification cards, refinements to existing identification methods, and other security topics. We can contribute to discussions about how improved sociotechnical systems can reduce the dangers of false positives in face recognition, biometrics, baggage checking, and biosensor networks. We can help clarify the utility of authentication (verifying registered individuals) compared with the difficulties of surveillance (broad searches based on profiles). Then we can work to determine if there are sufficient benefits to narrow-focus monitoring technologies, for example, scrutinizing selected email authors, identifying suspicious financial transactions, and comparing airline manifests against watch lists. Innovative solutions might avoid the tradeoffs we abhor. An even more positive outcome would be to improve transparency by increasing citizen rights to access, update, and view the usage logs of their financial, travel, or other records.

A systematic approach to terror prevention might emerge by developing process models of how terrorists act: from their recruitment, training, choice of targets, travel plans, border crossing, gaining identity cards, local preparations, and then their implementation. Interrupting this form of supply chain might be accomplished by more active early interventions and by repairing a nation's vulnerabilities. Modern information visualizations, already used by some law enforcement agencies, could be extended to support terror network activity analysis. Better tools could facilitate investigators who sift through the hundreds of thousands of citizen tips and other leads that emerge during investigations and interceptions.

Cyberterrorism is a specific threat we are most capable of dealing with. ACM should encourage increased research and raise the national priority of virus prevention software, server protection technology, and network reliability.

2. Strengthen communities. Strong communities would be more vigilant to threats, generate greater cooperation during attacks, and be more coordinated in coping with man-made or natural disasters. Since computer-mediated communications systems are a key technology, ACM can promote research conferences on open, yet safe, discourse methods. Such systems could strengthen physical communities by enlarging shared understandings and the common ground on which generalized reciprocity—the willingness to help others—flourishes.

Firefighters and law enforcement organizations that have well-developed experience with appropriate communications technologies are more effective in times of crisis. Responders to natural disasters, such as the Red Cross, have refined strategies for using communications tools to coordinate prompt and effective action. Better systems for interagency communication systems that also respect the unique needs of each agency while giving credit and clarifying responsibility could increase cooperation. Communicating is difficult enough with cooperative participants, but even greater challenges involve building systems that support users with opposing viewpoints. The ability to sustain consensus building leads to agreed-upon courses of action. Technologies to facilitate rational discourse would build public trust by enabling users to verify claims, limit disruptive rumors, provide summaries for newcomers, and record decision processes and votes.

We need to understand how to build more effective online communities that are safe places for constructive discussions. Improvements might include better authentication of senders (or controlled anonymity), mechanisms to support broad participation (turn-taking, required responses), and appropriate moderation tools (to filter out flames and off-topic notes).

How can information be made more trustworthy, especially in times of crisis when rumors and misinformation may circulate rapidly? Trust is the key to public confidence and constructive cooperation. Can we measure progress as designs of these sociotechnical systems are improved? Are there best practices that can be drawn from existing systems?

3. Broaden participation. Develop design principles for universal usability to achieve broad participation in information and communication technologies. Broad participation can help encourage activity among community groups to increase their vigilance and cooperate in times of emergency. In designing systems we find that diversity promotes quality; designing for and testing with multiple user communities often results in higher-quality products for all users.

To promote participation in the information society, ACM can do a great deal to ensure that new designs accommodate a diverse set of users (novice and expert, young and old, well-educated and poorly educated, coming from different cultures and using different languages). Equally important, ACM members can expand their efforts to accommodate a wide range of technologies, including slow and fast networks, old and new computers, desktop and portable devices, and small and large screens. Further projects would expand efforts to convert Web sites from text to voice or from one language to another. A key contribution could be increased research on online help, tutorials, helpdesk services, and other methods to bridge the gap between what users know and what they need to know.

The international dimension is important, but even within a single country there is a need to accommodate poorly educated users, poor readers, and those with low motivation. How can we foster research on the impact of technology in different cultures to understand how to design sociotechnical systems more responsive to different cultures?

There is strong evidence that open systems, such as Linux, offer alternative social mechanisms that generate a high degree of participation, pride, and protectiveness. The diversity and breadth of the Linux developer community intensifies its devotion to building better and more secure systems. Can it be true its commitment to openness in code and discussion generates greater robustness? Can we derive principles from such software development experiences that apply in larger social spaces?

4. Reduce inequities. Since terror and violence often emerge from troubling inequities, ACM should encourage appropriate infrastructure development for information and communications technologies in all countries. Many citizens are in desperate need of food, safety, or medical care. They don't need computers, but the organizations that can help them could benefit from improved technologies that operate in difficult physical and social environments. Lower-cost computer technology, such as the proposed Indian simputer (a simple low-cost, yet rugged machine for high-volume production) or Brazil's plan for building an information society should receive strong support from ACM members. Brazil's Rodrigo Baggio has fostered a network of almost 400 community centers in which access, training, and cooperation in technology are successfully practiced.

Software designs for developing nations would have a core set of reliable services whose instructions and help were written so they could be translated easily to multiple languages (much like what Caterpillar does for its construction equipment). Installation would be simplified and updates would guarantee backward compatibility. This would require substantial research, development, and testing, but it is a worthy and realizable goal.

Conference reports, Web sites, and publications featuring pilot projects that refine technology for disaster relief, community centers, and health clinics would provide better understanding of best practices. Improvements to educational facilities, local news sources, and networked communities in developing nations might be the best long-term hopes for economic growth and social improvement. Lessons from these projects also apply to the developing regions of the developed nations.

There are international development organizations already promoting technology projects and engaging computing professionals as volunteers or paid staff. The United Nations Development Program is at work on projects to which ACM members can contribute: democratic governance, poverty reduction, crisis prevention and recovery, energy and environment, and HIV/AIDS prevention/treatment. Other agencies include the UN's Information Technology Service; the UN's Food and Agricultural Organization; UNESCO's Management of Social Transformation (MOST); Volunteers in Technical Assistance (VITA); United States Agency for International Development; The Global Tech Corps (U.S. State Dept Program); Ashoka (international social entrepreneurs); and British Partnerships Online.

Initial versions of Web sites on these four challenges have already been established:

www.hcibib.org/preventterror
www.hcibib.org/communities
www.hcibib.org/participation
www.hcibib.org/development

Conclusion

The descriptions of these four challenges provide starting points for discussion and refinement. They may lead to promising technologies that would not only prevent some immediate terror threats, but also reduce the feelings of estrangement and alienation that raise sympathy for terrorism. Sociotechnical systems that respect human values, support economic development, and promote political participation can convert willingness to destroy into energy for development. Wherever poverty, civil war, and oppression limit aspirations, appropriate sociotechnical systems could be useful tools for those who strive to make their countries better.

These four initiatives could be launched immediately by electronic discussions within ACM and its varied special interests groups, which in turn may lead to panel discussions at conferences (such as SIGCHI where such discussions are already on the agenda for its upcoming CHI2002 conference in April). Moreover, ACM press releases could describe our initiatives and identify ACM members who would speak to the press or policymakers.

ACM Outreach Possibilities

In response to terrorism, ACM can focus its energies internationally by

- Establishing internal electronic discussions;
- Encouraging ACM conference organizers to directly address such issues as preventing future terrorism, strengthening communities, broadening participation, and reducing inequities;
- Developing informative Web sites on selected topics;
- Promoting research funding from corporate and government sources;
- Issuing position statements and press releases about these activities; and,
- Educating policymakers, business leaders, and the general public.

ACM could focus attention on these initiatives by proposing new topics for existing conferences as well as initiating entirely new conferences. Indeed, a truly ambitious effort would be a conference on information technologies in developing nations. The USACM (www.acm.org/usacm) should be commended to bringing ACM's positions to the policy community, and their experience will help in presenting ACM expertise to other arenas.

To support the four initiatives, ACM should encourage more research and development on these topics from universities, corporate sources, and government agencies. ACM might offer student fellowships in these areas and honor professionals who volunteer with appropriate organizations. Since ACM is an international organization, its white papers might be directed at funding agencies such as the U.S. National Science Foundation, Asian sources, or the European Commission. Letters signed by ACM in cooperation with other professional societies would have greater influence.

Skeptics may argue these problems are not primarily issues of computing technology. This is true, but appropriate sociotechnical systems can be part of the solution. Others will point out that terrorists can also benefit from advanced technologies. This is certainly a risk, but by our visible efforts in building constructive applications, we can do our part to shift the balance toward positive outcomes. Computing technology has been used for military applications, but it is also crucial for peacekeeping efforts such as detecting underground explosions, which helped bring about the Nuclear Test Ban Treaty.

These challenges may not attract every ACM member, but for those willing to respond to them, the Association should be a source of support. New ideas often take time to be widely accepted. Our contributions to constructive solutions to these serious problems will inspire others. The ACM community will be remembered for its role in increasing security and reducing social and economic inequities. This is our time to step forward and lead the way.

Contributing to this article were Ben Bederson, Gilbert Cockton, Joelle Coutaz, Allison Druin, Batya Friedman, Austin Henderson, Harry Hochheiser, Neville Holmes, Jeff Johnson, Clare-Marie Karat, John Karat, David Novick, Gary Perlman, Catherine Plaisant, Jennifer Preece, Kevin Schofield, Jean Scholtz, Barbara Simons, Alistair Sutcliffe, Loren Terveen, Ben White, Alan Wexelblat, Terry Winograd, and Dennis Wixon.

Ben Shneiderman (ben@cs.umd.edu) is a professor in the Department of Computer Science at University of Maryland, College Park, MD.

From *Communications of the ACM*, February 2002, pp. 31-34.

UNIT 8

Philosophical Frontiers

Unit Selections

Key Points to Consider

- 2003 marks the thirtieth anniversary of the publication of an essay entitled "Animals, Men and Morals" by Peter Singer in the *New York Review of Books*. This essay is often credited with beginning the animal rights movement. Singer argues that because animals have feelings, they can suffer. Because they can suffer, they have interests. Because they have interests, it is, among other things, unethical to conduct experiments on them. Suppose scientists succeed in developing machines that feel pain and fear. What obligations will we have towards them? If this is difficult to imagine, watch the movie *Blade Runner* with Harrison Ford. What do you think now?
- The overview to this unit says that the dollar value of the output of the meat and poultry industries exceeds the dollar value of the output of the computer industry. The overview mentions one reason why we hear so much more about software than chickens. Can you think of others?
- Neither author, Ray Kurzweil or Michael Dertouzos, thinks that we should limit certain lines of research. Do you? Why or why not?

Links: www.dushkin.com/online/
These sites are annotated in the World Wide Web pages.

Introduction to Artificial Intelligence (AI)
http://www-formal.stanford.edu/jmc/aiintro/aiintro.html

Kasparov vs. Deep Blue: The Rematch
http://www.chess.ibm.com/home/html/b.html

PHP-Nuke Powered Site: International Society for Artificial Life
http://alife.org/

According to U.S. Census Bureau statistics, the output of the meat and poultry industry is worth more than the output of the computer and software industries. Though this is not exactly a fair comparison—computers are used to build still other products—it does get at something significant about computers: They figure more importantly in our imaginations than they do in the economy. Why is this? Part of the answer has to do with who forms opinions in developed nations. The computer is an indispensable tool for people who staff the magazine, newspaper, publishing, and education sectors. If meat packers were the opinion makers, we might get a different sense of what is important. Recall "Five Things We Need to Know About Technological Change," in the first unit of this book. Neil Postman says that "Embedded in every technology there is a powerful idea. To a person with a computer, everything looks like data."

We can concede Postman's point but still insist that there is something special about computing. Before the computer became a household appliance, it was common for programmers and users alike to attribute human-like properties to it. Joseph Weizenbaum developed Eliza in the 1970s, a program that simulated a Rogerian psychotherapist. He became a severe critic of certain kinds of computing research, in part, because he noticed that staff in his lab had begun to arrive early to Eliza's advice. In 1956, a group of mathematicians interested in computing gathered at Dartmouth College and coined the term "Artificial Intelligence." AI, whose goal is to build into machines something that we can recognize as intelligent behavior, has become perhaps the best-known and most criticized area of computer science. Since intelligent behavior, like the ability to read and form arguments, is often thought to be the defining characteristic of humankind (we call ourselves, after all, *homo sapiens*), machines that might exhibit intelligent behavior have occupied the dreams and nightmares of Western culture for a long time. Rodney Brooks, whose mechanical insects were featured in the 1997 documentary, *Fast, Cheap and Out of Control*, claims, in "Humanoid Robots," that people have been trying to build them for at least 7,000 years.

Among the *New York Times* Best Sellers for 2003 is Michael Crichton's *Prey*, a distopian thriller about meat-eating robots. This one even caught the attention of physicist Freeman Dyson in the *New York Review of Books* (2/13/2003). (See unit 6 Key Points to Consider for Web site for this review.) Robots that can generate their own energy, as Fred Hapgood says, "are another illustration of this deep trend toward blurring the ancient distinction between biology and engineering." This is its real significance, however much fun it might be to imagine for a couple of hours that machines have taken over the world. The trend has its roots in two important discoveries of 1953. The first is well-known: the discovery of the chemical structure of DNA. The second is explained in "The Real Scientific Hero of 1953" by Steven Strogatz, a professor of applied mathematics. In 1953, Italian physicist Enrico Fermi, along with two colleagues, John Pasta and Stanislaw Ulam, performed the first computer experiment. They simulated entropy, the tendency of systems to move towards disorder, on MANIAC, the computer used in the development of the hydrogen bomb. Where these two discoveries meet is in the use of computers to understand complex systems, biological ones foremost among them. "Cancer will not be cured," writes Strogatz, by biologists working alone. Its solution will require "a melding of both great discoveries of 1953."

The important economic aspects of this melding, called "bioinformatics," are discussed in "The Race to Computerize Biology," where we learn that "biotech firms are now looking to computer modelling, data mining and high-throughput screening to help them discover drugs more efficiently." The English news weekly, *The Economist*, predicts that the bioinformatics market will be worth $40 billion by 2005, this for an industry so new that some word processing spell checkers have not yet added it to their lexicons.

The two different views in the next article—on the promises and perils of computing—grow out of an article that Bill Joy, of Sun Microsystems, wrote for *Wired* magazine, arguing that humanity should discontinue certain kinds of research. Ray Kurzweil in "Kurzweil vs. Dertouzos" says that he is often described as a "technology optimist." Though "a double-edged" sword, technology "represents vast power to be used for all humankind's purposes." Michael Dertouzos, on the other hand, reminds us that "when we marvel at the exponential growth of en emerging technology, we must keep in mind the constancy of human beings who will use it." It may come as a surprise that both of these commentators agree with Bill Joy that there are areas too dangerous to investigate, though for different reasons.

Our concluding article concerns present reality. Stephen Bertman's speech expounds on the accelerating velocity of everyday life and its implications for human nature and values. As always, the questions remain. Does technology stand apart from human values as Ray Kurzweil seems to imply or does it carry embedded ideas as Neil Postman argued in unit 1. Will the growth of unwanted e-mail sink the Internet? Should employers be able to intercept employee e-mail? Why are there so few women and people of color in computing? Have the courts really shifted the balance away from the public good in their current interpretation of intellectual property? Is the Web threatened by viruses and worms? Does high-tech immigration hurt developing countries? Should we forbid certain kinds of research? These eight questions, drawn from each of the eight units of *Computers in Society,* could be replaced by hundreds of others. Though we may never have answers, our hope is that through reading and reflecting on the kinds of ideas presented in this book, you can begin to formulate the important questions more clearly. To engage in reasoned discussion with friends, relatives, and neighbors is surely one of the first responsibilities of citizenship.

HUMANOID ROBOTS

The future promises lots of robots in our everyday lives; some, perhaps many, of them could look and behave like people but only if being humanoid represents a technological advantage over their relatively utilitarian counterparts.

Rodney Brooks

People have been interested in building "robots" in the form of humans for thousands of years. There were baked clay figures of humans in both Europe and China 7,000 years ago. At the height of Egyptian civilization 3,000 years ago, articulated statues could be controlled by hidden operators. At Thebes, the new king was chosen by an articulated statue of Ammon, one of the chief Egyptian gods (depicted as a human with a ram's head). Priests secredy controlled it as male members of the royal family paraded before it.

Leonardo da Vinci, the leading student of human anatomy in his time, designed a mechanical equivalent of a human—a humanoid robot—early in the 16th century; unfortunately, the design has still not been constructed.

Frenchman Jacques de Vaucanson early in the 18th century built three clockwork humanoids. One was a mandolin player that sang and tapped its foot as it played. Another was a piano player that simulated breathing and moved its head. A third was a flute player. All were reported to be very lifelike, though none could sense the environment; all were simple playback mechanisms.

Similar humanoids soon followed. In the 18th century Pierre Jacquet-Droz, a Swiss watchmaker, and his son Henri-Louis built a number of humanoids, including a female organ player that simulated breathing and gaze direction, looking at the audience, her hands, and the music. Henri Maillardet, also a Swiss watchmaker, built a boy robot in 1815 that could write script in both French and English and draw a variety of landscapes.

Modern Humanoids

The modern era of humanoid robots was ushered in during the early 1970s by Hirokazu Kato, a professor at Waseda University in Tokyo; he oversaw the building of Wabot-1, a robot that could walk a few steps on two legs, grasp simple objects with its two hands, and carry out some primitive speech interaction with people. But, as with the early humanoids, Wabot-1 was still essentially a playback mechanism.

Kato's next robot, Wabot-2, built in 1984, was much more than a playback mechanism. Like Wabot-1 it had two legs and two arms. Unlike Wabot-1, it could not stand but rather sat on a piano bench. Its feet were used to press the pedals of an organ, and its arms and hands were restricted to playing the organ's keyboard. It had five fingers on each hand and could move its arms from side to side when playing the keys. Its head was a large TV camera; when sheet music was placed on the music stand above the keyboard, it would read the music and play the piece. In some sense it, too, was a playback mechanism, but it played back standard musical notation, perceiving such notation through its vision system and responding appropriately.

By the mid-1990s many humanoid robot projects were under way, most notably in Japan, Germany, and the U.S. Today, more than 100 researchers work in humanoid robotics at Waseda University alone and a similar number at Honda Corp. just outside Tokyo. There are also large humanoid projects at Tokyo University, the Electro-Technical Laboratory (ETL) in Tsukuba, Advanced Telecommunications Research (ATR) in Kyoto, and at other Japanese locations. Germany's Bundeswehr University of Munich and the Technical University of Munich have hosted humanoid robot projects. The major projects in the U.S. have been at the University of Utah, Vanderbilt University, NASA-Houston, and MIT.

There have been many different motivations for building humanoid robots. Some formally announced ones include: investigating bipedal locomotion; building teleoperated robots to directly take the place of people (such as in spacewalks outside the International Space Station); building robots to maneuver in houses built to be convenient for people; investigating hand-eye coordination for tasks usually done by people; entertaining people; and functioning as a tool to study how people do what they do in the world.

MIT Humanoids

The humanoid robotics group at MIT (one of two groups in the Artificial Intelligence Laboratory working on humanoid robotics, the other concentrating on bipedal locomotion) started out developing humanoid robots as a tool for understanding humans' use of representations of the world around them [6]. Early plans were based on the work of the philosophers George Lakoff and Mark Johnson (best summarized in [8]) who posited that all of our under-standing of the world builds upon the embodied experiences we have when we are young. For instance, they argued that the concept of affection uses warmth as a metaphor because children are exposed to the warmth of their parents' bodies when shown affection. Thus we might say, "They greeted me warmly." Likewise, we tend to use bigness as a metaphor for importance, as in "tomorrow is a big day," because parents are important, big, and indeed dominate our visual experience when we are young. Higher-level concepts are built as metaphors less direct than these primary ones but nevertheless rely on our bodily experience in the world. For instance, for time, we use the metaphor of moving forward, walking or running in a straight line. Thus the future is ahead of us, the present is where we are, and the past is behind us.

As the first humanoid robot, called Cog, was being developed in the mid-1990s, many aspects of perception and motor control had yet to be solved [5]. Its developers realized there were important precursors to explicit representations of metaphors, as had been argued in earlier work on situated and embodied robots [4]. In the case of robots with humanoid form, intended to act in the world as people do, these precursors are social interactions [2], which are themselves based on emotional systems [7], facial expressions, and eye movements. The eye movements are driven by perceptual demands imposed by the underlying architecture of the eye [10]; in turn, they have been hijacked by evolution as significant components of human social interactions.

This realization prompted development of the robot Kismet in the late 1990s to study how social cues can be elicited from people by robots. Today, both robots are used for researching aspects of social interaction.

Active Vision

Vision systems with steerable cameras that move in purposeful ways as part of the perception process are called active vision systems [1]. A humanoid vision system with the same basic mechanical structure as humans and other mammals and that follows the same motion primitives used by humans appears to be animate and lifelike.

The human eye has a central fovea spanning about 5 degrees vertically and horizontally of the full 160 degrees the eye can see. The brightness and color receptors are much more densely packed in this area; more than half of the region of the brain that first processes signals from the eye is dedicated to the central 2% of the field of view. Humans move their eyes around rapidly, up to four times per second, to aim this high-resolution part of their eyes at whatever it is they are interested in. These rapid motions are called saccades and occur ballistically without feedback about their accuracy during their motion. They are under voluntary control, in that a person can consciously choose to saccade to a particular location, though most saccades are made completely involuntarily by some sort of attention mechanism. Something interesting is often in the low-resolution periphery of human perception, and the eye saccades to that target to see it with higher resolution.

Humans can also scan their eyes to follow something moving in their field of view. Called smooth pursuit, such scanning cannot be done voluntarily. People cannot scan their eyes smoothly from, say, left to right, unless there is a moving object they can lock onto and follow. Lastly, humans use their inner ears to detect head motion, feeding the signal forward to compensate with eye motion much more quickly than the vision system could track how the world appears to be slipping and compensate. This is known as the vestibular-ocular reflex.

These three capabilities—saccades, smooth pursuit, and the vestibular-ocular reflex—have been implemented repeatedly in both Cog and Kismet [5], operating with performance comparable to that of humans, though their cameras have much lower resolution overall than the human eye.

The robot's coherence of behavior is not determined by some internal locking mechanism but by its direction of gaze out into the world.

Humans also verge their eyes toward a target and estimate the gross depth by how far off parallel their eyes have to move to see the same point in space. Comparisons are then made between the images in the eyes to get a local relative depth map—the process of stereo vision. Cog and Kismet also have these capabilities and so are able to perceive 3D aspects of the world.

Cog and Kismet are able to detect human faces through a variety of methods [9] and estimate the gaze direction of a person by determining the direction their eyes are pointing. The robots are not able to do as good a job as the human visual system, however, but estimates with 3 to 5 degree accuracy are useful for social interactions.

Cog and Kismet each have their perception and control systems running on more than a dozen computers. There is no central executive and indeed no central locus of control for the robots. Nevertheless, they appear to be operating in a coherent manner. The low-level trick that allows this coherence to happen is the visual attention mechanism, which determines where the robot is looking; where it is looking determines what all the low-level perceptual processes will see. That in turn determines which of the robot's behaviors are active. The robot's coherence of behavior is not determined by some internal locking mechanism but by its direction of gaze out into the world.

Social Interaction

The Cog and Kismet visual systems are the bases for their social interactions. Even a naive human observer can understand what the robots are paying attention to by the direction of their gaze. Likewise, the robots can understand what a person is paying attention to by the direction of the person's gaze [9].

The visual attention system makes it completely intuitive for naive users to direct the robot's visual attention system to some particular objects. Cynthia Breazeal, now at the MIT Media Laboratory, describes a series of experiments in which subjects were asked to get the robot to pay attention to different objects [2]. Typically, they would bring the object into the field of view of the robot, then shake it and move it to the desired position, with the robot now smoothly pursuing it, paying attention to what the human subject wanted. The experimental subjects had no knowledge of how the robot's visual system operated but were able to use the same strategies they would use with a child, and they worked.

By manipulating the weighting the visual system applies to different visual cues, Kismet's high-level behaviors, such as dialogue turn-taking, can make it make or break eye contact, so indirectly, these high-level behaviors regulate social interaction. Moreover, Kismet expresses its internal emotional state through facial expressions and prosody in its voice. So, for instance, when someone comes very close to Kismet or waves something very quickly near its face, Kismet becomes more fearful. That emotional state is reflected in its posture; it draws back. This reaction triggers a complementary reaction in naive human subjects who also tend to draw back. Thus, Kismet, indirectly through its emotional system and its expression in the world, is able to manipulate people in social settings, just as humans unconsciously manipulate each other.

Kismet is also able to detect basic prosody in the voices of people and classify their speech as "praising," "prohibiting," "bidding for attention," or "soothing," four basic prosodic signals used in almost all human cultures by mothers with their babies. Kismet's detection of these cues changes its internal emotional state in appropriate ways; its outward demeanor changes, coupling in people who then intuitively react in appropriate ways.

Breazeal has reported on a number of experiments with human subjects [2]. Naive subjects in one set of experiments sat in front of the robot and were instructed to "talk to the robot." The robot could understand only their prosody and not the actual words they said. The robot generated speech with prosody, though it was always random strings of English phonemes with no intrinsic meaning.

Most subjects were able to determine when it was their turn to speak, but some did not know what to say. Others engaged in long conversations with the robot—even though there was no conventional linguistic transfer. The more basic social interactions often masked the lack of actual language. For instance, in one session a human subject said, "I want you to take a look at my watch," and Kismet looked right at the person's watch. The person had drawn up his left wrist to be in Kismet's field of view, then tapped his right index finger to the face of the watch. That was a sufficient cue to attract Kismet's attention system, and Kismet saccaded to the watch. Just as in human-to-human communication, layers of social interaction smoothed the process.

It would be desirable for robots to follow the path of embedded processors, rather than PCs, and produce little cognitive load on users.

Because Kismet's processing system made it a little slower at turn-taking than a human, careful examination of the video record showed frequent turn-taking errors (where the robot or the person interrupted the other) at the start of each session, but also that people soon adapted (the robot did not adapt), and that after a few minutes the errors were significantly less frequent. Video clips of many of these experiments are available at www.ai.mit.edu/projects/humanoidrobotics-group.

Humanoids Everywhere?

The first few domestic robots are already on the market, including lawnmowing robots and home floor-cleaning robots. All are easy to use, which will be very important as the functionality of domestic robots is developed further. We can compare robot ease of use with computer ease of use. There are two sorts of computers in people's homes: One is embedded processors in television sets, coffee machines, and practically any tool or appliance powered by electricity; they are trivial to interact with and induce almost no cognitive load on the human user. The other is home PCs with thousands of options that can be quite difficult to understand; they produce high cognitive loads on users. It would be desirable for robots to follow the path of embedded processors, rather than PCs, and produce little cognitive load. However, unlike today's embedded processors, robots will be highly visible because they will move around in home environments. Therefore, it will be desirable for them to understand human social conventions, so they can be unobtrusive; meanwhile, humans should be able to interact with them in the same kind of noncognitive ways they interact with other humans. For instance, it will be useful for a large mobile appliance and a person to be able to negotiate who goes first in a tight corridor with the same natural head, eye, and hand gestures all people understand already.

Should we expect these sociable robots to have humanoid form and be as commonplace in our lives as a number of Hollywood fantasies have portrayed? It is difficult to know today, but there are two compelling, and competing, arguments on opposite sides of this question:

The current infatuation with humanoid robots is a necessary but passing phase. It allows researchers to get at the essence of human-robot interactions, but the lessons learned will ultimately be applicable to robots with much more functional forms. For instance, we can expect driverless trucks in our residential neighborhoods. When human drivers stop at an intersection as other vehicles pull up on the cross street, they often engage in informal social interactions through eye contact, head nodding, and finger motions—social interactions ignored in the formal driving rules but that form a negotiation as to which driver should proceed first.

When another vehicle is a driverless truck, similar sorts of social negotiations should be possible to lubricate the safe flow of traffic. However, current experiences with humanoid sociable robots may well lead to development of social signals for the robot truck requiring no human form but rather signals that can tap into the same subconscious cues used by humans and by humans and humanoid robots.

It may be that the large number of humanoid robot projects under way today, especially in Japan, may produce enough successful prototype robots that people will find them naturally acceptable and expect them to have human form. It has become well understood over the past 20 years that the technologically superior solution may not be the one that wins out in the marketplace (in the same way the VHS video format won out over the Beta format). Rather, it depends on early market share and the little-understood dynamics of adoption. For this reason, humanoid robots might become common by accident. Or it may turn out there will be a discovery (not yet made) that they have some significant advantage over all other forms, and they will be common precisely because they are technologically superior.

The weight of progress in so many forms of robots for unstructured environments leads to the conclusion that robots will be common in people's lives by the middle of the century if not significantly earlier. Whether significant numbers of them will have human form is an open question.

REFERENCES

1. Blake, A. and Yuille, A., Eds. *Active Vision*. MIT Press, Cambridge, MA, 1992.
2. Breazeal, C. *Designing Sociable Robots*. MIT Press, Cambridge, MA, 2001.
3. Brooks, R. *Cambrian Intelligence*. MIT Press, Cambridge, MA, 1999.
4. Brooks, R. *Flesh and Machines: How Robots Will Change Us*. Pantheon, New York, 2002.
5. Brooks, R., Breazeal, C., Marjanovic, M., Scassellati, B., and Williamson, M. The Cog Project: Building a humanoid robot. *In Computation for Metaphors, Analogy, and Agents*, C. Nehaniv, Ed. *Lecture Notes in Artificial Intelligence 1562*. Springer Verlag, New York, 1999, 52–87.
6. Brooks, R. and Stein, L. Building brains for bodies. *Autonom. Robo. 1*, 1 (1994), 7–25.
7. Damasio, A. *The Feeling of What Happens: Body and Emotion in the Making of Consciousness*. Harcourt Brace, New York, 1999.
8. Lakoff, G. and Johnson, M. *Philosophy in the Flesh: The Embodied Mind and Its Challenge to Western Philosophy*. Basic Books, New York, 1999.
9. Scassellati, B. *Foundations for a Theory of Mind for a Humanoid Robot*. MIT Artificial Intelligence Laboratory, Ph.D. dissertation, 2001.
10. Yarbus, A. *Eye Movements and Vision*. Plenum Press, New York, 1967.

RODNEY BROOKS (brooks@ai.mit.edu) is Fujitsu Professor of Computer Science and Engineering and Director of the Artificial Intelligence Laboratory at the Massachusetts Institute of Technology, Cambridge, MA.

Article 43

The Real Scientific Hero of 1953

By STEVEN STROGATZ

ITHACA, N.Y.

Last week newspapers and magazines devoted tens of thousands of words to the 50th anniversary of the discovery of the chemical structure of DNA. While James D. Watson and Francis Crick certainly deserved a good party, there was no mention of another scientific feat that also turned 50 this year—one whose ramifications may ultimately turn out to be as profound as those of the double helix.

In 1953, Enrico Fermi and two of his colleagues at Los Alamos Scientific Laboratory, John Pasta and Stanislaw Ulam, invented the concept of a "computer experiment." Suddenly the computer became a telescope for the mind, a way of exploring inaccessible processes like the collision of black holes or the frenzied dance of subatomic particles—phenomena that are too large or too fast to be visualized by traditional experiments, and too complex to be handled by pencil-and-paper mathematics. The computer experiment offered a third way of doing science. Over the past 50 years, it has helped scientists to see the invisible and imagine the inconceivable.

Fermi and his colleagues introduced this revolutionary approach to better understand entropy, the tendency of all systems to decay to states of ever greater disorder. To observe the predicted descent into chaos in unprecedented detail, Fermi and his team created a virtual world, a simulation taking place inside the circuits of an electronic behemoth known as Maniac, the most powerful supercomputer of its era. Their test problem involved a deliberately simplified model of a vibrating atomic lattice, consisting of 64 identical particles (representing atoms) linked end to end by springs (representing the chemical bonds between them).

This structure was akin to a guitar string, but with an unfamiliar feature: normally, a guitar string behaves "linearly"—pull it to the side and it pulls back, pull it twice as far and it pulls back twice as hard. Force and response are proportional. In the 300 years since Isaac Newton invented calculus, mathematicians and physicists had mastered the analysis of systems like that, where causes are strictly proportional to effects, and the whole is exactly equal to the sum of the parts.

But that's not how the bonds between real atoms behave. Twice the stretch does not produce exactly twice the force. Fermi suspected that this nonlinear character of chemical bonds might be the key to the inevitable increase of entropy. Unfortunately, it also made the mathematics impenetrable. A nonlinear system like this couldn't be analyzed by breaking it into pieces. Indeed, that's the hallmark of a nonlinear system: the parts don't add up to the whole. Understanding a system like this defied all known methods. It was a mathematical monster.

Undaunted, Fermi and his collaborators plucked their virtual string and let Maniac grind away, calculating hundreds of simultaneous interactions, updating all the forces and positions, marching the virtual string forward in time in a series of slow-motion snapshots. They expected to see its shape degenerate into a random vibration, the musical counterpart of which would be a meaningless hiss, like static on the radio.

What the computer revealed was astonishing. Instead of a hiss, the string played an eerie tune, almost like music from an alien civilization. Starting from a pure tone, it progressively added a series of overtones, replacing one with another, gradually changing the timbre. Then it suddenly reversed direction, deleting overtones in the opposite sequence, before finally returning almost precisely to the original tone. Even creepier, it repeated this strange melody again and again, indefinitely, but always with subtle variations on the theme.

Fermi loved this result—he referred to it affectionately as a "little discovery." He had never guessed that nonlinear systems could harbor such a penchant for order.

In the 50 years since this pioneering study, scientists and engineers have learned to harness nonlinear systems, making use of their capacity for self-organization. Lasers, now used everywhere from eye surgery to checkout scanners, rely on trillions of atoms emitting light waves in unison. Superconductors transmit electrical current without resistance, the byproduct of billions of pairs of electrons marching in lock step. The resulting technology has spawned the world's most sensitive detectors, used by doctors to pinpoint diseased tissues in the brains of epileptics without the need for invasive surgery, and by geologists to locate oil buried deep underground.

But perhaps the most important lesson of Fermi's study is how feeble even the best minds are at grasping the dynamics of large, nonlinear systems. Faced with a thicket of interlocking feedback loops, where everything affects everything else, our familiar ways of thinking fall apart. To solve the most important problems of our time, we're going to have to change the way we do science.

For example, cancer will not be cured by biologists working alone. Its solution will require a melding of both great discoveries of 1953. Many cancers, perhaps most of them, involve the derangement of biochemical networks that choreograph the activity of thousands of genes and proteins. As Fermi and his colleagues taught us, a complex system like this can't be understood merely by cataloging its parts and the rules governing their interactions. The nonlinear logic of cancer will be fathomed only through the collaborative efforts of molecular biologists—the heirs to Dr. Watson and Dr. Crick—and mathematicians who specialize in complex systems—the heirs to Fermi, Pasta and Ulam.

Can such an alliance take place? Well, it can if scientists embrace the example set by an unstoppable 86-year-old who, following his co-discovery of the double helix, became increasingly interested in computer simulations of complex systems in the brain.

Happy anniversary, Dr. Crick. And a toast to the memory of Enrico Fermi.

Steven Strogatz, professor of applied mathematics at Cornell, is author of "Sync: The Emerging Science of Spontaneous Order."

The race to computerise biology

Bioinformatics: In life-sciences establishments around the world, the laboratory rat is giving way to the computer mouse—as computing joins forces with biology to create a bioinformatics market that is expected to be worth nearly $40 billion within three years

FOR centuries, biology has been an empirical field that featured mostly specimens and Petri dishes. Over the past five years, however, computers have changed the discipline—as they have harnessed the data on genetics for the pursuit of cures for disease. Wet lab processes that took weeks to complete are giving way to digital research done *in silico*. Notebooks with jotted comments, measurements and drawings have yielded to terabyte storehouses of genetic and chemical data. And empirical estimates are being replaced by mathematical exactness.

Welcome to the world of bioinformatics—a branch of computing concerned with the acquisition, storage and analysis of biological data. Once an obscure part of computer science, bioinformatics has become a linchpin of biotechnology's progress. In the struggle for speed and agility, bioinformatics offers unparalleled efficiency through mathematical modelling. In the quest for new drugs, it promises new ways to look at biology through data mining. And it is the only practical way of making sense of the ensuing deluge of data.

The changes wrought by computers in biology resemble those in the aircraft and car industries a decade or so ago, after the arrival of powerful software for CAD (computer-aided design) and CFD (computational fluid dynamics). In both industries, engineers embraced the new computational modelling tools as a way of designing products faster, more cheaply and more accurately. In a similar way, biotech firms are now looking to computer modelling, data mining and high-throughput screening to help them discover drugs more efficiently.

In the process, biology—and, more specifically, biopharmacy—has become one of the biggest consumers of computing power, demanding petaflops (thousands of trillions of floating-point operations per second) of supercomputing power, and terabytes (trillions of bytes) of storage. Bioinformatics is actually a spectrum of technologies, covering such things as computer architecture (eg, workstations, servers, supercomputers and the like), storage and data-management systems, knowledge management and collaboration tools, and the life-science equipment needed to handle biological samples. In 2001, sales of such systems amounted to more than $12 billion worldwide, says International Data Corporation, a research firm in Framingham, Massachusetts. By 2006, the bioinformatics market is expected to be worth $38 billion.

The opportunity has not been lost on information technology (IT) companies hurt by the dotcom bust and telecoms meltdown. Starting in 2000, IBM was the first to launch a dedicated life-sciences division. Since then, a host of other IT firms have jumped aboard the bioinformatics bandwagon. Along with IBM, Sun Microsystems has staked a claim on the computing and management part of the business. Firms such as EMC and Hewlett-Packard have focused on data storage. Agilent, SAP and Siebel provide so-called decision support. Even build-to-order PC makers such as Dell have entered the fray with clusters of cheap machines.

A swarm of small start-up firms has also been drawn in, mostly to supply data, software or services to analyse the new wealth of genetic information. Companies such as Accelrys in San Diego, California, Spotfire in Somerville, Massachusetts, and Xmine in Brisbane, California, are selling software and systems to mine and find hidden relationships buried in data banks. Others such as Open Text of Waterloo, Ontario, and Ipedo in Redwood

City, California, have built software that improves communication and knowledge management among different areas of pharmaceutical research. Gene Logic of Gaithersburg, Maryland, has created a business to collect samples and screen their genetic code for proprietary research libraries. And Physiome Sciences of Princeton, New Jersey, is providing computer-based modelling systems that offer an insight into drug targets and disease mechanisms.

> "In just a few years, gene chips have gone from experimental novelties to tools of the trade."

Bioinformatics is not for the faint of heart, however. Over the past year, the fortunes of a number of biotechnology firms have faltered, as venture-capital funds have sought alternative investments. Venerable names of biotechnology, including Celera Genomics of Rockville, Maryland, LION Bioscience of Heidelberg, Germany, and others, have found themselves scrambling to change the way they do business. Yet, for all the turbulence in the industry, the bioinformatics juggernaut remains on track, fuelled by new forces changing the pharmaceutical industry.

Gene genie

In retrospect, the marriage of genetics and computers was pre-ordained. After all, biotechnology is based on the genetic building-blocks of life—in short, on nature's huge encyclopedia of information. And hidden in the vast sequences of A (adenine), G (guanosine), C (cytosine) and T (thymine) that spell out the genetic messages—ie, genes—are functions that take an input and yield an output, much as computer programs do. Yet the computerisation of genetics on such a grand scale would not have occurred without the confluence of three things: the invention of DNA microarrays and high-throughput screening; the sequencing of the human genome; and a dramatic increase in computing power.

More commonly known as "gene chips", microarrays are to the genetic revolution of today what microprocessors were to the computer revolution a quarter of a century ago. They turn the once arduous task of screening genetic information into an automatic routine that exploits the tendency for the molecule that carries the template for making the protein, messenger-ribonucleic acid (m-RNA), to bind to the DNA that produces it. Gene chips contain thousands of probes, each imbued with a different nucleic acid from known (and unknown) genes to bind with m-RNA. The resulting bonds fluoresce under different colours of laser light, showing which genes are present. Microarrays measure the incidence of genes (leading to the gene "sequence") and their abundance (the "expression").

In just a few years, gene chips have gone from experimental novelties to tools of the trade. A single GeneChip from Affymetrix, the leading maker of microarrays based in Santa Clara, California, now has more than 500,000 interrogation points. (For his invention of the gene chip, Affymetrix's Stephen Foder won one of *The Economist*'s Innovation Awards for 2002.) With each successive generation, the number of probes on a gene chip has multiplied as fast as transistors have multiplied on silicon chips. And with each new generation has come added capabilities.

The sequencing of the human genome in late 2000 gave biotechnology the biggest boost in its 30-year history. But although the genome sequence has allowed more intelligent questions to be asked, it has also made biologists painfully aware of how many remain to be answered. The genome project has made biologists appreciate the importance of "single nucleotide polymorphism" (SNP)—minor variations in DNA that define differences among people, predispose a person to disease, and influence a patient's response to a drug. And, with the genetic make-up of humans broadly known, it is now possible (at least in theory) to build microarrays that can target individual SNP variations, as well as making deeper comparisons across the genome—all in the hope of finding the obscure roots of many diseases.

The sequencing has also paved the way for the new and more complex field of proteomics, which aims to understand how long chains of protein molecules fold themselves up into three-dimensional structures. Tracing the few thousandths of a second during which the folding takes place is the biggest technical challenge the computer industry has ever faced—and the ultimate goal of the largest and most powerful computer ever imagined, IBM's petaflop Blue Gene. The prize may be knowledge of how to fashion molecular keys capable of picking the lock of disease-causing proteins.

The third ingredient—the dramatic rise in computing power—stems from the way that the latest Pentium and PowerPC microprocessors pack the punch of a supercomputer of little more than a decade ago. Thanks to Moore's law (which predicted, with remarkable consistency over the past three decades, that the processing power of microchips will double every 18 months), engineers and scientists now have access to unprecedented computing power on the cheap. With that has come the advent of "grid computing", in which swarms of lowly PCs, idling between tasks, band together to form a number-crunching mesh equivalent to a powerful supercomputer but at a fraction of the price. Meanwhile, the cost of storing data has continued to fall, and managing it has become easier thanks to high-speed networking and smarter forms of storage.

Banking on failure

Despite such advances, it is the changing fortunes of the drug industry that are pushing biology and computing together. According to the Boston Consulting Group, the average drug now costs $880m to develop and takes almost 15 years to reach the market. With the pipelines of new drugs under development running dry, and patents of many blockbuster drugs expiring, the best hope that drug firms have is to improve the way they discover and develop new products.

Paradoxically, the biggest gains are to be made from failures. Three-quarters of the cost of developing a successful drug goes to paying for all the failed hypotheses and blind alleys pursued along the way. If drug makers can kill an unpromising approach sooner, they can significantly improve their returns. Simple mathematics shows that reducing the number of failures by 5% cuts the cost of discovery by nearly a fifth. By enabling researchers to find out sooner that their hoped-for compound is not working out, bioinformatics can steer them towards more promising candidates. Boston Consulting believes bioinformatics can cut $150m from the cost of developing a new drug and a year off the time taken to bring it to market.

That has made drug companies sit up. Throughout the 1990s, they tended to use bioinformatics to create and cull genetic data. More recently, they have started using it to make sense of it all. Researchers now find themselves swamped with data. Each time it does an experimental run, the average microarray spits out some 50 megabytes of data—all of which has to be stored, managed and made available to researchers. Today, firms such as Millennium Pharmaceuticals of Cambridge, Massachusetts, screen hundreds of thousands of compounds each week, producing terabytes of data annually.

The data themselves pose a number of tricky problems. For one thing, most bioinformatics files are "flat", meaning they are largely text-based and intended for browsing by eye. Meanwhile, sets of data from different bioinformatics sources are often in different formats, making it harder to integrate and mine them than in other industries, such as engineering or finance, where formal standards for exchanging data exist.

More troubling still, a growing proportion of the data is proving inaccurate or even false. A drug firm culls genomic and chemical data from countless sources, both inside and outside the company. It may have significant control over the data produced in its own laboratories, but little over data garnered from university research and other sources. Like any other piece of experimental equipment, the microarrays themselves have varying degrees of accuracy built into them. "What people are finding is that the tools are getting better but the data itself is no good," says Peter Loupos of Aventis, a French drug firm based in Strasbourg.

To help solve this problem, drug firms, computer makers and research organisations have organised a standards body called the Interoperable Informatics Infrastructure Consortium. Their Life Science Identifier, released in mid-2002, defines a simple convention for identifying and accessing biological data stored in multiple formats. Meanwhile, the Distributed Annotation System, a standard for describing genome annotation across sources, is gaining popularity. This is making it easier to compare different groups' genome data.

Tools for the job

Such standards will be a big help. One of the most effective tools for probing information for answers is one of the most mundane: data integration. Hence the effort by such firms as IBM, Hewlett-Packard and Accelerys to develop ways of pulling data together from different microarrays and computing platforms, and getting them all to talk fluently to one another. A further impetus for data integration, at least in America, is the Patent and Trademark Office's requirement for filings to be made electronically from 2003 onwards. The Food and Drug Administration is also expected to move to electronic filing for approval of new drugs.

It is in data mining, however, where bioinformatics hopes for its biggest pay-off. First applied in banking, data mining uses a variety of algorithms to sift through storehouses of data in search of "noisy" patterns and relationships among the different silos of information. The promise for bioinformatics is that public genome data, mixed with proprietary sequence data, clinical data from previous drug efforts and other stores of information, could unearth clues about possible candidates for future drugs.

"A big risk of computer modelling and other tools is to rely too much on them."

Unlike banking, bioinformatics offers big challenges for data mining because of the greater complexity of the information and processes. This is where modelling and visualisation techniques should come in, to simulate the operations of various biological functions and to predict the effect of stimuli on a cell or organ. Computer modelling allows researchers to test hunches fast, and offers a starting-point for further research using other methods such as X-ray crystallography or spectroscopy. It also means that negative responses come sooner, reducing the time wasted on unworkable target drugs.

Computational models have already yielded several new compounds. BioNumerik of San Antonio, Texas, has modelled the way certain drugs function within the human body. It has also simulated a specific region of a cell to observe the interaction between proteins and DNA. Thanks to its two Cray supercomputers running simulations that combine quantum physics, chemistry and biological models, BioNumerik has been able to get three compounds into clinical trials. Frederick Hausheer, BioNumerik's founder and chief executive, expects his firm's modelling technology to cut the time for discovering new drugs by a third to a half.

In a similar vein, Aventis has used several models of cells and disease mechanisms to discover a number of new compounds. And Physiome Sciences now sells a product that integrates various clinical and genomic data to generate computer-based models of organs, cells and other structures.

For all their power, these computer modelling techniques should be taken with at least a grain or two of salt. Although they allow researchers to tinker with various compounds, they will never replace clinical trials or other traditional methods of drug research. Even monumental bioinformatics efforts, such as the Physiome Project, will only help researchers refine their ideas before getting their hands wet. "If people haven't done this kind of work before, they won't understand how difficult it really is," says Dr Hausheer.

Indeed, a big risk of computer modelling and other information tools is to rely too much on them, says Martin Gerstel, chairman of Compugen, a maker of analytical and interpretation tools based in Jamesburg, New Jersey. Many researchers confuse the data generated by bioinformatics with information. The danger with all the computing power being brought to bear is that it is becoming seductively easy for biologists to rely on the number-crunching potential of computers and to ignore the scientific grind of hypothesis and proof. As the technology of bioinformatics outpaces the science of biology, the science risks becoming a "black box", the inner workings of which few will be able to comprehend.

To avoid this, biologists need an ever broader set of skills. For instance, the most pervasive impact of information technology on biology has been through wholesale quantification. Suddenly, biologists are being forced to become mathematicians in order to describe the biological processes and models involved. That implies a demand for wholly new sets of skills and educational backgrounds.

Such changes are not unlike those that affected physics and chemistry during the 1940s, when new computational paradigms created the foundations for nuclear energy and the age of plastics. Much as computing made physics more predictable and prolific, many believe that its new alliance with mathematics will make biology more powerful and definitive. But the marriage will experience some turbulent times before achieving the full flowering of its promise.

Kurzweil vs Dertouzos

In our September issue, Michael Dertouzos wrote a column, "Not by Reason Alone" (see www.technologyreview.com/articles/oct00/dertouzos.htm), that took Bill Joy of Sun Microsystems to task for a piece Joy had written in *Wired*. In his *Wired* article, Joy argued that humanity should renounce certain lines of research, including nanotechnology, because of the dangers they pose. Dertouzos argued that Joy's view was flawed because his predictions were based on reason which, taken alone, is an inadequate guide to the future. Dertouzos' column drew an impassioned response from Ray Kurzweil, author of *The Age of Spiritual Machines*. We print Kurzweil's letter and Dertouzos' rejoinder.

Ray Kurzweil

ALTHOUGH I AGREE WITH MICHAEL DERTOUZOS' CONclusion in rejecting Bill Joy's prescription to relinquish "our pursuit of certain kinds of knowledge," I come to this view through a very different route. Although I am often paired with Bill Joy as the technology optimist versus Bill's pessimism, I do share his concerns about the dangers of self-replicating technologies. Michael is being shortsighted in his skepticism.

Michael writes that "just because chips... are getting faster doesn't mean they'll get smarter, let alone lead to self-replication." First of all, machines are already "getting smarter."As just one of many contemporary examples, I've recently held conversations with a person who speaks only German by translating my English speech in real time into human-sounding German speech (by combining speech recognition, language translation and speech synthesis) and similarly converting their spoken German replies into English speech. Although not perfect, this capability was not feasible at all just a few years ago. The intelligence of our technology does not need to be at human levels to be dangerous. Second, the implication that self-replication is harder than intelligence is not accurate. Software viruses, although not very intelligent, are self-replicating as well as being potentially destructive. Bioengineered biological viruses are far behind. As for nanotechnology-based self-replication, that's further out, but the consensus in that community is this will be feasible in the 2020s, if not sooner.

Many long-range forecasts of technical feasibility in future time periods dramatically underestimate the power of future technology because they are based on what I call the "intuitive linear" view of technological progress rather than the historical exponential view. When people think of a future period, they intuitively assume that the current rate of progress will continue for the period being considered. However, careful consideration of the pace of technology shows that the rate of progress is not constant, but it is human nature to adapt to the changing pace, so the intuitive view is that the pace will continue at the current rate. It is typical, therefore, that even sophisticated commentators, when considering the future, extrapolate the current pace of change over the next 10 years or 100 years to determine their expectations. This is why I call this way of looking at the future the "intuitive linear" view.

But any serious consideration of the history of technology shows that technological change is at least exponential, not linear. There are a great many examples of this, including exponential trends in computation, communication, brain scanning, miniaturization and multiple aspects of biotechnology. One can examine this data in many different ways, on many different time scales and for a wide variety of different phenomena, and we find (at least) double exponential growth, a phenomenon I call the law of accelerating returns. The law of accelerating returns does not rely on an assumption of the continuation of Moore's law, but is based on a rich model of diverse technological processes. What it clearly shows is that technology, particularly the pace of technological change, advances (at least) exponentially, not linearly, and has been doing so since the advent of technology. That is why people tend to overestimate what can be achieved in the short term (because we tend to leave out necessary details) but underestimate what can be achieved in the long term (because exponential growth is ignored).

This observation also applies to paradigm shift rates, which are currently doubling (approximately) every decade. So the technological progress in the 21st century will be equivalent to what would require (in the linear view) on the order of 20,000 years.

EVEN THE TECHNO-SAVVY OVERLOOK TECHNOLOGY'S EXPONENTIAL GROWTH RATES.
—Kurzweil

Michael's argument that we cannot always anticipate the effects of a particular technology is irrelevant here. These exponential trends in computation and communication technologies are greatly empowering the individual. Of course, that's good news in many ways. These trends are behind the pervasive trend we see towards democratization, and are reshaping power relations at all levels of society. But these technologies are also empowering and amplifying our destructive impulses. It's not necessary to anticipate all of the ultimate uses of a technology to see that there is danger in, for example, every college biotechnology lab having the ability to create self-replicating biological pathogens.

However, I do reject Joy's call for relinquishment of broad areas of technology (such as nanotechnology) despite my not sharing Michael's skepticism on the feasibility of these technologies. Technology has always been a double-edged sword. We don't need to look any further than today's technology to see this. If we imagine describing the dangers that exist today (enough nuclear explosive power to destroy all mammalian life, just for starters) to people who lived a couple of hundred years ago, they would think it mad to take such risks. On the other hand, how many people in the year 2001 would really want to go back to the short, brutish, disease-filled, poverty-stricken, disaster-prone lives that 99 percent of the human race struggled through a couple of centuries ago?

People often go through three stages in examining the impact of future technology: awe and wonderment at its potential to overcome age-old problems, then a sense of dread at a new set of grave dangers that accompany these new technologies, followed, finally and hopefully, by the realization that the only viable and responsible path is to set a careful course that can realize the promise while managing the peril.

The continued opportunity to alleviate human distress is one important motivation for continuing technological advancement. Also compelling are the already apparent economic gains, which will continue to hasten in the decades ahead. There is an insistent economic imperative to continue technological progress: relinquishing technological advancement would be economic suicide for individuals, companies and nations.

Which brings us to the issue of relinquishment, which is Bill Joy's most controversial recommendation and personal commitment. Forgoing fields such as nanotechnology is untenable. Nanotechnology is simply the inevitable end result of a persistent trend toward miniaturization that pervades all of technology. It is far from a single centralized effort but is being pursued by a myriad of projects with many diverse goals.

Furthermore, abandonment of broad areas of technology will only push them underground, where development would continue unimpeded by ethics and regulation. In such a situation, it would be the less stable, less responsible practitioners (for example, the terrorists) who would have all the expertise.

The constructive response to these dangers is not a simple one: It combines professional ethical guidelines (which already exist in biotechnology and are currently being drafted by nanotechnologists), oversight by regulatory bodies and the development of technology-specific immune responses, as well as computer-assisted surveillance by law enforcement organizations. As we go forward, balancing our cherished rights of privacy with our need to be protected from the malicious use of powerful 21st-century technologies will be one of many profound challenges.

Technology will remain a double-edged sword, and the story of the 21st century has not yet been written. It represents vast power to be used for all humankind's purposes. We have no choice but to work hard to apply these quickening technologies to advance our human values, despite what often appears to be a lack of consensus on what those values should be.

Michael Dertouzos

IN MY COLUMN, I OBSERVED THAT WE HAVE BEEN INCAPABLE of judging where technologies are headed, hence we should not relinquish a new technology, based strictly on reason. Ray agrees with my conclusion, but for a different reason: He sees technology growing exponentially, thereby offering us the opportunity to alleviate human distress and hasten future economic gains. From his perspective, my point is "irrelevant", and my views on the future of technology are skeptical. Let's punch through to the underlying issues, which are vital, for they point at a fundamental and all-too-often ignored relationship between technology and humanity.

Ray's exponential-growth argument is half the story: No doubt, the number of transistors on a chip has grown and will continue to grow for a while. But transistors and the systems made with them are used by people. And that's where exponential change stops! Has word-processing software, running on millions of transistors, empowered humans to contribute better writings than Socrates, Descartes or Lao Tzu?

Technologies have undergone dramatic change in the last few centuries. But people's basic needs for food, shelter, nurturing, procreation and survival have not changed in thousands of years. Nor has the rapid growth of technology altered love, hate, spirituality or the building and destruction of human relationships. Granted, when we are in the frying pan, surrounded by the sizzling oil of rapidly changing technologies, we feel that everything around us is accelerating. But, from the longer range perspective of human history and evolution, change is far more gradual. The novelty of our modern tools is counterbalanced by the constancy of our ancient needs.

As a result, technological growth, regardless of its magnitude, does not automatically empower us. It does so only when it matches our ability to use it for human purposes. And that doesn't happen as often as we'd like. Just think of the growing millions of AIDS cases in Africa, beyond our control. Or, in the industrial world, ask yourself whether we are truly better off surrounded by hordes of complex digital devices that force us to serve them rather than the other way around.

Our humanity meets technology in other ways, too: In forecasting the future of technology, Ray laments that most people use "linear thinking" that builds on existing patterns, thereby missing the big "nonlinear" ideas that are the true drivers of change. Once again, this is only half the story: In the last three decades, as I witnessed the new ideas and the 50-some startups that arose from the MIT Laboratory for Computer Science, I observed a pattern: Every successful technological innovation is the result of two simultaneous forces—a controlled insanity needed to break away from the stranglehold of current reason and ideas, and a disciplined assessment of potential human utility, to filter out the truly absurd. Focusing only on the wild part is not enough: Without a check, it often leads to exhibitionistic thinking, calculated to shock. Wild ideas can be great. But I draw a hard line when such ideas are paraded in front of a lay population as inevitable, or even likely.

That is the case with much of the futurology in today's media, because of the high value we all place on entertainment. With all the talk about intelligent agents, most people think they can go buy them in the corner drugstore. Ray, too, brings up his experience with speech translation to demonstrate computer intelligence. The Lab for Computer Science is delightfully full of Victor Zue's celebrated systems that can understand spoken English, Spanish and Mandarin, as long as the context is restricted, for example to let you ask about the weather, or to book an airline flight. Does that make them intelligent? No. Conventionally, "intelligence" is centered on our ability to reason, even imperfectly, using common sense. If we dub as intelligent, often for marketing or wishful-thinking purposes, every technological advance that mimics a tiny corner of human behavior, we will be distorting our language and exaggerating the virtues of our technology. We have no basis today to assert that machine intelligence will or will not be achieved. Stating that it will go one way or the other is to assert a belief, which is fine, as long as we say so. Does this mean that machine intelligence will never be achieved? Certainly not. Does it mean that it will be achieved? Certainly not. All it means is that we don't know—an exciting proposition that motivates us to go find out.

THE NOVELTY OF MODERN TOOLS IS COUNTERBALANCED BY THE CONSTANCY OF ANCIENT NEEDS. *—Dertouzos*

Attention-seizing, outlandish ideas are easy and fun to concoct. Far more difficult is to pick future directions that are likely. My preferred way for doing this, which has served me well, though not flawlessly, for the last 30 years, is this: Put in a salad bowl the wildest, most forward-thinking technological ideas that you can imagine. (This is the craziness part.) Then add your best sense of what will be useful to people. (That's the rational part.) Start mixing the salad. If you are lucky, something will pop up that begins to qualify on both counts. Grab it and run with it, since the best way to forecast the future is to build it. This forecasting approach combines "nonlinear" ideas with the "linear" notion of human utility, and with a hopeful dab of serendipity.

Ray observes that technology is a double-edged sword. I agree, but I prefer to think of it as an axe that can be used to build a house or chop the head off an adversary, depending on intentions. The good news is that since the angels and the devils are inside us, rather than within the axe, the ratio of good to evil uses of a technology is the same as the ratio of good to evil people who use that technology...which stays pretty constant through the ages. Technological progress will not automatically cause us to be engulfed by evil, as some people fear.

But for the same reason, potentially harmful uses of technology will always be near us, and we will need to deal with them. I agree with Ray's suggestions that we do so via ethical guidelines, regulatory overviews, immune response and computer-assisted surveillance. These, however, are partial remedies, rooted in reason, which has repeatedly let us down in assessing future technological directions. We need to go further.

As human beings, we have a rational, logical dimension, but also a physical, an emotional and a spiritual one. We are not fully human unless we exercise all of these capabilities in concert, as we have done throughout the millennia. To rely entirely on reason is to ascribe omniscience to a few ounces of meat, tucked inside the skull bones of antlike creatures roaming a small corner of an infinite universe—hardly a rational proposition! To live in this increasingly complex, awesome and marvelous world that surrounds us, which we barely understand, we need to marshal everything we've got that makes us human.

This brings us back to the point of my column, which is also the main theme of this discussion: When we marvel at the exponential growth of an emerging technology, we must keep in mind the constancy of the human beings who will use it. When we forecast a likely future direction, we need to balance the excitement of imaginative "nonlinear" ideas with their potential human utility. And when we are trying to cope with the potential harm of a new technology, we should use all our human capabilities to form our judgment.

To render technology useful, we must blend it with humanity. This process will serve us best if, alongside our most promising technologies, we bring our full humanity, augmenting our rational powers with our feelings, our actions and our faith. We cannot do this by reason alone!

From *Technology Review,* January/February 2001, pp. 80-82, 84 by Ray Kurzweil and Michael Dertouzos.

Hyperculture —Stress

HOW FAST TIMES ARE TRANSFORMING AMERICA

Address by **STEPHEN BERTMAN**,
Professor of Classics,
University of Windsor, Windsor Ontario

Delivered to the United States Business and Industrial Council Educational Foundation, Madonna University, Livonia, Michigan, December 4, 1998

Early in World War II as England and Germany battled for supremacy in the skies over Europe, both sides raced to build faster and faster fighters and bombers. Allied and Axis planes, however, soon struck an invisible and deadly wall. As test pilots approached the speed of sound—about 760 miles per hour—they encountered a mysterious force that violently shook their fuselages and overpowered their controls.

What was this mysterious force?

As an airplane flies through the atmosphere, it creates waves of compressed air. Like invisible ripples, these waves rush outward from the plane at the speed of sound. As long as the plane itself flies at subsonic speed, the waves it generates run ahead of it. But as it nears the speed of sound, the plane begins to catch up with its own pressure waves. Should a plane attempt to penetrate such waves, their tremendous force can rip it apart in mid air.

Following a number of fatal crashes, aeronautical engineers finally figured out how to "break the sound barrier." They reduced the thickness of the wings and swept them back so they would knife through the air, and streamlined the plane's nose so it would puncture the invisible wall.

The principles of physics that explain the sound barrier can also help us understand the origin and nature of stress in our lives. As the velocity of everyday life increases—as we fly faster and faster through the atmosphere of daily experience—our "aircraft" encounters a turbulence it was never designed to withstand. As our speed increases, invisible pressures build up, pressures strong enough to shatter the structural integrity of our personalities and, our relationships. Ultimately, we may lose control, or the craft we fly may disintegrate.

The simple solution, of course, is to slow down. But if we cannot slow down—or choose not to the only remaining answer is to redesign our lives, to adapt structurally to our newfound speed.

But what does "adapt structurally" really mean? We are, after all, human beings, not machines.

There is no metal fuselage to streamline, no wings to sweep back. What parts of our lives, then, are we to alter?

And if the stress each of us feels is experienced socially as well as individually, what changes must society as a whole make to accommodate itself to faster times?

The answers to these questions will ultimately define the quality of American life. For the adaptations we make to speed alter the fundamental nature of our existence, not only in terms of our behavior but also in terms of our priorities. A faster America is a different America, different not merely in its velocity but in its values. Not stress but rather our accommodations to it will determine the future character of the American soul.

Social Acceleration

Speed-driven stress is not a new phenomenon in our history. During the Industrial Revolution, the steam engine accelerated transportation and manufacturing and, with them, the tempo of life. In the 1830's a French visitor to America's shores, Alexis de Tocqueville, noted how Americans always seemed in a hurry. And in 1845, Henry David Thoreau sought refuge at Walden Pond from what he perceived as the desperate, locomotive-like rush of society.

By the early 1900's the automobile had begun to change not only America's physical landscape but its mental landscape as well. Some, like author Booth Tarkington, foresaw the possibility of even greater changes. In his 1918 novel, The Magnificent Ambersons, he reflected on the automobile's potential cultural and psychological impact:

With all their speed forward they may be a step backward in civilization—that is, in spiritual civilization. It may be that they will not add to the beauty of the world, nor to the life of men's souls. I am not sure. But automobiles have come, and they bring a greater change in our life than most of us suspect. They are here, and almost all outward things are going to be different because of what they bring. They are going to alter war, and they are going to alter peace. I think men's minds are going to be changed in subtle ways because of automobiles; just how, though, I could hardly guess. But you can't have the immense outward changes that they will cause without some inward ones, and it may be... that the spiritual alteration will be bad for us.

While steam and gasoline engines were accelerating the movement of people and goods, electricity was speeding up the movement of ideas. The telegraph, the telephone, and radio—all 19th century inventions—quickened the flow of words by making rapid long-distance communication a reality.

In the 20th century, the technologies of speed were adapted to the purposes of global war and domestic peace, including the airplane, one of the century's earliest inventions.

Some technological changes are hard to appreciate because they do not occur dramatically.

Instead, they emerge gradually, infiltrating our everyday lives little by little even as they transform them. How much they transform them we can only see if we stop to take their sum, as author Jerry Mander has done:

"I was born in 1936. At that time there were no jet planes and commercial plane traffic was effectively non-existent. There were no computers, no space satellites, no microwave ovens, no electric typewriters, no Xerox machines, no tape recorders. There were no stereo music systems nor compact disks. There was no television in 1936. No space travel, no atomic bomb, no hydrogen bomb, no "guided missiles," as they were first called, no "smart" bombs. There were no fluorescent lights, no washing machines nor dryers, no Cuisinarts, no VCRs. There was no air conditioning. Nor were there freeways, shopping centers, or malls. There were no suburbs as we know them. There was no Express Mail, no fax, no telephone touch dialling, no birth-control pill. There were no credit cards, no synthetic fibres. There were no antibiotics, no artificial organs, no pesticides or herbicides.... During my lifetime all of this changed."

The inventions Mander lists are quite specific, but something far more subtle, and much more pervasive, was taking place as the decades rolled on. The very pace of life was picking up, quickened by new technologies that more and more began to typify American society.

Many of these were not mechanical technologies with turning gears and moving belts, but electronic ones that operated at the speed of light, 186,000 miles per second. In the time it takes for a human eye to blink, a signal could travel half-way to the moon.

But we weren't sending signals to the moon—at least, not yet. Instead, we were sending them to each other, with greater and greater frequency. In the '50's and '60's, America's phone was ringing, its radio was blaring, and its TV was on—all at the same time. And America's factories were cranking out more and more cars and appliances and gadgets for people to buy.

Back in 1950, fewer than one out of ten American households had a TV set. By 1955, seven out of ten did, an increase of 30 million households in just five years. And by 1970, television was being watched in 96% of America's homes.

Television was more than just a medium of mass entertainment. It was a device that cancelled distance, delivering in an instant the images of objects thousands of miles away.

But just as potent as television's speed was its power as an instrument of social change. It changed how America's days and evenings were spent. It changed how family members interacted. It even changed where furniture was placed. But more than all these things, it changed us as a culture by making the technology of speed a central feature of our national experience. Never before in history had speed been so intimate a component of personal and social life.

However dazzling technological progress was, its own speed and the social acceleration it produced made greater and greater demands upon the human nervous system. By 1970, author Alvin Toffler was describing the symptoms of a new disease he said he had discovered, a disease he called "future shock." According to Toffler, future shock was a psychobiological condition induced by subjecting individuals to "too much change in too short a time." Toffler argued that technological and social changes were taking place so rapidly that people could no longer adapt to them. "Future shock," he wrote, "is the dizzying disorientation brought on by the premature arrival of the future.... [U]nless man quickly learns to control the rate of change in his personal affairs as well as in society at large, we are doomed to a massive adaptational breakdown."

Since the publication of Future Shock in 1970, the rate of social change has radically increased. Largely responsible for this increase has been the rapid development and deployment of older technologies and the swift introduction and growth of new ones. Supported by an electronic network of instantaneous communications, our culture has been transformed into a nationally and globally integrated system in which the prime and unchallenged directive is to keep up with change.

The computer received scant attention in Future Shock—and understandably so. After all, the first word processor did not appear until 1970; the first silicon chip, not until 1971; the first personal computer, not until 1975. Even as late as 1984, only 8 out of 100 American households had a computer.

In just two years, however, the figure doubled. And by 1994, there was a computer in more than one out of every three American homes. Meanwhile, during the same period, computer speed was increasing at a rate of 55% a year, and E-mail and Internet use were just starting to become commonplace.

At the same time, other technologies were revving America up. Sales of cell phones and fax machines, numbered in the low hundreds of thousands in the 1980's, climbed to seven million a year in just a decade. And by 1997, some two million Americans were carrying electronic pagers.

Yet more important than the popularity of any one of these technologies is their combination, which radically reinforces and intensifies the accelerative effect that each separate technology would have had alone. It is their electronic linkage that keeps pictures, sounds, and data continually coursing on a non-stop, high-speed track, saturating our environment with instancy. And the more our society depends upon electronic information flow and entertainment, the more our everyday lives need to keep up with its speed-of-light pace, since our economic and emotional existence is wired into its circuitry.

Without question, this speed can be exhilarating. It brings us what we need and want faster than ever before. But that same speed can also add stress to our lives.

For example, in a national survey conducted in 1986 by the Louis Harris organization, one out of three Americans said they lived with stress nearly every day. And six out of ten said they experienced "great stress" once or twice a week. In addition, in 1994, two out of ten people questioned reported feeling great stress almost every day, according to the findings of the Prevention Index survey.

In addition, studies by University of Maryland sociologist John Robinson have revealed a progressive increase in hurriedness over the years. In 1965, 25% of those surveyed said their lives were rushed all the time. By 1975, the figure had risen to 28%. By 1985, it had climbed to 32%. And, more recently in 1992, Penn State researchers Geoffrey Godbey and Alan Graefe put the figure at 38%, almost a 850% increase from 1965. Strikingly, those who lived in small towns felt as rushed as those who lived in big cities. Just as strikingly, both groups felt their lives were hurried not only at work but also at play. The presence of stress in our lives is also revealed by the printed word. In the last five years, almost 400 articles on stress and time management have appeared in popular national magazines. In addition, there are some 900 books currently in print on these topics. All these publications do more than just show how popular a subject stress is. They also demonstrate how little control we seem to have over it.

Like it or not, we've all been drafted into an army, a peacetime army that fights its battles on the battlefield of everyday life. It's "time wars" we wage, to use Jeremy Rifkin's term, wars between the slower pace our minds and bodies crave and the faster tempo our technology demands. And in such wars all of us are combat veterans.

As the speed of everyday life has risen, Americans have come closer and closer to an invisible "sound barrier." Already we can feel the fuselage shutter as it begins to enter a zone of air turbulence that can rend it apart. Already we can feel the controls becoming resistant to our will.

When we land, the engineers who debrief us redesign our plane, and in a matter of time we are airborne again, questing anew for greater and greater speed, striving once again, to break the barrier that stopped us before.

But unlike the science of aeronautics, the modifications in design we accept represent changes in ourselves. For in order to maintain acceleration, we will need to accommodate the quality of our lives to the demands of an artificial environment comprised of incredibly swift but unfeeling electrons. Thus it will not be the plane alone that will be transformed, but its pilot as well.

What lies on the other side of the barrier is not simply more speed but another kind of us, a kind we are already becoming.

Like the crew of the Starship Enterprise, "boldly go[ing] where no man has gone before," we are approaching a velocity called "warp speed," a velocity that can warp our behavior and our most basic values even as it desensitizes us to the metamorphosis we undergo. It is a velocity generated by our own inner need and sustained by the powerful technology at our touch, a velocity sanctioned by a society committed to speed.

Warp speed produces its effects by changing our very relationship to time.

First, warp speed disengages us from the past. The speed of our ascent leaves the past far behind us, like a receding landscape viewed from the rear of a roaring rocket, a landscape so progressively miniaturized by increasing velocity that its features lose all recognizable form. Traditions become incomprehensible; history, irrelevant; memories, a blur.

Second, warp speed plunges us toward the future. The features of the future rush toward us like the fireballs of a meteor storm, blinding us to what lies farther ahead hidden in the cosmic night. Brilliant inventions, glittering products, glistening data, and luminous celebrities each swarm brighter than the last—sweep past us in successive waves, dazzling our eyes.

Nullifying a vision of the past and negating a true view of the future, warp speed isolates us in the present. Marooned there, we turn to the present as our exclusive basis for fulfilment and gratification, as our sole source of security in a cosmos where all other sources of security have been stripped from us by our onrushing speed. Hurtling through time, we cling to the moment.

The Power of Now

As we travel at warp speed, we fall under the sway of a new force, the power of now. The power of now is the intense energy of an unconditional present, a present uncompromised by any other dimension of time. Under its all-consuming power, the priorities we live by undergo transformation in a final act of adaptation to electronic speed. Our lives cease to be what they once were, not so much because life itself has changed, but because the way we see it has.

The power of now replaces the long-term with the short-term, duration with immediacy, permanence with transience, memory with sensation, insight with impulse.

Unlike the monastery or the desert where mystics once attained transcendent perspective by withdrawing from the world, the realm of now is an environment of pervasive sensory stimulation and swift flux, a continually altered cosmos that offers us no fixed horizon. As a consequence, our lives come to be characterized more by their random trajectory than by any reasoned destination.

The individual, the family, and society at large are all being transformed by the power of now.

Not only is the power of now altering their nature, it is changing the very meaning these words have in our minds. Thus, under its influence, both reality and our understanding of reality are being reshaped.

The Fluid Individual

As individuals, the power of now immerses us in an atmosphere of transience and flux. We float on the current of an electromagnetic sea, a sea whose waves are visible on the screens of television sets and computers. Even as it seductively entertains or informs us with its content, each medium indoctrinates us with its form, a form characterized by instantly changing images. As a result, we become progressively desensitized to the importance of continuity and wholeness in our lives. Inured to what is temporary, we lose touch with the permanent.

In a culture fed by a fast-moving electronic stream, those who "go with the flow" to find excitement and fulfillment inexorably speed up their lives. More than simply inducing stress, the prolonged acceleration of behavior can lead to marked changes in personality, changes evident in one's Plastic external appearance and inner sensibilities. Through diets and surgery, individuals today seek the transformation of the outer self in the shortest possible time. Meanwhile, through psychotropic drugs and teachings that promise shortcuts to happiness and well-being, they seek the transformation of the inner self as well.

By assigning the highest priority to speed, the power of now undermines the value of those experiences and activities that require slowness to develop: psychological maturation, the building of meaningful and lasting human relationships, the doing of careful and responsible work, the creation and appreciation of the arts, and the search for answers to life's greatest problems and mysteries. At the same time, by encouraging the immediate gratification of the senses, the power of now obscures the need to cultivate those skills and virtues—patience, commitment, self-denial, and even self-sacrifice—without which no civilization can long endure.

Fulfilling the need to feel a certain way, satisfying the desire to look a certain way, the power of now shapes the individual within and without. Like a chameleon, whose colors change to match the background against which it moves, the individual fluidly glides across the landscape of time, continually altered in body and mind by the addictive energy of an artificial present.

The Centrifugal Family

The symbolic gravity that once let families keep their feet on the ground has been replaced by a new, whirling momentum that has torn the traditional family asunder, confusing old identities and relationships. As a result, the "centrifugal family" has become one of the most salient features of American society.

The force of social acceleration has in fact modified the very definition of love. Influenced by high-speed technology and a culture of quick turnaround time and instant results, individuals expect life to express-deliver the love they need, and grow restive when it does not. We come to expect the imperfect human beings in our lives to operate as efficiently as our computers, quickly losing patience with those we might otherwise love if they do not answer as swiftly, or respond as rapidly, or obey as readily, as the machines we know.

As a consequence, marriage—a "diachronic" pursuit implying a commitment that reaches across time—is fast becoming an anachronism. The fact that our material culture is characterized by things that do not last and, indeed, were never intended to last imparts the expectation of impermanence to our human relationships as well. Traditional marriage thus becomes vulnerable to wear precisely because it stands as an affirmation of constancy in an increasingly inconstant world.

Even anniversary gifts have been redefined by technology and speed. The traditional gift for a first wedding anniversary used to be paper, but now it is clocks. The traditional fourth anniversary present used to be fruit or flowers; now it is electrical appliances. The fourteenth anniversary was once commemorated with crystal; today it is celebrated with watches.

Social acceleration is also responsible for a deterioration in the meaning of parenthood and childhood. In a fast-moving, sensually-oriented society like ours, the virtues of sacrifice and long-term commitment—so essential to effective parenthood—become rare. At the same time, acceleration corrupts the meaning of childhood. Children born in a microwave culture absorb its tempo internally and "mature" too fast, precociously experimenting with behaviors from spending to sex, while lacking the judgement that only gradual maturation can provide.

At the other end of the biological spectrum, the elderly suffer the effects of rapid and turbulent change. In a society governed by the pull of the present, the old are looked upon as more and more irrelevant—even by themselves—as they continue to lose touch with the quickly-shifting topography of the land they once knew. Their most socially acceptable option is to look and act young and not dwell on the past. As a result, the family and society itself come to lose one of their most precious possessions, a sense of connectedness with the past that could, like a gyroscope, stabilize them in turbulent times.

It is no accident that the life of the family is in such danger today. Diachronic commitment, so necessary for family survival, is a concept alien to our society. Alien also is the concept of continuity. Continuity is different from mere transience, for continuity emphasizes not moment but meaning, the meaningful connection of parts—female and male, young and old—into a living whole bonded by common purpose, a whole in which energy (in the family, the energy of love) is given and shared. The increased incidence of family breakdown today permeates the environment in which people live with an atmosphere of impermanence that seeps into the interstices of every human relationship. Family fragmentation rather than being an exception has become the rule.

One thing is certain: never before in history has a civilization been so deprived of the cohesiveness of family as a defense against the centrifugal force of change.

Hypercultural

In a fluid social environment, the acceleration of one activity tends to induce acceleration in other activities. Thus speed begets more speed. While electronic connectivity gives contemporary culture its cohesion, it also sustains its acceleration. The social consequence of connectivity and speed is a synchronous society, a society unified by instancy and acutely attuned to the moment. In such a society, people are not separated by rigid barriers of space or time but coexist synergistically, joined by neural networks governed by the principles of data consumption and sensory gratification.

The end product of such high-speed synergy is a "hyperculture," a culture whose most distinguishing trait is a pathological, self-justifying speed inimical to humane values. In such a culture, so-called deviant behavior, including violent and criminal acts, is actually not an anomaly but is in fact consistent with society's highest goal: get as much as you can as fast as you can.

Democracy is peculiarly susceptible to a hyperculture's power. While all forms of government change to some degree, democracy is especially vulnerable because it is designed to respond to the potentially unstable moods and variable sentiments of a large populace. The only stabilizing influences on a democracy are its traditions. A speed-driven hyperculture, however, is anti-traditional. Focused almost exclusively on the present and thereby deprived of long-term historical memory, citizens in a hurried society lack the knowledge and perspective they need to make wise political decisions. The nature of the power of now thus poses a profound challenge to the longevity of our republic.

The Time Machine

Over a century ago, H.G. Wells wrote The Time Machine a tale of a daring adventurer who travelled through the fourth dimension. Journeying faster than the speed of light, he landed on an Earth he barely recognized, a future world of both savage desolation and tender promise in which creatures of darkness battled creatures of light in a struggle that would determine our planet's destiny.

By the standards of 1895, Wells' machine was state-of-the-art—"a glittering metallic framework" fashioned of ivory and brass and transparent crystal, a device fitted with a saddle and two white levers: one for moving forward into the future, the other for moving back into the past.

Accustomed as we now are to space exploration, Wells' design may seem technically naive. But simplistic as it was, it nevertheless embodied a visionary concept: that human beings by their inventive genius might someday be able to break the restraining bonds of time and travel to other eras, future or past.

Though the fulfilment of such a dream may be far off, a time machine of sorts already exists—in fact, one more powerful than Wells' imagination could ever have conceived. The machine can accommodate not merely one passenger but an entire society. And it is energized not by a mysterious crystal but by the spirit of technology itself. Unlike Wells' time-traveller, we shall not arrive on an alien landscape. For it will not be the world, as much as ourselves, that will be altered. For we are being transformed, even at this very moment, by our extraordinary velocity and by the emergence of a newly insistent force—the power of now.

It is impossible to know the long-term effects of our transformation. The one thing we can be sure of is we will never be the same.

Speed and Education

One force that can slow down an irrationally accelerated society is the force of education, for education connects us with the abiding values of an earlier time and with the humane traditions of our race.

At its best, a university seeks to promote the permanent and enduring, as opposed to what Pope John Paul II in his recent encyclical called the "fleeting and provisional." The traditional liberal arts college and university stands for the ideal, not the pragmatic; the genuine, not the artificial; the spiritual, not the commercial.

Yet higher education today is not impervious to the pressures of the power of now and its enticements. So much in our society has already been commercialized, commodified, and quantified. It is no wonder then that our educational institutions are being similarly transformed. Today, like any good corporation, the university consults its sales charts and marketing surveys to determine what should be taught. It aims for higher productivity and judges the merits of its workers by the number of units produced, failing to realize that some disciplines will never be cost-efficient because they are so labor-intensive. The university turns to technology (TV monitors, computers) and large classrooms to multiply its achievements, forgetting that humane arts must be humanly transmitted on a human scale else their intrinsic value is lost.

Notwithstanding logos, slick packaging, and mission statements, few institutions take the time to contemplate what the irreducible core is without which a university ceases to deserve the name.

The typical university of today teaches customers how to make a living instead of teaching students how to live. It mistakes data for wisdom, while its classrooms become more networked but less intimate, more virtual but less real.

Herein lies the supreme challenge the humanities will face in the 21st century. In a fast-paced society governed by commerce and technology, the humanities stand as an anomaly. The more a university aligns itself with commerce and technology, the more the humanities will become isolated. Naked and exposed, their vulnerability will only invite calculated acts of "ethnic cleansing" undertaken in the name of profitability and the greater good.

A hypercultural environment pollutes a campus in other ways. In the first place, it devalues those activities that are inherently slow and time-intensive: contemplation, reflection, meditation, appreciation. Such activities are just so much "down time" in a computer-driven world. Secondly, high speed severs from the past and from a sense of history, thereby robbing us of the one standard by which we could measure the present. To a society on the move, history is just so much excess baggage.

Like so many colleges and universities, the one I teach at has a motto: "Bonitatem et disciplinam et scientiam doce me." It means "Teach me goodness and judgment and knowledge."

The motto is in Latin, the language of the Catholic Church and, before that, the Roman Empire. But its origin is much older still. The words come from the Old Testament, a verse from an ancient Hebrew song (Psalm 119:66) in which the worshipper prays to God to instruct him in the ways of righteousness. The words of the motto are in Latin because they are taken from a translation made by St. Jerome around the year 400. Since my university was originally founded by Basilian priests, it is the Latin version they chose.

The motto embodies a set of priorities. The first and most important thing the psalmist prays to be taught is "bonitas" (goodness), then "discipline" (judgment), and lastly "scientia" (factual knowledge). The spiritual basis for this gradation is clear: facts alone are inadequate unless we possess a capacity for critical judgment; yet even that capacity is inadequate if not infused with goodness. Thus, of all subjects the most important is moral.

Over the more than thirty years I have been a professor at my university, I have seen changes in its curriculum that parallel changes in society. It is "scientia" (factual knowledge) that has risen and "bonitas" (goodness) that has fallen as a subject worthy of study. As courses in natural and social sciences have multiplied, programs in religion, philosophy, and literature have declined, often not because of a lack of genuine student interest as much as administrative bias.

To be fair, the administrators are right. They, better than I, know what is popular. And their judgment is confirmed by graphs reflecting enrollment patterns for the last three decades in colleges and universities across America.

Each year I quiz my students to see if they recognize "Bonitatem et disciplinam et scientiam." A couple of hands may go up in a class of a hundred. These are the students who recognize their school's motto. If, however, I then ask the class what the words mean, not a single hand is raised.

These test results reflect not just the decline of Latin or of Biblical literacy, but something much deeper: the forgetting of both words and their symbolic meaning. By losing touch with a motto, my students have lost touch with an outlook on life.

It may well be argued that the world no longer needs spiritual guidance, that secular values are sufficient to take us into—and beyond—the 21st century. But what disturbs me is that my students are not granted the power to choose. Materialism and technology have in effect revised the curriculum, foreclosing not only whole subjects but an entire set of human alternatives once known but now deliberately ignored.

In the future, speed-of-light technology will more and more come to dominate our lives and define our values. In a world with so many insensate forces arrayed against the flowering of the human spirit, it is precisely the humanities that society will so desperately need. The humanities are not all we need or will ever want. But without them we will remain forever poor.

As I make clear in my book, Hyperculture, if we can just do three things—restrain our technology, retain our history, and regain our senses—we may, just may, reclaim our lives.

Index

F

G

H

I

J

K

L

M

N

O

P

Q

R

S

T

U

V

W

Y

Z

Test Your Knowledge Form

We encourage you to photocopy and use this page as a tool to assess how the articles in *Annual Editions* expand on the information in your textbook. By reflecting on the articles you will gain enhanced text information. You can also access this useful form on a product's book support Web site at *http://www.dushkin.com/online/*.

NAME: DATE:

TITLE AND NUMBER OF ARTICLE:

BRIEFLY STATE THE MAIN IDEA OF THIS ARTICLE:

LIST THREE IMPORTANT FACTS THAT THE AUTHOR USES TO SUPPORT THE MAIN IDEA:

WHAT INFORMATION OR IDEAS DISCUSSED IN THIS ARTICLE ARE ALSO DISCUSSED IN YOUR TEXTBOOK OR OTHER READINGS THAT YOU HAVE DONE? LIST THE TEXTBOOK CHAPTERS AND PAGE NUMBERS:

LIST ANY EXAMPLES OF BIAS OR FAULTY REASONING THAT YOU FOUND IN THE ARTICLE:

LIST ANY NEW TERMS/CONCEPTS THAT WERE DISCUSSED IN THE ARTICLE, AND WRITE A SHORT DEFINITION:

We Want Your Advice

ANNUAL EDITIONS revisions depend on two major opinion sources: one is our Advisory Board, listed in the front of this volume, which works with us in scanning the thousands of articles published in the public press each year; the other is you—the person actually using the book. Please help us and the users of the next edition by completing the prepaid article rating form on this page and returning it to us. Thank you for your help!

ANNUAL EDITIONS: Computers in Society 04/05

ARTICLE RATING FORM

Here is an opportunity for you to have direct input into the next revision of this volume.
We would like you to rate each of the articles listed below, using the following scale:

1. **Excellent: should definitely be retained**
2. **Above average: should probably be retained**
3. **Below average: should probably be deleted**
4. **Poor: should definitely be deleted**

Your ratings will play a vital part in the next revision.
Please mail this prepaid form to us as soon as possible.
Thanks for your help!

RATING	ARTICLE
________	1. From Movable Type to Data Deluge
________	2. Whom to Protect and How?
________	3. Five Things We Need to Know About Technological Change
________	4. Beyond the Bar Code
________	5. How You'll Pay
________	6. You've Got Spam
________	7. Start-Up Finds Technology Slump Works in Its Favor
________	8. The Computer and the Dynamo
________	9. Bringing Linux to the Masses
________	10. Brain Circulation: How High-Skill Immigration Makes Everyone Better Off
________	11. The Perils of E-Mail
________	12. The Great Prosperity Divide
________	13. "You're Hired, Now Go Home"
________	14. Dealing With Tech Rage
________	15. They're Watching You
________	16. Security vs. Privacy
________	17. Searching for Answers
________	18. Is That a Computer in Your Pants?
________	19. Do Cheaters Ever Prosper? Just Ask Them
________	20. Why Women Avoid Computer Science
________	21. Cyber-Stars
________	22. The World According to Google
________	23. Bad Documents Can Kill You
________	24. The Digital Dilemma
________	25. The Control of Ideas
________	26. Democracy in an IT-Framed Society
________	27. Should Democracy Online Be Quick, Strong, or Thin?
________	28. As Goes Software...
________	29. Governing the Internet
________	30. Homeland Insecurity
________	31. Are You the Weak Link?
________	32. Code Red for the Web
________	33. Networking the Infrastructure
________	34. Will Spyware Work?
________	35. The Shock of the Old
________	36. Data Extinction
________	37. Immigration and the Global IT Workforce
________	38. Wiring the Wilderness in Alaska and the Yukon
________	39. The Quiet Revolution
________	40. Dot Com for Dictators
________	41. ACM's Computing Professionals Face New Challenges
________	42. Humanoid Robots
________	43. The Real Scientific Hero of 1953
________	44. The Race to Computerise Biology
________	45. Kurzweil vs. Dertouzos
________	46. Hyperculture—Stress: How Fast Times Are Transforming America

(Continued on next page)

BUSINESS REPLY MAIL
FIRST-CLASS MAIL PERMIT NO. 84 GUILFORD CT

POSTAGE WILL BE PAID BY ADDRESSEE

McGraw-Hill/Dushkin
530 Old Whitfield Street
Guilford, Ct 06437-9989

ABOUT YOU

Name Date

Are you a teacher? ❒ A student? ❒
Your school's name

Department

Address City State Zip

School telephone #

YOUR COMMENTS ARE IMPORTANT TO US!

Please fill in the following information:
For which course did you use this book?

Did you use a text with this ANNUAL EDITION? ❒ yes ❒ no
What was the title of the text?

What are your general reactions to the *Annual Editions* concept?

Have you read any pertinent articles recently that you think should be included in the next edition? Explain.

Are there any articles that you feel should be replaced in the next edition? Why?

Are there any World Wide Web sites that you feel should be included in the next edition? Please annotate.

May we contact you for editorial input? ❒ yes ❒ no
May we quote your comments? ❒ yes ❒ no